Frontiers in Civil Justice

Frontiers in Civil Justice

Privatisation, Monetisation and Digitisation

Edited by

Xandra Kramer

Professor of Private Law, Erasmus School of Law, Erasmus University Rotterdam, the Netherlands and Professor of Private International Law, Utrecht University, the Netherlands

Jos Hoevenaars

Postdoc Researcher, Erasmus School of Law, Erasmus University Rotterdam, the Netherlands

Betül Kas

Postdoc Researcher, Erasmus School of Law, Erasmus University Rotterdam, the Netherlands

Erlis Themeli

Postdoc Researcher, Erasmus School of Law, Erasmus University Rotterdam, the Netherlands

EE Edward Elgar PUBLISHING

Cheltenham, UK • Northampton, MA, USA

Cover image: Johannes Plenio on Unsplash.

Published by
Edward Elgar Publishing Limited
The Lypiatts
15 Lansdown Road
Cheltenham
Glos GL50 2JA
UK

Edward Elgar Publishing, Inc.
William Pratt House
9 Dewey Court
Northampton
Massachusetts 01060
USA

A catalogue record for this book
is available from the British Library

Library of Congress Control Number: 2022938615

This book is available electronically in the **Elgar**online
Law subject collection
http://dx.doi.org/10.4337/9781802203820

Printed on elemental chlorine free (ECF)
recycled paper containing 30% Post-Consumer Waste

ISBN 978 1 80220 381 3 (cased)
ISBN 978 1 80220 382 0 (eBook)

Printed and bound in the USA

Contents

Contributors

Masood Ahmed is an Associate Professor at the University of Leicester (UK), focusing on civil justice. He was a member of the Civil Procedure Rule Committee and worked with members of the judiciary and leading practitioners in implementing major civil justice reforms. He is the ADR and case note editor for the Civil Justice Quarterly; commentator of the Civil Procedure Rules; and editorial member of the Journal of Personal Injury Law. At the Leicester Law School, he convenes the Dispute Resolution Research Cluster and is the founder and convenor of the Civil Justice Systems and ADR stream for the Socio-Legal Studies Association (SLSA) Annual Conference. He has written extensively on civil justice and reform, civil procedure and ADR.

Naomi Appelman is PhD researcher at the Institute for Information Law (IViR) and part of the Digital Transformation of Decision-Making team at the Amsterdam Law School. She has an academic background in political philosophy and information law. In her research she focuses on democratising online speech regulation and enabling the contestation of automated decision-making by content moderation systems. She has co-authored several reports and publication on related issues and is a co-founder of the Racism and Technology Center.

Joanna van Duin is Assistant Professor of Private Law and Civil Procedure at the Amsterdam Centre for Transformative Private Law (ACT) and part of the Digital Transformation of Decision-Making team. After graduating from both Leiden and Oxford University she worked for six years as an attorney-at-law. Her research revolves around the fundamental right to access to court and an effective remedy in the context of EU (consumer) law, online dispute resolution and digital justice.

Martin Ebers is Associate Professor of IT Law at the University of Tartu, Estonia and permanent Fellow (Privatdozent) at the Law Faculty of the Humboldt University of Berlin, Germany. He is the author and editor of 16 books and over 100 articles. In 2017, he co-founded the Robotics & AI Law Society (RAILS), which he also presides. In 2020, he published the books *Algorithms and Law* (Cambridge University Press), *Rechtshandbuch Künstliche Intelligenz und Robotik* (Beck) and *Algorithmic Governance and Governance of Algorithms* (Springer).

Ronan Fahy is a Senior Researcher at the Institute for Information Law (IViR), where his research focuses on freedom of expression and platform regulation. He is a joint-lead of the Digital Services Act (DSA) Observatory at IViR.

Marco Giacalone is a Marie Sklodowska-Curie fellow at Seraphin.Legal, and a post-doctoral researcher at Vrije Universiteit Brussel. His research focuses on the transformations of law in the field of access to justice with a focus on ADR, ODR, EU regulations and the application of economic principles in the law area. He is currently conducting the research project NEMESIS (Negotiation and Mediation Sensible Issues' Solutions), examining the application of advanced e-negotiation and e-mediation models for resolving civil disputes.

Catalina Goanta is Assistant Professor in Private Law and Technology at Maastricht University. After completing her PhD in European private law at Maastricht University, she was a Niels Stensen fellow and visited the University of St Gallen and Harvard University between 2018 and 2019. She is an editor of the *European Journal on Consumer and Market Law*, and a member of the organising committee of the Natural Legal Language Processing workshop. She is also a non-residential fellow of the Stanford Transatlantic Technology Law Forum.

Natali Helberger is a Distinguished University Professor in law and digital technology, with a special focus on AI. She is based at the Institute for Information Law (IVIR) at the University of Amsterdam. She is an elected member of the Dutch Royal Academy of Arts and Sciences (KNAW).

Joris van Hoboken is Associate Professor at the Institute for Information Law (IViR) and Professor of Law at the Vrije Universiteit Brussels (VUB). He specialises in data protection, algorithmic governance and the regulation of internet intermediaries. He is a leading member of the Digital Transformation of Decision-Making research initiative, and also leading the Digital Services Act (DSA) Observatory at IViR.

Jos Hoevenaars is a postdoctoral researcher at Erasmus University Rotterdam. His research is part of the ERC consolidator project 'Building EU Civil Justice: challenges of procedural innovations – bridging access to justice' (www.euciviljustice.eu) in which he focuses on self-representation and the significance of legal representation in civil justice. He has a PhD in legal sociology and his research focuses in particular on matters of access to justice, legal professions and the EU legal system, using a contextual approach to law in practice.

Betül Kas is a postdoctoral researcher at Erasmus School of Law. Her research is part of the ERC consolidator project 'Building EU Civil Justice: challenges of procedural innovations – bridging access to justice' (www.eucivijustice.eu) in which she focuses on the privatisation of civil justice. She holds a PhD degree and an LLM from the European University Institute (Florence), an LLM in Globalisation and Law and an LLB in European Law from the University of Maastricht. Her research mostly concerns the areas of European law and European private law.

Xandra Kramer is Professor of Private Law at Erasmus University Rotterdam and of Private International Law at Utrecht University, and a deputy judge in the District Court of Rotterdam. She has been involved in multiple studies for the European Parliament, the European Commission, and the Dutch Ministry of Justice, and was a reporter in the project leading to the ELI-Unidroit Model European Rules of Civil Procedure (2020). She is an elected member of the Dutch Royal Academy of Arts and Sciences (KNAW).

Nicolas Kyriakides obtained an LLB from the University of Athens, LLMs from UCL and NYU and his DPhil at Oxford under the supervision of Adrian Zuckerman. He is partner at a leading law firm in Cyprus. He has been a Visiting Researcher at Harvard Law School. He teaches Civil Procedure and Banking Law at the University of Nicosia. He is the author of the book *Cyprus Banking Law* and multiple journal articles. He is the co-founder and co-director of the Procedural Law Unit at the University of Nicosia.

Anna Nylund is Professor of Law at the University of Bergen, Norway. Her research and teaching mainly concern national, comparative and European civil procedure and alternative dispute resolution, as well as children's participation rights. She is a member of several academic associations, including the Norwegian Academy of Science and Letters.

Pietro Ortolani is a Professor of Digital Conflict Resolution at Radboud University, Nijmegen. He holds a law degree from the University of Pisa and a PhD in arbitration from LUISS Guido Carli University, Rome. Before joining Radboud University, he was a Senior Research Fellow at the Max Planck Institute Luxembourg for Procedural Law, a Research Associate at the University of Pisa and a Law Research Associate at Queen Mary, University of London.

Catherine Piché, LLM (magna cum laude, Ottawa, 1997), LLB (Dalhousie University, 1999), LLM (NYU, 2001), DCL (McGill, 2011) is a full Professor in the Faculty of Law of the University of Montréal, specialising in civil procedure and evidence law, complex litigation and class actions, comparative law and conflicts of laws. She is the cofounder and Scientific Director of the first law reform commission of the province of Quebec, the Institut Québécois de

Réforme du Droit et de la Justice. She is the founder and director of the Class Actions Lab.

Anna Plevri is an Assistant Professor of Civil Procedure and ADR at the School of Law at the University of Nicosia and a licensed lawyer both in Greece and Cyprus. She is a legal scholar, author of many books and papers on civil procedure, ADR, private law and law and technology. She is an accredited Mediator on Civil, Commercial, Family, Workplace, Financial Disputes and ODR, a certified Mediator's Trainer and an independent Arbitrator (MCIArb, ICC Hellas). She is the co-founder and director of the Procedural Law Unit at the University of Nicosia.

Seyedeh Sajedeh Salehi is a doctoral candidate at Vrije Universiteit Brussel, Belgium. Her research is mainly focused on the application of alternative (online) dispute resolution mechanisms for resolving civil and commercial disputes in connection with promoting consumer access to justice in the EU.

Astrid Stadler holds a chair of private law, civil procedure law, private international and comparative law at the University of Konstanz, Germany, and has had a part-time chair of comparative mass litigation at Erasmus University, Rotterdam (2011–2015). Her fields of research are civil procedure law (national and international) with a focus on collective redress, but also contract law, and property law. She is vice-president of the German Association of Civil Procedural Law and co-editor of the German 'Juristenzeitung' (JZ).

Erlis Themeli is a postdoctoral researcher at Erasmus University Rotterdam. He is part of the ERC consolidator project 'Building EU Civil Justice: challenges of procedural innovations – bridging access to justice' (www.euciviljustice.eu) in which he conducts research on digitisation of justice and artificial intelligence. For his PhD, he researched how the civil justice systems of different European countries compete to attract commercial cases in their courts.

Ilja Tillema is a trainee judge at the Rotterdam District Court. Previously, she worked as an Assistant Professor at the Erasmus University Rotterdam, after having obtained her PhD degree based on her dissertation 'Entrepreneurial Mass Litigation: Balancing the Building Blocks', under supervision of Professors Willem van Boom and Siewert Lindenbergh.

Stefaan Voet is an Associate Professor at KU Leuven and a host Professor at the University of Hasselt. He is also a Programme Affiliate at the CMS/Swiss Re Research Programme on Civil Justice Systems at the CSLS at the University of Oxford, a member of the Class Actions Exchange Network spearheaded by the universities of Stanford, Oxford and Tilburg and an affiliate at the Class

Action Lab of the University of Montréal. Stefaan is also a practicing lawyer and a substitute justice of the peace.

Brahim Zarouali is Assistant Professor in Persuasive Communication at the Amsterdam School of Communication Research, and member of the Information, Communication and the Data Society research initiative. His research can be situated at the intersection of persuasive communication and new media technologies, with a specific focus on how these technologies shape individuals' views, attitudes and behaviours.

Yomna Zentani is an incoming Trainee Solicitor at Clifford Chance (London). She obtained her Bachelor of Law degree in the Republic of Cyprus, where she graduated top of her cohort and received the Highest Achiever Award, in addition to the University Champions Award for 'Academic and Research Engagement.' She then went on to secure two academic scholarships at the University of Cambridge to pursue a Master of Law degree – the Rowan Williams Cambridge Studentship and the AlThuraya Foundation Cambridge Studentship.

Preface

Civil justice systems are a continuous topic of discussion and subject to reforms at national, European and global level with a view to improving access to justice. While traditionally focusing on basic requirements to secure the efficiency and quality of justice, new developments in the broader arena of civil justice, including technological advancements, follow each other in rapid fashion. The present book studies three connected and cross-cutting issues in civil justice which require a deeper and renewed reflection considering their contribution in facilitating access to justice and current debates in Europe. These are the interaction between formal and informal justice against the background of the growth of ADR; the key importance of different forms of digitised justice; and the collectivisation of civil justice, more in particular the funding of collective redress. These three frontiers of civil justice are viewed from different perspectives and jurisdictions as well as from a pan-European level as EU civil justice is increasingly important.

We are grateful to all contributors to this book, each of whom drew on their experience as an academic, policy maker, or practitioner in the field of civil justice to provide a unique perspective on the current frontiers of civil justice development. Many thanks to Ilja Tillema, formerly a colleague at Erasmus University, and now a trainee judge at the Rotterdam District Court, for her assistance in the preparation of this book, and thanks to Edward Frisken for the language editing of some chapters. We would like to thank the other members of the ERC team, Georgia Antonopoulou and Emma van Gelder and finally, many thanks to our student assistant, Edine Apeldoorn, for her vital help in finalising the manuscript.

This book is made possible by funding from the European Research Council (ERC) under the European Union's Horizon 2020 research and innovation programme. It is part of the ERC consolidator research project 'Building EU Civil Justice: challenges of procedural innovations – bridging access to justice' (2017–2022), carried out at Erasmus School of Law.

Information on the ERC consolidator project 'Building EU Civil Justice' is available at www.euciviljustice.eu. The editors are Principal Investigator and postdoc researchers.

Rotterdam, The Netherlands, December 2021

Xandra Kramer
Jos Hoevenaars
Betül Kas
Erlis Themeli

1. Frontiers in civil justice – privatising, digitising and funding justice[1]

Xandra Kramer, Jos Hoevenaars and Erlis Themeli

1.1 NEW PATHWAYS AND FRONTIERS IN CIVIL JUSTICE

A well-functioning civil justice system is pivotal for enforcing rights of consumers and businesses, protecting fundamental rights, and facilitating trade and economic growth. Yet, for many decades civil justice systems have been under pressure and criticised for their inability to provide affordable, expedient, and simple procedures for dispute resolution. The turn of the century saw the 'civil justice crisis'[2] and the right to a fair trial as encompassed in Article 6 of the European Convention on Human Rights (ECHR) is among the most violated human rights.[3] Attempts at securing the fundamental right of access to justice have traditionally focused mainly on the key hurdles of costs, complexity and delays of civil procedures. These have resulted in legislative amendments aimed at increasing efficiency, simplifying procedures, and reducing costs. While these continue to be important, successive civil justice reforms in Europe and beyond have only moderately contributed to effectively securing access to justice. In more recent years, justice reforms have taken a more fundamental turn in many European countries. These reforms in civil procedure are in part triggered by the need to more assertively take the right

[1] This research has received funding from the European Research Council (ERC) under the European Union's Horizon 2020 research and innovation programme (grant agreement No 726032), ERC consolidator project 'Building EU Civil Justice: challenges of procedural innovations – bridging access to justice'; see <www.euciviljustice.eu>.

[2] Adrian A.S. Zuckerman (ed), *Civil Justice in Crisis* (Oxford University Press 1999).

[3] See e.g., European Court of Human Rights, Annual Report 2020, 164; The European Court of Human Rights, 50 Years of Activity: Some Facts and Figures, 6.

of access to justice seriously, but have also been driven by societal changes, austerity measures following the economic crisis of 2008, and, perhaps most forcefully, by technological advancements. At the same time, at the European Union level, civil justice cooperation has become increasingly important, and policy initiatives and new legislative instruments are shaping civil procedure in Europe.

New pathways in dispute resolution have been paved by the digitisation of justice, the gradual privatisation of justice and emerging alternative dispute resolution (ADR) providers and platforms, and an increase in possibilities for self-representation – often supported by technology. Lastly, in international commercial dispute resolution, where arbitration has become commonplace rather than an alternative route of dispute resolution, the rise of international commercial courts is remarkable. These new pathways, that were discussed in a recent book, have changed the face of civil justice.[4] The present book builds on these pathways and zooms in on the most promising as well as challenging frontiers in advancing civil justice. Three interrelated cross-cutting developments that are central in this book are: the interaction between formal and informal justice; developments in different forms of digitised justice; and the funding and collectivisation of civil justice.

First, the growth of ADR in practice, along with national, European, and global legislative instruments require a renewed reflection on the balance between these various forms of informal justice and the courts. Most notably, at the EU level the consumer ADR Directive and ODR Regulation were adopted and have been in effect as of 2015 and 2016 respectively.[5] Recognising the indisputable importance of both routes of justice, it is essential to scrutinise their relationship, interaction, and the possible directions of communication between them. Second, sweeping technological developments continuously require a reassessment of the efficiency and efficacy of the civil justice system. On the one hand, the increasing amount of social interaction and commerce that takes place in an online environment requires a civil justice system that can respond to the ever-changing nature of the civil dispute landscape. On the other hand, the digitisation of the civil justice system itself has gained new momentum and has become one of the spearheads of civil

4 X.E. Kramer, A. Biard, J. Hoevenaars and E. Themeli (eds), *Pathways to Civil Justice in Europe* (Springer 2021).

5 Directive 2013/11/EU of 21 May 2013 on alternative dispute resolution for consumer disputes and amending Regulation (EC) No. 2006/2004 and Directive 2009/22/EC (Directive on consumer ADR) [2013] OJ L165/63; Regulation (EU) 524/2013 of 21 May 2013 on online dispute resolution for consumer disputes and amending Regulation (EC) No. 2006/2004 and Directive 2009/22/EC (Regulation on consumer ODR) [2013] OJ L165/1.

justice cooperation in EU policy-making. Technological developments and emerging technologically assisted services are increasingly influencing the entire justice chain: starting from e-negotiations, through online dispute resolution (ODR) platforms to fully automatic decision-making by algorithmic judges. Third, pivotal in effectuating access to justice is funding of litigation. The high costs of litigation as well as retrenching governments have resulted in a shift from public to private funding. This is particularly visible in high value and public interest cases, hence the focus in the present work is on the funding of collective redress as a frontrunner mechanism to bring these cases to court. Acknowledging that public funding continues to be essential, the rise of private funding and the balance between these two requires further scrutiny.

This book studies these three frontiers in civil justice both from a European and a national perspective, combining theory with policy and insights from practice. It scrutinises the peculiarities of these seminal areas of change and the interrelation between them. These three frontiers are viewed against the backdrop of the requirements of effective access to justice and the overall goal of establishing a sustainable civil justice system in Europe. Part I is dedicated to the interaction between public and private justice, viewed from a pan-European perspective and zooming in on several European jurisdictions. Part II deals with digitisation of dispute resolution, another key topic in the current civil justice debate, spanning both private justice (e-negotiations, private forms of ODR) and court litigation, and including the rapid development and use of advanced forms of Artificial Intelligence. Part III turns to collective redress – both collective settlements and collective actions – and in particular the funding thereof by means of private funding and common funds. The final chapter views the latter from the Canadian perspective, a frontrunner jurisdiction in many respects, to illustrate what is likely to also become important in Europe.

The present chapter reflects on the development of civil justice in Europe, focusing on current challenges and opportunities, and the three frontiers that are central in this book (1.2). It then turns to discussing the interaction between private and public justice (1.3), digitising public and private justice (1.4), and funding collectivised justice (1.5), on the basis of the chapters included in this book. It concludes with an assessment of how these three key issues will further shape the future of civil procedure in Europe (1.6).

1.2 CIVIL JUSTICE IN EUROPE: DEVELOPMENTS AND CHALLENGES

While civil procedural law has traditionally been a topic of domestic law and is closely interwoven with national legal culture and the judicial system, European developments and EU law have become more important over the past two decades.[6] First, the right of access to justice and a fair trial have been shaped by the ECHR, and in particular the case law of the European Court of Human Rights on Article 6 thereof, as well as the Resolutions of the Council of Europe. In the EU, Article 47 of the Charter on Fundamental Rights, plays an increasingly important role in protecting fundamental procedural rights, and is advanced by the expanding case law of the European Court of Justice.

Third, and most importantly in the present context, a vast number of legislative instruments have been brought about that not only influence national civil procedure, but that have created a self-standing European civil procedural system. Many of these are brought about on the pillar of judicial cooperation in civil matters, introduced in 1999, as laid down in Article 81 of the Treaty on the Functioning of the European Union (TFEU). Increasingly, also Article 114 TFEU serves as a legislative basis for procedural law instruments, which – unlike Article 81 – not only harmonise cross-border civil procedure, but also apply in domestic cases. Three main strands of legislation can be discerned.[7] The first strand consists of the regulations dealing with typical private international law and international litigation issues, including international jurisdiction, the recognition and enforcement of judgments, the cross-border service of documents, and the taking of evidence. The second strand of unification consists of several instruments that have introduced pan-EU civil procedures or that aim at harmonising specific topics of civil procedure in cross-border cases. These include the Regulations on a European Order for Payment Procedure, the European Small Claims Procedure, the European Account Preservation

---

[6] This is also evident from a range of edited volumes focusing on the Europeanisation of civil procedure in recent years. This includes, among others, B. Hess, M. Bergström and E. Storskrubb (eds), *EU Civil Justice: Current Issues and Future Outlook* (Hart Publishing 2016); B. Hess and X.E. Kramer (eds), *From Common Rules to Best Practices in European Civil Procedure* (Nomos/Hart Publishing 2017); A. Nylund and H.B. Krans (eds), *European Union and National Civil Procedure* (Intersentia 2016); A. Nylund and M. Strandberg (eds), *Europeanisation of Civil Procedure: Overcoming Follow-Up Fragmentation through Bottom-Up Harmonisation?* (Cambridge University Press 2019); B. Hess and K. Lenaerts (eds), *The Fiftieth Anniversary of the European Law of Civil Procedure* (Nomos 2020); Kramer, et al (n 4).

[7] See X.E. Kramer, 'Strengthening Civil Justice Cooperation: The Quest for Model Rules and Common Minimum Standards of Civil Procedure in Europe' in Marco Antonio Rodrigues and Hermes Zaneti Jr, Coleção Grandes Temas do Novo CPC - v.13 - *Cooperação Internacional* (Editora Juspodivm 2019) 591-607.

Order[8] as well as the Mediation Directive.[9] What these have in common is that their scope of application is limited to cross-border cases.[10] A third category of harmonised EU civil procedural rules are the sector-specific rules dealing with a specific substantive area, most notably consumer law.[11]

The topics central in this book appear in all of these three categories. First, reviewing policy and legislative developments reveals that court litigation, in other words: formal justice, has been at the forefront at least from a legislative perspective. The regulations that fall into the first and second category, encompassing those concerned with international litigation and creating uniform cross-border procedures or procedural rules, are primarily intended for court procedures. Recommendations dating from 1998 and 2001 already acknowledged the importance of out-of-court dispute resolution,[12] but the first legislation was the Mediation Directive, which was brought about in 2008.[13] While this Directive regulates only a few specified topics, including the obligation to ensure quality and confidentiality of mediation and the enforcement of a settlement agreement, it sketched the first contours of regulating both formal and informal justice. It applies to both mediation initiated by parties and to court-ordered mediation, and specifically aims at ensuring a balanced relationship between mediation and judicial proceedings.[14] While the Commission aimed at having an instrument that would apply to both domestic and cross-border cases,[15] the vast majority of Member States were

---

[8] Regulation (EU) 2015/2421 of 16 December 2015 amending Regulation (EC) 861/2007 establishing a European Small Claims Procedure and Regulation (EC) 1896/2006 creating a European order for payment procedure [2015] OJ L341/1; Regulation (EU) 655/2014 of 15 May 2014 establishing a European Account Preservation Order to facilitate cross-border debt recovery in civil and commercial matters [2014] OJ L189/59.

[9] Council Directive 2008/52/EC of 21 May 2008 on certain aspects of mediation in civil and commercial matters [2008] OJ L136/3.

[10] These legislative instruments based on Art 81 TFEU, limited to matters having cross-border implications. These are generally defined as cases in which at least one of the parties is domiciled or habitually resident in a Member State other than the Member State of the court or tribunal seized for the dispute, see e.g., Art 3 of the European Order for Payment and Small Claims Regulations.

[11] These are based on Art 114 TFEU.

[12] Commission Recommendation 98/257/EC on the principles applicable to the bodies responsible for the out-of-court settlement of consumer disputes, OJ L115, 17 April 1998; Commission Recommendation 2001/310/EC on the principles of out-of-court bodies involved in the consensual resolution of consumer ADR, OJ L109, 19 April 2001.

[13] Directive 2008/52/EC (n 9).

[14] Article 1 Mediation Directive.

[15] Proposal for a Directive of the European Parliament and of the Council on certain aspects of mediation in civil and commercial matters, 22 Oct. 2004, COM(2004)718 final.

against an instrument on domestic cases. At the sectorial level, however, ADR could advance, and consumer ADR became one of the spearheads. In 2013 the Consumer ADR Directive was established, which applies to both cross-border and domestic cases. Its primary aim is to set quality standards for ADR entities by introducing a certification system.[16] This is complemented by the ODR Regulation, which has introduced an EU-wide ODR platform to facilitate the resolution of disputes resulting from online sales and services.[17] Alongside, and sometimes in part resulting from EU legislative instruments, ADR has further developed at the national level. In a couple of Member States and other European countries, forms of mandatory mediation in particular cases are also emerging, including in Italy[18] and in the three jurisdictions covered in this volume, Belgium,[19] England and Wales,[20] and Norway.[21] Importantly, ADR and the interaction between formal and informal justice have also received attention in soft law instruments. Most prominent is the ELI-ENCJ Statement on formal and informal justice which was adopted in 2018.[22] In the 2020 ELI-Unidroit Model European Rules on Civil Procedure, which focus on court procedures, one of the three main overarching rules concerns the obligation of the parties and the role of the court in seeking consensual dispute resolution.[23] Lastly, a reference is made to settlements in the European Parliament Recommendation for a Directive on Minimum standards of civil procedure of 2017.[24] An integrated approach to public and private dispute resolution is, however, still lacking both at the EU and national level.

Second, digitisation of justice occurs at different speeds in the individual EU Member States. While a couple of Member States are well underway in digitising justice, others are lagging behind. Digitising justice has been a focal point

---

[16] See, *inter alia*, A. Biard, 'Monitoring Consumer ADR in the EU: A Critical Perspective', (2018) 2 *European Review of Private Law* 171–96.

[17] See, *inter alia*, E.M. van Gelder, 'The EU Approach to Consumer ODR' (2019) *International Journal of Online Dispute Resolution* 219–26.

[18] E. Silvestri, 'Too much of a good thing: Alternative Dispute Resolution in Italy' (2017) Nederlands-Vlaams tijdschrift voor Mediation en conflictmanagement 77–90.

[19] S. Voet, 'Formal and Informal Justice in Belgium' (Chapter 3).

[20] M. Ahmed, 'Formulating a more principled approach to ADR within the English civil justice system' (Chapter 4).

[21] A. Nylund, 'Alternative Dispute Resolution, Justice and Accountability in Norwegian Civil Justice' (Chapter 5.)

[22] ELI-ENCJ statement on The Relationship between Formal and Informal Justice: The Courts and Alternative Dispute Resolution, adopted by ELI and ENCJ in 2018.

[23] ELI-Unidroit Model European Rules of Civil Procedure (adopted by ELI and Unidroit in 2020), Rules 9 and 10. Also throughout the Rules, reference is made to ADR and settlements.

[24] European Parliament Recommendation on common minimum standards of civil procedure in the EU, 2015/2084(INL) of 6 June 2017.

of EU justice policy with the primary aim of improving judicial cooperation for over a decade.[25] In the last few years, policy and legislative activities have intensified. While previous editions of the EU Justice Scoreboard included some information on ICT, the 2021 EU Justice Scoreboard contains more elaborate data referencing digitisation as a way to promote efficient and accessible justice systems. More recently, digitisation has gained extra attention as a way of keeping courts functioning during the Covid-19 pandemic.[26] Using different criteria to assess digitisation, including for instance the availability of online information of the court system, the availability of electronic communication tools and digital solutions to initiate proceedings, a certain pattern can be determined.[27] Also, a Member State such as the Netherlands that is technologically highly developed, has a very high internet penetration, and accessible online public information on justice, still experiences difficulties in advancing digitising court communication and court procedures.[28] At the EU level, advancing digitisation has been complicated due to these national differences, the decentralised approach that has been taken requiring national systems to be interoperable, and – also resulting from the principles of subsidiarity and proportionality – a large degree of voluntariness. Being a horizontal matter, references to digital communication and other electronic means can be found in a series of instruments on cross-border litigation and in sectorial instruments. While the earlier versions of the Service and Evidence Regulations enabled digital communication, in 2020 both regulations were revised to

---

[25] See e.g., X.E. Kramer, 'Access to Justice and Technology: Transforming the Face of Cross-Border Civil Litigation and Adjudication in the EU' in K. Benyekhlef, J. Bailey, J. Burkell and F. Gélinas (eds), *E-Access to Justice* (Ottawa: University of Ottawa Press 2016) 351–75.

[26] The 2021 EU Justice Scoreboard, Communication from the Commission to the European Parliament, the Council, the European Central Bank, the European Economic and Social Committee and the Committee of the Regions, COM(2021) 38, 1. The Scoreboard uses nine criteria for evaluating digitisation, including for instance the availability of online information about the judicial system, procedural rule allowing digital technology in courts, the use of digital technology by courts and the availability of electronic communications tools. See 31–37.

[27] For instance, Estonia scores first on a number of criteria, and scores well overall, while among others Cyprus and Greece have lower scores overall.

[28] In 2018, an ambitious programme was largely discontinued due to difficulties, see e.g., X.E. Kramer, E. Themeli and E.M. van Gelder, 'e-Justice in the Netherlands: The Rocky Road to Digitised Justice' in M. Weller and M. Wendland (eds), *Digital Single Market: Bausteine eines Rechts in der Digitalen Welt* (Tübingen: Mohr Siebeck 2018) 209–35. While progress has been made in the last few years, it is still lagging behind in enabling online submissions of claims and communication with the court.

further strengthen and to some extent oblige the use of e-communication.[29] The European Order for Payment and Small Claims Regulations also facilitate and encourage the use of e-communication and (for the latter) videoconferencing, and these procedures have been subject of e-Codex pilots. The launch of the e-Justice portal in 2010 has greatly facilitated access to information, and with regard to ADR, the above-mentioned establishment of the ODR platform in 2016 was an important step in simplifying online access to justice. An overarching framework, however, is still lacking. In 2021, an extensive impact assessment was made for the further digitisation of both civil and criminal justice. On 1 December 2021, the Commission published its proposal for a Regulation on the digitalisation of judicial cooperation and access to justice. This aims at making digital communication equal to other forms of communication, introducing a common approach to the use of modern technologies and the setting up of a decentralised IT system for the exchange of communication between courts and competent authorities and of these entities with natural and legal persons.[30]

Third, funding of justice systems and of litigation in particular is still predominantly a domestic issue in Europe, being interwoven with financing the judicial system as a whole. The costs of litigation are generally high, and this is in part what explains the rise of ADR being a cheaper alternative, and what triggers investments in digitisation of justice. That costs are a sensitive issue in the EU became clear with the revision of the European Small Claims Procedure, where the European Commission attempted to set a maximum court fee for this procedure.[31] This proposal was dismissed by the Member States and considered to be beyond the competence of the EU. Legal aid is at the forefront of securing the right of access to justice and embedded in Article 6 ECHR and – more prominently – in Article 47 EU Charter, as is also clear from the case law. However, this is limited to the obligation to provide some form of legal aid to people who cannot afford the costs of litigation. Apart

---

[29] Regulation (EU) 2020/1784 of the European Parliament and of the Council of 25 November 2020 on the service in the Member States of judicial and extrajudicial documents in civil or commercial matters (service of documents) (recast), OJ L405/40.

[30] Proposal for a Regulation of the European Parliament and of the Council on the digitalisation of judicial cooperation and access to justice in cross-border civil, commercial and criminal matters, and amending certain acts in the field of judicial cooperation, COM(2021) 759 final. This proposal was put forward while this manuscript was in the final stages of editing and is not discussed in the various chapters.

[31] Proposal for a Regulation of the European Parliament and of the Council amending Council Regulation (EC) 861/2007 of 11 July 2007 establishing a European Small Claims Procedure and Council Regulation (EC) 1896/2006 of the European Parliament, and of the Council of 12 December 2006 creating a European order for payment procedure, COM(2013) 794 final, Art 2.

from the Legal Aid Directive, which aims to guarantee the same standards for cross-border litigation in the EU,[32] there is little regulation so far.[33] Meanwhile, in several Member States different forms of private funding of litigation have been developed, including legal aid insurance and more recently third-party litigation funding by commercial funders. It is primarily the rise of collective redress in Europe that is the gamechanger for the funding of litigation. This in part takes place at the national level but the issue of funding a collective redress has meanwhile also reached the EU level. Collective redress has been one of the most debated topics in the EU for more than ten years. This is due to a great diversity among Member States in the regulation of collective redress, and in about half of the Member States appropriate mechanisms are still lacking. In 2013, a non-binding Recommendation on Collective Redress was put forward.[34] Due to the need for effective enforcement of consumer law and mass damages – as recently in the Volkswagen diesel emissions scandal – a sectorial approach was taken as the more feasible one. This resulted in the adoption of the Representative Actions Directive for consumers (RAD) in November 2020 which will be effective as of 25 June 2023.[35] This Directive includes a few provisions on funding. It only allows non-profit designated Qualified Entities to bring a claim,[36] but as is clear from Article 10, funding by a commercial party is possible as far as allowed under national law and provided that it is secured there is no conflict of interest. Article 12 implements the loser pays rule with certain restrictions for consumers. In addition, according to Article 20, Member States are required to take measures to ensure funding for collective redress. Interesting in this regard is the possibility of 'cy pres distribution' in Article 9(7), according to which Member States can use unclaimed proceeds to feed into legal aid or a fund.[37] Interestingly, following a study of the European

---

[32] Council Directive 2002/8/EC of 27 January 2003 to improve access to justice in cross-border disputes by establishing minimum common rules relating to legal aid for such disputes [2002] OJ L26/41.

[33] The European Parliament Recommendation of 2017 (n 24) also included a few provisions on costs and funding, requiring proportionality of court fees, laying down the loser pays principle and securing legal aid (Arts 13–15 proposed directive).

[34] Commission Recommendation 2013/396/EU of 11 June 2013 on common principles for injunctive and compensatory collective redress mechanisms in the Member States concerning violations of rights granted under Union Law [2013] OJ L201.

[35] Directive (EU) 2020/1828 of the European Parliament and of the Council of 25 November 2020 on representative actions for the protection of the collective interests of consumers and repealing Directive 2009/22/EC, OJ L 409/1.

[36] Art 4(3)(c) RAD.

[37] I.N. Tzankova and X.E. Kramer, From Injunction and Settlement to Action: Collective Redress and Funding in the Netherlands, in Alan Uzelac and Stefaan Voet, *Class Actions in Europe: Holy Grail or a Wrong Trail?* (Springer 2021) 97–130 at 124, 125.

Parliament Research Service,[38] the European Parliament Committee published a Draft Report with recommendations to the Commission on Responsible Private Funding of Litigation.[39] While it remains to be seen how the RAD will be implemented and whether the Commission will take up the European Parliament recommendations, these are promising first steps towards regulating funding of civil justice, and collective redress in particular.

1.3 BALANCING AND CONNECTING PRIVATE AND PUBLIC JUSTICE

Privatised justice is a vital part of today's civil justice systems. As discussed in Section 1.2 above, there are different forms of informal justice by private providers and in the context of court proceedings by way of court-ordered or court-annexed mediation, or more informal attempts of settlement. A challenge created by the growth of ADR and in particular more recent forms of ODR is how to secure the quality of dispute resolution. In the EU, the ADR Directive was an important step in regulating the quality requirements. Recognising the indisputable importance of both public courts and private routes to dispute settlement, it has become crucial to address the interaction between these. The contributions in Part I of this book address the development of public and private justice in the EU alongside emerging forms of mandatory ADR and judicial oversight or other forms of accountability. After reflecting on consumer ADR in the EU, drawing on examples from specific jurisdictions (Belgium, England & Wales, and Norway) Part I dissects this first of the three frontiers of current civil justice development.

In Chapter 2, **Betül Kas** traces the development of consumer ADR in the EU and highlights the potential that lies in an investigation of the interactions between informal and formal justice for the future development of an effective framework for the resolution of consumer disputes in the EU. It is highlighted how the Court of Justice of the European Union has played a key role in giving impetus to the EU's efforts of promoting the availability of high-quality ADR in the EU and in legitimising the Member States' experimentation with mandatory pre-trial ADR in order to further the effective administration of

---

[38] J. Saulnier, K. Müller and I. Koronthalyova, 'Responsible Private Funding of Litigation. European Added Value Assessment' [2021] European Parliament Research Service. See on this study X.E. Kramer and I. Tillema, 'The Funding of Collective Redress by Entrepreneurial Parties: The EU and Dutch Context' (2020) 2 Revista Ítalo-Española de Derecho Procesal 165–81 at 174–75.

[39] European Parliament, Draft Report with recommendations to the Commission on Responsible private funding of litigation (2020/2130(INL)), 17 June 2021.

justice.[40] However, the Court's favourable position towards ADR has not yet led to a broader European-level discussion about the proper relationship between ADR and the courts. So far, the EU framework requires the Member States to set up ADR entities that are standing next to the courts, giving rise to a 'multi-option system', which leaves the question of whether a dispute is resolved by ADR or court primarily to the parties' choice. While the ELI-ENCJ Statement on formal and informal justice provides a useful starting point to envisage the role of the judge in encouraging the 'responsible' use of ADR processes, the question how ADR processes could contribute towards upholding the fundamental role of the courts remains unaddressed. The development of a synergetic relationship between the courts and ADR by the EU still constitutes an untapped potential.

Over the last years, Belgium has seen several procedural reforms. In every reform there was a (large or minor) focus on different forms of informal justice: consumer ADR, conciliation, judicial and extra-judicial mediation, and collaborative mediation. Over the years, new dispute resolution avenues have come to the fore. Today, all these forms belong to the alternative dispute resolution options within the Belgian dispute resolution landscape. There is a consensus that in some circumstances they are a better, quicker, and cheaper alternative than judicial adjudication. However, it remains a difficult relationship to disentangle. In that sense, critical questions remain. Should some of these forms of informal justice be made mandatory before going to court? What about the 'quality' of the non-judicial deciders and solvers? Does an informal justice process offer the same procedural guarantees as a formal justice process? How can/should the outcomes of informal justice processes be enforced? How to design appropriate forms of interaction, interconnection, and integration between formal and informal justice processes? In Chapter 3, **Stefaan Voet** assesses these questions from a Belgian perspective. In light of the fading division between public and private enforcement, a plea is made for an integrated dispute resolution framework in which all options are connected in order to avoid enforcement gaps.

Although successive English civil justice reforms have embraced ADR as an important aspect of the civil justice process, the issue of whether the courts possess the power to compel non-consenting litigating parties to engage with ADR has been a controversial one. The orthodox judicial approach has been to dismiss the notion of compulsory ADR on the grounds that it would unduly

---

40 Joined cases C-317/08, C-318/08, C-319/08 and C-320/08 *Rosalba Alassini v Telecom Italia SpA, Filomena Califano v Wind SpA, Lucia Anna Giorgia Iacono v Telecom Italia SpA and Multiservice Srl v Telecom Italia SpA* EU:C:2010:146; Case C-75/16 *Livio Menini and Maria Antonia Rampanelli v Banco Popolare – Società Cooperativa* EU:C:2017:457.

restrict the constitutional rights of the parties to access the courts. In the English civil justice system however, a divergent judicial approach has emerged which, although officially rejecting compulsory ADR, impliedly compels the parties to engage with ADR through the threat of cost sanctions. Consequently, the evolving ADR jurisprudence has been inconsistent, contradictory, and confusing. In Chapter 4, **Masood Ahmed** critically considers English judicial approaches to compulsory ADR and argues, considering current digitisation reforms, including the introduction of the Online Civil Money Claims and recent landmark decisions of the Court of Appeal, that it is time for the courts to reject the orthodox approach to compulsory ADR and to fully embrace their case management powers in making ADR orders. Ultimately, Ahmed argues, this will allow the senior courts to develop a consistent and coherent message for the courts, litigants, and the legal profession.

Proponents of ADR praise its qualitative and quantitative advantages for being a flexible, cost-efficient, and swift process that promises party self-determination and mutually agreeable, sound outcomes. In practice, many ADR processes do not match the rhetoric and fail to provide a genuine alternative process. Regulation is often inadequate since it fails to recognise ADR as a range of processes (many of which are dominated by quasi-adjudicative practices) and it does not consider that many disputants are unable to make informed decisions regarding the procedure and outcome. In Chapter 5, **Anna Nylund** identifies the palpable gap that exists between ADR theory and practice and argues that the development of a theory of ADR that is better aligned with ADR as an integral part of the justice system could serve to improve the quality and accessibility of dispute resolution. By exploring key factors underpinning the gap between ADR theory and practice and through explicating concepts of justice in ADR, she addresses the accountability gap in ADR, and puts forth suggestions for mechanisms of accountability. After formulating parameters for justice and accountability she applies them to the three most-used processes in Norway and evaluates their ability to provide just outcomes and processes and render the ADR system accountable. She discusses how the formal justice system could enhance the quality and appeal of out-of-court dispute resolution by addressing ADR processes as they are practiced.

1.4 DIGITISING PRIVATE AND PUBLIC JUSTICE: NEW TECHNOLOGIES, ARTIFICIAL INTELLIGENCE, AND ONLINE PLATFORMS

The use of digital technologies has seen a rapid rise in both the private and public justice field, and at present is perhaps the most important topic at the EU level, as also highlighted in Section 1.2 above. Part II of this book is dedicated to new technologies, Artificial Intelligence (AI) and emerging online platforms. There is no doubt that these digital technologies reduce costs, improve communication both in cross-border and domestic cases and simplify access to justice. Many law firms, courts, and public institutions offer better and faster services thanks to them. And even though we cannot say that technology has solved access to justice problems, such as complex procedures, long adjudication time, and high costs, we can say that it has changed our life. Now more than ever online trade is very common, online platforms are growing in number and types, and social media is ubiquitous. Sadly, this has led to new access to justice problems for online consumers, and platform and social media users. Finding redress for a small online purchase, for example, can be quite challenging considering the costs and lengthy procedures involved. It is even harder for platform or social media users to find legal support or protect their rights. In Europe this situation is more challenging in cross-border situations where physical distance, language barriers, legal uncertainties, and the possibility to enforce rights across borders create even more hurdles.

Digital technologies, however, can help improve this situation by offering alternatives to court litigation, by improving communication between citizens and institutions, and by providing better access to information. As **Erlis Themeli** explains in Chapter 6, the EU has approved a series of action plans with the goal of supporting the adoption of digital technologies in the field of justice within its borders. The action plans emphasise the importance of digital technologies both for public institutions and for citizens. In particular, they aim at improving the communication between institutions and their constituents, and at dematerialising cross-border judicial proceedings. Themeli argues that the Action Plans should be viewed in conjunction with other activities of the EU, such as legislative reform and the general promotion of digitisation. The EU Justice Scoreboard is one of the examples of how the EU tries to promote the adoption of digital technologies in the justice field. At the same time some cross-border civil justice regulations, among others the European Small Claims Procedure and the European Order for Payment Procedure, have been amended to include digital communications more prominently. Themeli adds, as part of the digitisation of justice, the legislative work on AI for which the EU has approved an Ethics Guideline for Trustworthy AI and has prepared a Regulation on AI. The importance of AI cannot be understated and as the next chapter illustrates the challenges it brings are many.

In Chapter 7, **Nicholas Kyriakides, Anna Plevri and Yomna Zentani** argue that the use of AI has the potential to improve access to justice to an even greater degree by encouraging cost savings large enough to reverse the corrosive effect that the lack of access has had on the rule of law and public confidence. They build upon findings made by Adrian Zuckerman to delve into the possible benefits and risks associated with utilising AI to facilitate broad access to justice. Using Zuckerman's work as a launchpad, this chapter seeks to encourage further critical debate on AI's role in court adjudication and to elucidate its possible impact on key stakeholders such as the public and potential litigants. The key issue at stake is the legitimacy of the justice system as a whole; were AI to systemically penetrate it, the system would become unrecognisable. Therefore, potential consequences of such a transformation must be carefully considered. Should the transition into AI-led adjudications lead to the loss of perceived legitimacy, this may have profound undesirable consequences on the rule of law, and, therefore, undermine efforts to provide quality access to justice to citizens throughout the EU.

Recently, AI is increasingly used in consumer online dispute resolution (cODR) to diagnose problems, predict outcomes, influence negotiations, limit bias, reduce unrealistic settlement points, and facilitate the resolution of disputes by the removal of human interventions. As such, cODR is becoming increasingly automated. The use of AI based techniques in cODR creates opportunities for consumers and the justice system in general, especially by the increasing speed and costs, but also raises concerns in terms of fair trial rights and due process standards. Within this context, **Martin Ebers** presents a critical evaluation of AI systems in cODR, dealing especially with the extent to which AI systems can meet or violate due process standards and whether there is a need to regulate the role of AI in cODR, in Chapter 8.

Negotiations take up a significant portion of interactions, and many disputes find their resolution in mutual agreements between parties. Within the ODR and AI context, e-negotiation is a process that uses negotiation support systems, including computers or other forms of electronic communications, to enable parties to reach an agreement. In Chapter 9, **Marco Giacalone and Seyedeh Sejeden Salehl** explore the concept of e-negotiation and its existing applications for resolving disputes in the EU. The authors point to the fact that in Europe, despite prominent examples from the United States, Canada, and Australia, the topic of e-negotiation has thus far received rather limited discussion. Assessing several widely used e-negotiation systems, and discussing their strengths and weaknesses, they identify the great potential of e-negotiation, and its application through the EU ODR Platform in particular, in ameliorating many of the existing barriers in citizens' access to justice.

Concerns about access to justice have found a new dimension in today's data-driven economy and online social media platforms, which enable an ever-growing range of interactions between individual users. Unavoidably, these interactions give rise to disputes: social media behaviour can, for instance, result in claims for copyright infringement, unfair commercial practices, or privacy violations. Yet, these claims are rarely adjudicated by public courts; most of these disputes are resolved internally by the platforms, through techniques known as 'content moderation'. In Chapter 10, **Catalina Goanta and Pietro Ortolani** unpack content moderation and show how, behind this label, platforms operate as veritable online civil courts. As such, they explore the platforms' failure to ensure adequate access to justice through content moderation. The authors comparatively analyse the reporting systems of four social media platforms (Facebook, Twitch, TikTok and Twitter) and propose a hierarchy of 'actionable' content, as well as the underlying procedural rights of users to file complaints. Additionally, the authors explore the responsibility of social media platforms as adjudicators, to determine what role traditional principles of dispute resolution (such as independence and impartiality) play in their private spheres. Finally, they propose a normative framework for private access to justice in the context of harms arising out of social media content.

The publication and dissemination of unlawful online content and the lack of effective remedies to stop it has proven to be a persistent problem. In Chapter 11, **Naomi Appelman, Joanna van Duin et al.** report on the findings of empirical research, commissioned by the Dutch government, on the possible need for procedural innovation in the Netherlands to quickly take down online content that causes personal harm – i.e., a wide variety of Article 8 ECHR claims that impact people's private life. The results of this interdisciplinary study, combining law and communication science perspectives, show that, even though a significant minority of the Dutch population has personal experience with harmful content, the available means of recourse are often not utilised. This appears to be partly due to a lack of knowledge, as well as the length, complexity, and costs of a legal procedure. Other obstacles concern the specialised nature of the problem and the difficulty for injured parties to find the appropriate actor to address. There is also tension between the need for routes that are fast, accessible, and scalable, and the need to ensure procedural safeguards and the protection of fundamental rights – in particular the right to freedom of expression. Appelman and van Duin suggest ways to improve remedies for the removal of unlawful online content and propose a roadmap that provides injured parties with a step-by-step plan or escalation model, according to e.g., the different types of content at issue and the actors involved.

1.5 FUNDING CIVIL JUSTICE AND COLLECTIVE REDRESS

One of the most persistent barriers in access to justice remains the costs associated with litigation. As discussed in Parts I and II, this is also one of the reasons why private forms of justice and online dispute resolution have gained importance, while also digitalisation of court litigation reduces costs. A special category of litigation that is of particular importance for access to justice due to economies of scale is that of collective redress. Mass damage, complex and public interest cases, are generally not suitable for ADR mechanisms and benefit only to a limited extent from digitisation of procedures. It is in this area specifically that costs and funding have been discussed mostly in recent years, as was addressed in Section 1.2. Part III of this book focuses on the funding of litigation and of collective redress in particular. The contributions explore the opportunities and drawbacks of three funding routes: collective actions by or via public funding entities, semi-public consumer organisations and private entrepreneurial entities. The chapters address these focusing on three distinct jurisdictions, The Netherlands, Germany and Canada (Quebec). The first is one of the frontrunners in the EU both as regards collective redress and funding, while also in Germany an important collective redress mechanism is in place and has been the centre of the Volkswagen diesel scandal litigation. Canada, and Quebec in particular, has a well-developed system of collective actions and settlements and the financing through public funds can serve as an example for Europe.

As was mentioned above (Section 1.2), the Netherlands is one of the frontrunners in collective redress, and in the last decade entrepreneurial parties have started to diversify the Dutch mass litigation landscape. This is in part incentivised by the potential large earnings that such litigation provides. In Chapter 12, **Ilja Tillema** discusses several Dutch cases in which entrepreneurial parties have been involved, focusing on the pros and cons of their involvement, and the ways in which the legislator and courts have addressed this development so far. By juxtaposing the possible benefits of entrepreneurial parties – such as the facilitation of access to justice, increased competition, increased quality of claims, (e)quality of representation and the alignment of interest – with the 'dark side' of the coin – fostering a claim culture, inefficient competition, adverse selection, abusive behaviour and conflicts of interest – Tillema provides lessons learned from the Dutch cases and sketches an idea of what to expect in the future of mass litigation and entrepreneurial parties. So far, entrepreneurial lawyering seems not to have resulted in excessive litigation. Dutch developments cannot be detached from European developments. Both legislation and case law demonstrate that a move towards a stricter approach in the Netherlands is beginning to take shape. Dutch courts will continue to face challenges in the assessment of the business model of representative organisations, and that the political debate on entrepreneurial parties will continue. She concludes that to maintain an effective and trustworthy collective action system, it is essential to combine transparency and accountability with the sustainability of entrepreneurial parties and describes this as a balancing act.

Astrid Stadler delves into recent German case law on litigation funding issues in Chapter 13. Two Federal High Court decisions of 2018 explicitly forbid consumer associations to use the services of a commercial third-party funder for actions skimming-off illegally gained profit in consumer cases. Another highly topical issue is the funding of mass claims based on the assignment model which plays an important role in cartel damage litigation and in the VW Dieselgate case. Legaltech companies and Special Purpose Vehicles (SPVs) offer debt collection free of charge and risk, but charge success fees. Despite a quite liberal decision of the Federal High Court in 2019, lower courts clearly tend to declare assignments to legaltech platforms like 'myRight' or SPVs void, due to an alleged violation of the German Act on Legal Services – a set of rules which de facto provides a monopoly for lawyers. The conflict is rooted in an obvious mismatch and the lack of a level playing field: whereas contingency fees are not allowed for lawyers under German law, there is no equivalent ban for SPVs and legal tech platforms. Finally, Stadler reflects critically on the German VW Dieselgate settlement in spring 2020 and how German law has inadvertently imported typical US class actions conflicts of interests. She concludes that in the long term, there is a definite need for a legislative framework on third-party funding, but also for the establishment of a fund for representative actions under the Representative Actions Directive.

In Chapter 14, **Catherine Piché** focuses on the public forms of financing class litigation and argues that financing class actions publicly through assistance by entities such as the Canadian province of Quebec's *Fonds d'aide aux recours collectifs* (the assistance fund for class action lawsuits; the Fonds) is the most appropriate and effective way to finance class action litigation, whenever available. She explains how the Fonds entity is not only effective as a class litigation funding mechanism but also as a mandatory independent oversight body beneficial to the class action system and the industry as a whole, that it should be recognised as such and serve as a model for reform of other legal systems. She argues that for the objectives and public policy purposes of class actions to be fulfilled, successful cases must be used to help finance unsuccessful ones. Assistance must be provided to legitimate and promising cases from entities with proper motivations: that is, to provide a way to fund this kind of litigation, to provide true access to justice. Because the Fonds' right to compensation applies to all class actions in Quebec, every class action case initiated in the province – whether it is funded or not – helps finance the next one. Furthermore, the Fonds' motive to assist class plaintiffs in a neutral manner helps provide access to worthwhile cases. As such, the very structure and functioning of Quebec's public class action assistance fund immunises it from potential conflicts of interest and the risk of agency cost in representative actions.

1.6 CONCLUDING REMARKS: THE ROAD AHEAD

Civil justice and the concept of access to justice are changing. Traditional approaches have focused primarily on increasing access to courts, securing that legal aid is available for those without sufficient means, simplifying procedural rules and increasing efficiency to meet the requirement that judgment is given within reasonable time. While these continue to be essential, the legal landscape is changing along with society and technological developments. There is a need for different forms of dispute resolution, technology has become a vital element in both private and court justice, and mass damages – for instance in consumer, cartel, and environmental cases – require appropriate collective redress mechanisms with funding that goes beyond legal aid to individuals by the government. In terms of regulatory attention, we have reached the next stage in EU civil justice. While the 2008 financial crisis and Brexit seemed to have slowed down developments,[41] it now seems to be at full speed in a more encompassing and integrated civil justice system. This chapter described the three main frontiers in the development of such an integrated system capable of addressing current access to justice issues.

ADR mechanisms have so far been developing as a separate track, while mediation and settlements within the court system have largely been voluntary and – in many countries – often incidental. The inherent limitations of the court system, limited legal aid and the ad hoc establishment of private ADR and ODR entities and platforms call for a more integrated approach. A step in the right direction at the EU level is the ADR Directive laying down quality requirements. In 2022, the ADR Directive and ODR Regulation will be evaluated, and it is expected that this will lead to further improvements, also in the monitoring of these quality requirements and in the operation of the ODR platform. Both for ensuring quality standards and for potential litigants to find their way, it is important that formal and informal justice become more integrated. An example in the EU, though be it a small step, is that the User Guide and Practice Guide on the European Small Claims Procedure after its revision in 2019, also refer to the possibility of ADR and to the operation of the ODR platform.[42] Similarly, the ODR platform should refer to this procedure as an option in case ADR fails. Apart from these references by way of signposting, a more advanced system of integrating formal and informal justice is needed, as is also suggested by Kas and Voet in the present book, and following up on the ELI-ENCJ Statement mentioned above.[43] One of the means is making mediation more compulsory and guided, which, as Ahmed discusses in relation to England and Wales, can also be part of the court's case management system. A more inter-connected system of formal and informal justice, along with what Nylund in assessing developments in Norway refers to as semi-formal justice, also requires a clear organisational framework and

[41] Kramer et al (n 4) 16–17.

[42] A Guide for Users to the European Small Claims Procedure and Practice Guide for the Application of the European Small Claims Procedure, available on the e-Justice Portal (the first author of this chapter was involved in revising these guides in 2019).

[43] Section 1.2; n 21.

accountability of ADR processes. The expansion of ADR and the expectation that these different forms of informal justice along with the need to administer cases in courts, calls for a more fundamental rethinking of an integrated justice system, both at the national and the EU level.

Another layer to the civil justice system, and one that is also important for cross-fertilisation and connection to private dispute resolution and court adjudication is technology. Technology develops fast and often follows trends in society, such as the importance of social media. Private dispute resolution entities seem to be more flexible in responding to these than public courts. Online service providers and sellers like eBay are at the forefront of technology development and have created their own forms of dispute resolution, as Goanta and Ortolani and Ebers discuss in the present book. This requires a strong commitment of legislators and the developers to uphold high-quality standards and to protect fundamental rights, including that of fair trial and privacy. The benefits of digital technology are also evident in courts, and the Covid-19 pandemic has showed the importance of a resilient judicial system and digital communication. The above-mentioned Commission proposal put forward on 1 December 2021, is an important step towards a more horizonal and encompassing approach to digital communication and justice and alignment between Member States.[44] Most developments are expected in further advancing the use of AI in dispute resolution, as is illustrated in several chapters of the present book. Also in this regard, private dispute resolution platforms have made big steps. The use in courts differs greatly per country, but also there it is clear that AI is very promising as it can compile arguments and read files faster than humans and it can already be used to resolve non-complex cases. It would not be surprising if a robot judge will replace a human judge for some types of cases in public courts in the near future. However, more structurally replacing human judges with robots involves social, political, and human aspects that will need further deliberation. Ultimately, the legal community will need to face this challenge and consider the risks it poses to procedural rights and the right to a fair trial, but also the benefits that AI will bring.

For the protection of consumer rights in particular, not only an integrated system of public and private dispute resolution and digitised justice is important, but also advancing collective redress and the funding thereof. It is also in the area of collective redress where public and private, or formal and informal justice go hand in hand in the form of collective actions and settlements. Collective redress is at the same time an area where private and (semi) public interests come together as by definition it affects large groups of individuals. The establishment of the Representative Action Directive is a huge step in

---

[44] Section 1.2; n 29.

regulating collective redress and its regulatory and factual implementation in the next years creates an opportunity to bring Member States on board that do not yet have suitable mechanisms to collectively deal with cases that cannot be resolved individually. Collective redress, however, cannot exist and grow without funding, and traditional legal aid by the government cannot provide this. This also explains the rise of entrepreneurial parties, as Tillema discusses in the present book, and in the same vein Stadler rightfully argues that third-party funding is inevitable. But as for private dispute resolution, public regulation is required, and entrepreneurial lawyering will not take care of every case that needs legal address. The example Piché illustrates for public funds in Quebec can serve as an example of how such funds strike a balance between different interests in furthering access to justice.

The key issues and examples addressed in the different chapters of this book will continue to shape the future of civil justice development and underscore the complexity of present-day civil justice challenges, while at the same time pointing to opportunities available for addressing them. Taken together, the three identified frontiers in the development of a civil justice system capable of dealing with current and emerging issues of access underscore the need for a comprehensive and integrated approach.

PART I

ADR and the courts – shaping the interaction between public and private justice

2. The untapped potential of a structured interaction between courts and ADR for the resolution of consumer disputes in the EU[1]

Betül Kas

2.1 INTRODUCTION

In 2013, the EU adopted the ADR Directive 2013/11/EU and the ODR Regulation 524/2013 in order to encourage the use of alternative dispute resolution mechanism in consumer disputes.[2] The regulatory package constitutes the most far-reaching project of the EU in the area of alternative dispute resolution. The promotion of ADR by the EU challenges the conventional picture and the traditional instruments of European integration. Traditionally, European integration has been depicted as a rights-based process, in which the European and national judiciaries play a leading role.[3] Accordingly, EU consumer policies have been sought to be realised through the conferral of

[1] This research has received funding from the European Research Council (ERC) under the European Union's Horizon 2020 research and innovation programme (grant agreement No 726032), ERC consolidator project 'Building EU Civil Justice: challenges of procedural innovations – bridging access to justice'; see www.euciviljustice.eu, accessed 30 March 2022.

[2] Directive 2013/11/EU of the European Parliament and of the Council of 21 May 2013 on alternative dispute resolution for consumer disputes and amending Regulation (EC) No 2006/2004 and Directive 2009/22/EC (Directive on consumer ADR) [2013] OJ L165/63; Regulation (EU) No 524/2013 of the European Parliament and of the Council of 21 May 2013 on online dispute resolution for consumer disputes and amending Regulation (EC) No 2006/2004 and Directive 2009/22/EC (Regulation on consumer ODR) [2013] OJ L 165/1.

[3] On the role of the law in the European integration process, see Mauro Cappelletti, Monica Seccombe and Joseph Weiler, 'Integration Through Law: Europe and the American Federal Experience' in Mauro Cappelletti, Monica Seccombe and Joseph Weiler (eds), *Integration Through Law*, book 1, vol 1 (European University Institute, 1986); on the role of national courts, see for instance Bruno de Witte, Juan A. Mayoral,

substantive consumer rights and their enforcement before the national civil courts. The latter have been equipped with instruments to actively protect the weaker position of consumers in civil proceedings and became thereby enforcers of EU law.[4] By opening a space for out-of-court dispute resolution, the EU thus breaks with the conventional understanding of European integration and the established instruments of consumer protection. ADR is endorsed by the EU in view of the lengthy, costly and complex nature of court proceedings. Out-of-court dispute resolution promises instead a rapid, easy and cheap route to redress for individual consumers. The EU's push towards ADR has not been however universally welcomed. Not only have ADR's promises been defined in contraposition to court proceedings, but also its risks and dangers. That ADR might undermine substantive consumer rights and offer no more than a second-class justice system have been frequent observations.[5]

The aim of this chapter is to trace the development of Consumer ADR in the EU and highlight the potential that lies in an investigation of the interactions between informal and formal justice. For that purpose, the chapter will first set the scene by briefly reconstructing the emergence of Consumer ADR in the EU, setting out the main features and provisions of the ADR Directive and the future policy challenges of the ADR framework (section 2.2). Subsequently, the chapter will explore how the Court of Justice of the European Union (hereafter 'CJEU' or 'Court') took a leading role in affirming the EU's policy approach by accommodating the promotion of ADR within the justified limitations of Article 47 EU Charter (section 2.3). Next, the chapter will highlight proposals for a complementary relationship between ADR and the courts (section 2.4). On the basis of the overall examination, the chapter's conclusion calls for the development of a structured interaction between courts and ADR (section 2.5).

Urszula Jaremba, Marlene Wind and Karolina Podstawa (eds), *National Courts and EU law: New Issues, Theories and Methods* (Edward Elgar 2016).

4 Anthi Beka, *The Active Role of Courts in Consumer Litigation* (Intersentia 2018); Chantal Mak and Betül Kas, *Civil Courts and the European Polity. The Constitutional Role of Private Law Adjudication in Europe* (Hart Publishing 2022).

5 Horst Eidenmüller and Martin Engel, 'Against False Settlement: Designing Efficient Consumer Rights Enforcement Systems in Europe' (2014) 29 *Ohio State Journal on Dispute Resolution* 261; Gerhard Wagner, 'Private Law Enforcement Through ADR: Wonder Drug or Snake Oil?' (2014) 51(1) *Common Market Law Review* 165; Per Henrik Lindblom, 'ADR – The Opiate of the Legal System?' (2008) 16(1) *European Review of Private Law* 63.

2.2 THE DEVELOPMENT OF CONSUMER ADR IN THE EU

2.2.1 The Emergence of Consumer ADR

ADR was for the first time included in the EU discussion on consumer access to justice by the Commission's 1993 Green Paper 'Access of Consumers to Justice and the Settlement of Consumer Disputes in the Single Market'.[6] At that time, access to justice was still understood to mean access to court. In that sense, the Green Paper stressed the constitutional dimension of access to justice, which constitutes a core principle of the rule of law and a human right.[7] It identified as a key problem that legal norms established by the Community legal order rely for their enforcement on the national courts, which adhere to the procedures of their respective Member State. Specifically, barriers of access to justice at the national level hamper the effectiveness and non-discriminatory application of Community law.[8]

In order to start a discussion on access to justice in consumer matters, the Green Paper provided a comparative survey on the situation in the Member States. This led, among others, to the finding that alongside (or upstream of) court procedures, a number of alternatives (or supplementary) dispute resolution instruments have been developed at national level. The Commission observed that the 'multiplicity of initiatives (and the welcome many of them have received) proves that the "demand" for justice, as regards consumer disputes, is not "satisfied" in certain Member States by existing court procedures'.[9] Specifically, their cost and duration are very often disproportionate to the value of the dispute. The suspicion is expressed that '[t]his trend, in the absence of measures designed to facilitate "public" access to justice, is likely to continue'.[10]

The Green Paper contained no hints that ADR would become an integral part of the EU's consumer policy. Instead, the Commission highlighted the problems associated with ADR, specifically:

> the extent to which the guarantees of independence (at least impartiality), which in rule-of-law states are invested in the judiciary, can be assured by the new 'judges'

---

[6] European Commission, *Access of consumers to justice and the settlement of consumer disputes in the single market* (Green Paper, COM(93) 576 final).
[7] Ibid., 5.
[8] Ibid., 6.
[9] Ibid., 58.
[10] Ibid.

> who are increasingly being called on to settle disputes outside the framework of the courts proper.[11]

However, importantly, one of the main tools of the EU's future policy was already highlighted, namely the role of minimum quality standards in ensuring that 'consumer will trust instances other than the courts' and counter the risk of "misleading advertising" which in the medium term could jeopardise the very idea of 'alternative' justice'.[12]

Three years later, the Commission followed up with the Communication 'Action Plan on consumer access to justice and the settlement of consumer disputes in the internal market'.[13] The Communication further problematised consumer disputes in view of the typical disproportion between the economic sum at stake and the cost of its legal resolution, raising the question as to how to reconcile the requirement that justice be rendered without discrimination with the constraints of the budget for the administration of justice. With respect to the former requirement, the Commission refers once more to the human rights dimension of the issue, reasoning that the right to a fair trial in Article 6 ECHR 'knows no exceptions as regards the value of the issue at stake, and applies also to what are considered as small disputes (by the administration of justice, but not by the citizens concerned)'.[14] The citizen-dimension is emphasised: 'it is the small disputes of everyday life that give ordinary citizens an opportunity to gauge the effectiveness of the law – and not the headline-making court cases, which rarely concern them'.[15] Next to that, the Communication highlights the internal market dimension of the problem: the barriers which stem from and are related to the judicial settlement of cross-border consumer disputes hinder the smooth functioning of the internal market, on the same line as technical and tax barriers.[16]

Instead of engaging with simplified court procedures, the Commission decided that the initial focus of the Community must be on out-of-court procedures. It reasoned that the proliferation of out-of-court bodies at national level should not be ignored by the Community but should be rendered fruitful for the internal market. National experience has shown the key role of certain minimum criteria for establishing trust among consumers. Thus, the inten-

---

11 Ibid.

12 Ibid., 83.

13 European Commission, *Action plan on consumer access to justice and the settlement of consumer disputes in the internal market* (Communication, COM/96/0013 FINAL).

14 Ibid., 5, footnote 3.

15 Ibid., 5.

16 Ibid., 8.

tion was set to adopt a list of minimum criteria for out-of-court settlement procedures for consumer disputes to support and supplement the policies of the Member States that have chosen to promote a 'conciliation culture' in the domain of consumer disputes.[17] With the support of the European Parliament,[18] the Commission adopted two Recommendations containing minimum quality requirements for the out-of-court resolution of consumer disputes. While Recommendation 98/257/EC's scope encompasses procedures, which lead to the settling of a dispute through the active intervention of a third party, who proposes or imposes a solution,[19] Recommendation 2001/310/EC applies to third-party procedures that involve an attempt to bring the parties together to convince them to find a solution.[20]

Around ten years later, the shortcomings of the EU's soft law approach were identified, namely geographic and sectoral gaps in ADR coverage, low awareness among consumers caused by lack of information, non-compliance with the quality principles, and, on that basis, non-effective resolution of disputes, particularly when e-commerce transactions were concerned.[21] As a response, the ADR Directive 2013/11/EU and the ODR Regulation 524/2013 were adopted in 2013. The ADR Directive requires the Member States to guarantee the availability of ADR entities that comply with binding quality requirements. The ODR Regulation builds on the infrastructure of quality-certified ADR entities. It provides a multilingual interactive platform that allows consumers to submit online their disputes over online purchases, informs the parties on the quality-certified ADR entities competent to handle their case and transmits the dispute to the ADR entity on which the parties have agreed.[22] As typical for the area of EU consumer law, both legal acts have chosen the EU's internal

---

[17] Ibid., 14.

[18] European Parliament, *Resolution on the Commission communication 'Action plan on consumer access to justice and the settlement of consumer disputes in the internal market'* (COM (96)0013 – C4-0195/96) [1996] OJ C 362/275.

[19] Commission Recommendation of 30 March 1998 on the principles applicable to the bodies responsible for out-of-court settlement of consumer disputes [1998] OJ L 115/31.

[20] Commission Recommendation of 4 April 2001 on the principles for out-of-court bodies involved in the consensual resolution of consumer disputes [2001] OJ L 109/56.

[21] Commission Staff Working Paper, Executive Summary Of The Impact Assessment, Accompanying the document Proposal for a Directive of the European Parliament and of the Council on Alternative Dispute Resolution for consumer disputes (Directive on consumer ADR) and Proposal for a Regulation of the European Parliament and of the Council on Online Dispute Resolution for consumer disputes (Regulation on consumer ODR) (COM(2011) 793 final).

[22] Since the platform has been set up as a mere referral system that does not itself provide for an actual tool for the resolution of disputes, the focus of this chapter will be laid on the ADR Directive's regulatory framework.

market competence in Article 114 TFEU as legal basis. As specified in their first recitals, the EU legislature seeks a 'high level' of consumer protection in line with Article 169 TFEU and Article 38 EU Charter.

2.2.2 Key Features of the ADR Directive

The ADR Directive guarantees the consumer's right to access a quality-certified ADR entity to resolve disputes with EU traders over purchases of products or services.[23] For that purpose, the Member States are under an obligation to ensure the availability of quality-certified ADR entities[24] for domestic and cross-border disputes throughout the Union[25] and in virtually all retail sectors (so-called 'full ADR coverage'),[26] irrespective of whether the purchase was made offline or online.

The Member States are given the possibility of fulfilling their obligation by building on existing ADR entities and adjusting their scope of application, if needed, or by providing for the creation of new ADR entities. In order to ensure full coverage, they may set up a residual ADR entity which is competent to deal with those disputes for the resolution of which no existing ADR entity is competent.[27] In contrast to the citizen's constitutional guarantee of access to a court, the Member States are however not obliged to operate ADR entities themselves through public funding. The availability of ADR processes can be assured through public or private funding or a combination thereof.[28] In addition, the directive does not prescribe a specific type of ADR process, thus allowing for processes where an ADR entity proposes or imposes a solution or brings the parties together with the aim of facilitating an amicable solution.[29]

The directive's core is constituted by the harmonised minimum quality principles, which should strengthen both consumers' and traders' confidence in ADR processes.[30] Compliance is ensured through a specific certification and monitoring mechanism: Member States designate national competent authorities that establish and maintain national lists of ADR entities whose

---

23 ADR Directive, art 5(1). The directive deals exclusively with disputes of consumers against traders, see art 2(2)(g) and recital 16.

24 ADR entities are established on a durable basis, offer the resolution of a dispute through an ADR procedure, and are listed in accordance with the directive's certification procedure, see art 4(1)(h).

25 ADR Directive, art 5(2)(e).

26 ADR Directive, art 2(2), with the exception of non-economic services of general interest, health and education.

27 ADR Directive, art 5(3).

28 ADR Directive, recital 46.

29 ADR Directive, art 2(1) and (4), see also recital 21.

30 ADR Directive, recital 37.

compliance with the quality requirements they have certified. The national authorities are required to monitor ADR entities' compliance on an ongoing basis and only compliant ADR entities may remain listed.[31] In the following, the main features of the directive's principles will be briefly set out:

Expertise, independence and impartiality

Natural persons entrusted with the resolution of disputes must possess the necessary knowledge and skills in the field of alternative or judicial resolution of consumer disputes and a general understanding of law in order to understand the legal implications of the dispute.[32] In addition, it is required that the person in charge is appointed for a term of office of sufficient duration, not subject to any instructions from either party or their representatives and remunerated in a way that is not linked to the outcome of the procedure.[33] Where the decision maker is a collegial body, an equal number of representatives for consumers' interests and of representatives for traders' interests has to be ensured.[34] Although consumer complaint-handling systems operated by the trader are not covered by the scope of the Directive,[35] the establishment of ADR entities with a link to businesses is possible under stricter requirements.[36]

Transparency

Transparency entails two different components: on the one hand, with regard to access to and information about the ADR entity,[37] and, on the other hand, with regard to the conduct, the various steps and outcome of the dispute resolution process.[38] Notably, an obligation has been included to publish information about systematic or significant problems that frequently lead to disputes between consumers and traders, which may be accompanied by rec-

---

[31] ADR Directive, arts 19–20. The practical application of this mechanism has been extensively studied by Biard, see Alexandre Biard, 'Monitoring Consumer ADR Quality in the EU: A Critical Perspective' (2018) 26(2) *European Review of Private Law* 171; Alexandre Biard, 'Impact of Directive 2013/11/EU on Consumer ADR: Evidence from France and the UK' (2018) *Journal of Consumer Policy* 1; Alexandre Biard, 'Towards High-Quality Consumer ADR: The Belgian Experience' in Loïc Cadiet, Burkhard Hess and Marta Requejo Isidro (eds), *Privatizing Dispute Resolution. Trend and Limits* (Nomos 2019) 79.

[32] ADR Directive, art 6(1)(a).

[33] ADR Directive, art 6(1)(b)–(c).

[34] ADR Directive, art 6(5).

[35] ADR Directive, art 2(2)(b).

[36] ADR Directive, art 6(3) and (4).

[37] ADR Directive, art 7(1)(a)–(f).

[38] ADR Directive, art 7(1)(g)–(o).

ommendations as to how such problems can be avoided or resolved in future.[39] The recitals clarify the aim of this obligation to raise traders' standards and to facilitate the exchange of information and best practices.[40]

Effectiveness

According to Article 8 ADR Directive, the essential features of an effective ADR procedure are constituted by easy access and speedy conflict resolution. Particularly, the procedure should be easily accessible online and offline, not require a lawyer or legal adviser, generate little or no costs for the consumer, and should generally be concluded within 90 days of receipt of the complaint file.

Fairness

Fairness consists of two main elements. First, it sets out in basic terms the adversarial nature of the procedure and the parties' right to be heard.[41] Secondly, it safeguards the voluntary nature of ADR processes which aim at resolving the dispute by proposing a solution.[42] Voluntariness comprises both participation in the procedure and acceptance of the outcome. It is secured by the possibility of withdrawing from the procedure at any stage. While national law may require the mandatory participation by traders,[43] the consumer must always be able to exit the procedure.[44] The voluntary nature of ADR is rendered effective by requiring that the parties must be informed that participation in the procedure does not preclude the possibility of seeking redress through court proceedings, that the proposed solution may be different from an outcome determined by a court applying legal rules, and about the legal effect of agreeing to or following a proposed solution.[45]

Liberty

Member States are obliged to ensure that pre-dispute agreements to lodge a complaint with an ADR entity are not binding on consumers if they were concluded before the dispute arose and if they deprive the consumer of the right to resort to the courts.[46] Moreover, ADR procedures are permitted to impose a binding solution only if the consumer has been informed about the

---

39 ADR Directive, art 7(2)(b).
40 ADR Directive, recital 30.
41 ADR Directive, art 9(1).
42 ADR Directive, art 9(2).
43 ADR Directive, recitals 43 and 49.
44 ADR Directive, art 9(2)(a) and (b).
45 ADR Directive, art 9(2)(b)(ii) and art 9(2)(c).
46 ADR Directive, art 10(1).

binding nature in advance and has expressly accepted this. Specific acceptance by the trader is not required if national law requires that solutions are binding on traders.[47] Although formally not part of the principle of liberty, it is noteworthy in this context that according to Article 12(1), the Member States must ensure that limitation or prescription periods are suspended during the conduct of the ADR process.

Legality

Article 11 ADR Directive safeguards that the consumer is not deprived of the protection by mandatory consumer protection rules if the ADR body imposes a solution on the consumer.

2.2.3 Future Policy Challenges for Consumer ADR

In September 2019, the European Commission published its first report on the application of the ADR Directive. The Commission found that the availability and quality of ADR have been reinforced in the entire Union. The report problematises however that ADR has not yet realised its potential due to its slow uptake among consumers and traders.[48] ADR is still underused. The Commission identified three main challenges that limit the current framework's full effectiveness: First, awareness levels among both consumers and traders are still insufficient.[49] Second, the diversity of ADR landscapes makes them difficult to navigate for consumers and traders, in particular in Member States with a large number of certified ADR entities.[50] Third, the report notes that it is insufficient that currently only one in three retailers is willing to use ADR, even if overall traders' participation in ADR has increased.[51] The 2021 Consumer Conditions Survey confirmed a low popularity of ADR and ODR among consumers. Notably, in the event of experiencing future problems, only 8 per cent of consumers have indicated that they would approach an ADR body, while 15 per cent would try to take the provider to court.[52]

---

47 ADR Directive, art 10(2).

48 European Commission, Report on alternative dispute resolution for consumer disputes and Regulation (EU) No 524/2013 of the European Parliament and of the Council on online dispute resolution for consumer disputes (COM(2019) 425 final).

49 Ibid., 9.

50 Ibid., 10.

51 Ibid., 10. The findings of the Commission are largely shared by the European Consumer Organisation, see BEUC, Stepping up the Enforcement of Consumer Protection Rules (BEUC-X-2020-083 – 11/09/2020).

52 European Commission, Consumer Conditions Survey: Consumers at home in the single market – 2021 edition, Key highlights, 9.

2.3 THE ROLE OF ARTICLE 47 EU CHARTER IN REGULATING CONSUMER ADR

The CJEU took a leading role in legitimising the promotion of Consumer ADR as a tool for enhancing access to justice in the EU. The reception and integration of ADR in the CJEU's case law have been of particular interest. The Court played a prominent role in constructing the EU legal order through the conferral of individual legal rights and the so-called 'Europeanisation' of national remedies and procedures according to the principles of equivalence, effectiveness and effective judicial protection.[53] Two preliminary references by the Italian judiciary gave the Court an opportunity to engage with ADR in consumer disputes. Although Article 47 EU Charter governs formally merely the right to access a court, the rulings reveal how the provision has concurrently (i) accommodated a broad notion of access to justice that encompasses both the courts and ADR, and (ii) set boundaries to restrictions of the autonomy of consumers to choose freely between the courts and ADR.

2.3.1 Accommodating a Broad Notion of Access to Justice in Article 47 EU Charter

Before the adoption of the ADR Directive, the CJEU had been asked to assess the relationship between the promotion of ADR processes and the judicial protection of rights conferred by the EU legal order. Specifically, *Alassini and Others*[54] concerned the Italian transposition of the Universal Service Directive, which harmonises not only certain rights of end-users of telecom services; it also requires that the Member States ensure that transparent, simple and inexpensive out-of-court procedures are available for the fair and prompt resolution of consumer disputes relating to issues covered by the Directive.[55] The applicants in the dispute underlying the preliminary reference initiated legal proceedings against two telecom companies in order to obtain damages for breach of contracts. The companies objected that these actions were inadmissible, since the applicants had not first sought an out-of-court settlement, in accordance with Italian law. The referring court questioned the compliance

53 Most prominently, Walter van Gerven, 'Of Rights, Remedies and Procedures' (2000) 37(3) *Common Market Law Review* 501.

54 Joined cases C-317/08, C-318/08, C-319/08 and C-320/08 *Rosalba Alassini v Telecom Italia SpA, Filomena Califano v Wind SpA, Lucia Anna Giorgia Iacono v Telecom Italia SpA and Multiservice Srl v Telecom Italia SpA* EU:C:2010:146.

55 See Art 34 of Directive 2002/22/EC of the European Parliament and of the Council of 7 March 2002 on Universal Service and users' rights relating to electronic communications networks and services [2002] OJ L 108/51.

of national law with EU law, insofar as it made access to court subject to the mandatory condition of a prior attempt to settle the dispute.

The Court reviewed the Italian provisions against the Universal Service Directive and the right to effective judicial protection. In this context, it drew to the tension that results at least partly also from within EU law itself: On the one hand, the Court noted that national law rendering out-of-court procedure mandatory strengthens the effectiveness of the Universal Service Directive.[56] On the other hand, it equally recognised that making the admissibility of legal proceedings conditional upon the prior implementation of an out-of-court settlement procedure affects the exercise of rights conferred on individuals by the same directive.[57]

As it falls within the Member State's procedural autonomy to introduce a mandatory ADR process, the principles of equivalence and effectiveness are applicable. Under the principle of effectiveness, national procedural rules are precluded by EU law if they render it practically impossible or excessively difficult for individuals to exercise their rights conferred by EU law. The CJEU held that a mandatory attempt at settlement does not conflict with the principle of effectiveness provided that certain requirements are met,[58] namely that (1) the outcome of the settlement procedure is not binding on the parties;[59] (2) the settlement procedure does not result in a substantial delay for the purposes of bringing legal proceedings;[60] (3) for the duration of the settlement procedure, the period for the time-barring of claims is suspended;[61] (4) the settlement procedure does not entail significant costs;[62] (4) the procedure could be accessed not only online, but also offline;[63] (5) where the urgency of the situation requires interim measures, the settlement procedure allows, or does not preclude, the adoption of such measures.[64]

The Court confirmed subsequently that this outcome is also in line with the principle of effective judicial protection as enshrined in Articles 6 and 13 of the ECHR and Article 47 of the EU Charter, even though a mandatory settlement procedure inserts an additional step for access to the courts.[65] The

---

56 Joined cases C-317/08, C-318/08, C-319/08 and C-320/08 *Rosalba Alassini v Telecom Italia SpA, Filomena Califano v Wind SpA, Lucia Anna Giorgia Iacono v Telecom Italia SpA and Multiservice Srl v Telecom Italia SpA* EU:C:2010:146, para 45.

57 Ibid., para 52.

58 Ibid., para 53.

59 Ibid., para 54.

60 Ibid., para 55.

61 Ibid., para 56.

62 Ibid., para 57.

63 Ibid., para 58.

64 Ibid., para 59.

65 Ibid., para 62.

right to access a court is not absolute and may be subject to justifiable limitations.[66] The Court held that the restrictions resulting from the Italian legislation pursued legitimate objectives in the general interest, namely the quicker and less expensive settlement of disputes and a lightening of the burden on the court system. In addition, subject to the previously mentioned five requirements, the imposition of a mandatory out-of-court settlement procedure cannot be considered disproportionate.[67] Affirming the view of Advocate General Kokott, the Court underlined that no less restrictive alternative to the implementation of a mandatory procedure exists, since the introduction of an optional procedure is not as efficient a means of achieving those objectives.[68]

While *Alassini* concerned the specific issue of mandatory ADR, the Court's reasoning gives wider-ranging insights. Although Article 47 of the EU Charter formally guarantees merely the right to access a court, the ruling illustrates that the provision gives space for a broad notion of effective access to justice, which encompasses both the courts and ADR.[69] The Court recognised that the promotion of ADR pursues legitimate objectives, namely the effective administration of justice. As the effective administration of justice as such is a prerequisite to render the individual's right to access a court effective, it could be even argued that problems in the administration of justice may oblige a Member State to consider introducing a mandatory pre-trial attempt of ADR.[70] The Court made however equally clear that ADR's legitimacy is conditional on the fulfilment of its promises in terms of offering an accessible and efficient dispute resolution process. Thus, the Court gave further impetus to the EU's approach based on the introduction of quality standards for ADR. The Court's requirements have been indeed subsequently integrated in the ADR

---

66 Ibid., para 63.

67 Ibid., para 64.

68 Ibid., para 65.

69 Chantal Mak, 'Rights and Remedies. Article 47 EUCFR and Effective Judicial Protection in European Private Law Matters' in Hans W. Micklitz (ed), *Constitutionalization of European Private Law* (OUP 2014), 236–58, 258; prominently, a broad notion of access to justice that includes ADR processes has been proposed by Mauro Cappelletti and Bryant Garth, 'Access to Justice: The Worldwide Movement to Make Rights Effective. A General Report' in Mauro Cappelletti and Bryant Garth (eds), *Access to Justice. A World Survey* vol I, book 1 (Sijthoff Giuffrè 1978) 6–9.

70 Similarly, Advocate General Saugmandsgaard Øe in his opinion in Case C-75/16 *Livio Menini and Maria Antonia Rampanelli v Banco Popolare – Società Cooperativa*, EU:C:2017:132, para 76: '(…) since the aim of that obligation is allegedly to lighten the burden on the court system — an objective which the Court has recognised as being legitimate –, it also promotes, indirectly, access for consumers to the judicial system (…)'.

Directive, rendering them thereby relevant not only for mandatory pre-trial out-of-court procedures, but for all quality-certified ADR processes in the EU.

2.3.2 Upholding ADR's Voluntary Basis Through Article 47 EU Charter

While the Court's interpretation of Article 47 EU Charter gave support to the promotion of high-quality ADR processes, it also underlined the importance of maintaining ADR's voluntary basis. This aspect has been elaborated by the Court in its subsequent ruling in *Menini and Rampanelli*, which succeeded the ADR Directive and arose out of another preliminary reference by an Italian court. The case dealt with two consumers who brought an appeal against an order for payment obtained against them by a bank following the grant of a credit by the latter. The referring court took the view that Italian law makes it necessary to dismiss the application for suspension of provisional enforcement as the consumers must, in order for the appeal to be admissible, use a mediation procedure. However, the national court noted the rather ambiguous wording of Article 1 of the ADR Directive, which in its first sentence requires the Member States to ensure that *consumers can, on a voluntary basis*, submit complaints against traders to an ADR entity and in its second sentence provides for the possibility, for the Member States, of making *participation in ADR procedures mandatory,* provided that such legislation does not prevent the parties from exercising their right of access to the judicial system. The Italian court thus decided to ask the CJEU whether a mandatory recourse to a mediation procedure as a condition for the admissibility of legal proceedings is compatible with the directive.

The CJEU held that the Member States retain under the ADR Directive their full legislative autonomy in making ADR processes mandatory or optional, on condition that the parties' right of access to the judicial system is maintained.[71] With regard to the latter aspect, the Court confirmed the applicability of its ruling in *Alassini* and the relevance of the requirements established therein for mediation procedures.[72] Going beyond its ruling in *Alassini*, the Court provided more detailed explanations on the voluntary nature of ADR processes. The Court derived guidance from recital 13 of the Mediation Directive 2008/52,[73] which explains that the voluntary nature of mediation lies not in the freedom of

---

[71] Case C-75/16 *Livio Menini and Maria Antonia Rampanelli v Banco Popolare – Società Cooperativa* EU:C:2017:457.

[72] Ibid., para 61.

[73] Directive 2008/52/EC of the European Parliament and of the Council of 21 May 2008 on certain aspects of mediation in civil and commercial matters [2008] OJ L 136/3.

the parties to choose whether or not to use that process but in the fact that the parties are themselves in charge of the process, may organise it as they wish and terminate it at any time.[74] Accordingly, in order to secure the consumer's right of access to the judicial system, the Court stressed the importance of the right to withdraw from the mediation procedure and to reject its outcome. Both aspects are secured through the ADR Directive. Regarding the former, Article 9(2)(a) ADR Directive requires the Member States to ensure that the parties have the possibility of withdrawing from the procedure at any stage if they are dissatisfied with its performance or operation. In that respect, the Court clarified that national legislation may not restrict the consumer's right to withdraw from a mediation procedure to the extent that she/he demonstrates the existence of a valid reason in support of that decision. To the contrary, the consumer must be able to bring the procedure to an end without restriction immediately after the first meeting with the mediator.[75] Regarding the latter, in accordance with Article 9(2)(b) of ADR Directive, at the end of the ADR procedure, a solution is merely proposed to the parties and they have the choice as to whether or not to agree to or follow it. Even though Article 9(3) establishes the possibility for national legislation to provide that the outcome of ADR procedures is binding on traders, such a possibility requires that the consumer has previously accepted the proposed solution.[76]

Menini and Rampanelli has shown how the right to access a court has the ability to uphold ADR's voluntary basis and thus limit mandatory features to a pre-trial attempt. The voluntary nature of ADR is not only essential to secure access to the judiciary, but also to maintain the fundamental nature of ADR as such. Traditionally, party autonomy and consent form the fundamentals of legitimising out-of-court dispute resolution. Differently to court procedures, ADR processes are considered able to account for parties' self-determination, which forms the basis for mutually acceptable and lasting outcomes.[77] Hence, compelling the parties who are opposed to ADR to the use of such a process beyond an initial attempt obstructs not only the fundamental right to access to a court but risks also undermining the effectiveness of the ADR process as such.

---

[74] Case C-75/16 *Livio Menini and Maria Antonia Rampanelli v Banco Popolare – Società Cooperativa* EU:C:2017:457, para 50.

[75] Ibid., paras 66–70.

[76] Ibid., para 58.

[77] Burkhard Hess, 'Privatizing Dispute Resolution and its Limits' in Loïc Cadiet, Burkhard Hess and Marta Requejo Isidro (eds), *Privatizing Dispute Resolution. Trend and Limits* (Nomos 2019), 17, 22.

2.4 SHAPING THE INTERACTION BETWEEN ADR AND THE COURTS

The CJEU has played a key role in giving impetus to the EU's efforts of promoting the availability of high-quality ADR in the EU and in legitimising the Member States' experimentation with mandatory pre-trial ADR in order to further the effective administration of justice. However, the Court's favourable position towards ADR has not yet led to a broader discussion about the proper relationship between ADR and the courts.[78] The EU requires the Member States to set up ADR entities that are standing next to the courts. Hence, the European framework does not enable a so-called 'multi-door courthouse model' but gives rather rise to a 'multi-option system'.[79] Such a system leaves the question of whether a dispute is resolved by ADR or court to the parties' choice. The development of a synergetic relationship between the courts and ADR constitutes still an untapped potential.

Giving the judge the power to refer disputes to ADR could, on the one hand, lead to a 'responsible' delegation of disputes to ADR and easing of the judiciary's caseload, and, on the other hand, increase public confidence in ADR. Such an approach is promoted by the ELI-ENCJ Statement on formal and informal justice, which constitutes the most prominent (soft law) instrument dealing with the question of how courts and judges should interact with ADR processes at European level.[80] The Statement sees in the courts a key player that could encourage ADR. Enhancing the judge's role in referring disputes to ADR processes would strengthen the so-called 'managerial role' of the judge, who has to engage in a balancing act between the need for a legal pronouncement and the parties' concerns about speed and costs.

The question about how ADR processes could contribute towards upholding the fundamental role of the courts which lies in developing and clarifying the law remains largely unaddressed.[81] The fundamental legal importance of a legal dispute is not explicitly included among the grounds on the basis of which the Member States may permit ADR entities to refuse to deal with

[78] Xandra Kramer, Jos Hoevenaars and Erlis Themeli, 'Frontiers in Civil Justice – Privatizing, Digitizing and Funding Justice' (Chapter 1).

[79] On the difference, see Tania Sourdin, 'The Role of Courts in the New Justice System' (2015) 7 *Yearbook on Arbitration and Mediation* 95.

[80] ELI-ENCJ statement on The Relationship between Formal and Informal Justice: The Courts and Alternative Dispute Resolution, adopted by ELI and ENCJ in 2018.

[81] On the role of courts, see Owen Fiss, 'Against False Settlement' (1984) 93 *Yale Law Journal* 1073, 1085; Hazel Genn, 'What Is Civil Justice For? Reform, ADR, and Access to Justice' (2012) 24(1) *Yale Journal of Law & the Humanities* 397.

a dispute according to the ADR Directive.[82] It is indeed questionable whether it is legitimate to deny a consumer access to an ADR process on the basis of such a ground. It implies the risk that the consumer will be denied any redress if she/he shies away from initiating possibly complex, lengthy and costly court proceedings. ADR processes often constitute the only proportionate route to redress for low value claims.

In the literature, proposals have been made to place ADR bodies under a duty or to enable them to refer preliminary references to the courts in case disputes raise points of law that have not yet been clarified by the courts. Such test cases could serve the clarification of statutory interpretations and assure greater consistency. A national court could in turn raise the matter to the CJEU.[83] It seems that such a solution has not yet been implemented in practice. The question is what role should be given to the parties' interests in the ADR body's decision of referring a preliminary question to court. It should be cautioned that such an approach could considerably delay the ADR process against the interests of the parties, which might have chosen ADR precisely in order to reduce complexity and find a flexible solution.

As has been shown by the discussion of *Menini and Rampanelli*, it is a key feature of the EU's multi-option system that the question of whether a dispute reaches court is left to the consumer's choice in line with Article 47 EU Charter.[84] However, whether the consumer has *in fact* a choice can be debated. While the outcome of the ADR process may not be legally binding on the consumer, it may be factually binding. There is a risk that the consumer will accept the outcome reached by ADR rather than filing a lawsuit even if the agreement is disadvantageous for the consumer. The ADR entity's authority as validated by the certification process, the typical discourse on the disadvantages of court procedures and the advantages of ADR processes in terms of costs, time and outcome, as well as the prospect of an immediate compensation by the trader, make it seem plausible that a consumer will rather refrain from a new, time-consuming and costly – and in the end uncertain – court procedure and agree to the settlement. Thus, an outcome that is disadvantageous for

---

82 ADR Directive, art 5(4). However, the Member States may allow ADR entities to refuse dealing with complex disputes that would seriously impair the effective operation of the ADR entity.

83 Pablo Cortés and Rafał Mańko, 'Developments in European Civil Procedures' in Pablo Cortés (ed), *The New Regulatory Framework for Consumer Dispute Resolution* (OUP 2016), 41, 57–58; Marco Loos, 'Enforcing Consumer Rights through ADR at the Detriment of Consumer Law' (2016) 24(1) *European Review of Private Law* 76–78.

84 On the importance of informed consent, see Jacqueline Nolan-Haley, 'Informed Consent in Mediation: A Guiding Principle for Truly Educated Decisionmaking' (1998) *Notre Dame Law Review* 775.

the consumer can trigger rational apathy on the side of the consumer with respect to taking action before court. Particularly in cases of legal uncertainty, instead of choosing recourse to the courts, it is conceivable that the consumer rather accepts the settlement than risks receiving nothing. The consumer's conflict behaviour may be also negatively impacted if its complaint is found to be unfounded, particularly if the neutral person in charge of the process is accorded a high level of recognition.

To counter these problems, the ADR Directive enhances the consumer's autonomous and educated decision-making by requiring ADR entities to provide the parties with information on the consequences of the choices made in the context of the ADR process.[85] This approach is in line with the CJEU's recent case law. In *Ibercaja Banco SA*, the Court highlighted that 'the right to effective consumer protection includes the option to waive the exercise of one's rights'.[86] Specifically, the Court accepted that a consumer may waive the right to rely on the unfairness of a contractual term in the context of a novation agreement, provided that that waiver is the result of free and informed consent.[87] That means that, at the time of the waiver, the consumer must have been aware of the non-binding nature of that term and of the consequences resulting from it.[88] Particularly where the consumer is not assisted by a lawyer, the person in charge of the ADR process has a key role in providing consumers with adequate information to ensure its informed consent, thus guaranteeing that the right to access a court is not undermined.

2.5 CONCLUSIONS AND OUTLOOK

The benefits of, but also criticism on, the promotion of Consumer ADR have been primarily developed by comparing ADR processes to court procedures. Accordingly, the courts are seen as the main parameter for assessing all aspects of the ADR process: from the forms of protection that can be obtained, the procedural guarantees to be observed, the substantive outcome reached, to the legal effects of the final agreement. This perspective has led to useful results in improving the quality of ADR as reflected in the minimum procedural guarantees, thus enhancing the role of ADR in guaranteeing access to a fair process. The EU's approach to ADR appears to rely on the findings of procedural justice theory, which contend that the substantive outcome reached through a process will be seen to be fair by the litigants if the process as such and the treatment

---

85 ADR Directive, recital 42; see also the elaborations on the principle of fairness in section 2.2.2 of this chapter.

86 Case C-452/18 *XZ v Ibercaja Banco SA* EU:C:2020:536, para 25.

87 Ibid., para 28.

88 Ibid., para 29.

of the parties within that process are fair.[89] Indeed, while the ADR Directive's quality principles have been found to reflect to some extent the core features of the fundamental right to a fair trial,[90] they leave the normative basis of the outcome reached by ADR processes unaddressed. This aspect has been subject to criticism in the literature, which underlines the need for a rights-based process in consumer disputes. The further ADR processes are however assimilated to those of the court's, the greater the risk of undermining the nature and benefits of ADR, while obscuring at the same time the potential for the search for more innovative solutions. The search for interactions between ADR and other mechanisms could potentially lead to more promising avenues for future development. For instance, with respect to the enforcement of consumer law, it has been shown that the data collected by ADR entities could be valuable for identifying systemic sectoral trends and facilitating market surveillance by regulators.[91] When it comes to the relationship between ADR and the courts, the EU does not offer yet a vision. So far, it pursues a multi-option system, which offers the well-informed consumer the opportunity to switch from ADR to court if she/he is dissatisfied with the ADR process or its outcome. In that respect, the CJEU case law has allowed the Member States to experiment with mandatory pre-trial ADR under the ADR Directive. The ELI-ENCJ Statement on formal and informal justice proposes how judges could encourage the use of and public confidence in ADR processes by either informing the parties about their availability or referring suitable disputes to them. On the other hand, the question about the approach that ADR processes should adopt in interacting with courts and judges remains largely unaddressed at European level.

---

[89] Rebecca Hollander-Blumoff and Tom R. Tyler, 'Procedural Justice in Negotiation: Procedural Fairness, Outcomes Acceptance, and Integrative Potential' (2008) 33 *Law & Society Inquiry* 473.

[90] Anne Kamphorst, 'The Right to a Fair Trial in Online Consumer Dispute Resolution' (2019) 8(5) *Journal of European Consumer and Market Law* 175.

[91] Cooperation between ADR entities and national authorities enforcing consumer law is supported by the ADR Directive, see art 17; see on this aspect Christopher Hodges, 'Consumer Redress: Implementing the Vision' in Pablo Cortés (ed), *The New Regulatory Framework for Consumer Dispute Resolution* (OUP 2016) 351; Christopher Hodges, 'The consumer as regulator' in Dorota Leczykiewicz and Stephen Weatherill (eds), *The Images of the Consumer in EU Law: Legislation, Free Movement and Competition Law* (OUP 2016) 245.

3. Formal and informal justice in Belgium

Stefaan Voet

3.1 INTRODUCTION

Disputes are traditionally resolved through the formal court system which involves a trial where a judge decides who is right or wrong. In Belgium, this is no different. As a consequence, and as in many European jurisdictions, the Belgian judiciary has been faced with a judicial backlog for decades. This is exacerbated by the fact that access to Belgian courts is generally easy: court fees are low[1] and lawyers are, at least compared to their neighbouring colleagues, not very expensive.

Within this formal court system, there are mechanisms in place allowing for the resolution of disputes without judicial adjudication. Two are discussed here: judicial (or court-connected) mediation (section 3.2.1) and judicial conciliation (section 3.2.2), the latter mainly being used by justices of the peace to settle small claims.

On the other hand, and over the years, the Belgian legislator has focused on, and increasingly incentivized, informal justice systems. These are disputes resolution processes that take place outside the formal court system, and that have a certain degree of stability, institutionalization, and legitimacy. Just like formal justice systems, they offer redress (remedies) but within a non-judicial context.

The traditional informal justice systems are arbitration (section 3.3.1) and out-of-court mediation (section 3.3.2). Their rules are laid down in the Belgian Judicial Code (hereafter: BJC). In 2018, the Belgian legislator introduced another option: collaborative negotiations (section 3.3.3).

[1] For the justices of the peace and the police courts the court fee is 50 EUR. For the courts of first instance and the commercial courts the court fee is 165 EUR. For the courts of appeal the court fee is 400 EUR. For the Court of Cassation the court fee is 650 EUR. These fees apply in all cases, irrespective of the value of the claim.

New forms of informal justice systems are appearing in Belgium. Under the influence of European legislation – and with the goal of facilitating and strengthening a real internal market for consumers – Belgium has created a robust, and compared to many other European jurisdictions, efficient and effective consumer dispute resolution (CDR) framework (section 3.3.4). At the centre is the Consumer Mediation Service, Belgium's residual ADR entity. In its capacity as a unique portal, it dispatches consumer complaints to specialized (and accredited) ADR entities. When no such entity exists, it deals with the dispute itself. Over the course of the years, the Consumer Mediation Service has become the dispute hub for consumers. On the other hand, but still in its infancy, another technique comes peeping over the mountain: regulatory redress, which is redress that is ordered or brought about by the intervention of public enforcers (section 3.3.5). It is a novel and controversial technique. Nevertheless, also in Belgium, it has proven its potential in offering quick and efficient redress.

These latter new forms of informal justice – CDR and regulatory redress – are an illustration of the fading division between public and private enforcement. In light of this, a plea is made for an integrated dispute resolution framework in which all options are connected in order to avoid enforcement gaps (section 3.4).

3.2 FORMAL JUSTICE SYSTEMS

3.2.1 Judicial (or Court-Connected) Mediation[2]

In 2005, the Belgian Mediation Act entered into force.[3] The Act added a new Part VII to the BJC. It broadened the scope of mediation from family cases

---

2 This subchapter is largely based on Piet Taelman and Stefaan Voet, 'Mediation in Belgium: A Long and Winding Road' in Carlos Esplugues and Louis Marquis (eds), *New Developments in Civil and Commercial Mediation. Global Comparative Perspectives* (Springer 2015) 89–112.

3 Loi du 21 fevrier 2005 modifiant le Code judiciaire en ce qui concerne la médiation, *Moniteur Belge* 22 mars 2005, 12.772. For an analysis see Benoît Allemeersch and others (eds), *De nieuwe wet op de bemiddeling* (die Keure 2005); Benoît Allemeersch, 'Een geactualiseerde inleiding tot de bemiddelingswet' in Raf Van Ransbeeck (ed), *Bemiddeling* (die Keure 2008); Annette Bridoux, *Les écrits en médiation selon le Code judiciaire et le Code de déontologie des médiateurs* (Larcier 2021); Olivier Caprasse, 'Médiation et arbitrage – Quinze ans d'évolutions du Code judiciaire' in Georges de Leval (ed), *La jurisprudence du Code Judiciaire commentée. Textes, annotations, jurisprudence et commentaires* (die Keure 2012); Michel Gonda, *Droit et pratique de la médiation, 2e édition* (Larcier 2021); Pierre-Paul Renson, *La médiation civile et commerciale. Comment éviter les aléas, le coût et la durée d'un procès* (Anthemis 2010).

to mediation in all types of civil, commercial and social cases. The Belgian Mediation Act therefore applies to mediation in all those cases. In 2018, the rules were amended.[4] However, the framework remained the same.

Mediation is defined as a confidential and structured process of voluntary deliberation between conflicting parties with the collaboration of an independent, neutral and objective third party who facilitates communication between the parties and assists them to find a solution by themselves.[5]

The most essential feature of mediation is that a mediator does not impose a solution. Unlike a judge, a mediator does not decide the dispute, but helps the parties to communicate so they can try to settle the dispute themselves. Mediation leaves the control of the outcome with the parties.

Belgian law distinguishes between out-of-court mediation and judicial (or court-connected) mediation. Out-of-court mediation is freely chosen by the parties before, during or after judicial proceedings,[6] without prompting or other involvement by the judge. This is a form of informal justice and is discussed more in detail below (section 3.3.2).

Judicial mediation is court-connected mediation: mediation that is ordered, with the consent of the parties, by the judge in the framework of a pending court procedure. However, in both cases (judicial and out-of-court mediation) participation is entirely voluntary, and any party can stop the procedure at any time.

One of the most important innovations of the 2018 reform is that the judge may now decide to impose a mediation process. In every stage of the proceedings (even in summary proceedings), a court may at the request of the parties or *sua sponte* but with the consent of the parties order mediation, as long as the

---

For an analysis in English see Michael Traest, 'Belgium' in Carlos Esplugues Mota, José Luis Iglesias and Guillermo Palao Moreno (eds), *Civil and Commercial Mediation in Europe. National Mediation Rules and Procedures. Vol. I* (Cambridge 2012) and Ivan Verougstraete, 'The Belgian Law on Mediation' in Institut de Formation Judiciaire (ed), *Family Mediation and Guidance in Cross-Border Disputes within the EU: How to improve Practices?* (Institut de Formation Judiciaire 2012). For a recent and comprehensive overview see Maxime Berlingin and Catherine Delforge (eds), *Modes amiables de règlement des conflits/Minnelijke geschillenoplossing* (die Keure 2021); Maxime Berlingin (coord), *Le temps des MARCs* [Modes alternatifs de résolution des conflits] (Larcier 2021) and Charles Devillers et Martin Marnix (eds), *Les alternatives au(x) procès classique(s)* (Anthemis 2021).

[4] Loi du 18 juin 2018 portant dispositions diverses en matière de droit civil et des dispositions en vue de promouvoir des formes alternatives de résolution des litiges, *Moniteur Belge* 2 juillet 2018, 53.455. See Stefaan Voet, 'Bemiddeling en andere vormen van alternatieve geschillenoplossing' in Piet Taelman and Benoît Allemeersch (eds), *Het burgerlijk proces opnieuw hervormd* (Intersentia 2019).

[5] Article 1723, §1 BJC.

[6] Article 1730, §1 BJC.

final arguments have not been concluded and the judge has not taken the case in deliberation.[7] Since the parties may only oppose it jointly, it is sufficient for one party to be in favour of mediation to obtain a court order imposing it on the parties.[8]

It is important to underline that if the parties agree to initiate judicial mediation, this does not have any impact on the claims they have brought or will bring before the court, nor does it on the merits of the case.

The decision ordering judicial mediation explicitly mentions the agreement of the parties to try mediation and the name, the capacity and the address of the mediator. The decision also states the timeframe provided for the parties to reach a solution (this cannot be longer than six months) and the date a court hearing will be held. The day of this court hearing should be the first possible day in court after the time allotted for mediation has expired.[9] At the hearing, the parties inform the judge about the outcome of the mediation process. If they have not reached an agreement they can opt for a new term or ask the judge to resume the judicial procedure.[10] In cases where the parties want an extension of the mediation period, the judge may grant it, but may limit this period in order to avoid an abuse of proceedings.[11]

During the (judicial) mediation process, the case technically remains under the management of the court. Any of the parties may ask the court to order provisional measures (e.g., to hear witnesses or to order the production of evidence). At the request of the mediator or one of the parties, the judge can end the mediation even before the end of the allotted mediation term.[12]

In case of judicial mediation, the statute of limitations is automatically tolled because judicial mediation is considered to be part of the judicial proceedings (as the case is still pending before the court during the mediation).

The course of judicial mediation is similar to voluntary mediation.[13] Parties have to conclude a mediation protocol and, in case of success, a mediation agreement. At the end of his or her mission, the mediator informs the judge in writing about the outcome of the mediation and whether the parties have reached an agreement. If so, the parties or one of them can initiate a homologation procedure. In case the mediation has led to a partial agreement, the judicial procedure will be continued.

---

7 Article 1734, §1 BJC.
8 Article 1734, §1 BJC.
9 Article 1734, §2 BJC.
10 Article 1734, §3 BJC.
11 Verougstraete (n 3) 155.
12 Article 1735, §3 BJC.
13 Article 1736, BJC.

3.2.2 Conciliation

Conciliation, as a method of settlement in court, necessarily involves a judge acting as a conciliator. This informal and quite often successful way of resolving disputes – especially before justices of the peace[14] – is governed by Articles 730/1-734 of the BJC. The rules were slightly amended by the 2018 Act.

It has to be underlined that the judge has no adjudicative power in such a case. As a rule,[15] proceedings may not yet have been commenced at the moment the judge will be requested to conciliate between the parties. The BJC provides that before going to court, a party and/or some of them and/or all the parties can voluntarily submit the dispute to the judge exclusively with the view of obtaining a settlement. Parties can simply write a letter to the clerk of the court asking to summon the opposing party or parties. The judge has to draft a procès-verbal of the conciliation session.[16] There are no costs.

The 2018 Act expanded the toolbox of the conciliation judge.[17] Except in summary proceedings, the judge can ask the parties how they have tried to settle the case before going to court. He can inform them about the possibilities to do so. The judge even can order the personal appearance of the parties. At the request of the parties, or if the judge deems it necessary, the case can be postponed for a maximum of one month to allow the parties to settle the case out of court.

In practice judges often make use of negotiation or mediation skills in their attempt to bring parties to an agreement. They suggest possible solutions for the dispute and even try to nudge the parties gently in the direction of a settlement. If an agreement is reached, it will be laid down in the procès-verbal of the conciliation session and will be enforceable as a judgment.[18] Under no circumstance can the agreement be appealed. In cases where the conciliation fails, the judge will draft a procès-verbal of non-settlement and each party may consider judicial proceedings.

However, some judges behave much more reluctant by giving the parties a voice and/or putting some question to them, without any formal attempt to reach a settlement. Such is in particular the case when an attempt to conciliate is compulsory, e.g., in labour cases.[19] It is generally accepted that a judge

---

[14] These are small claims courts dealing with cases of a value of lower than 5,000 EUR and rental disputes.

[15] Exceptions to that rule are labour law cases.

[16] Article 731 BJC.

[17] Article 730/1 BJC.

[18] Article 733 BJC.

[19] Pursuant to Article 972 BJC an expert appointed by a court has among others a duty to encourage a conciliation between the parties.

seized with a case should withdraw from it, at least if he made a formal or active attempt to conciliate the parties which failed. Such attempts of judges compromise their impartiality. Mandatory conciliation does not work well and is considered as an expensive nuisance rather than a useful tool. People go through the motions, but the exercise is generally unproductive. The same argument has been used by opponents of mandatory mediation.[20]

Conciliation has to be distinguished from mediation. While a conciliator quiet often indirectly recommends a solution, a (facilitative) mediator does not give any advice upon the resolution of the dispute. The mediator only assists the parties in working towards a self-negotiated settlement.

3.3 INFORMAL JUSTICE SYSTEMS

3.3.1 Arbitration

The Belgian rules on arbitration were amended in 2013,[21] largely inspired by the UNCITRAL Model Law.[22] The structure of Part VI of the BJC has been changed and the order of the articles been shuffled, but the content of the law has not been altered dramatically.[23] As arbitration law merely serves as a roadmap, parties are allowed to a large extent to set up their own arbitration rules or may use rules composed by an arbitration institute, such as the Belgian Center for Mediation and Arbitration (CEPANI).[24]

According to Belgian law, an arbitration agreement is an agreement by the parties to submit to arbitration all or certain disputes which have arisen, or which may arise between them in respect of a defined legal relationship, whether contractual or not.[25]

---

20 Verougstraete (n 3).

21 Loi du 24 juin 2013 modifiant la sixième partie du Code judiciaire relative à l'arbitrage, *Moniteur Belge* 28 juin 2013, 41.263. A translation in English is available at https://www.cepani.be/arbitration-what-is/ accessed 25 June 2021. See Niuscha Bassir and Maarten Draye (eds), *Arbitration in Belgium. A Practitioner's Guide* (Kluwer 2016).

22 Maud Piers and Dirk De Meulemeester, 'The Adoption of the UNCITRAL Model Law Encourages Arbitration in Belgium' [2013] 2 b-Arbitra 367 and Denis Philippe, 'Modernisation of the Belgian Law on Arbitration' [2014] 109 Revue internationale du droit des affaires 5.

23 Piers and De Meulemeester (n 22) 83.

24 https://www.cepani.be/ accessed 25 June 2021. See Benoît Allemeersch, Olivier Caprasse, Dirk De Meulemeester, Benoît Kohl and Emma Van Campenhoudt, *Guide to the CEPANI Arbitration Rules* (Kluwer 2021).

25 Article 1681 BJC.

Anyone who has the capacity or is empowered to make a settlement may conclude an arbitration agreement.[26] Any pecuniary claim may be submitted to arbitration. Non-pecuniary claims with regard to which a settlement agreement may be made may also be submitted to arbitration.[27]

The court before which a dispute that is also the object of an arbitration agreement is brought, shall declare itself without jurisdiction at the request of a party, unless the arbitration agreement is invalid with regard to this dispute or has ceased to exist. The plea must be raised before any other plea or defence, failing which it shall be inadmissible.[28]

The arbitral tribunal may rule on its own jurisdiction, including any objections with respect to the existence or validity of the arbitration agreement. For that purpose, an arbitration agreement which forms part of a contract shall be treated as an agreement independent of the other terms of the contract. A decision by the arbitral tribunal that the contract is null and void shall not entail ipso jure the invalidity of the arbitration agreement.[29]

The arbitral tribunal may order any interim or conservatory measure it deems necessary. It may not authorize attachment orders.[30] An interim or protective measure issued by an arbitral tribunal shall be recognized as binding and, unless otherwise provided by the arbitral tribunal, enforced by the Court of First Instance, irrespective of the country in which it was issued.[31] This is a unilateral procedure.[32]

Notwithstanding any agreement to the contrary, the parties shall be treated with equality and each party shall be given a full opportunity of presenting his case, pleas in law and arguments in conformity with the principle of adversarial proceedings. The arbitral tribunal shall ensure that this requirement as well as the principle of fairness of the debates is respected.[33]

The parties are free to agree on the procedure to be followed by the arbitral tribunal in conducting the proceedings. Failing such agreement, the arbitral tribunal may, subject to the arbitration rules as provided in the BJC, determine the rules of procedure applicable to the arbitration in such manner as it considers appropriate.[34]

---

26 Article 1676, §2 BJC. This also includes public legal entities (Article 1676, §3 BJC).
27 Article 1676, §1 BJC.
28 Article 1682, §1 BJC.
29 Article 1690, §1 BJC.
30 Article 1691 BJC.
31 Article 1696, § 1 BJC.
32 Article 1696, §1/1 BJC.
33 Article 1699 BJC.
34 Article 1700, §1–2 BJC.

Unless otherwise agreed by the parties, the arbitral tribunal shall freely assess the admissibility and weight of the evidence. The arbitral tribunal shall set the necessary investigative measures unless the parties authorize it to entrust this task to one of its members.[35]

The parties are free to agree on the language or languages to be used in the arbitral proceedings. Failing such agreement, the arbitral tribunal shall determine the language or languages to be used. This agreement or determination, unless otherwise specified therein, shall apply to any communication between the parties, any hearing and any award, decision or other communication by the arbitral tribunal.[36]

Unless the parties have agreed that no hearings shall be held, the arbitral tribunal shall hold such hearings at an appropriate stage of the proceedings, if so requested by a party. The chairman of the arbitral tribunal shall set the schedule of the hearings and shall preside over them.[37]

The arbitral tribunal shall decide the dispute in accordance with such rules of law as are chosen by the parties as applicable to the substance of the dispute. Any designation of the law of a given State shall be construed, unless otherwise expressed, as directly referring to the substantive law of that State and not to its conflict of laws rules. Failing any designation by the parties, the arbitral tribunal shall apply the law determined by the conflict of laws rules which it considers applicable.[38]

The arbitral tribunal shall make a final decision or render interlocutory decisions by way of one or several awards. The parties may determine the time limit within which the Arbitral Tribunal must render its award, or the terms for setting such a time limit. Failing this, if the arbitral tribunal is late in rendering its award, and a period of six months has elapsed since the date on which the last arbitrator has been appointed, the President of the Court of First Instance, at the request of one of the parties, may impose a time limit on the arbitral tribunal.[39]

The arbitral award rendered in Belgium or abroad may only be enforced after the Court of First Instance has granted enforcement in full or in part. The court can render the award enforceable only if it can no longer be contested before the arbitrator(s) or if the arbitrators have declared it to be provisionally enforceable notwithstanding an appeal.[40] This is a unilateral procedure.

---

[35] Article 1700, §3–4 BJC.

[36] Article 1703, §1 BJC.

[37] Article 1705 BJC.

[38] Article 1710, §1–2 BJC.

[39] Article 1713, §1–2 BJC.

[40] Article 1719 BJC.

Recognition and enforcement can only be refused based on a limited number of grounds.[41]

3.3.2 Out-of-Court Mediation

As mentioned above, Belgian law distinguishes between out-of-court mediation and judicial (or court-connected) mediation. Out-of-court mediation is freely chosen by the parties before, during or after judicial proceedings, without prompting or other involvement by the judge.

The Belgian legislator explicitly opted for a privatization of mediation: only private persons (such as lawyers, notaries or social workers) can be mediators within the framework of the BJC. Belgium has no judge-mediators. Parties involved in a dispute are not obliged to try mediation within the legal framework. They can mediate according to their own rules (so-called free or wild mediation). However, as a consequence, their agreement will not be susceptible to homologation by the judge, making it not (directly) enforceable.

Any contract may contain a mediation clause.[42] This is an agreement according to which the parties commit themselves to try mediation first to resolve possible disputes regarding the validity, realization, interpretation, enforcement or termination of a contract, before using other forms of dispute resolution. A mediation clause, which is binding upon the parties to the contract, does not prevent them from seeking provisional or conservatory measures (e.g., the appointment of an expert or a standstill measure), since this does not imply that parties waive mediation.[43]

Every time a judge or an arbitrator decides a case in which a mediation clause applies, one of the parties can invoke, *in limine litis*, the 'mediation exception' or 'mediation plea'. If the clause is valid, the case is suspended until the parties or one of them have informed the clerk of the court or the arbitrator that the mediation process has ended.[44]

The Mediation Act establishes a (Belgian) Federal Mediation Commission,[45] composed of a commission for the recognition of Belgian and foreign medi-

---

[41] Article 1721 BJC.

[42] Article 1725, §1 BJC. The mediation agreement (or mediation clause) was thoroughly analysed by Andries (Ken Andries, *Het bemiddelingsbeding: geldigheid, effect, inhoud en afdwingbaarheid* (Larcier 2007) and Ken Andries, 'Bemiddelingsbeding' [2011] 242 Nieuw Juridisch Weekblad 318).

[43] Article 1725, §3 BJC.

[44] Article 1725, §2 BJC.

[45] Article 1727 BJC. See Bernard Asscherickx, 'Taken van de federale bemiddelingscommissie en de nieuwe erkenningscriteria voor de bemiddelaars' in Raf Van Ransbeeck (ed), *Bemiddeling* (die Keure 2008).

ators, a commission for the recognition of training and continuing education and a discipline commission that also deals with complaints.[46] The Ministry of Justice provides the Federal Mediation Commission with staff and resources.[47]

A mediator can be accredited by the Federal Mediation Commission. There is no legal obligation to be accredited, but an agreement reached after the mediation process assisted by a non-accredited mediator is not eligible for judicial homologation, making it non-enforceable. If, in other words, the parties want to obtain an enforceable agreement at the end of the mediation, they have to make an appeal to an accredited mediator. In case of judicial mediation, the mediator appointed by the judge is in principle an accredited mediator.

Mediation stands or falls with confidentiality. Belgian law explicitly deals with this feature.[48] All documents, statements and communications made during and for the benefit of the mediation process are confidential. They cannot be used in judicial, administrative or arbitral procedures or in any other dispute resolution procedure. Since 2018, there are a number of exceptions to these rules. For example, the parties can jointly decide to lift the confidentiality veil of documents or to extend the confidentiality to documents, statements and communications made before the mediation process.

The mediator is bound by a duty of professional secrecy. He or she cannot testify in civil and administrative procedures concerning facts and information he or she acquired during the mediation process. Testifying in criminal procedures is not legally excluded.[49] When a mediator violates his or her professional secrecy, he or she commits a crime and can be prosecuted.

If parties agree to out-of-court mediation, a mediation protocol has to be drafted. It forms the mediation framework in which the parties, in consultation with the mediator, mutually determine all the rules about the mediation process, including its duration. The mediation protocol is signed by the parties and the mediator. The mediation protocol acts as a contract between the parties and the mediator. It should contain a number of minimum requirements.[50]

A successfully ended mediation process results in a mediation agreement between the parties. This agreement ends their dispute. It is laid down in a dated document signed by them and the mediator. If such is the case, it

---

46 Article 1727, §1 BJC.

47 Article 1727, §3 BJC.

48 Article 1728 BJC.

49 Benoît Allemeersch and Peter Schollen, 'De wet tot wijziging van het Gerechtelijk Wetboek in verband met de bemiddeling' [2005] 38 Rechtskundig Weekblad 1481, 1494.

50 Article 1731, §2 BJC.

mentions the accreditation of the mediator. The agreement contains the precise obligations of all parties.[51]

The parties or one of them can ask the judge to approve or homologate the mediation agreement,[52] which means that it will become enforceable as a regular judgment. Homologation can only be granted when parties concluded a mediation protocol and if an accredited mediator was involved in the mediation. To protect the parties in mediation, only agreements made under proper assistance of such a mediator can be the object of judicial homologation.

Unfortunately, there is not a lot of data available regarding mediation in Belgium. Every two years bMediation – an accredited training centre for mediation in civil and commercial matters – publishes some data in its mediation barometer, which it collects among all accredited mediators. According to its 2018 report:[53]

- 60–70 per cent of all judicial mediations and 75 per cent of all out-of-court mediations end in a settlement;
- on average, mediation cases take 45 days;
- in 45 per cent of the cases no lawyers are present;
- most cases deal with real estate, shareholder disputes, neighbour disputes and commercial disputes;
- the average cost is 150 EUR per hour; an average mediation procedure costs around 3,000 EUR.

3.3.3 Collaborative Negotiations

The 2018 Act, which amended the existing rules on mediation, also introduced a new ADR track: collaborative negotiations.[54] This is a structured, voluntary and confidential method of negotiation where specifically trained and accredited lawyers closely accompany their clients during the negotiation process, in order to work towards a resolution for the dispute. A judge can only order collaborative negotiation following a joint request of the parties and after having heard the parties about the process. He can do so at any stage of the proceedings.

---

[51] Article 1732 BJC.

[52] Article 1733 BJC.

[53] 'BMediation publiceert de bemiddelingsbarometer van 2018' (*bMediation*, 7 February 2019) https://www.bmediation.eu/bmediation-publiceert-de-bemiddelingsbarometer-van-2018-een-samenvatting-van-bemiddelingen-in-belgie/?lang=nl accessed 27 June 2021. The data only concerns civil and commercial mediation cases.

[54] Articles 1738–1747 BJC.

The main difference with mediation is the absence of a third party, a mediator. The process is steered by the collaborative lawyers of the parties. They do not act like a mediator, in the sense that they continue to advise their clients. A collaborative lawyer represents his clients in the framework of an exclusive and limited mandate of assistance and consultancy for the purpose of a negotiated agreement. In this process he is to be considered as a professional negotiator who wishes to settle the dispute out of court. As a collaborative counsel lawyer takes on such an active role, he is expected to sign the collaborative negotiation protocol as well. This protocol can be seen as a framework agreement in which the parties make arrangements regarding the negotiation process.

If the negotiation fails, the lawyers involved must withdraw and they can no longer assist their clients in a possible later judicial proceeding. This guarantees the confidentiality of the procedure.

3.3.4 Consumer Dispute Resolution

Recently, new alternative ways of redress (or justice) have come to the fore in Europe.[55] The first is the out-of-court resolution of consumer disputes: the world of CDR (consumer dispute resolution).[56] CDR uses the traditional ADR techniques but within the context of a dispute resolution structure that is entirely separate from the courts. The CDR architecture encompasses a number of possible structures: arbitration, sometimes with mediation as a first stage; official quasi-arbitration but non-binding adjudication; regulated arbitration; complaint functions within public regulatory authorities; private sector ombudsmen, sometimes regulated; and statutory ombudsmen. CDR also encompasses ODR (online dispute resolution), which uses technology (the internet) to facilitate ADR.[57] The model here is usually binding arbitration, although the process, arbitrators and systems are not always transparent. However, online platforms also usually provide a direct communication channel between consumer and trader, which has a high success rate of nego-

---

[55] This subchapter is largely based on Stefaan Voet, 'Class Actions in Belgium: Evaluation and the Way Forward' in Alan Uzelac and Stefaan Voet (eds), *Class Actions in Europe Holy Grail or a Wrong Trail?* (Springer 2021).

[56] Naomi Creutzfeldt, 'The Origins and Evolution of Consumer Dispute Resolution Systems in Europe' in Christopher Hodges and Astrid Stadler (eds), *Resolving Mass Disputes. ADR and Settlement of Mass Claims* (Edward Elgar 2013). See also Christoper Hodges, 'Unlocking Justice and Markets: The Promise of Consumer ADR' in Joachim Zekoll, Moritz Bälz and Iwo Amelung (eds), *Formalisation and Flexibilisation in Dispute Resolution* (Brill 2014).

[57] Julia Hörnle, *Cross-Border Internet Dispute Resolution* (Cambridge University Press 2009).

tiated and voluntary redress where the platform includes a self-regulatory feedback feature.

CDR gained momentum in 2013 when the European Parliament and the Council adopted a new Consumer ADR Directive and a Consumer ODR Regulation.[58] The Regulation establishes a free and interactive pan-European ODR platform through which consumers and traders can initiate ADR in relation to disputes concerning online transactions (offline transactions are excluded). National ADR entities receive the complaint electronically and seek to resolve the dispute through ADR. The ODR platform was launched in the spring of 2016.[59] The Consumer ADR Directive promotes ADR by encouraging the use of approved ADR entities that ensure the following minimum quality standards: the entities should be impartial and provide transparent information, offer their services at no or nominal cost, and hear and determine complaints within 90 days of referral. The Directive applies to domestic and cross-border disputes concerning complaints by a consumer resident in the EU against a trader established in the EU.

CDR has two added values. First, although not particularly designed for this, many CDR regimes have the potential of processing mass problems. They are capable of identifying and processing multiple (similar or identical) claims and have developed aggregation techniques – similar to how courts aggregate bulks of claims – that deliver consistency of outcomes. For example, in the Netherlands the Consumer Complaint Commissions regularly allocate a series of similar cases for hearing on the same day, thereby providing consistency of adjudication. The results of these cases are then communicated to the parties of other (suspended) cases and these parties are invited to settle their case.[60] Second, if well designed, CDR can go beyond mere dispute resolution. Hodges identified the five functions of CDR: (1) consumer advice; (2) dispute resolution; (3) aggregation of data; (4) publication of the aggregated data, as feedback to traders/sectors and information to consumers, competitions, regulators and investors; and (5) improving market behaviour.[61]

---

[58] Directive of the European Parliament and of the Council (EU) 2013/11 on alternative dispute resolution for consumer disputes and amending Regulation (EC) No 2006/2004 and Directive 2009/22/EC [2013] OJ L165/63 (Consumer ADR Directive) and Regulation of the European Parliament and of the Council (EU) 524/2013 on online dispute resolution for consumer disputes and amending Regulation (EC) No 2006/2004 and Directive 2009/22/EC [2013] OJ L165/1 (Consumer ODR Regulation).

[59] https://webgate.ec.europa.eu/odr accessed 1 July 2021.

[60] Franziska Weber and Christoper Hodges, 'The Netherlands' in Christopher Hodges, Iris Benöhr and Naomi Creutzfeldt-Banda (eds), *Consumer ADR in Europe* (Hart Publishing 2012) 148.

[61] Christopher Hodges, 'Consumer Redress. Implementing the Vision' in Pablo Cortés (ed), *The New Regulatory Framework for Consumer Dispute Resolution* (Oxford University Press 2016) 353.

In the meantime, almost all Member States have implemented the Consumer ADR Directive,[62] including Belgium.[63]

In 2015, the Consumer Mediation Service,[64] Belgium's residual ADR entity, was set up. It is an autonomous public body with legal personality, which is composed of a front office and a service for the out-of-court resolution of consumer disputes. The Consumer Mediation Service has a particular structure, in the sense that it is composed of the existing federal economic ombudsman services and two private ombudsman services.[65] The latter two were chosen not only because they administer a large number of complaints, but also because their services are similar to the public ombudsman services.

Every year, the Consumer Mediation Service publishes an activity report. Besides statistical information about the number of complaints, this report can contain recommendations about systematic or significant problems that occur frequently and lead to consumer disputes. These structural recommendations can indicate how such problems can be avoided or resolved in the future. The goal is to enhance traders' performance and to facilitate the exchange of information and best practices. This statistical information can also play a key role in detecting mass cases and in exposing rogue traders. They can give rise to regulatory interventions (i.e., investigations, the imposition of (administrative) sanctions or criminal prosecution).[66]

Table 3.1 below gives an overview of the most recent data.[67]

Finally, it should be mentioned that the Consumer Mediation Service also has standing to bring a consumer class action,[68] which is an example of the interaction between an ADR entity and formal justice. There are three class action prerequisites: the violation of a Belgian or European consumer regulation or statute, an adequate class representative (i.e., a consumer association or the Consumer Mediation Service) and the superiority of the class action

---

[62] For an overview see Pablo Cortés ibid.

[63] Loi du 4 avril 2014 portant insertion du Livre XVI, 'Règlement extrajudiciaire des litiges de consommation' dans le Code de droit économique, *Moniteur Belge* 12 mai 2014, 38. 262.

[64] https://consumerombudsman.be/en accessed 1 July 2021.

[65] Two members of the Telecom Mediation Service, two members of the Ombudsman Service for the Postal Sector, two members of the Ombudsman Service for Energy, two members of the Mediator for Rail Passengers, the Ombudsman in Financial Matters and the Insurance Ombudsman.

[66] The exchange of data is facilitated by Article 17 of the Consumer ADR Directive dealing with the 'cooperation between ADR entities and national authorities enforcing Union legal acts on consumer protection'.

[67] This was compiled on the basis of the 2019, 2020 and 2021 annual reports.

[68] Stefaan Voet, 'Consumer Collective Redress in Belgium: Class Actions to the Rescue?' [2015] 1 *European Business Organization Law Review* 121.

Table 3.1 *Recent consumer mediation service data*

Total number of new cases					
2019		**2020**		**2021**	
8.653		15.014		14.488	
2019		**2020**		**2021**	
1.330		4.562		4.377	
2019		**2020**		**2021**	
2.779		3.915		3.536	
2019		**2020**		**2021**	
4.544		6.537		6.575	
admissible	not admissible	admissible	not admissible	admissible	not admissible
2.774	1.770	4.330	2.207	4.100	2.475
2019		**2020**		**2021**	
settlement: 47% recommendation: 47% closure: 6%		settlement: 51% recommendation: 43% closure: 7%		49% 40% 11%	
2019		**2020**		**2021**	
64 days		55 days		59 days	

mechanism. The procedure consists of four phases: a certification phase (in its certification decision, the court can freely choose between an opt-in or opt-out regime), a mandatory negotiation phase, a possible phase on the merits of the case, and an enforcement phase under the supervision of an out-of-court collective claims settler. Any collective settlement is approved by the court. There is no *pro forma* approval. The court can refuse approval if for example the agreed redress is evidently unreasonable.

The class action can only be brought by an adequate class representative.[69] Only authorized consumer associations and authorized non-profit organizations whose statutory aim corresponds with the collective harm, have standing to bring a class action.[70] The Consumer Mediation Service only has standing to

[69] Article XVII.36, 2° CEL (Code of Economic Law).
[70] Article XVII.39 CEL.

initiate a class action and to negotiate a collective settlement.[71] If a settlement cannot be reached, and the court has to decide the merits of the case, a consumer association has to step in to continue the procedure.[72]

The Consumer Mediation Service has brought one case to date. It was brought at the instigation of the Energy Ombudsman on behalf of approximately 40,000 consumers against eight energy companies for unfair subscription fees.[73] In its decision of 14 April 2021, the Court of Appeals of Brussels declared the action inadmissible.[74]

3.3.5 Regulatory Redress

Within the broader context of the transformation of (public and private) enforcement,[75] other new trends and approaches emerge. One example is regulatory redress, which is redress that is ordered or brought about by the intervention of public enforcers.[76] Its strength is the combined weight of public/regulatory enforcement tools and civil/compensatory tools. The advantage, and at the same time incentive, for businesses is that all aspects of a (mass) harm situation are resolved in one process, thereby avoiding sequential public (i.e., criminal and/or regulatory) and private procedures and costs. Providing redress can be incentivized by leniency in enforcement policies or by the advantage of maintaining high commercial reputation. It goes without saying that in order for regulatory redress to fulfil its potential, there need to be suffi-

---

[71] Article XVII.39, 3° CEL.

[72] Article XVII.40 CEL.

[73] Voet (n 55) 146.

[74] Court of Appeals Brussels 14 April 2021, 2019/AR/1763. See Hakim Boularbah and Maria-Clara Van den Bossche, *Country Report Belgium* [2021] 2 Mass Claims 140.

[75] See Hans Micklitz and Andrea Wechsler (eds), *The Transformation of Enforcement. European Economic Law in a Global Perspective* (Hart Publishing 2016).

[76] Christopher Hodges and Stefaan Voet, *Delivering Collective Redress. New Technologies* (Hart Publishing 2018) 153-210 and Stefaan Voet, '"Where the Wild Things Are". Reflections on the State and Future of European Collective Redress' in Ann L.M. Keirse and Marco B.M. Loos (eds), *Waves in Contract and Liability Law in Three Decades of Ius Commune* (Intersentia 2017) 133–35. For a typology see Christopher Hodges, 'Mass Collective Redress: ADR and Regulatory Techniques' [2015] 5 *European Review of Private Law* 829, 841–45 (removing illicit profits; ordering redress to be paid; bringing a collective action; piggybacking civil claimants in public enforcement proceedings; referring assessment of loss to the court; ordering an infringer to create a restoration scheme; ordering an infringer to propose a compensation scheme; approving a compensation scheme proposed by one or more parties; referring a proposed compensation scheme to a court for approval; ordering an infringer to negotiate; etc.).

cient resources and more importantly, safeguards to protect the independence of the public enforcement agencies (such as publication of enforcement policies, fair procedural rules, a predictable and transparent process, ministerial and stakeholder oversight, the possibility for courts to impose more serious sanctions and a mechanism for appeals, etc.).[77]

There are multiple public enforcers or regulators in Belgium, but generally their powers regarding restitution or civil sanctions are limited.[78] The focus is on deterrence rather than restitution. Nevertheless, victims can claim compensation following a public enforcement decision (*follow-up*), arguing that the tort (or at least the fault element) has been proven by the finding of a violation by the regulator.

However, some remarks have to be made regarding two important regulators and their link with redress: the Financial Services and Markets Authority (FSMA)[79] and the Commission for the Regulation of Electricity and Gas (CREG).[80] A first remark relates to the general finding that restitution and civil sanctions are not the main focus of public regulators or enforcers. One could take the example of the FSMA. When a supervised trader does not comply with the regulations in place, the FSMA has a wide array of instruments to deal with this non-compliance and to sanction the trader.[81] The (administrative) sanctioning has to be situated in the relationship between the FSMA and the supervised trader, not vis-à-vis the financial consumer. Although a consumer's complaint might trigger an investigation and administrative action, a harmed financial consumer will need to have recourse to other instruments outside the regulatory framework.

One should nevertheless pay attention to the possibility of including the consumer indirectly in a settlement between the FSMA and the non-complying trader. The fact that the consumer is not a party to that settlement, does not imply that the consumer cannot be kept in mind when drafting the terms of the settlement. A settlement concerning interest rate derivatives to cover variable rate loans to SMEs between the FSMA and a number of financial institutions

---

77 Voet (n 55) 158.

78 Stefaan Voet, 'Public Enforcement and A(O)DR as Mechanisms for Resolving Mass Problems: A Belgian Perspective' in Christopher Hodges and Astrid Stadler (eds), *Resolving Mass Disputes: ADR and Settlement of Mass Claims* (Edward Elgar 2013) 274.

79 http://www.fsma.be/ accessed 7 July 2021.

80 https://www.creg.be/en accessed 7 July 2021.

81 For instance, require the publishing of a correction, inspections, publishing warnings, suspend trading, striking an intermediary from the register, revoking authorization, imposing fines or penalties.

provides an excellent example.[82] After inspection, the FSMA concluded that not all rules regarding the duty of care and the supply of information were observed by the financial institutions concerned so that the FSMA pressed for several interventions. Some only regarded the institutions, such as their duty to make sure that their employees are qualified to assume the responsibility imposed onto them. Yet, the consumer was not forgotten. The financial institutions concerned agreed to pay each client a certain amount of money by way of commercial compensation. That way, compensation was provided to the consumers although the settlement was only reached between the FSMA and a number of financial institutions.

In addition to including consumers' redress in settlements, the statutory framework can also provide some assistance to financial consumers. In that regard, Article 30*ter* of the Act of 2 August 2002[83] is exemplary. It contains a rebuttable presumption that in cases where a financial consumer is harmed by a transaction and a trader has committed a certain breach as a result of that transaction, the transaction at hand is presumed to be the result of the breach. This means that the presumption entails that the investor would not have made the same decision without the breach.

A second remark concerns the CREG. The statutory framework provides for the creation of a Dispute Resolution Chamber (*Chambre d'appel*) which would resolve disputes between the network administrator and the network users regarding the duties of the network administrator, the distribution network administrators and the administrators of closed industrial networks. Disputes regarding contractual rights and obligations however, are excluded.[84] The *law in the books* certainly leaves room for offering redress to consumers, but the *law in practice* has not yet developed since the Dispute Resolution Chamber is currently unable to operate due to a lack of appointment of its members.

3.4 CONNECTING THE DOTS

How to assess these evolutions?[85] An overall conclusion is that the binary and traditional classification of private vs public enforcement is outdated. Traditional private law has become public private law and public law has been privatized. Both have been replaced by a 'multilayered framework of regu-

---

[82] https://www.fsma.be/sites/default/files/public/sitecore/media%20library/Files/fsmafiles/news/2015-05_rentederivaten.pdf accessed 7 July 2021.

[83] Loi du 2 August 2002 relative à la surveillance du secteur financier et aux services financiers, *Moniteur Belge* 4 septembre 2002, 39.121.

[84] Loi du 11 mai 1999 relative à l'organisation du marché de l'électricité of 29 April 1999, *Moniteur Belge* 11 mai 1999, 16.264 (Article 29).

[85] This subchapter is largely based on Voet (n 76).

lation, lawmaking and law application'.[86] ADR entities, such as the Belgian Consumer Mediation Service, which primarily focuses on private redress for consumers, performs a quasi-public function in the sense that its actions have, albeit implicit, regulatory consequences. Another example can be found in the collective redress area where empirical research shows 'that a public/private dichotomy is of little use in analysing legal responses to mass harms. Their relationship is more like a complex origami figure than two adjacent boxes. Actors, processes and outcomes overlap and intersect on a number of levels'. Hensler and Thornburg discern three levels: (1) public processes often rely on private fact-gathering and the viability of private processes often depends on the outcome of public regulatory investigations and criminal prosecutions; (2) the actors in these mass action dramas play multi-faceted roles (e.g., public entities appearing in private litigation); and (3) the outcomes of actions that are conventionally labelled as public and private overlap and interact (redress can act as regulation and public regulatory or criminal findings can provide a legal basis for redress).[87]

On the other hand, there are clear policy shifts. New approaches of enforcement and redress are emerging: 'a range of new techniques are being developed to deliver the objectives of behavioural compliance and of redress. Those objectives constitute restatements of what used to be called regulation and compensation, respectively delivered through criminal, administrative and/or regulatory structures and private law'.[88] According to Hodges and Creutzfeldt three aspects of the traditional public-private division have changed: (1) substantive law: the principles of the private law of damages still underpin payment of compensation or redress when a compensation order or consumer redress scheme is invoked in criminal or regulatory processes, but the details of damages law are in practice often of little importance' (2) forum: there is a shift from courts to CDR entities, ombudsmen and regulators' and (3) actors:

---

[86] This is a translation from Dutch to English of the title of the pivotal work in Belgium of Van Gerven and Lierman: Walter Van Gerven and Steven Lierman, *Algemeen Deel. Veertig jaar later. Privaat- en publiekrecht in een meergelaagd kader van regelgeving, rechtsvorming en regeltoepassing* (Kluwer 2010) 515–23.

[87] Deborah Hensler and Elizabeth Thornburg, 'The Public Dimension of Private Collective Litigation: A Comparative Analysis' in Deborah Hensler, Christopher Hodges and Ianika Tzankova (eds), *Class Actions in Context. How Culture, Economics and Politics Shape Collective Litigation* (Edward Elgar 2016) 276.

[88] Christopher Hodges and Naomi Creutzfeldt, 'Transformations in Public and Private Enforcement' in Hans Micklitz and Andrea Wechsler (eds), *The Transformation of Enforcement. European Economic Law in a Global Perspective* (Hart Publishing 2016) 128.

besides lawyers in private litigation, regulators and CDR bodies have entered the stage.[89]

The Belgian example shows that new enforcement and redress mechanisms are appearing. If well designed, CDR can capture and resolve mass problems. Because many CDR schemes can aggregate data, that can be exchanged with regulators, the mechanism can go beyond mere dispute resolution. Regulatory redress, which is redress that is ordered or brought about by the intervention of public enforcers, is still terra incognita. Nevertheless, the examples mentioned above show that it works and that in some contexts it can offer real, sustainable and impressive solutions – again, if it is well designed. There need to be sufficient resources and safeguards to protect the independence of the public enforcement agencies.

Although one may criticize these changes, and despite the existence of caveats, these techniques are here to stay. Sometimes CDR and regulatory redress are not the consequence of a well-targeted policy, but were developed and implemented by the sectors and actors themselves, making them market driven and thus unstoppable.

The goal, and the challenge should be an integrated and holistic framework. Arguments to 'replace' public enforcement mechanisms by private or other mechanisms, or vice versa, are based on the wrong premise. The focus should be on exploring and optimizing *all* options for redress. Even more important is to connect these options so they can form an integrated (dispute resolution) framework. Only a broad and integrated instrumentarium, as a 'dispute resolution continuum', which can avoid enforcement gaps, is effective and efficient.[90]

Many models are possible. In the CDR orbit, statutory forms of cooperation exist. Article 16 of the Consumer ADR Directive provides for cooperation and exchanges of experience between CDR entities. Member States have to ensure that CDR entities cooperate in the resolution of cross-border disputes and conduct regular exchanges of best practices as regards the settlement of both cross-border and domestic disputes. A network of national CDR entities has been set up. Article 17 focuses on the cooperation between CDR entities and public regulatory authorities, including the exchange of information on practices in specific business sectors about which consumers have repeatedly

---

[89] Ibid., 131.

[90] Egelyn Braun, 'Collective alternative dispute resolution (ADR) for the private enforcement of EU competition law' (LLM thesis, European University Institute 2016), 1 http://cadmus.eui.eu/handle/1814/44324 accessed 9 July 2021: 'ultimately, the enforcement toolbox should be diversified not only to ensure the successful fulfilment of the regulatory goals, but also to facilitate the transformations that are occurring in the enforcement landscape more broadly.'

lodged complaints. It also supports feedback on market behaviour to traders, competitors and customers.

One of the conclusions of a study, analysing the implementation of the Consumer ADR Directive in the various Member States, is the need for interconnection between courts, enforcement bodies and CDR.[91] In this study, Hodges notes that:

> A pathway should be built between [CDR] entities and the courts as well as regulators when statutory interpretation is at stake. A system of preliminary reference between [CDR] entities and regulators, which could in turn trickle up from regulators to national courts, should be put in place to ensure an adequate application of consumer law.[92]

Graham notes 'that an added value of [CDR] is that it can go beyond individual complaints, and provide redress to others entitled to it, but who have not complained'.[93] In other words, 'when integrated into regulatory systems, [CDR] and dispute resolution models can enable private redress, enhanced public norms enforcement, and regulatory objectives of economic and market re-balancing (reallocating the cost burden of illicit behaviour from consumers to perpetrators), monitoring and behaviour control'.[94]

---

[91] Pablo Cortés, 'Conclusion. Ensuring the Provision of Consumer Dispute Resolution' in Pablo Cortés (ed), *The New Regulatory Framework for Consumer Dispute Resolution* (Oxford University Press 2016) 465–66.

[92] Ibid., 465 and Hodges (n 61) 351–69.

[93] Cortés (n 91) 465.

[94] Rebecca Money-Kyrle, 'Legal Standing in Collective Redress Actions for Breach of EU Rights: Facilitating or Frustrating Common Standards and Access to Justice?' in Burkhard Hess, Maria Bergström and Eva Storskrubb (eds), *EU Civil Justice. Current Issues and Future Outlook* (Hart Publishing 2016) 247–48.

4. Formulating a more principled approach to ADR within the English civil justice system[1]

Masood Ahmed

4.1 INTRODUCTION

The English civil justice system is, once more, undergoing substantial procedural reform. The fundamental aim of the latest reform programme is to modernise the civil justice system by moving away from an expensive, complex, and slow paper-based system to an efficient online court process that is 'just, proportionate, and accessible to everyone.'[2] Increasing access to justice through the digitisation of the civil justice system is a key priority for policy makers and the senior judiciary.[3] Currently, litigants may issue and defend small money claims through the Online Civil Money Claims (hereafter 'OCMC') which includes an opt-out mediation stage before the matter can proceed to judicial determination.[4] The senior judiciary is seeking to go further in creating a fully integrated online system in the management and

---

[1] I am grateful to Betul Kas for her helpful comments on an earlier draft of this chapter.

[2] The Lord Chancellor, the Lord Chief Justice, and the Senior President of Tribunals, 'Transforming Our Justice System' [15 September 2016] https://assets.publishing.service.gov.uk/government/uploads/system/uploads/attachment_data/file/553261/joint-vision-statement.pdf accessed 19 March 2021.

[3] Ibid., also see The Rt Hon Sir Ernest Ryder, Senior President of Tribunals, 'The Modernisation of Access to Justice in Times of Austerity' (5th Annual Ryder Lecture, University of Bolton, 3 March 2016); Sir Terrance Etherton, Master of the Rolls, 'The Civil Court of the Future' (The Lord Slynn Memorial Lecture, 14 June 2017); Sir Ernest Ryder, Senior President of Tribunals, 'Assisting Access to Justice' (Keele University, 15 March 2018); The Rt Hon The Lord Burnett of Maldon (Association of District Judges Annual Conference, 13 April 2018).

[4] 51R Practice Direction.

resolution of disputes. Sir Geoffrey Vos, the current Master of the Rolls,[5] is an ardent supporter of the use of technology and artificial intelligence[6] and he recently explained his future vision of an online civil justice system with 'a single funnel' through which all disputes would proceed and be directed to suitable dispute resolution procedures.[7] To facilitate the consensual settlement of disputes, the new system will integrate sophisticated alternative dispute resolution (hereafter 'ADR') procedures.

ADR forms is an integral part of the civil justice landscape. It is an important aspect of the overriding objective – the heart of the Civil Procedure Rules (hereafter 'CPR') – which enables the courts to deal with cases justly and at proportionate cost.[8] Disputing parties are also obliged to consider and engage with ADR processes both before, at the pre-action stage of litigation,[9] and during the litigation process. Furthermore, the courts are equipped with appropriate powers to penalise parties which failed to consider ADR or unreasonably refused to engage with it.[10]

Although successive English civil justice reforms have embraced and enthusiastically promoted the virtues of ADR and encouraged its use,[11] the issue of whether the courts should *compel* disputing parties to engage with ADR

---

[5] The Master of the Rolls is the second most senior judge in England and Wales after the Lord Chief Justice. As President of the Court of Appeal's Civil Division, the Master of the Rolls is responsible for the deployment and organisation of the work of the judges of the division as well as presiding in its courts, often hearing the most complex cases across the full range of civil, family and tribunal matters.

[6] Sir Geoffrey Vos, 'Technological Challenges for English Law and Jurisdiction' (ISDA Virtual Annual Forum, 10 March 2021). Similarly, see the comments of the Deputy Head of Civil Justice for England and Wales, Lord Justice Birss, 'Online Future of Civil Justice' (Fordham IP Conference, New York, Fordham Law School, 2021).

[7] Vos (n 6) para 32.

[8] CPR 1.4 (2)(e) provides that the case management duties of the court include: 'encouraging the parties to use an alternative dispute resolution procedure if the court considers that appropriate and facilitating the use of such procedure'.

[9] Before proceedings are issued the parties will be obliged to engage with the pre-action protocols. For a list of the current pre-action protocols see Ministry of Justice, 'Pre-Action Protocols – Civil Procedure Rules' www.justice.gov.uk/courts/procedure-rules/civil/protocol accessed 9 May 2021.

[10] CPR 44. For a discussion of the various methods by which the courts may encourage ADR, see Shirley Shipman, 'Court Approaches to ADR in the Civil Justice System' (2006) 15 CJQ 181.

[11] The Rt Hon Lord Woolf, *Access to Justice Interim Report* (Lord Chancellor's Department 1995); The Rt Hon Lord Woolf, *Access to Justice Final Report* (Lord Chancellor's Department 1996); Sir Rupert Jackson, *Review of Civil Litigation Costs Final Report* (The Stationery Office 2009); Lord Justice Briggs, *Chancery Modernisation Review: Final Report* (2013); Lord Justice Briggs, *Civil Courts Structure Review: Interim Report* (Judiciary of England and Wales, 2015); Lord Justice

has had a turbulent and difficult procedural history. The senior judiciary have traditionally rejected the argument that parties should be obliged to engage with ADR because to do so would undermine the fundamental constitutional right of the parties to access the courts in the vindication and enforcement of their legal rights.[12] This narrow interpretation of access to justice was reiterated by the UK Supreme Court in the landmark decision of *R (on the application of Unison) v Lord Chancellor*[13] in which the President of the Supreme Court, Lord Reed, defined access to justice as 'access to the courts (and tribunals: *R v Secretary of State for the Home Department, Ex p Saleem* [2001] 1 WLR 443)'.[14]

Judicial resistance to the notion of compulsory ADR has its jurisprudential roots in the leading but controversial decision of *Halsey v Milton Keynes General NHS Trust*[15] in which the Court of Appeal observed that to compel non-consenting parties to engage with ADR 'would be regarded as an unacceptable constraint on the right of access to the court and, therefore, a violation of article 6'[16] of the European Convention of Human Rights.[17] Rather than laying the foundations for the development of a consistent jurisprudential body of case law, *Halsey's* misconceived stance on the article 6 issue has led to the evolution of two divergent and opposing judicial schools of thought. The first is consistent with the 'orthodox' approach: it officially rejects the idea of compelling non-consenting parties to engage with ADR and thereby seeks to uphold and protect their rights to access the courts. The second school of thought officially rejects the idea of compulsory ADR but *impliedly* compels parties to consider and engage with ADR through the threat and use of cost sanctions.[18] Thus, the jurisprudence is in a highly unsatisfactory state: it is

---

Briggs, *Civil Courts Structure Review: Final Report* (Judiciary of England and Wales, 2016).

12 Ibid.

13 *R (on application of Unison) v Lord Chancellor* [2017] UKSC 51.

14 Ibid., [66].

15 *Halsey v Milton Keynes General NHS Trust* [2004] 1 WLR 3002.

16 Ibid., [9].

17 Article 6 provides:
In the determination of his civil rights and obligations or of any criminal charge against him, everyone is entitled to a fair and public hearing within a reasonable time by an independent and impartial tribunal established by law. Judgment shall be pronounced publicly but the press and public may be excluded from all or part of the trial in the interest of morals, public order or national security in a democratic society, where the interests of juveniles or the protection of the private life of the parties so require, or to the extent strictly necessary in the opinion of the court in special circumstances where publicity would prejudice the interests of justice.

18 Masood Ahmed, 'Implied Compulsory Mediation' (2012) 31(2) CJQ 151–75.

contradictory, confusing, and has the potential to increase costs, delays, and complexity through unnecessary satellite litigation.

This chapter critically considers the issue of ADR compulsion through an analysis of the current digitisation reforms and developments within the jurisprudence. In doing so, the recent decision of *Lomax v Lomax*[19] will be considered in which the Court of Appeal confirmed that the courts could, as part of their case management powers, compel non-consenting parties to engage with a specific type of ADR procedure – judicial early neutral evaluation (hereafter 'ENE'). It is argued that the reasoning of the Court provides the basis upon which the courts can develop a more principled approach to the issue of compulsion, as well as applying more generally to other types of ADR, including mediation orders. These jurisprudential developments and the implementation of OCMC reinforce the call for the article 6 point in *Halsey* to be reappraised and to be dismissed. The chapter will also consider a recent Civil Justice Council (CJC) report which confirmed that, in its view, appropriate forms of compulsory ADR, where the parties can return to the courts, are lawful.[20]

This chapter is organised into four sections. Section 4.2 considers the latest digitisation reforms. Section 4.3 critically considers the issue of compulsion and its impact on the development of ADR jurisprudence. In Section 4.4, recent divergent Court of Appeal decisions are discussed, and a detailed analysis is given of *Lomax*. Finally, the chapter concludes with proposals for reform.

4.2 DIGITISATION REFORMS, ADR, AND OPT-OUT MEDIATION

A substantial aspect of the digitisation reforms is the implementation of OCMC. The objective of OCMC, which is currently subject to a pilot scheme,[21] is to increase access to justice, in particular for litigants in person, by digitising and simplifying the civil court procedure for small money claims. Claimants may issue proceedings online for claims of up to £10,000 and defendants may contest those claims online.

To better understand OCMC and its enhanced focus on ADR, we must first appreciate Lord Justice Briggs' dispute resolution philosophy which he formulated in his *Chancery Modernisation Review* in 2013.[22] In that review, Briggs LJ recommended a culture change in the courts' management of disputes so

---

19 *Lomax v Lomax* [2019] EWCA Civ 1467.

20 Civil Justice Council, 'Compulsory ADR' (June 2021), https://www.judiciary.uk/wp-content/uploads/2021/07/Civil-Justice-Council-Compulsory-ADR-report-1.pdf accessed 12 August 2021.

21 51R Practice Direction.

22 Briggs, *Chancery Modernisation Review* (n 11).

that disputes are managed in the *widest possible sense*. This new way of managing disputes should, Briggs LJ explained, include not only the determination and enforcement of rights via court adjudication but should also include the consensual settlement of disputes. As his Lordship put it, the courts must adopt 'a more active role in the encouragement, facilitation and management of disputes in the widest sense, rather than merely case preparation for trial'.[23]

In his subsequent *Civil Courts Structure Review*,[24] Briggs LJ gave effect to his dispute resolution philosophy by making a radical proposal: the introduction of an online court for the resolution of low value money claims. He drew inspiration from the earlier recommendations made by the Civil Justice Council[25] which emphasised the virtues of online dispute resolution procedures in the early resolution of disputes. Similarly, Briggs LJ proposed a three-stage online court that would form part of the mainstream civil justice system with an enhanced focus on ADR. His Lordship explained the structure of the online court as follows:

> stage 1 will consist of a mainly automated process by which litigants are assisted in identifying their case (or defence) online in terms sufficiently well ordered to be suitable to be understood by their opponents and resolved by the court, and required to upload (i.e. place online) the documents and other evidence which the court will need for the purpose of resolution. Stage two will involve a mix of conciliation and case management, mainly by a Case Officer, conducted partly online, partly by telephone, but probably not face-to-face. Stage 3 will consist of determination by judges…either on the documents, on the telephone, by video or at face-to-face hearings, but with no default assumption that there must be a traditional trial.[26]

Although OCMC is not an integrated online court, it does reflect certain aspects of Briggs LJ's vision. After pleadings have been filed through OCMC, the parties are invited to participate in mediation, which is conducted via telephone, to explore whether their dispute can be resolved without continuing to trial. The mediation stage is an opt-out process for cases worth up to £500, that is, disputes are automatically referred to mediation unless one or both of the parties elect not to have their dispute referred to mediation. In the event that

---

23 Ibid., 68.

24 Briggs, *Civil Courts Structure Review: Interim Report* (n 11); Briggs, *Civil Courts Structure Review: Final Report* (n 11).

25 Civil Justice Council, 'Online Dispute Resolution for Low Value Civil Claims Report' (February 2015), https://www.judiciary.gov.uk/wp-content/uploads/2015/02/Online-Dispute-Resolution-Final-Web-Version1.pdf accessed 9 May 2021; see also JUSTICE, 'Delivering Justice in an Age of Austerity—A Report' (2015) https://files.justice.org.uk/wp-content/uploads/2015/04/06172133/JUSTICE-working-party-report-Delivering-Justice-in-an-Age-of-Austerity.pdf accessed 9 May 2021.

26 Briggs, *Civil Courts Structure Review: Interim Report* (n 11) 76.

the dispute is settled through mediation, the parties' agreement is recorded in a settlement agreement. If the mediation does not result in a settlement, then the matter continues through OCMC and eventually to trial.

The opt-out mediation stage may be criticised for its failure to truly integrate ADR within the online platform in order to provide court users with what is more commonly referred to as online dispute resolutions procedures ('ODR', which are ADR procedures that are conducted through the online processes). Indeed, there is increasing support, at least in the context of consumer disputes, for the greater use of ODR as shown by the recent EU consumer scoreboard for 2021.[27] Other jurisdictions, like China, are moving at a far quicker pace in integrating ODR within their civil justice architecture.[28] In China, online pre-trial mediation platforms have been incorporated within the smart court architecture. This ODR procedure is designed to deal with both basic and complex, high value disputes. For example, in 2018, ten personal injury cases were brought in the former Beijing Railway Transportation Court which involved 25 claimants suing a railway company.[29] Given the fact that most of the parties were residing outside Beijing, the court used its online mediation platform. In preparing for the mediation, the judge communicated online with all the parties to ensure that they had reasonable expectations regarding the process. The parties logged onto the court's online mediation system and undertook identity verification, filed statements of case and defence, submitted evidence, and conducted negotiations. The entire mediation process was recorded and saved online. All of the cases were successfully mediated and concluded with the e-signing of the mediation agreements. Zhou has praised the use of online mediation and observes that the successful conclusion of these disputes demonstrates 'the possibility for the swift, cost-effective resolution of personal injury claims that can significantly reduce the parties' litigation burden'.[30]

Although OCMC does not currently integrate ODR, it does provide a strong basis upon which the system can build and expand to incorporate ODR procedures. The opt-out mediation stage ushers in a significant philosophical and practical culture shift in the manner in which disputes are to be resolved and

---

[27] European Commission, 'Key consumer data 2020, The new online Consumer Scoreboard' https://ec.europa.eu/info/policies/consumers/consumer-protection/key-consumer-data_en accessed 9 May 2021.

[28] For a detailed discussion of mediation in China, see Peter C.H. Chan, *Mediation in Contemporary Chinese Civil Justice: A Proceduralist Diachronic Perspective* (Brill Nijhoff 2017).

[29] Mimi Zou, '"Smart courts" in China and the Future of Personal Injury Litigation' (2020) 2 JPIL 135; also see Jingjing Hao and Meng Chen, 'The Expansion of Technology in the Chinese Judicial System' [2020] available at https://doi.org/10.31124/advance.12402980.v1 accessed 9 May 2021.

[30] Zou (n 29) 140.

gives effect to Briggs LJ's wider notion of dispute resolution. By formally directing the parties to mediation, it helps to focus their minds on the early settlement of their dispute, and obliges them to make a conscious decision on opting out of the process. It is no longer desirable nor feasible for all disputes to simply proceed to a hearing before a judge. Disputes are to be directed to *appropriate* resolution procedures, including ADR, which will, in turn, help to further the principle of proportionality and, consequently, facilitate greater access to justice.

It is essential that all dispute resolution procedures uphold and protect the principle of procedural justice. Substantive justice[31] is concerned with the courts correctly applying the law to true facts or, to put it another way, deciding the case on its substantive merits.[32] It is this exercise of determining the dispute through the application of law to true facts by the courts that gives life to the principle of substantive justice which is lacking in popular forms of non-adjudicative ADR procedures such as mediation, conciliation and negotiation.[33] Sorabji explains the court's role in securing substantive justice thus:

> All civil justice systems are committed, to varying degrees, to determining civil disputes through ascertaining true facts and applying it to right law in order to secure an accurate decision. In that way they arrive at substantive justice.[34]

Procedural justice, which consists of the rules of court as well as principles such as equality before the law, impartiality, and proportionality, is the means by which the courts discharge their constitutional function of vindicating and enforcing rights and thereby upholding the rule of law.

De Girolomo explains that procedural justice is a concept that rests on certain elements of process that, if present, result in party perceptions of fairness in the dispute resolution process experienced by them.[35] If parties perceive those processes to be fair then they are likely to respect and accept any outcomes from those processes because parties care about the process by which

---

31 Jeremy Bentham, 'Rationale of Judicial Evidence' in John Bowring (ed), *The Works of Jeremy Bentham*, vol 6 (William Tait 1843) 212–213. For an interesting discussion of the significance of truth in the pursuit of justice see Remco van Rhee and Alan Uzelac, 'The Pursuit of Truth in Contemporary Civil Procedure Revival of Accuracy or a New Balance in Favour of Effectiveness' in Remco van Rhee and Alan Uzelac (eds), *Truth and Efficiency in Civil Litigation* (Intersentia 2012).

32 John Sorabji, *English Civil Justice after the Woolf and Jackson Reforms: A Critical Analysis* (CUP 2013).

33 Compared with adjudicative forms of ADR such as arbitration.

34 Sorabji (n 32) 31.

35 Debbie De Girolomo, 'The Mediation Process: Challenges to Neutrality and the Delivery of Procedural Justice' (2019) 39(4) OJLS 4-5.

outcomes are reached. Hollander-Blumoff and Tyler contend that an outcome reached through a consensual process will be seen to be fair if the process leading to the outcome and the treatment of the parties within that process are fair.[36] Similarly, others have argued that procedural fairness applies to both court adjudication and mediation procedures and that mediation delivers procedural justice if all its elements are met, including allowing participants to 'tell their story', and making them part of the decision-making process.[37]

It is essential that the opt-out mediation stage is robustly evaluated and tested to ensure that it is procedurally fair, especially from the perspective of users.[38] By doing this, procedural weaknesses in the system can be identified and improvements can be made in-line with reliable user data. Ultimately, users will have confidence in opt-out mediation and they are more likely to accept and comply with outcomes.

4.3 THE CONTINUING PROBLEM OF *HALSEY*

The orthodox judicial school of thought on the issue of compulsory ADR has its jurisprudential roots in *Halsey*. The main issue for the Court of Appeal in that case was whether the defendants in two personal injury claims should be penalised in costs for refusing to mediate. Mediation had been offered by the claimants in both actions, and, in one case, a court had actually recommended it. Dyson LJ, giving the leading judgment, rejected the argument that the courts should compel parties to mediation. He reasoned that compulsion would breach the right to a fair trial enshrined in article 6 ECHR but went on to stress that the courts could, however, encourage the parties to consider mediation. The strongest form of encouragement would be in the form of an ADR order (an order made in the Commercial Court which requires the parties to not only engage in ADR but also to provide reasons to the court if the ADR is unsuccessful). If a party subsequently failed to comply with such an order, that would amount to unreasonable litigation behaviour and would justify the courts penalising that party in costs.[39]

---

[36] Rebecca Hollander-Blumoff and Tom R. Tyler, 'Procedural Justice in Negotiation: Procedural Fairness, Outcomes Acceptance, and Integrative Potential' (2008) 33 *Law & Society Inquiry* 473.

[37] Jonathan M. Hyman and Lela P. Love, 'If Poria Were a Mediator: An Inquiry into Justice in Mediation' (2020) 9 *Clinical Law Review* 157, 192.

[38] see e.g., Natalie Byrom, *Digital Justice: HMCTS data strategy and delivering access to justice. Report and Recommendations* (The Legal Education Foundation, October 2019).

[39] *Halsey* (n 15) [31].

The decision in *Halsey* reflects a tension between the formal rejection of compulsory ADR and the acknowledgement of the courts' powers to 'encourage' parties to engage in ADR. To say that parties should not be compelled to ADR but then to indicate that 'encouragement' may be robust and in the form of a court order appears to be contradictory. It is highly unlikely that parties, even if they are opposed to ADR, will decline to abide by a court order: such parties would clearly face severe cost consequences under CPR 44.[40] A court order and the threat of severe cost consequences would impliedly force the parties to ADR, rendering Dyson LJ's position on article 6 obsolete.

More importantly, the Court of Justice of the European Union (CJEU) in *Alassini v Telecom Italia Spa*,[41] a decision which came after the *Halsey* decision, dealt directly with the issue of whether compulsory mediation was a breach of article 6.[42] *Alassini* concerned an action which was brought by customers of two telecom companies for breach of contract. The Italian government made legal action relating to issues covered by the EU Universal Service Directive[43] conditional on a prior attempt to reach a settlement. The Italian law, in the opinion of Advocate General Kokott, pursued legitimate objectives in the general interest in the quicker and less expensive resolution of disputes. Advocate General Kokott found that the measure of requiring parties to engage in settlement discussions before commencing court proceedings was proportionate because no less restrictive alternative existed to the implementation of a mandatory procedure, since the introduction of an out-of-court settlement procedure which is merely optional is not as efficient a means of achieving those objectives.[44] The Court agreed with the assessment of Advocate General Kokott, and thus held that the Italian law did not seek to replace court proceedings and therefore access to the court was not denied but, at worst, delayed by 30 days. Similarly, in *Menini and another v Banco Popolare*[45] the CJEU held that EU Member States could compel parties to mediate before raising an

---

40 CPR 44 contains the general rules on costs.

41 Case C-317/08 *Alassini v Telecom Italia SpA* [2010] EU:C:2010:146.

42 The CJEU judgment is based on article 47 EU Charter and the EU principle of effective judicial protection. Although the ECHR and the case law of the ECtHR serve as reference points for the CJEU, they remain two separate regimes.

43 Directive 2002/22/EC of the European Parliament and of the Council of 7 March 2002 on universal service and users' rights relating to electronic communications networks and services (Universal Service Directive), OJ L 108/51. The Directive is no longer in force as it has been repealed by Directive (EU) 2018/1972 of the European Parliament and of the Council of 11 December 2018 establishing the European Electronic Communications Code (Recast), PE/52/2018/REV/1, OJ L 321/36.

44 *Alassini* (n 41) [67].

45 Case C-75/16 *Menini and another v Banco Popolare Società Cooperativa* [2017] EU:C:2017:132.

action in court, although they were not permitted to dictate how the mediation was to be conducted.

The *Halsey* article 6 point has also been criticised by Lord Clarke MR.[46] He observed that European states such as Belgium, a signatory to the ECHR, had introduced compulsory ADR schemes without a successful article 6 challenge. Lord Clarke MR also cast doubt over the use of the ECtHR decision in *Deweer*[47] in *Halsey*. That case was one which dealt with the claimant, a Belgian national, agreeing to pay an amount in settlement of a fine and thereby waiving his right to referring the dispute to a tribunal. The ECtHR in that case held that the claimant's waiver did not amount to a violation of his right to a fair trial. Therefore, mediation did not waive a party's right to a fair trial. Lord Clarke MR recognised the court's jurisdiction to require parties to engage in mediation when he said 'Despite the Halsey decision it is at least strongly arguable that the court retains jurisdiction to require parties to enter into mediation' and that mediation could 'be factored into and become an integral part of standard directions and the court's power would derive from its general case management powers under the CPR'.[48] In *Halsey*, the Court appears to have misunderstood the nature of mediation, a process from which the parties are at liberty to withdraw before reaching a settlement, and arbitration, an adjudicative process which the parties cannot leave if they have agreed to refer their dispute to an arbitral tribunal. It was this misunderstanding which reinforced the Court's conclusion that compulsory mediation would undermine access to the courts because the parties would not only be obliged to engage with mediation but would be obliged to settle their dispute without the liberty to withdraw from the process. In view of the jurisprudential developments that followed *Halsey*, Lord Dyson, in his speech at the *Chartered Institute of Arbitrators Third Mediation Symposium*, acknowledged the courts' powers to order the parties to engage in mediation when he said 'in and of itself compulsory mediation does not breach article 6' but that 'compulsory mediation is more effective when it is voluntary.'[49]

A further point to note is *Halsey's* failure to address previous decisions which appeared to have embraced the notion of compulsory ADR. Blackburn J in *Shirayama Shoukusan Co v Danovo*[50] had no doubt that the courts have assumed the jurisdiction to order parties to mediation and he drew support from Arden J's (as she was then) decision in *Kinstreet Ltd v Balmargo Co*,[51] in

46 Lord Clarke MR, 'The Future of Civil Mediation' (2008) 74 *Arbitration* 419.
47 *Deweer v Belgium* (1980) 2 EHRR 439.
48 Lord Clarke MR, 'The Future of Civil Mediation' (n 46).
49 Lord Dyson, 'A Word on Halsey', (2011) 77(3) *Arbitration* 337–41.
50 *Shirayama Shokusan Co Ltd v Danovo Ltd (No. 1)* [2003] EWHC 3306 (Ch).
51 *Kinstreet Ltd v Balmargo Co* [1999] 8 WLUK 24.

which the parties were ordered to mediation. Further, Coleman J in *Cable & Wireless plc v IBM United Kingdom Ltd*[52] confirmed that the courts maintained the power to order unwilling parties to engage in ADR in the Commercial Court and it went on to make such an order. Coleman J stated:

> I have no doubt that the overall interests of all parties...would be best served if the whole group of disputes between C and RHL was referred to mediation before any further substantial costs are incurred either in pursuing or defending satellite litigation...In many respects this series of disputes with its particular commercial background is the paradigm of a case which is likely to be settled by mediation.[53]

4.4 RECENT JURISPRUDENTIAL INCONSISTENTIES AND *LOMAX*

The two schools of thought have created inconsistencies within the jurisprudence, which has, in turn, given contradictory messages to court users on the extent of their ADR obligations and the approach the courts will adopt if ADR is rejected. However, the recent Court of Appeal decision in *Lomax* has provided the grounds upon which the courts are able to formulate a more principled approach to the issue of compulsory ADR, but the article 6 issue in *Halsey* must be reappraised and formally rejected.

4.4.1 Jurisprudential Inconsistencies

Two recent Court of Appeal decision neatly illustrate the tensions within the jurisprudence. The principal issue in *Thakkar v Patel*[54] was the defendants' failure to engage with the claimants' invitation to mediate. Both had requested a stay for ADR on their respective allocation questionnaires and both parties had expressed a willingness to try to mediate. The claimants made arrangement for a mediation and identified possible mediators for consideration by the defendants. The defendants, by contrast, were slow to respond to the claimants' letters and, as Jackson LJ put it, 'raised all sorts of difficulties'.[55] Eventually, the claimants wrote to the defendants setting out the history of their attempts to arrange a mediation and stated that they no longer had confidence that a mediation could be arranged given the defendants' failure to co-operate.

The matter proceeded to trial at which the claimants were awarded £44,933.52 on their claim and the defendants were awarded £16,750 on their

---

52 *Cable & Wireless plc v IBM United Kingdom Ltd* [2002] EWHC 2059 (Comm).

53 Ibid. Reference in the judgement to 'C and RHL' is to the parties in the case.

54 *Thakkar v Patel* [2017] EWCA Civ 117.

55 Ibid., [10].

counterclaim. Turning to the issue of costs, the judge examined the parties' conduct during the litigation process and, in particular, in relation to the claimants' invitation to mediation. He found that the claimants' had been more proactive in their attempts in arranging a mediation whereas the defendants were 'less keen to participate'.[56] The judge went on to say that there were real prospects of settlement if a mediation had taken place. After weighing up all the circumstances, the judge ordered the defendants to pay 75 per cent of the claimants' costs of the claim. The defendants appealed on the ground that the judge had erred in the exercise of his discretion concerning costs.

On the mediation issue, Jackson LJ noted that the claimants had taken proactive steps to set up a mediation. Although recognising the fact that the defendants had not refused to mediate outright, they had 'dragged their feet and delayed for so long that the claimants lost confidence in the process'.[57] Jackson LJ agreed with the judge's finding that there was a real chance that the matter would have settled had it gone to a mediation and he provided five reasons for agreeing with the judge's conclusions. First, the dispute was a commercial one which was purely about money. Secondly, the differences between the parties' respective settlement offers (of approximately £10,000) were very close. Thirdly, the costs of the litigation were vastly greater than the sums in issue. Fourthly, bilateral negotiations between the parties had been unsuccessful. Finally, a skilled mediator would have assisted the parties by pointing to the small gap between their respective positions and the huge future costs of the litigation. Given those circumstances, Jackson LJ stated that he 'would be astonished if a skilled mediator failed to bring the parties to a sensible settlement'.[58]

Jackson LJ went on to cite *PGF II SA v OMFS Co 1 Ltd*[59] in which the Court of Appeal held that silence in the face of an offer to mediate was, as a general rule, unreasonable conduct meriting a costs sanction. That was so even if an outright refusal to mediate might have been justified. His Lordship explained that, although the defendants in the present appeal had not refused to mediate,

---

[56] Ibid., [15].

[57] Ibid., [27].

[58] Ibid., [27].

[59] *PGF II SA v OMFS Co 1 Ltd* [2013] EWCA Civ 1288. For a discussion of various aspects of this case, see Patrick Taylor, 'Failing to Respond to an Invitation to Mediate' (2014) 80 *Arbitration* 470; Masood Ahmed, 'Silence in the Face of Invitations to Mediate' (2014) 73(1) *CLJ* 35; Gary Meggitt, 'PGF II SA v OMFS Co and Compulsory Mediation' (2014) 33 CJQ 335; Sir Bernard Rix, 'The Interface of Mediation and Litigation' [2014] 80 Arbitration 21; John McQuater, 'The Future of Part 36 (Part 8)' (2015) *1 Journal of Public International Law* 49; and Erich Suter, 'Unreasonable Refusal to Mediate and Costs' (2015) 81 *Arbitration* 2.

they had 'dragged their feet'[60] until the claimants had lost confidence in the settlement process. Although Jackson LJ remarked that the judge's costs order was 'a tough order'[61] it was nevertheless justified. Jackson LJ concluded in the following strong terms:

> The message which this court sent out in PGF II was that to remain silent in the face of an offer to mediate is, absent exceptional circumstances, unreasonable conduct meriting a costs sanction, even in cases where mediation is unlikely to succeed. The message which the court sends out in this case is that *in a case where bilateral negotiations fail but mediation is obviously appropriate, it behoves both parties to get on with it.* If one party frustrates the process by delaying and dragging its feet for no good reason, that will merit a costs sanction. In the present case, the costs sanction was severe, but not so severe that this court should intervene.[62]

Both PGF and Thakkar oblige litigating parties to actively engage with a call to mediation and to respond in a constructive and co-operative manner. Simply remaining silent and thereby ignoring an invitation to mediation or dragging one's feet runs counter to the very nature of ADR and undermines the philosophy of encouraging party dialogue in the early settlement of disputes. Further, both cases are consistent with the approach previously taken by the Court of Appeal in the leading case of *Dunnett v Railtrack plc*.[63]

A mere four months after the decision in Thakkar, the Court of Appeal took a completely divergent approach in Gore v Naheed.[64] That case concerned a boundary dispute. The defendants' invitation to mediation was rejected by the claimant. The defendants lost at first instance and they appealed both on the substantive issues and the costs order which was made against them. On the issue of costs, the defendants, relying on PGF, argued that the judge should have made some allowance in their favour for the fact that the claimant had refused to engage with their invitation to mediation.

Giving the leading judgment, Patten LJ rejected the defendants' arguments on the issue of mediation. His Lordship adopted a completely opposite approach to that in PGF and Thakkar when he said:

> Speaking for myself, *I have some difficulty in accepting that the desire of a party to have his rights determined by a court of law in preference to mediation can be said to be unreasonable conduct particularly when, as here, those rights are ultimately vindicated.* But, as Briggs LJ makes clear in his judgment, a failure to engage, even

60 *Thakkar* (n 54) [27].
61 Ibid., [30].
62 Ibid., [31] (emphasis added).
63 *Dunnett v Railtrack Plc Dunnett v Railtrack plc* [2002] EWCA (Civ) 303.
64 *Gore v Naheed* [2017] EWCA Civ 369.

> if unreasonable, does not automatically result in a costs penalty. It is simply a factor to be taken into account by the judge when exercising his costs discretion.[65]

His Lordship agreed with the judge's conclusion that it had not been unreasonable for the claimant to have declined to mediate; the claimant's solicitor had considered that mediation had no realistic prospect of succeeding and would only add to costs. Patten LJ also approved of the judge's opinion that the case raised complex questions of law which made it unsuitable for mediation. Consequently, Patten LJ held that the judge's 'refusal to make an allowance on these grounds cannot in my view be said to be wrong in principle'.[66]

The decision in *Gore* clearly contradicts and undermines the decisions in *PGF* and *Thakkar* which require the parties to seriously consider and engage with an invitation to mediate, regardless of the relevance of their belief in the strength of their cases. *Gore* is, therefore, illustrative of the diverging, inconsistent and unclear messages emanating from the Court of Appeal on the issue of the parties' duties to engage with ADR.

4.4.2 *Lomax*

A clearer approach emerged in the decision of the Court of Appeal in *Lomax v Lomax*. That case concerned a family inheritance dispute which was governed by the CPR. The claimant applied for an ENE or a Financial Dispute Resolution (hereafter 'FDR') hearing, which the defendant opposed. Could the court make an ENE order regardless of whether the parties consented to it being made?

At first instance,[67] Parker J held 'on the finest of fine balances'[68] that she could not order an ENE or FDR without the consent of both parties. A close analysis of the language of the CPR was, according to Parker J, directed at *facilitation* rather than compulsion.[69] As Parker J explained, 'My overall conclusion is that the current rules are insufficiently precise in their formulation for me either to conclude, or be confident that the rule-maker intended, that the judge is permitted to give directions which lead to a non-consensual ENE.'[70] This conclusion did not, however, detract from her view that this was a case '*which cries, indeed screams out*, for a robust judge-led process to focus on the

---

65 Ibid., [49] (emphasis added).
66 Ibid., [50].
67 *Lomax v Lomax* [2019] EWHC 1267 (Fam).
68 Ibid., [111].
69 CPR 1.4(2).
70 *Lomax* (n 67) [119].

legal and factual issues … and perhaps even craft a proposed solution for the parties to consider'.[71]

Giving the judgment of the Court of Appeal, Moylan LJ noted that, because the wording of CPR r.3.1(2)(m) did not contain an express requirement for party consent before an ENE could be ordered, the issue was whether such a limitation could be implied by the rule. In distinguishing the decision in Halsey, Moylan LJ stated that it was a case which concerned whether a court could oblige unwilling parties to submit their disputes to a specific type of ADR procedure: mediation. Halsey did not assist in the task of interpreting CPR r.3.1(2)(m) because it was concerned with whether parties could be compelled to take part in mediation that was outside the court process, whereas ENE formed a part of the court process. Despite distinguishing Halsey, Moylan LJ did recognise that 'the court's engagement with mediation has progressed significantly since Halsey was decided'[72] and, as a consequence, appeared to indirectly cast doubt on the continuing validity of the reasoning in Halsey.

Moylan LJ also rejected the argument that ordering ENE prevented the parties from having their dispute determined by the courts. His Lordship explained that, in the event that the matter could not be settled as a result of the parties engaging with ENE, this 'did not, in any material way, obstruct a party's access to the court'.[73] At most, an ENE was an additional step in the court process and therefore was 'not in any sense an 'unacceptable constraint' on the parties' rights to access the courts'.[74] Court-ordered ENE was, in Moylan LJ's view, 'a step in the process which can assist with the fair and sensible resolution of cases'.[75] In fact, an ENE in which a judge provides his neutral evaluation of the merits of the parties' respective positions had the positive effect of focusing the parties' minds on the issues and on settlement, which would save both the parties' and the courts' time and cost.

The decision is a significant development in strengthening the relationship between ADR and the civil process. By recognising that the courts have the power to compel non-consenting parties to engage in ENE, the Court of Appeal has reinforced and further enhanced the role played by ADR in the resolution of civil disputes during the court process. The wording of CPR r.3.1(2)(m) is deliberately widely drafted with the intention of providing the courts with the necessary discretion to manage disputes effectively in order to further the overriding objective. Ordering ENE in appropriate cases is an important part of those judicial functions. To accept the argument that party consent should

---

71 Ibid., [123] (emphasis added).
72 *Lomax* (n 19) [27].
73 Ibid., [26].
74 Ibid.
75 Ibid.

be implied into CPR r.3.1(2)(m) would be to place an unnecessary fetter on the court's case management powers and undermine the overriding objective of dealing with cases justly and at proportionate cost. It would also beg the question of which other aspects of the court's case management powers were subject to party consent given the complete absence of any explicit reference to consent in CPR r.3.1. The decision, therefore, is consistent with the central aims of the overriding objective and, more significantly, upholds and gives effect to the principle of proportionality. Accordingly, the courts should consider the effect decisions in individual cases have on the civil justice system as a whole. A commitment to the principle of proportionality reduces the possibility of achieving substantive justice as it requires a compromise between the resources made available to each claim and securing a substantively just decision in individual claims. In this respect, judicial ENE provides a unique opportunity to the parties because the issues are dealt with in an authoritative manner whilst also upholding the principle of proportionality.

ENE, like mediation, is not a hindrance to the parties' rights to access the courts because the parties are at liberty to choose not to be bound by the expert's evaluation and to revert to the court process for judicial determination of their dispute. It is a procedure which assists the parties to obtain a judge's opinion on the merits of the parties' respective positions and to focus their minds on settlement; the parties are not bound by that opinion unless they choose to be. If they choose not to be bound by the expert's opinion, it can still be used to narrow the issues between the parties and can help facilitate settlement through another ADR procedure such as negotiation or mediation.

Traditionally, there was a tendency among the judiciary to vigorously promote mediation as the preferred ADR procedure. This overzealous judicial emphasis on mediation within the jurisprudence has restricted the wider concepts of ADR and 'dispute resolution' which in turn has created what this author has termed 'judicial mediation bias'.[76] This phenomenon has also developed an understanding of the civil justice system as a two-stream process of mediation and litigation. However, the Court of Appeal's decision in *Lomax* demonstrates a judicial shift away from 'judicial mediation bias'. The courts appear to be willing to critically consider the nature of various ADR procedures and to identify those that are suited to the circumstances of the case rather than simply recommending mediation, the most common form of ADR procedure used by the parries and preferred by the courts. Parker J

[76] Masood Ahmed, 'Moving on from Judicial Preference for mediation to Embed Appropriate Dispute Resolution' (2019) 70(3) *Northern Ireland Legal Quarterly* 331–353.

cited *Bradley v Heslin*[77] in which Norris J recommended the use of ENE over mediation in providing the parties with an effective method of resolving their boundary dispute. Parker J noted that 'Mediation (even by a legally trained mediator, if one should be found to assist where the issues were specialised) is unlikely to approach the issues in an authoritative way, as Norris J said in Seals'.[78] Similarly, in his judgment, Moylan LJ also discussed in detail the nature of ENE and its practical and economic virtues for the courts and the parties. Thus, both decisions reflect a wider understanding and appreciation of what is meant by dispute resolution and the judicial activities related to ADR. The classic perception of the role of a judge is limited to formal adjudication. In reality, however, the promotion of settlement is also a mainstream judicial activity, and perhaps even more so than formal adjudication considering the fact that a vast majority of claims issued in the civil courts are undisputed. The claimant's choice of ENE as opposed to simply opting for mediation caused Parker J to engage with a wider consideration of dispute resolution, including engaging in a critical comparison between ENE and mediation, which has been inherently absent from the jurisprudence.[79]

A further policy rationale can be made to justify the call to extend the reasoning in Lomax to mediation in the court process. By engaging the court process, the parties are consciously and willingly submitting their dispute to be managed by the courts to *a resolution process*. Those resolution processes include various ADR procedures as well as traditional judicial determination and the parties should expect the courts, who are tasked with furthering the overriding objective in dealing with cases justly and at proportionate cost, to manage their dispute in the most appropriate manner. This also reinforces Briggs LJ's approach that courts should manage disputes in the widest possible sense in which 'a trial is statistically unlikely to be its conclusion.'[80] In doing so, the courts should take a more active role in the encouragement, facilitation and management of dispute resolution in the widest sense, including ADR as part of that process, rather than merely focusing on case preparation for trial.

There is, however, a fundamental shortcoming with Lomax; it is the Court of Appeal's failure to comprehensively reappraise and dismiss the ADR compulsion issue. Rather, Moylan LJ simply by-passed Halsey by distinguishing it on weak grounds and to indirectly cast doubt on Halsey by saying: 'I would only comment that the court's engagement with mediation has progressed

77 *Bradley v Heslin* [2014] EWHC 3267 (Ch).

78 *Lomax* (n 67) [123].

79 Masood Ahmed, 'Moving on from judicial preference for mediation to embed appropriate dispute resolution' (n 76).

80 Briggs, *Chancery Modernisation Review* (n 11).

significantly since Halsey was decided.'[81] This is disappointing, given the unsatisfactory state of the ADR jurisprudence on the issue of compulsion. The Court of Appeal should have directly addressed Halsey to make clear that an order for mediation *during the court process*, like ENE, does not hinder the parties' rights to access the courts but rather it reinforces and promotes a wider and more effective approach to the management and resolution of disputes and, fundamentally, assists the courts to further the overriding objective.

4.4.3 CJC Report

The CJC,[82] the non-governmental body responsible for overseeing and co-ordinating the modernisation of the civil justice system, has recently confirmed that appropriate forms of compulsory ADR 'where a return to the normal adjudicative process is always available, are capable of overcoming the objections voiced in the case law…'[83] Although the CJC did not make detailed proposals for reform, it made three observations: where ADR is free to the parties then it is unlikely to be controversial; greater use of compulsory judge-led ADR processes will prove acceptable; and compulsory mediation may be considered, provided it is sufficiently regulated. The CJC report is significant because it confirms and reinforces the argument that consensual forms of ADR where the parties are free to withdraw from the process and continue to access the courts do not undermine Article 6. It also recognises and embraces the continued importance of ADR within the civil justice system and its wider economic and practical benefits to litigants and the courts. Although it does not make proposals for reform, it does recognise the role of judge-led ADR which further develops the skills and experiences of the judiciary in managing and resolving civil disputes other than through the traditional court process.

4.5 REFORM AND CONCLUSION

Halsey is clearly wrong on the Article 6 issue: ordering parties to engage with ADR is *not* a violation of their rights to access to the courts because they are at liberty to withdraw from that process and proceed to judicial determination; access to the courts would only be undermined if the parties are ordered to reach a settlement during the ADR process. The overriding objective and, in

---

[81] *Lomax* (n 19) [27].

[82] The primary role of the Civil Justice Council is to advise the Lord Chancellor, the judiciary and the Civil Procedure Rule Committee on civil matters. The chairman of the Civil Justice Council is the Master of the Rolls.

[83] *Civil Justice Council,* 'Compulsory ADR' (n 20).

particular, the increasing need for the parties and the courts to incur proportionate costs further reinforces the call to finally abandon judicial resistance to the issue of compulsion.[84] The early settlement of disputes preserves the courts' finite resources and investing those resources in those cases which genuinely cannot be resolved through ADR and therefore require judicial attention.

A more radical approach to the observations made by the CJC must be taken to finally introduce clarity and consistency in the jurisprudence. Thus, the Article 6 issue in *Halsey* must be reappraised and finally dismissed in order for the courts to develop a clearer and more consistent body of case law. A failure to address the current jurisprudential inconsistences is unsatisfactory from a legal, policy, and practical perspective. Court users are given contradictory messages and guidance on the extent of their ADR obligations which consequently undermines civil justice reforms which seek to enhance the role and impact of ADR. Given the Court of Appeal's responsibility in implementing, developing, and supervising civil justice reforms, it will be for that court to dismiss the *Halsey* Article 6 issue and for a more principled approach towards the issue of compulsion to develop.

The courts should take confidence from the decision in *Lomax* and continue to embrace their case management powers, including the full range of ADR procedures, and be more willing to make ADR orders in appropriate cases. The reasoning in *Lomax* also extends to the making of mediation orders, an observation previously made by this author[85] and which was also echoed by the court in *McParland & Partners Ltd and Anor v Whitehead*.[86] In that case, Sir Geoffrey Vos recommended early neutral evaluation to the parties and in doing so he explained that *Lomax* 'inevitably raised the question of whether the court might also require parties to engage in mediation despite the decision in Halsey'.[87] Not only does *Lomax* undermine *Halsey* on the Article 6 point but it provides strong justification for the courts to make orders compelling parties to engage with mediation and, by further extension, other types of ADR procedures. Furthermore, the opt-out mediation stage of OCMC is a further representation of the desire of policy makers and the judiciary to not only

---

84 John Sorabji, *English Civil Justice after the Woolf and Jackson Reforms: A Critical Analysis* (CUP 2014) 168–89.

85 Masood Ahmed, 'Compelling Parties to ADR' (*The Law Society Gazette*, 16 September 2019) https://www.lawgazette.co.uk/legal-updates/compelling-parties-to-adr/5101419.article accessed 9 May 2021; Masood Ahmed and Fatma Arslan 'Compelling Parties to Judicial Early Neutral Evaluation but a Missed Opportunity for Mediation' (2020) 39(1) CJQ 1.

86 *McParland & Partners Ltd & Anor v Whitehead* [2020] EWHC 298 (Ch).

87 Ibid., [42]. In *Telecom Centre (UK) Ltd v Thomas Sanderson Ltd* [2020] EWHC 368 (QB) Master McCloud provided valuable guidance on the procedure for conducting JENE in the Queen's Bench Division.

embrace ADR but also to give practical effect to a cultural change in the way in which disputes are resolved within the civil justice system.

More should be done by the courts to engage with the parties and to explain the nature of ADR, the role of the third-party neutral, and, more significantly, the freedom of the parties to withdraw from the process (before a settlement is concluded) and to have their dispute heard by a judge. Support for this approach can be taken from the Statement of the European Law Institute and of the European Network of Councils for the Judiciary which recommends greater training of the judiciary on ADR matters. In particular, Article 18 provides that the courts should ensure that the parties understand whether the ADR process that is being recommended is mandatory or voluntary, and Article 19 recommends that the courts explain the nature of ADR and its relationship with the court process.[88] The process of informing and 'educating' the parties of ADR should not simply be left to the parties' lawyers and their appointed party neutral, but should also include judges. This will help to reinforce the parties' understanding of the nature of ADR and their willingness to constructively engage with the settlement process. It will also reinforce the principle of procedural justice in the court ordered ADR procedure by ensuring the parties understand the procedure and the opportunity for them to tell their story and to be part of the decision-making process if the parties decided to settle their dispute.

The current digitisation reforms and the future vision of an online civil court process with integrated sophisticated ADR procedures have the potential to truly revolutionise the English civil justice system and increase access to justice for all. However, the tension within the ADR jurisprudence has the potential to undermine those reforms and, therefore, it will be for the Court of Appeal to finally dismiss the *Halsey* Article 6 point to allow for a more principled and modern approach to develop on the issue of compulsory ADR.

---

[88] The European Law Institute and the European Network of Councils for the Judiciary, 'The Relationship between Formal and Informal Justice: the Courts and Alternative Dispute Resolution' (European Law Institute 2018) https://www.europeanlawinstitute.eu/fileadmin/user_upload/p_eli/Publications/ADR_Statement.pdf accessed 9 May 2021.

5. Alternative dispute resolution, justice and accountability in Norwegian civil justice

Anna Nylund

5.1 INTRODUCTION

Alternative dispute resolution (ADR) promises to increase access to justice by delivering better, cheaper and faster justice than litigation in courts does. Critics argue that ADR as part of the justice system reduces access to justice,[1] and recurrent examples of how ADR fails to provide a fair process and just outcomes sustain resistance against ADR across Europe. Moreover, researchers have identified a palpable gap between ADR theory and practice that has repercussions on the quality of ADR. Developing a theory of ADR that is better aligned with ADR as an integral part of the justice system could serve to improve the quality and accessibility of dispute resolution.

Settlement and pragmatic outcomes are highly valued in the Norwegian civil justice system.[2] These values are manifested in the omnipresence of ADR, both within and outside courts. The most important systems for civil, non-family disputes based on the number of cases are court-connected mediation, Conciliation Boards as a mandatory first instance for small claims, and consumer dispute resolution (CDR). The number of cases in Conciliation Boards and CDR far exceeds the number of civil court cases.[3]

---

[1] E.g., Hazel Genn, *Judging Civil Justice. The Hamlyn Lectures* (Cambridge University Press 2010) 78ff.

[2] Anna Nylund, 'Institutional Aspects of the Nordic Justice Systems: Striving for Consolidation and Settlements' in Laura Ervo, Pia Letto-Vanamo and Anna Nylund (eds), *Rethinking Nordic Courts* (Springer 2021) 187.

[3] In 2020, there were 12,983 incoming civil and family cases in Norwegian courts; 72,988 cases in Conciliation Boards, most of which are uncontested; and 9,805 (2019 figures) CDR cases in the public system alone, according to the Annual Reports of the Norwegian Courts Administration https://www.domstol.no/domstoladministrasjonen/publikasjoner/arsrapporter/arsrapport-2020/ accessed 5 July 2021; the Norwegian

This chapter starts by exploring key factors underpinning the gap between ADR theory and practice (section 5.2). Then, the concepts of justice in ADR and a suggestion for standards of justice appropriate for ADR as an integral part of the justice system are developed (section 5.3). In section 5.4, the accountability gap in ADR is addressed, and suggestions for mechanisms for accountability are put forth. The final section uses the parameters for justice and accountability in ADR in order to evaluate the three most-used processes in Norway. It attempts to evaluate whether the Norwegian processes provide just outcomes and processes and render the neutral[4] and the justice system accountable.

5.2 THE GAP BETWEEN ADR THEORY AND PRACTICE

The terminology and taxonomy of ADR processes have been a continuous source of debate and disagreement since the 1980s.[5] Still today, ADR, mediation and conciliation are imprecisely defined and are often used interchangeably as umbrella terms to refer to a range of different dispute resolution processes.[6] Mediation theory operates with three major forms of mediation: facilitative, evaluative and transformative mediation. The latter is seldom used in legal settings. In facilitative mediation, the mediator facilitates negotiations and interests-based outcomes, whereas in evaluative mediation, the mediator often recommends an outcome based on the likely litigated outcome.

Police, which administers the Conciliation Boards https://www.politiet.no/globalassets/05-om-oss/rapporter/politiets-arsrapport-2020.pdf accessed 5 July 2021, 10; and the Norwegian Consumer Council https://fil.forbrukerradet.no/wp-content/uploads/2020/03/aarsrapport-2019-redusert.pdf accessed 5 July 2021, 38.

[4] In this text, the word *neutral* is used to define a person who assists the disputants in resolving their dispute.

[5] E.g., Carrie Menkel-Meadow, 'Pursuing Settlement in an Adversary Culture: A Tale of Innovation Co-Opted or "The Law of ADR"' (1991) *Florida State University Law Review* 1; Carrie Menkel-Meadow, 'When Dispute Resolution Begets Disputes of Its Own: Conflicts Among Dispute Resolution Professionals' (1997) *UCLA Law* Review 1871; John Lande, 'Moving Negotiation Theory from the Tower of Babel Toward a World of Mutual Understanding' (2017) *Journal of Dispute Resolution* 1.

[6] E.g., Silvia Barona and Carlos Esplugues, 'ADR Mechanisms and their Incorporation into Global Justice in the Twenty-First Century: Some Concepts and Trends' in Carlos Esplugues and Silvia Barona (eds), *Global Perspectives on ADR* (Intersentia 2014); The European Law Institute and the European Network of Councils for the Judiciary, 'The Relationship between Formal and Informal Justice: the Courts and Alternative Dispute Resolution' (European Law Institute 2018) https://www.europeanlawinstitute.eu/fileadmin/user_upload/p_eli/Publications/ADR_Statement.pdf accessed 5 July 2021.

The term 'evaluative mediation'[7] is inaccurate, because it refers to a wide range of practices. James Alfini describes three varieties of evaluative mediation. To pressure parties to lower their expectations and produce swift settlement, 'trashers' 'tear apart' the parties' cases by stressing weaknesses and overplaying risks of litigation.[8] 'Bashers' do not in fact evaluate the case but rather persuade the parties to make 'realistic' settlement offers and continue haggling until they arrive at a figure both accept. Trashing and bashing are also referred to as 'muscle mediation'.[9] Other 'evaluative' mediators listen to a first round of arguments in a joint session, then proceed to private sessions and soon deliver an assessment of the likely litigated outcome, 'hashing'. The mediator then recommends that the parties settle based on the predicted outcome in court or on equivalent terms.[10] Since the mediation proceeds almost exclusively in private meetings (caucuses), parties have an incentive to act strategically to attempt to spin the mediator to view their arguments overly positively[11] and to make unrealistically high or low settlement offers to ensure that the haggling goes their way.[12] This type of 'mediation' represents a 'distorted and diminished' version of adjudication.[13]

Concomitantly, 'evaluative mediation' also refers to practices wherein the mediator discusses the strengths and weaknesses of the parties' cases and is hesitant to provide an exact estimation of the likely litigated outcome. The mediator is unwilling to evaluate both because the evaluation could form an anchoring bias, which could lead the mediator and parties to discard other options and to overlook weaknesses of the evaluation, and because the evaluation is necessarily based on limited information.[14] Labelling all processes

---

7 This term was originally coined by Leonard L. Riskin, 'Understanding Mediators' Orientations, Strategies, and Techniques: A Grid for the Perplexed' (1996) *Harvard Negotiation Law Review* 7, 23–24. Later, Riskin used the terms elicitive and directive: Leonard L. Riskin, 'Decisionmaking in Mediation: The New Old Grid and the New New Grid System' (2003) *Notre Dame Law Review* 1.

8 James J. Alfini, 'Trashing, Bashing, and Hashing it Out: Is This the End of "Good Mediation"?' (1991) *Florida State University Law Review* 47.

9 E.g., Riskin, 'Understanding Mediators' Orientations' (n 7) 28 and 31; Nancy A. Welsh, 'You've Got Your Mother's Laugh: What Bankruptcy Mediation Can Learn from the Her/History of Divorce and Child Custody Mediation' (2009) *American Bankruptcy Institute Law Review* 427, 438.

10 E.g., Eric R. Galton, *Ripples from Peace Lake: Essays for Mediators and Peacemakers* (Trafford Publishing 2004); Dwight Golann, *Mediating Legal Disputes* (ABA Publishing 2009).

11 E.g., Welsh, 'Mother's Laugh' (n 9) 445 and 448–449.

12 E.g., Welsh, ibid.

13 Bryan Clark, *Lawyers and Mediation* (Springer 2012) 166.

14 E.g., Golann, *Mediating Legal Disputes* (n 10) 145ff.

'evaluative mediation' thus conceals their profound differences and renders the terminology inaccurate.

'Trashing' and 'bashing' bear little resemblance to the collaborative, problem-solving process that mediation theory originally envisioned. Such a process would enable the parties to address their 'business' and 'economic' interests; their personal, professional and relational issues;[15] community interests, such as the wish to prevent similar problems from arising in the future;[16] or any combination of these according to the desires of the parties. Mediation should aspire to empower the parties to exercise self-determination.[17] However, critics argue that modern mediation and other ADR do not render justice, nor do they empower the parties.[18]

Felix Steffek and associates have developed a fine-grained taxonomy of ADR processes,[19] which appears to rest on a tacit assumption that ADR takes place outside courts and that the parties are able to make informed decisions regarding the process. The taxonomy uses dichotomic categories: mandatory/voluntary processes, interest-based/rights-based processes, the disputants/neutral control of the content of the outcome, the disputants/neutral control of the process, and the disputants control/do not control the effects of the outcome. Although this taxonomy represents an advance for ADR theory and could be helpful for commercial disputes with repeat-player disputants, it is problematic because it does not reflect ADR as it is practiced in many settings. Research shows that mediators do not practise the model they purport to practise; lawyers tend to use the quasi-adjudicative practices with a narrow legal scope in which they have been trained.[20] The taxonomy does

---

[15] E.g., Roger Fisher and Daniel Shapiro, *Beyond Reason. Using Emotions as You Negotiate* (Penguin 2005) 15; Leonard L. Riskin and Nancy A. Welsh, 'Is That All There Is: The Problem in Court-Oriented Mediation' (2008) *George Mason Law Review* 863, 886–890.

[16] Riskin, 'Understanding Mediators' Orientations' (n 7) 18–23.

[17] E.g., Roselle Wissler, 'Court-Connected Arbitration in the Superior Court of Arizona: A Study of its Performance and Proposed Rule Changes' (2007) *Journal of Dispute Resolution* 65, 90–91; Ellen Waldman and Lola Akin Ojelabi, 'Mediators and Substantive Justice: A View from Rawls' Original Position' (2016) *Ohio State Journal on Dispute Resolution* 391; Debbie De Girolamo, 'Sen, Justice and the Private Realm of Dispute Resolution' (2018) *Journal of Law in Context* 353.

[18] E.g., Riskin and Welsh (n 15) 893ff; Nancy A. Welsh, 'Making Deals in Court-Connected Mediation: What's Justice Got to Do with It' (2001) *Washington University Law Quarterly* 787, 797–799.

[19] Felix Steffek, 'Principled Regulation of Dispute Resolution: Taxonomy, Policy, Topics' in Felix Steffek and others (eds), *Regulating Dispute Resolution: ADR and Access to Justice at the Crossroads* (Hart Publishing 2013).

[20] E.g., Roselle L. Wissler, 'Court-Connected Mediation in General Civil Cases: What We Know from Empirical Research' (2002) *Ohio State Journal on Dispute*

not address the gap between theory and practice, such as misleading labels. Thus, although the disputants have selected a 'facilitative' neutral to get a facilitative, interest-based process, the neutral might deliver a rights-based, quasi-adjudicative process, and vice versa. Misleading labels are particularly problematic for self-represented and one-shot disputants. These disputants also lack the knowledge to ensure that the neutral acts according to the standards of the process.

Several commentators have noted that ADR processes thus form a continuum rather than clear-cut categories.[21] Moreover, empirical research suggests that successful mediators use a variety of interventions;[22] hence, categorizing processes based on interventions or prohibiting the use – or non-use – of a specific intervention may be counterproductive.

In ADR processes that are deeply entangled with the justice system, features reducing the disputants' self-determination are common, such as mandatory mediation, strong incentives to mediate or sanctions for failing to mediate or for rejecting a reasonable settlement offer.[23] Jacqueline Nolan-Haley notes that '[w]here there is no effective recourse to the court system for poor people, …, parties are in a weak bargaining position in ADR processes.'[24] Agreeing to settle in ADR is sometimes the only option that disputants have to resolve their dispute.[25] Courts uphold agreements made in ADR because they assume that the agreement is a result of voluntary and informed decisions. Hence, the parties

---

Resolution 641, 685; Kimberlee K. Kovach, 'Privatization of Dispute Resolution: In the Spirit of Pound, but Mission Incomplete: Lessons Learned and a Possible Blueprint for the Future' (2007) *South Texas Law Review* 1003, 1020; James A. Wall and Timothy C. Dunne, 'Mediation Research: A Current Review' (2012) *Negotiation Journal* 217.

21 E.g., Jean R. Sternlight, 'ADR is Here: Preliminary Reflections on Where It Fits in a System of Justice' (2002) *Nevada Law Journal* 289, 294; Thomas J. Stipanowich and Véronique Fraser, 'The International Task Force on Mixed Mode Dispute Resolution: Exploring the Interplay between Mediation, Evaluation and Arbitration in Commercial Cases' (2017) *Fordham Int'l LJ* 839.

22 E.g., Wall and Dunne (n 20); John Lande, 'A Framework for Advancing Negotiation Theory: Implications from a Study of How Lawyers Reach Agreement in Pretrial Litigation' (2014) *Cardozo Journal of Conflict Resolution* 1, 44; Donna Shestowsky, 'How Litigants Evaluate the Characteristics of Legal Procedures: A Multi-Court Empirical Study' (2016) *UC Davis Law Review* 793, 803.

23 E.g., Jacqueline M. Nolan-Haley, 'Is Europe Headed Down the Primrose Path with Mandatory Mediation?' (2011) *North Carolina Journal for international Law and Commercial Regulation* 981; Jacqueline Nolan-Haley, 'Mediation: The New Arbitration' (2012) *Harvard Negotiation Law Review* 61.

24 Jacqueline Nolan-Haley, 'Does ADR's Access to Justice Come at the Expense of Meaningful Consent' (2018) *Ohio State Journal on Dispute Resolution* 373, 383.

25 Mariana Hernandez Crespo, 'A Systemic Perspective of ADR in Latin America: Enhancing the Shadow of the Law Through Citizen Participation' (2008) *Cardozo Journal of Conflict Resolution* 108, 115; Genn (n 1) 125.

have no effective protection from mediator pressure. Furthermore, upholding the settlement aligns with prevailing policies favouring settlement, which legitimizes coercive ADR practices.[26] Unsurprisingly, interest-based mediation has often had to yield to rights-based, and even coercive, approaches.[27]

Mediation theory postulates that disputants prefer to maximize self-determination. However, research has uncovered that many disputants want the neutral to inform them about the likely litigated outcome, to assess the strengths and weaknesses of their cases, or both. Disputants also prefer to retain control of the outcome by making decisions in light of the information from the neutral and do not want the neutral to advocate for a specific settlement.[28] These findings suggest that parties might not want a purely facilitative process and that the parties seek, at least partially, 'justice through the law'.[29] The parties wish to make decisions 'in light of the law',[30] and, to accomplish that goal, self-represented parties need assistance from a lawyer or from the neutral.[31]

Commentators note how confidentiality has become the 'defining feature of mediation'[32] and many other forms of ADR, as well as how it is interpreted

---

[26] Jacqueline M. Nolan-Haley, 'Judicial Review of Mediated Settlement Agreements: Improving Mediation with Consent?' (2013) *Yearbook on Arbitration and Mediation* 152, 154.

[27] Bobbi McAdoo and Nancy A. Welsh, 'Look Before You Leap and Keep on Looking: Lessons from the Institutionalization of Court-Connected Mediation' (2005) *Nevada Law Journal* 399, 401; Welsh, 'Mother's Laugh' (n 9) 438; Genn (n 1) 124; Jacqueline Nolan-Haley, 'Mediation, Self-Represented Parties, and Access to Justice: Getting There from Here' (2019) *Fordham LR* 1, 6–7.

[28] Wissler, 'Court-Connected Mediation' (n 20) 664 and 684–685; McAdoo and Welsh (n 27) 425; Welsh, 'Mother's Laugh' (n 9) 440–441; Donna Shestowsky and Jeanne Brett, 'Disputants' Perception of Dispute Resolution Procedures: An Ex Ante and Ex Post Longitudinal Empirical Study' (2008) *Connecticut Law Review* 63; Shestowsky (n 22) 825–826.

[29] Jacqueline M. Nolan-Haley, 'Court Mediation and the Search for Justice through the Law' (1996) *Washington University Law Quarterly* 47.

[30] Ulla Glässer, 'Linking ADR Discourses – Nine Lessons learned from Mediation Development for the Implementation of the EU Directive on Consumer ADR' in Michael Stürner, Fernando Gascón Inchausti and Remo Caponi (eds), *The Role of Consumer ADR in the Administration of Justice. New Trends in Access to Justice under EU Directive 2013/11* (DeGruyter European Law Publishers 2014) 120–121.

[31] Jacqueline Durand, 'The Institutionalization of Mediation and its Effect on Unrepresented Parties: Is Justice Really the Goal of Court-Mandated Mediation?' (2016) *Georgetown Journal of Legal Ethics* 973; Nolan-Haley, 'Mediation, Self-Represented Parties' (n 26).

[32] Nancy A. Welsh, 'Dispute Resolution Neutrals' Ethical Obligation to Support Measured Transparency' (2019) *Oklahoma Law Review* 823, 875. See also Judith Resnik, 'The Contingency of Openness in Courts: Changing the Experiences and

and applied in a manner that renders control practically impossible and allows disputants and lawyers to behave badly.[33] Recent research has identified an accountability gap in ADR.[34] Nancy Welsh notes that 'most courts do very little to assure the accountability of the mediation process, individual mediators, or mediated outcomes'.[35] The accountability deficit becomes particularly acute when ADR belongs to, or serves the goals of, the domain of the formal justice system.

We need to found ADR on the most recent research advances regarding how different types of ADR can produce just processes and outcomes in various contexts, as well as how neutrals and the justice system can be held accountable.[36]

5.3 ADR IN SERVICE OF JUSTICE

Justice comes in many forms. It can be defined by formal legal rules, other social norms, the interests, needs and preferences of the parties. It encompasses distributive, reparative, retributive, procedural, relational, and psychological aspects.[37] The aspects are partly interconnected, e.g., the opportunity

---

Logics of the Public's Role in Court-Based ADR' (2014) *Nevada Law Journal* 1631, 1683–1685.

33 Welsh, 'Dispute Resolution Neutrals' Ethical Obligation' (n 32) 875.

34 Lisa Blomgren Amsler and Jessica Sherrod, 'Accountability Forums and Dispute System Design' (2017) *Public Performance & Management Review* 529, 530; Nancy A. Welsh, 'Bringing Transparency and Accountability (with a Dash of Competition) to Court-Connected Dispute Resolution' (2020) *Fordham LR* 2449.

35 Nancy A. Welsh, 'The Place of Court-Connected Mediation in a Democratic Justice System' (2004) *Cardozo Journal of Conflict Resolution* 117, 139.

36 E.g., Michael T. Colatrella Jr, 'Informed Consent in Mediation: Promoting Pro Se Parties' Informed Settlement Choice While Honoring the Mediator's Ethical Duties' (2014) *Cardozo Journal of Conflict Resolution* 705; Jean-François Roberge and Dorcas Quek Anderson, 'Judicial Mediation: From Debates to Renewal' (2018) *Cardozo Journal of Conflict Resolution* 613; Welsh, 'Dispute Resolution Neutrals' Ethical Obligation' (n 32) 880–881; Dorcas Quek Anderson, 'The Evolving Concept of Access to Justice in Singapore's Mediation Movement' (2020) *International Journal of Law in Context* 128; Erin R. Archerd, 'Evaluating Mediation's Future' (2020) *Journal of Dispute Resolution* 31, 51–55; Mary Anne Noone and Lola Akin Ojelabi, 'Alternative Dispute Resolution and Access to Justice in Australia' (2020) *International Journal of Law in Context* 108.

37 E.g., Carrie Menkel-Meadow, 'The Lawyer as Consensus Builder: Ethics for a New Practice' (2002) *Ten L Rev* 63, 88; Nancy A. Welsh, 'Perceptions of Fairness' in Andrea Kupfer Schneider and Christopher Honeyman (eds), *The Negotiator's Fieldbook* (ABA Publishing 2006); Charlie Irvine, 'What Do "Lay" People Know about Justice? An Empirical Enquiry' (2020) *International Journal of Law in Context* 146, 156–158.

to speak directly to the other party could contribute to relationship repair, procedural justice[38] and interests-based outcomes. In some contexts, it might be appropriate to allow the parties to select the type(s) of justice they wish to achieve, whereas in other contexts it might be more appropriate to operate with pre-defined standards of justice.[39] Additionally, ADR processes should render procedural justice; that is, the disputants should be allowed to express themselves freely, and the neutral should listen to them and should treat the disputants even-handedly and with dignity and respect.[40]

ADR processes can be classified according to the type of justice they primarily aspire to produce. Formal processes seek to produce 'justice through the law'.[41] Informal processes aspire to provide distributive, retributive, reparative, social, psychological or relationship-based justice, or any combination of these. Semiformal processes attempt to balance formal and informal justice, whereby legal rights, other types of social norms, and other forms of justice are amalgamated according to the preferences of the parties.[42] According to Ellen Waldman's terminology, these processes could be labelled norm-advocating, norm-creating and norm-educating.[43]

Formal justice necessitates a process whereby the parties are given an adequate opportunity to present the relevant legal and factual arguments and evidence supporting them, as well as to comment on and rebut the arguments and evidence of the other party. The neutral(s) must give grounds for the 'ruling', which enables the parties to detect any weaknesses in the reasoning of the neutral, to ensure that the neutral has considered all arguments and evidence,[44] and to prevent arbitrary outcomes.[45] Informal justice requires a process whereby the role of the neutral is to assist the parties in identifying their interests and needs and in creating options that address those interests and

---

[38] Irvine, ibid., 154.

[39] Welsh, 'Dispute Resolution Neutrals' Ethical Obligation' (n 32) 880–881.

[40] Rebecca Hollander-Blumoff and Tom R. Tyler, 'Procedural Justice and the Rule of Law: Fostering Legitimacy in Alternative Dispute Resolution' (2011) *Journal of Dispute Resolution* 1, 5–6.

[41] Carrie Menkel-Meadow, 'Regulation of Dispute Resolution in the United States of America: From the Formal to the Informal to the "Semiformal"' in Felix Steffek and others (eds), *Regulating Dispute Resolution: ADR and Access to Justice at the Crossroads* (Hart 2013).

[42] Lande, 'A Framework' (n 22) 36–39.

[43] Ellen A. Waldman, 'Identifying the Role of Social Norms in Mediation: A Multiple Model Approach' (1997) *Hastings LJ* 703.

[44] See, e.g., the reasoning of the European Court of Human Rights in *Magnin v France* App no 26219/08 (ECtHR, 10 May 2012), para 29.

[45] See, e.g., *Fazliyski v Bulgaria* App no 40908/05 (ECtHR, 16 April 2013), para 69.

needs. The neutral facilitates communication, cooperation, and the negotiation of a mutually acceptable outcome.[46] The neutral must refrain from being directive. Party self-determination through free and informed decision-making is the key to a quality process and outcome.[47]

Semiformal processes are underdeveloped in ADR theory.[48] However, early neutral evaluation (ENE) is an exception.[49] Based on summaries of the case and brief discussions, in which information is openly available to both disputants, the neutral assesses the likely litigated outcome. To ensure the quality of the evaluation and informed decision-making, the neutral is encouraged to disclose assumptions, conditions, and contingencies underpinning the evaluation. The neutral also assists the parties in identifying the core disputed issues and in pinpointing common ground. The neutral is allowed to discuss the broader interests and needs of the disputants and assist them in identifying outcomes that could cater to these. If the parties so desire, the neutral assists them in negotiating a settlement agreement. Semiformal processes, however, do not necessitate a prediction of the likely litigated outcome. The evaluation can be limited to a single issue, or the neutral can limit the discussion to the strengths and weaknesses of the parties' cases, the applicable legal norms, and the litigation risks and tangible and intangible litigation costs.[50] European civil justice systems have not embraced ENE, however.

ADR processes should be categorized based on the aims underpinning the interventions and the combined effect of interventions, rather than the use of specific interventions. For instance, a judge or arbitrator can encourage the disputants to consider their broader interests, without the process changing character from formal to semiformal.[51] Similarly, giving self-represented disputants information regarding the applicable substantive and procedural rules does not render the process formal. Information could be pivotal for enabling a disputant to exercise self-determination and to vindicate his or her

---

46 E.g., Laurence Boulle and Miryana Nesic, *Mediator Skills and Techniques: Triangle of Influence* (Bloomsbury Professional 2010); Shirly Shipman, Ben Waters and William Wood, *Brown & Marriott's ADR: Principles and Practice* (4th edn, Sweet & Maxwell 2019).

47 E.g., Nancy Welsh, 'Do You Believe in Magic? Self-Determination and Procedural Justice Meet Inequality in Court-Connected Mediation' (2017) *Southern Methodist University Law Review* 721; Nolan-Haley, 'ADR's Justice' (n 24).

48 Penny Broker, *Mediation Law – Journey through Institutionalism to Juridification* (Routledge 2013) 239ff; Menkel-Meadow, 'Regulation of Dispute Resolution' (n 41).

49 Wayne D. Brazil, *Early Neutral Evaluation* (ABA Publishing 2012) 6–8.

50 Michaela Keet, Heather Heavin and John Lande, *Litigation Interest and Risk Assessment* (ABA Publishing 2020) 65ff.

51 E.g., ELI/Unidroit, 'Model European Rules of Civil Procedure: From Transnational Principles to European Rules of Civil Procedure', Rules 10(1) and 49.

rights. Accordingly, the fundamental issue is whether the intervention, in the specific context and the manner in which it is executed, is likely to render a just outcome or not.

In legal disputes, disputants wish to vindicate their legal rights. Consequently, they need an ADR process that is designed to enable them to do so. Processes aspiring for informal justice are often incompatible with this goal, particularly for self-represented disputants, who need information on legal norms and the likely 'litigated' outcome to make an informed decision on settlement. Thus, information should be incorporated into the ADR process or provided as an auxiliary service.[52]

ADR processes should serve as a supplement to litigation either by diversifying the type of justice that dispute resolution processes can provide, by enabling citizens to enforce claims that were previously unenforceable due to the high costs of litigation, or both. Formal ADR processes contribute to increased access to justice only if they provide a swifter and cheaper process than courts do. Semiformal ADR processes contribute to access to justice when the parties are able to 'customize' the outcomes rendered by formal justice. Informal processes increase access to justice when the outcome is compatible with any standard of justice selected by the disputants or determined by the norms governing the process, such as the best interests of the child in parental responsibility ADR processes. Hence, in implementing and evaluating ADR processes, the type of justice delivered is vital.

5.4 THE ACCOUNTABILITY DEFICIT IN ADR

To close the accountability gap in ADR, and in particular ADR processes embedded in the justice system, we need to devise appropriate accountability mechanisms for formal, informal and semiformal justice and to ensure that the neutral employs interventions in a manner that supports accountability.[53]

The 'open' character of formal processes is a key factor producing accountability. The parties have access to all information that is transmitted to the neutral, and the neutral must give at least brief grounds for the outcome. Making the outcome subject to review enhances accountability. Confidentiality is problematic in this regard. However, arbitration illustrates

---

52 E.g., Gary Friedman and Jack Himmelstein, *Challenging Conflict. Mediation through Understanding* (ABA Publishing 2008) 139ff; Glässer (n 30) 120-121.

53 Much of the current research on regulation of ADR draws on the perspective of international private law and does not address ADR from the point of view of the justice system and one-shot litigants; see, e.g., Nadja Alexander, 'Introducing Regulatory Robustness Rating for Mediation Regimes in the EU' in Nadja Alexander, Sabine Walsh and Martin Svatos, *EU Mediation Law Handbook* (Wolters Kluwer 2017).

how confidentiality can be combined with accountability by limiting confidentiality to third parties while retaining full openness to the parties. The parties have access to hearings and all documents that the other party presents to the arbitration tribunal, and the arbitrators are, as a rule, obliged to give grounds for the award.[54] Furthermore, repeat-player legal counsel can sanction arbitrators indirectly by influencing the business and reputation of the arbitrator: rendering poor-quality awards has repercussions for the business of the arbitrator. However, self-represented parties and one-shot legal counsel are barred from exercising this type of informal power. This is one factor explaining why many European countries, including Norway, restrict the use of arbitration clauses in consumer, tenancy, and labour contracts.[55]

Currently, the paramount challenge of 'evaluative' mediation, as it is practiced in Europe and elsewhere, is opaqueness, or a lack of openness. The extensive use of private meetings prevents the parties from appraising the quality of assessments of strengths, weaknesses and likely litigated outcomes and rendering the neutral accountable. The neutral could even present different evaluations to each party without the parties being aware of this.

In formal and semiformal processes, interventions aiming at producing, or informing the parties of, formal justice should, therefore, be open at least to the parties and to bodies monitoring the quality of the ADR process. Assessments of the strengths and weaknesses of the parties' cases and the likely litigated outcome should be made contingent on both parties having had sufficient opportunity to present their legal arguments and evidence supporting them and having had access to – and the opportunity to comment on – the arguments and evidence of the opposite party. The neutral should also explain the reasoning underpinning the assessment. Such openness is likely to protect the parties

[54] E.g., UNCITRAL Arbitration Rules (General Assembly resolution 68/109), art 17(4) states that '[a]ll communication to the arbitral tribunal by one party shall be communicated by that party to all other parties.' Art 34(3) of the rules states that '[t]he arbitral tribunal shall state the reasons upon which the award is based'. The UNCITRAL Arbitration Rules are available at https://uncitral.un.org/sites/uncitral.un.org/files/media-documents/uncitral/en/uncitral-arbitration-rules-2013-e.pdf accessed 5 July 2021. See also, e.g., International Chamber of Commerce, '2021 Arbitration Rules', arts 22–27 and 32, available at https://iccwbo.org/dispute-resolution-services/arbitration/rules-of-arbitration/#article_22 accessed 5 July 2021.

[55] Act relating to arbitration (lov om voldgift) of 14 May 2004 no 25, s 11, unofficial English translation available at https://lovdata.no/dokument/NLE/lov/2004-05-14-25 accessed 5 July 2021; Tenancy Act (lov om husleieavtaler) of 28 March 1999 no 17, ss 12-10, available at https://lovdata.no/dokument/NL/lov/1999-03-26-17 accessed 5 July 2021; Act relating to working environment, working hours and employment protection (Lov om arbeidsmiljø, arbeidstid og stillingsvern mv. (arbeidsmiljøloven)) of 17 June 2005 no 62, ss 15-16, unofficial English translation available at https://lovdata.no/dokument/NLE/lov/2005-06-17-62 accessed 5 July 2021.

from assessments that are premature and based on insufficient or erroneous information. When the neutral is not to decide the case, the neutral could be prohibited from evaluating the likely litigated outcome or suggesting a specific figure for settlement.[56] Instead, the neutral could be required to indicate a range of outcomes rather than a specific figure, as well as to stress the caveats of the evaluation by indicating the contingencies, the fact that the assessment is based on limited information, and the fact that the assumptions on which it is based might be incorrect. The neutral could also be required to discuss litigation risks and costs in a balanced manner. If the neutral provides the (self-represented) information regarding applicable legal rules or other social norms, a written outline of the key information should be provided to ensure that the information is balanced and correct.[57]

In informal and semiformal processes, informal justice needs to be protected as well. Positive protection is needed to ensure that the interests of the parties are explored, and communication and collaboration enhanced. The neutral could be required to elicit and explicitly discuss the interests and goals of the parties and two or more options that satisfy these interests.[58] The parties should be required to attend mediation in person to enable them to exercise self-determination. Extensive use of joint meetings to allow the parties to have 'reciprocal voice and understanding' should be encouraged.[59] Research suggests that relationship repair and creative, interest-based outcomes are associated with a longer duration of the mediation session.[60] Hence, the neutral should not have an incentive to unduly reduce the duration of the process.

---

[56] Golann, *Mediating Legal Disputes* (n 10) 162ff; Keet, Heavin and Lande (n 50) 65ff and 129–136.

[57] Welsh, 'Bringing Transparency' (n 32) 2845 quoting the ABA Advisory Committee on Dispute Resolution Research, 'Preliminary Recommendations on Data Elements for Court to Collect Regarding ADR/Settlement Assistance' [2019] version 2.0.

[58] E.g., Jonathan M Hyman, 'Swimming in the Deep End: Dealing with Justice in Mediation' (2004) *Cardozo Journal of Conflict Resolution* 19; Welsh, 'Do You Believe in Magic?' (n 47) 756–757.

[59] E.g., Dwight Golann, 'Is Legal Mediation a Process of Repair – or Separation? An Empirical Study, and Its Implications' (2002) *Harvard Negotiation Law Review* 301; Nancy A. Welsh, 'Stepping Back through the Looking Glass: Real Conversations with Real Disputants about Institutionalized Mediation and Its Value' (2003) *Ohio State Journal on Dispute Resolution* 573, 639.

[60] Golann, 'Legal Mediation' (n 59); Lin Adrian Lin and Solfrid Mykland, 'Creativity in Court-Connected Mediation: Myth or Reality?' (2014) *Negotiation Journal* 421. Facilitative interventions have a positive impact on relationships and on settlement rate, see ABA Section of Dispute Resolution, 'Report of the Task Force on Research on Mediator Techniques' (12 June 2017) https://www.americanbar

Moreover, informal justice should have negative protection to shield the parties from undue pressure to settle, adopt a specific view of the outcome, or both. 'Cooling off' periods, wherein the parties are given time to consider or reconsider the terms of the settlement or a draft settlement or to be allowed to withdraw from the settlement, could be an appropriate tool to reduce the pressure to settle in this regard.[61] The ratio of settlements as a standard for the quality of mediation should be replaced by a broader approach that measures party satisfaction and the perception of the parties regarding the process and outcomes.[62]

When ADR hinges on the justice system, either due to the courts or other organs of the justice system providing ADR processes or due to the justice system actively promoting – or even mandating – the use of ADR, the justice system must be made accountable for the quality of the ADR processes.[63] Many ADR programmes run with limited oversight.[64] To save costs, the justice system adopts strong incentives for settlement but it is less concerned about justice, fairness and quality of ADR processes and the outcomes they produce.[65] Commonly used performance indicators, such as settlement rates, are not sufficient to ensure that ADR processes deliver on their promise to offer substantive justice, that is a fair and balanced outcome according to some standard of justice (i.e., distributive, formal legal, relational, or social justice), legitimacy and integrity.[66] On the contrary, they might encourage coercive ADR practices.[67]

To increase accountability, the quality of procedures and outcomes needs to be monitored. Providers of ADR should be compelled to collect and publish data on, inter alia, whether the parties were present during ADR, the approximate ratio between joint and private meetings, whether the neutral predicted

---

.org/content/dam/aba/administrative/dispute_resolution/2019-mediation-research-task-force-report.pdf accessed 5 July 2021, 31–37.

[61] Timothy Hedeen, 'Coercion and Self-Determination in Court-Connected Mediation: All Mediations Are Voluntary, But Some Are More Voluntary Than Others' (2005) *Justice System Journal* 273, 286.

[62] Welsh, 'Mother's Laugh' (n 9) 458.

[63] Glässer (n 30) 125; Amsler and Sherrod (n 34); Roberge and Andersson (n 36); Welsh, 'Dispute Resolution Neutrals' Ethical Obligation' (n 32); Noone and Ojelabi (n 36).

[64] Wayne D. Brazil, 'Court ADR 25 Years after Pound: Have we Found a Better Way?' (2002) *Ohio State Journal on Dispute Resolution* 93, 128; Noone and Ojelabi (n 36); Welsh, 'Bringing Transparency' (n 34) 2482.

[65] See above nn 17–21.

[66] Lisa Bingham Amsler, Janet K. Martinez and Stephanie E. Smith, 'Christina Merchant and the State of Dispute System Design' (2015) *Conflict Resolution Quarterly* 7; Amsler and Sherrod (n 34) 540ff; Roberge and Andersson (n 36).

[67] Genn (n 1).

the likely litigated outcome, and whether the neutral recommended a specific outcome.[68] Neutrals could also be required to report the outcome to the organization providing the ADR service. In this way aggregate data on settlements could be made available.[69] Moreover, data on how disputants perceive the quality of the procedure and the outcome should be collected.[70] Further, neutrals should be required to acquire and advance the knowledge, skills and tools needed to provide quality dispute resolution through training, peer mentoring and co-mediation.[71] Since many self-represented parties and one-shot litigants are unable to make an informed decision regarding the ADR process, the justice system should design ADR accordingly by limiting the processes available and by maximizing the transparency of each process.

5.5 ADR PROCESSES IN NORWAY – JUSTICE AND ACCOUNTABILITY

5.5.1 Court-connected Mediation

Court-connected mediation (*rettsmekling*) was first introduced in Norway in 1997 to diversify dispute resolution to include interest-based, individualized justice and to render a faster and cheaper dispute resolution process.[72] As a rule, mediation is a court service with judges serving as mediators, and the mediation process is covered by regular court fees. Mediation is voluntary, and courts may not order the parties to mediate against their will.[73] The systems have put no formal incentives to mediate or settle in place, nor are parties

---

[68] Welsh, 'Bringing Transparency' (n 34) 2486.

[69] Welsh, 'Dispute Resolution Neutrals' Ethical Obligation' (n 32) 876.

[70] E.g., Rebecca L. Sandefur, 'Paying Down the Civil Justice Data Deficit: Leveraging Existing National Data Collection' (2017) *S C L Rev* 295, 296; Welsh, 'Dispute Resolution Neutrals' Ethical Obligation' (n 32) 872–873; Welsh, 'Bringing Transparency' (n 34) 2487–2488.

[71] Julie Macfarlane, 'Mediating Ethically: The Limits of Codes of Conduct and the Potential of a Reflective Practice Mode' (2002) *OsgoodeHall LJ* 49; Rochelle Arms Almengor, 'Reflective Practice and Mediator Learning: A Current Review' (2018) *Conflict Resolution Quarterly* 21.

[72] NOU 2001: 32. Rett på sak, Rett på sak — Lov om tvisteløsning (tvisteloven). Utredning fra Tvistemålsutvalget, 224–226. Denmark and Finland have similar systems that are based on the Norwegian system.

[73] Act relating to mediation and procedure in civil disputes (hereafter 'Dispute Act') (Lov om mekling og rettergang i sivile tvister) of 17 June 2005 no 90, s 8-3, unofficial English translation available at https://lovdata.no/pro/#document/NLE/lov/2005-06-17-90 accessed 5 July 2021.

sanctioned for failure to mediate or settle.[74] Judges are expected to suggest that the parties attempt to mediate whenever mediation appears to be appropriate. In addition, judges are required to facilitate settlement within the parameters of regular civil proceedings when appropriate.[75]

Court-connected mediation is popular in Norway: 20–25 per cent, and in some courts up to 35 per cent, of general civil cases are mediated. Approximately 65 per cent of the mediations end in settlement.[76] Additionally, some cases settle after the mediation has ended. A recent study found that Norwegian lawyers are more likely than their Scandinavian colleagues to prefer litigation over arbitration.[77] The court-connected mediation scheme is likely to be an important factor in this regard.

The mediator facilitates negotiations and communication and assists the parties in identifying their needs and interests and options that fulfil these.[78] Although Dispute Act section 8-5 explicitly allows the mediator to make suggestions for outcomes, the preparatory works, which are an important source of law, emphasize that mediators shall not predict the likely litigated outcome, because the mediation process does not result in an adequate basis for a quality prediction.[79] The mediator shall refrain from recommending a specific outcome or any other move that could amount to indirect or direct pressure to settle or to accept a specific outcome and shall protect the weaker party from pressure exerted by the stronger party.[80] The mediator may, however, discuss the strengths and weaknesses of the parties' cases. The parties are obliged to attend mediation in person.

In two studies on settlement agreements in court-connected mediation, Lin Adrian and Solfrid Mykland found that approximately two-thirds of the set-

---

74 The parties might still feel pressure to attend mediation and to settle, to appease the case-managing judge.

75 Dispute Act (n 73) ss 8-1 and 8-2.

76 NOU 2020: 11, Den tredje statsmakt — Domstolene i endring. Utredning fra Domstolkommisjonen 274; Dokument 3:3 (2019–2020) Riksrevisjonens undersøkelse av saksbehandlingstid og effektivitet i tingrettene og lagmannsrettene 12, 83–84 and 122. The Finnish system has almost equal success both in the ratio of mediations and in settlement rates. Statistics from the Finnish Court Administration are on file with the author.

77 Prospera and Roschier, 'Roschier Disputes Index 2021, A survey on facts and trends in international dispute resolution from a Nordic Perspective' (2021) https://www.roschier.com/publications/RDI2021/#p=1 accessed 5 July 2021.

78 Information regarding court-connected mediation can be found on the website of the Norwegian Courts Administration https://www.domstol.no/sivil-sak/sakstyper/rettsmekling/ accessed 5 July 2021; NOU 2001: 32 (n 72) 228 and 723; Ot.prp. nr 51 2004–2005 Om lov om mekling og rettergang i sivile tvister (tvisteloven) 126.

79 Ot.prp. nr. 51 (n 78) 126.

80 NOU 2001: 32 (n 72) 217, 221, and 595.

tlements contained at least one issue that could not be found in the statement of claim and statement of defence.[81] Some agreements included remedies that a court could not have ordered, such as making obligations contingent, or the employer writing a letter of recommendation to the former employee, which is vital for the future employment prospects of the employee. These findings indicate that many mediations are (partially) interest-based.

A study conducted at the Oslo District Court found that two-thirds of the parties believed that the mediator facilitated dialogue and interest-based outcomes, and many appreciated the mediator's discussion of the strengths and weaknesses of their case.[82] However, in most cases, the parties did not experience an improved relationship.[83] The fact that the initial and final sessions were the only joint sessions in 81 per cent of the mediations helps to explain this,[84] as the parties had limited opportunities to collaborate and communicate directly with each other. Furthermore, the study found indications that the mediator pressured the parties to settle and that many mediators predicted the likely litigated outcome.[85] Some parties described the mediator as 'pushy' and indicated that the mediator had told them that they would lose the case.[86] Nonetheless, the study could not quantify the prevalence of mediator pressure and predictions of the litigated outcome.

Norwegian court-connected mediation rests on a tacit ideal of semiformal justice. Nevertheless, many judge-mediators still operate in an adjudicative, rights-centred mode that makes parties susceptible to mediator pressure and premature assessments of the litigated outcome. Today, judge-mediators are informally rewarded for settlement because settlements reduce court dockets and case processing times. Inadequate mediation training and an erroneous belief that private meetings form the core of mediation are likely to contribute to 'evaluative' mediation practices.

The system lacks appropriate mechanisms for quality control. Mediators who press parties and evaluate the likely litigated outcome do not face any sanctions. The Disciplinary Council for Judges has repeatedly accepted strong

---

81 Adrian and Mykland, 'Creativity in Court-Connected Mediation' (n 60); Lin Adrian and Solfrid Mykland, 'Unwrapping Court-Connected Mediation Agreements' in Anna Nylund, Kaijus Ervasti and Lin Adrian (eds), *Nordic Mediation Research* (Springer 2018).

82 Ragnar Lindefjell and Hanne Sofie Bjelland, Rettsmekling i Oslo tingrett fra partenes og advokaters perspektiv. Masteroppgave (Københavns universitet 2020) 49.

83 In some mediations, the relationship between the disputants improved, but in other mediations it deteriorated, Lindefjell and Bjelland (n 82) 42.

84 Ibid., 43.

85 Ibid., 44–46 and 51.

86 Ibid.

settlement pressure, even within the course of regular civil proceedings.[87] The quality of mediation is not monitored systematically, and, hence, information on, inter alia, party satisfaction and the prevalence of mediators pressuring the parties to settle is inadequate. Moreover, we do not know whether some mediators routinely employ coercive interventions or predict the likely litigated outcome while other mediators refuse to do so, nor whether and how these differences influence the outcome and party satisfaction.

In conclusion, the Norwegian system is largely successful in producing semiformal justice, but the protection against mediator pressure is insufficient. The inclusion of a variety of standards of justice and, when appropriate, relationship repair needs to be safeguarded, to avoid a narrow legal scope of mediation. Moreover, mechanisms making the mediator and courts accountable for the quality of the process and outcome need to be implemented, and the incentives to produce swift settlement should be replaced by incentives to utilize joint meetings and to deliberate different types of justice.

5.5.2 Conciliation Boards

Conciliation Boards, although not formally courts, are the *de facto* first instance in civil cases where the amount in dispute is less than NOK 200,000 (approx. €20,000).[88] As the name suggests, Conciliation Boards strive for settlements between the parties, and they can only decide cases at the request of both parties, or at the request of one party if the case is sufficiently simple and clear. The Boards consist of three lay members who have only received a few hours of training. The process mimics the one in courts, but if the parties declare that they do not want the Board to make a final ruling, the Board may suggest solutions and express its views on the disputes. The panel hearing the case cannot have private meetings with the parties. The hearings are short, often lasting no more than an hour.

Since the members are not trained lawyers, they cannot render formal justice. The members do not have mediation training, and the preparatory works clearly state that the Board shall not provide interest-based mediation.[89] Hence, Conciliation Boards lack the adequate means to produce formal and informal justice. The main standard of justice is whatever the panel hearing the case considers to be an equitable outcome in the case at hand. There are no mechanisms providing accountability in 'mediation' because no data regarding

---

[87] See cases TU 19-001, 19-034, TU 18-040 and TU 16-065.

[88] For more detailed information on Conciliation Boards, see Anna Nylund, *Civil Procedure in Norway* (Wolters Kluwer 2020) 83–91.

[89] NOU 2001: 32 (n 72) 227.

disputant satisfaction are collected, nor do the panel members risk sanctions. The only recourse is to commence court proceedings; however, since the panel consists of lay people, the outcome in court is likely to have a very limited, if any, impact on them. Conciliation Boards also publish very limited information on the proceedings, which renders them even less accountable.

If the parties commence court proceedings, their case will be assigned to the small claims track, which does not allow court-connected mediation. Hence, the Norwegian court system does not provide access to quality ADR for small claims.

5.5.3 Consumer Dispute Resolution

Originally, the Norwegian – and Scandinavian[90] – consumer dispute resolution systems were designed to render formal justice by providing a cheap and swift procedure for vindicating claims that are too small to litigate.[91] Since the implementation of the EU Consumer Dispute Resolution Directive,[92] the systems have been remodelled to provide 'mediation' in addition to an (quasi-) adjudicative process. This chapter is limited to the public CDR scheme, which has competence to hear all claims except those where a private CDR body is competent.[93] In Norway, both consumers and traders can initiate CDR.

The first step of CDR is mediation in the Consumer Council. The Council is a public organ, and most of the employees are lawyers. To enable the parties to make informed decisions, the council can give the parties information regarding, inter alia, the applicable legal rules and the type of evidence they need to produce to prove their case, as well as inform them on the costs for producing such evidence. The employee in charge of the case can discuss the interests of the parties and suggest an equitable outcome to produce a balanced settlement

---

[90] The other Scandinavian countries have similar systems. In Finland and Sweden, the outcome in CDR is not binding.

[91] NOU 2010: 11, Nemndsbehandling av forbrukertvister, ch 3 and 6.

[92] Parliament and Council Directive 2013/11/EU of 21 May 2013 on alternative dispute resolution for consumer disputes and amending Regulation (EC) 2006/2004 and Directive 2009/22/EC (Directive on consumer ADR) [2013] OJ L165/63.

[93] The largest private CDR bodies, such as the Norwegian Financial Services Complaints Board, have a similar structure to the public CDR system. The outcomes are, however, not enforceable as a court ruling; see Act relating to authorization of alternative dispute resolution entities in consumer matters of 17 June 2016 no 29 (Lov om godkjenning av klageorganer for forbrukersaker), unofficial English translation is available at https://lovdata.no/pro/#document/NLE/lov/2016-06-17-29 accessed 5 July 2021.

that serves the interests of both parties.[94] To reduce pressure to settle and to ensure that the settlement is informed, the CDR body must inform the parties that the suggested outcome might deviate from the litigated outcome and the legal consequences of settlement.[95] The parties must have adequate time to consider the suggested outcome; that is, they shall not be pressured to accept it upfront. Moreover, the Consumer Council has a duty to be impartial at all stages of the procedure.[96]

If the preparatory stage does not result in settlement, the Consumer Disputes Commission decides the case. Members of the commission are trained lawyers, and decisions are binding and enforceable unless one party lodges court proceedings. Proceedings in private CDR bodies follow approximately the same model. Decisions of private CDR bodies are not binding, but courts tend to uphold their decisions, since they are usually well-argued.[97] Additionally, the public CDR system is competent to hear disputes regarding the purchase of goods and services between private individuals.[98]

The mediation stage serves semiformal justice, and the second stage serves formal justice. Hence, they increase access to justice both by offering accessible dispute resolution for claims that are too petty for litigation and by enlarging the types of justice available. The 'educative' interventions and the 'cooling off' period facilitate informed decision-making and also reduce pressure to settle. The second, adjudicative stage ensures efficient enforcement of consumer rights.

The Consumer Council staff are required to make brief notes on the information they give to the parties or on suggested settlements.[99] Moreover, CDR as a voluntary scheme depends on the trust of traders and consumer organizations, which creates incentives to deliver quality results. The Consumer Council monitors user satisfaction continuously. The Consumer Dispute Commission publishes its 'rulings', and the rulings are subject to 'appeal' to the courts, which produces accountability. Hence, the Norwegian public CDR system has implemented adequate mechanisms for accountability.

---

[94] The outcome does not have to mirror the litigated outcome, but it needs to be reasonable for the consumer; see Act regarding consumer dispute resolution in the Consumer Authority and the Consumer Disputes Commission (hereafter 'Consumer Complaints Act') (Lov av 23. juni 2020 nr. 98 om behandling av forbrukerklager i Forbrukertilsynet og Forbrukerklageutvalget) of 23 June 2020 no 98, s 11 sub-s 3.

[95] Consumer Complaints Act (n 94) s 11.

[96] Ibid., s 5.

[97] Denmark has similar rules. In Finland and Sweden, the outcome is non-binding, but in most cases, traders still respect the outcome.

[98] This is a unique trait of the Norwegian system.

[99] Prop.55 L (2019–2020) Lov om behandling av forbrukerklager i Forbrukertilsynet og Forbrukerklageutvalget (forbrukerklageloven) 37.

5.6 CONCLUDING REMARKS ON ADR IN NORWAY

The Norwegian court-connected mediation system illustrates the gap between a process that is regulated mainly as an informal process but renders in practice semiformal justice by way of evaluative mediation. While court-connected mediation serves to diversify dispute resolution processes and renders justice in most cases, the weak protection against mediator pressure and premature assessments of the likely litigated outcome put parties at risk of being denied the opportunity to customize the outcome and even to receive procedural and substantive justice. Better mechanisms for ensuring semiformal justice and the accountability of the court and neutral for the process and outcome are needed. Moreover, implementing a process inspired by ENE, alongside court-connected mediation, could clarify the nature of the process and help courts develop two distinct semiformal processes: ENE for parties who desire more formal elements and mediation for those who prefer more informal elements. For small claims, the public CDR system renders primarily formal justice through a modified adjudicative process, in which the parties are informed of their legal rights and the outcome should reflect consumer law. Nevertheless, the parties are encouraged to customize the outcome, while the CDR body still protects the rights of the consumer, inter alia, by ensuring that the consumer understands the implications of the settlement. Public records of the process and outcome put the parties and consumer and trader organizations in the position to monitor the quality and hold the CDR system accountable. Norwegian public CDR serves as a blueprint of a system that offers both semiformal and formal justice to self-represented parties in a two-stage process where a norm-educative semiformal process is followed by an adjudicative process.

The Conciliation Boards are an example of the opposite situation – that is, a process that is neither suitable for producing formal nor informal justice, due to an inadequate organizational framework and inadequate training of the members of the Boards. The Boards seem to rest on an assumption that settlement in itself is a token of substantive and procedural justice. In contrast to CDR, Conciliation Boards reflect an undefined concept of substantive justice, and an inadequately designed process that does not align well with informal, semiformal or formal justice. The system is opaque and provides very limited mechanisms for accountability.

PART II

Digitising private and public justice

6. The frontiers of digital justice in Europe[1]

Erlis Themeli

6.1 INTRODUCTION

For some time now, a concern of the European Commission has been to make Europe fit for the digital age. The penetration and importance of digital technologies in our societies have been continuous, but its speed has been different depending on the field, trade, society, culture, and geographical location. Consequently, the approach of many regulators to digitisation has been fragmented and spontaneous. Perhaps that is even more true when we consider the digitisation of justice. While technology has slowly but steadily entered courts and the legal profession, the response from the European Commission or individual Member States has been patchy and uncoordinated. But this has changed in recent years and the European Commission has been very active in pursuing EU instruments (or initiatives). However, technological advancement is not the only drive for this change. The determination of EU institutions to develop further the digitisation of justice has deep roots in the history of EU institutions. There is an intrinsic need to facilitate European citizens and companies to freely move across the Union and be legally secured in each step. Physical distance, language barriers, legal uncertainty, and the possibility to enforce rights are some of the hurdles for cross-border mobility. Technology is often mentioned as a tool that removes hurdles and therefore increases mobility, but technology used in a wrong way can be a hurdle itself.[2]

[1] This research has received funding from the European Research Council (ERC) under the European Union's Horizon 2020 research and innovation programme (grant agreement No 726032), ERC consolidator project 'Building EU Civil Justice: challenges of procedural innovations – bridging access to justice'; see www.euciviljustice.eu.

[2] On the benefits that digital technologies can bring to justice: E. Themeli and S. Philipsen, 'AI as the Court: Assessing AI Deployment in Civil Cases' in K. Benyekhlef (ed), *AI and Law. A Critical Overview* (Éditions Thémis, Montreal 2021); T. Sourdin, B. Li and D. M. McNamara, 'Court Innovations and Access to Justice in Times of

Therefore, the regulators' continuous search to find the right balance between the right amount of technology and the effective protection of rights has led to numerous instruments and initiatives. In this chapter, I discuss some of these activities, among others, the e-Justice Action Plans, the e-Justice Portal, and the procedures it supports, E-CODEX, and Artificial Intelligence (AI). It serves as an introductory chapter to the other chapters of this part which address specific topics in the area of digitisation of justice in the EU.

6.2 DIGITISATION OF JUSTICE AND ACCESS TO JUSTICE

While individual Member States take care of access to justice within their own borders, the EU attaches considerable importance to access to justice across borders. In these situations, delays, costs, and legal uncertainties increase the hurdles of accessing justice.[3] At the same time, digitisation has made it possible for everyone to interact with others across the border. But there is a paradox here. While it is easier to interact and trade remotely with people across borders, it is more difficult to resolve conflicts. Courts are far away, costs of cross-border litigation are high, procedures are complex, and dealing with foreign languages makes it an even bigger challenge.[4] Under these conditions, many see access to justice only as a slogan. The Covid-19 pandemic exacerbated this situation and demonstrated too well how fragile the freedom of movement, the justice system, and the ability of the justice system to provide effective access to justice are. Travel restrictions were put in place and the possibility to go to court and resolve a conflict in person became a Herculean labour. For many, during the pandemic, the only form of mobility was digital mobility. So, the possibility to digitally resolve conflicts is not only a luxury or a show of technological advancement, but it is a necessity.

Crisis' (2020) 9(4) *Health Policy and Technology* 447. On the problems that digital technology can cause: D. Amoroso and G. Tamburrini, 'The Human Control Over Autonomous Robotic Systems: What Ethical and Legal Lessons for Judicial Uses of AI?' in: X. E. Kramer and others (eds), *New Pathways to Civil Justice* (Springer 2021); N. Vermeys, 'The Computer As the Court: How Will Artificial Intelligence Affect Judicial Processes?' in: Kramer and others, ibid.

[3] A. Biard, J. Hoevenaars, X. E. Kramer and E. Themeli, 'Introduction: The Future of Access to Justice – Beyond Science Fiction' in: Kramer and others, ibid.

[4] See for the example how costs affect choice of court and the willingness to litigate abroad: E. Themeli, *Civil Justice System Competition in the European Union: The Great Race of Court* (Eleven International Publishing 2018) 266–275, 288–301.

The recent revisions of the European Small Claims Procedure (ESCP), the European Payment Order (EPO), the Regulations on Service of Documents,[5] and Taking of Evidence[6] illustrate the efforts of the Commission to improve access to justice by using more digital technologies. These revisions have more prominently incorporated digital communication to reduce costs and speed-up procedures.[7] As I explain in section 6.4, the EPO and the ESCP are supported by the e-Justice Portal, a website intended as an information hub and support tool for justice in the EU. But the revised regulations have not been an isolated effort. European plans to digitise justice have been materialised with the approval of the e-Justice Action Plans, which are renewed every four years. The Plan, however, should not be seen as a standalone effort, because implementing reforms in the field of justice for the whole EU is never easy. Different legal settings, legal nationalism, technical difficulties, and finances are some of the difficulties that reforms encounter. On top of these, digital technologies evolve fast which makes it hard to implement a certain solution because of the risk of it becoming obsolete. As a result, the EU tries to nudge Member States to use more digital technologies in court or the justice system at large also by providing data about it at the EU Justice Scoreboard. While the effects of the Scoreboard may be weak, they may be the drop that spills the glass. Recently, the Commission communicated its plans for a regulation on the digitalisation of judicial cooperation.[8] As the title suggests, this proposed regulation's goal is to require all Member States' courts and public authorities to accept electronic communications from natural and legal persons in cross-border judicial procedures. However, these persons will keep the right to use traditional forms of communications, which should be equal in value to electronic communications. If the proposal passes without changes, it will

---

[5] Regulation (EC) 1393/2007 of the European Parliament and of the Council of 13 November 2007 on the service in the Member States of judicial and extrajudicial documents in civil or commercial matters (service of documents), and repealing Council Regulation (EC) 1348/2000 [2007] OJ L324, 79–120. Amended by Regulation (EU) 517/2013 of 13 May 2013.

[6] Council Regulation (EC) No 1206/2001 of 28 May 2001 on cooperation between the courts of the Member States in the taking of evidence in civil or commercial matters [2001] OJ L174, 1–24. Amended by Regulation (EC) 1103/2008 of The European Parliament and of The Council of 22 October 2008.

[7] X. E. Kramer, 'Access to Justice and Technology: Transforming the Face of Cross-Border Civil Litigation and Adjudication in the EU' in: Karim Benyekhlef, Jane Bailey, Jacquie Burkell and Fabien Gélinas (eds), *E-Access to Justice* (University of Ottawa Press 2016) 351–375.

[8] European Commission, 'Proposal for a Regulation on the digitalisation of judicial cooperation and access to justice in cross-border civil, commercial and criminal matters, and amending certain acts in the judicial cooperation' COM(2021) 759 final, 1.12.2021.

affect also the EPO and ESCP procedures, together with a number of other regulations dealing with cross-border judicial cooperation and procedures. In addition to civil and commercial matters, the proposal covers also criminal proceedings. Moreover, the EU is also very active in regulating and promoting the use of AI. While not always related to access to justice or the justice system, AI promises to solve some of the problems faced by the justice system. In the following sections, I am going to follow this outline to discuss the frontiers of digital justice in Europe.

6.3 E-JUSTICE ACTION PLANS

Since 2007, a barrage of communications, strategies, and regulations has created the foundations for the digitisation of justice in Europe. The 2007 Justice and Home Affairs Council indicated that work is needed to increase the use of information and communication technologies (ICT) in the field of justice. At that time, studies showed that ten million people were involved in cross-border civil proceedings, a number that would only increase in the future.[9] Cross-border disputes are particularly challenging because of mobility and information costs.[10] As a result, people with no experience or financial possibilities have more difficulty finding a legal professional from afar and without references, and for them travelling to another jurisdiction to follow the procedure may be financially prohibitive. Not only people, but also public institutions have difficulty communicating legal acts or accessing legal information across the border. Against this background, the European Commission and the Council of the EU approved the Multiannual e-Justice Action Plan 2009–2013 in 2008.[11] The Action Plan fully supported the establishment of a European e-Justice Portal with information on the justice system of all Member States, but also practical information on finding legal professionals, the courts system of a Member State, and so on.[12] The Portal's goal was to improve access to information on cross-border civil and commercial judicial matters, improve e-communication between judicial authorities, and improve

---

[9] European Commission, *Towards a European e-Justice Strategy* (Communication from the Commission to the Council, the European Parliament and the European Economic and Social Committee SEC (2008)1947 SEC (2008)1944, 2008).

[10] Information costs are often increased by differences in language and culture. Moreover, official information on websites if often directed at residents and therefore difficult to understand for a foreigner.

[11] Multi-annual European e-Justice action plan 2009-2013, *OJ C75, 31.3.2009, p. 1–12.*

[12] European Commission, 'E-Justice Portal' (*European E-Justice*) https://e-justice.europa.eu/?action=home&plang=en accessed 07 May 2022.

interoperability between Member States' judicial electronic systems. Perhaps more importantly, the Action Plan establishes three functions for the European e-Justice. First, e-Justice should provide information on the field of justice. This means improving the possibilities to access exiting information, improving intercommunication between local and cross-border institutions, and digitising more databases so that they can be reached electronically. Second, dematerialisation of proceedings. This means that cross-border judicial proceedings should be made with electronic means as much as possible. Third, it is important to simplify and encourage the communication between judicial authorities. These functions indicate the importance of communication and the hope of the Commission that digitisation will help to improve it.

It is difficult to assess the success of this action plan, but the fact that it was followed by the 2014–2018 Action Plan shows that the European institutions are serious about their actions.[13] This second action plan reaffirmed the essential role of digital technologies in increasing the efficiency of justice in Europe. The e-justice Portal received another round of support and the promise to be expanded and developed further. An important issue was the promise to make national legislation more accessible by using digital technology to improve information spread and overcome language obstacles. The most recognisable examples of these activities are the interconnected register of insolvencies, which allows interested parties in all Member States to see if a company is under bankruptcy procedures,[14] and the lawyers[15] and the notaries[16] registries which allow anyone to search for a lawyer or notary in any EU Member State. In terms of uniformity, the Action Plan introduced the idea of a single European case law identifier (ECLI), which would allow judicial decisions to have a similar name and therefore would be easier to search for or record them. And finally, the Action Plan voiced its support on the use of videoconferencing in judicial procedures.

Currently, the third Action Plan 2019–2023[17] goes in tandem with the 2019–2023 e-Justice Strategy (from here on the Strategy).[18] The third action plan reaffirms the aims and the mission of its predecessor. The e-Justice Portal

---

[13] Multiannual European e-Justice Action Plan 2014-2018, *OJ C182, 14.6.2014, p. 2–13*.

[14] This section of the Portal is available here: European Commission, 'Bankruptcy and insolvency registers' (*European E-Justice,* 8 October 2020) https://e-justice.europa.eu/110/EN/bankruptcy_and_insolvency_registers accessed 07 May 2022.

[15] This section of the Portal is available here: 'Lawyers' (*European E-Justice*) https://e-justice.europa.eu/334/EN/lawyers accessed 07 May 2022.

[16] This section of the Portal is available here: 'Notaries' (*European E-Justice)* https://e-justice.europa.eu/335/EN/notaries accessed 07 May 2022.

[17] 2019–2023 Action Plan European e-Justice, *OJ C 96, 13.3.2019, p. 9–32*.

[18] 2019–2023 Strategy on e-Justice, *OJ C 96, 13.3.2019, p. 3–8*.

remains the central point for the Action Plan, but its functionality has been improved and the amount of information it contains has been increasing.

What is the next step of the EU after the Action Plan expiration date in 2023? For sure the Action Plan will be updated with a 2024-2029 Action Plan. The Commission has identified as important elements the following: improve secure communication channels between institutions, further develop secured digital judicial proceeding, improve digital information for citizens on legal provisions, and maintaining the digital registers.[19] The end goal is a digital-by-default approach which when harmonised with the e-Government initiatives should further integrate and improve both initiatives.[20] Hot on the agenda should be the monitoring of artificial intelligence and distributed ledger technologies (DLT, more commonly known as the blockchain technology) to identify possible solutions for e-justice problems. At this point it should be reminded that the Action Plans and the Strategy serve as some sort of constitution for the digitisation of justice and the development of electronic means to improve access to justice in Europe. Thus, we can read both documents as a collection of principles.

The Strategy lays down the necessary link between e-Government and e-Justice principles. As explained in the document itself, these principles call for a digital-by-default approach which means that all Member States should give citizens the possibility to communicate and reach public institutions digitally. In addition, websites and the digital communication with citizens should be user-friendly. This is important because while information may be available it may be buried in hidden corners of a website. And here we may add that user-friendliness should also consider a user that comes from a different Member State and is not used to the local digital culture or does not know the local language. Moreover, the strategy calls for the interoperability of the different systems in each Member State. Even the smallest difference between operational systems may hinder the communication between them. But this is hard to achieve and often the solution is a European-wide central point that would ensure interoperability of the different national systems, or similar.

Going forward, the Commission's aim is to harmonise the e-Justice with the e-Government principles. First, any project should be evaluated based on its priority. Mature technologies which can be implemented with reasonable costs

---

19 n 16 item 5.

20 E-Government is part of the EU's effort to digitise cross-border public services. Considering how important public institutions are in creating the conditions for access to justice, the need to coordinate both e-justice and e-government is evident. A dedicated page on e-government reforms is available here: European Commission, 'Shaping Europe's digital future' (*European Commission*) https://digital-strategy.ec.europa.eu/en/policies/egovernment accessed 07 May 2022.

will get priority to save costs but also ensure user-friendliness. Second, Action Plans should have a continuity between each other, which would guarantee the sustainability and the progress of present projects. Third, the Action Plan should be able to evolve and thus adapt to new technologies and needs. Fourth, practitioners should be involved in the development and launch of new digital tools. While it makes sense to involve practitioners, this principle should also put citizens in the equation as they suffer more from a lack of access to justice and often are those that find it hard to catch up with technology when compared to practitioners.

6.4 THE E-JUSTICE PORTAL AS A DIGITAL SUPPORT TOOL

The e-Justice Portal[21] is the most visible product of the Action Plans so far. Among others, it offers information on family matters, monetary claims, court procedures, legal actions, and legislation. In addition, it provides help in finding a legal professional in the EU and help to access, among others, registers on companies, lawyers, and notaries in Europe. The Portal is user-friendly and provides considerable details from an average user perspective. Often, the information is repeated in different parts of the website to deal with intertwined procedures. Moreover, the information is available in all official EU languages. In addition to serving as an information hub, the Portal serves as a support tool for several EU regulations. It is not clear how successful this website is and how many visitors it receives, but we should not be fast to dismiss its importance. In an age where you can easily find information online, it is equally easy to get lost under the avalanche of results from an online search. The e-Justice portal, however, provides concise and clear information categorised in topics such as family matters and inheritance, monetary claims, court procedures, and taking legal action. EU residents facing a cross-border legal matter should consider this website the starting point when trying to solve their issue.

Overall, the Portal is laudable as more and more information is added, and the interface has improved in recent years. It provides valuable but not exhaustive information. However, work is needed to increase the Portal's visibility and its user friendliness.[22] While it is a valuable tool for legal professionals, for the average person, for instance a consumer, or someone involved in a family

---

[21] The website can be accessed here: https://e-justice.europa.eu/home accessed 07 May 2022.

[22] J. Hoevenaars and X. E. Kramer, 'Improving Access to Information in European Civil Justice: A Mission (Im)Possible?' in: J. von Hein and T. Kruger (eds), *Informed Choices in Cross-Border Enforcement* (Intersentia 2020) 503–525.

dispute, the information may be difficult to navigate. Cross-border judicial issues, nevertheless, are numerous and intertwined so a single website cannot resolve all problems inherent to these cases. A lot of information about laws and procedures is contained in websites managed by Member States in their own language. So, to help foreigners, to improve access to information and justice, to fertilise cross-border interaction, and to reinforce the idea of an EU without inner borders, Member States should try to provide information also in a language that can be understood by people coming from across the border.

In addition to providing information, the Portal serves as a tool that helps laypeople to fill in forms for certain cross-border legal instruments or simply download an editable version of them.[23] Two of the supported instruments

---

[23] These forms provided by the portal relate to judgments in civil and commercial matters (concerning Regulation (EU) 1215/2012 of 12 December 2012 and Council Regulation (EC) 44/2001 of 22 December 2000 on jurisdiction and the recognition and enforcement of judgments in civil and commercial matters); national information and online forms on legal aid (concerning Council Directive 2003/8/EC of 27 January 2003 to improve access to justice in cross-border disputes by establishing minimum common rules relating to legal aid for such disputes); maintenance obligations forms (concerning Council Regulation (EC) 4/2009 of 18 December 2008 on jurisdiction, applicable law, recognition and enforcement of decisions and cooperation in matters relating to maintenance obligations); matrimonial matters and matters of parental responsibility forms (concerning Council Regulation (EC) 2201/2003 of 27 November 2003 concerning jurisdiction and the recognition and enforcement of judgments in matrimonial matters and the matters of parental responsibility, repealing Regulation (EC) 1347/2000); serving documents forms (concerning Regulation (EC) 1393/2007 of the European Parliament and of the Council of 13 November 2007 on the service in the Member States of judicial and extrajudicial documents in civil or commercial matters (service of documents), and repealing Council Regulation (EC) 1348/2000); taking of evidence forms (concerning Council Regulation (EC) 1206/2001 of 28 May 2001 on cooperation between the courts of the Member States in the taking of evidence in civil or commercial matters); European enforcement order forms (concerning Regulation (EC) 805/2004 of the European Parliament and of the Council of 21 April 2004 creating a European Enforcement Order for uncontested claims); European Account Preservation Order forms (concerning Regulation (EU) 655/2014 of the European Parliament and of the Council of 15 May 2014 establishing a European Account Preservation Order procedure to facilitate cross-border debt recovery in civil and commercial matters); compensation to crime victims forms (concerning Council Directive 2004/80/EC of 29 April 2004 relating to compensation to crime victims); public documents forms (concerning Regulation (EU) 2016/1191 of the European Parliament and of the Council of 6 July 2016 on promoting the free movement of citizens by simplifying the requirements for presenting certain public documents in the European Union and amending Regulation (EU) 1024/2012); national information and online form concerning the European Certificate of Succession (Regulation (EU) 650/2012 of the European Parliament and of the Council of 4 July 2012 on jurisdiction, applicable law, recognition and enforcement of decisions and acceptance and enforcement of authentic instruments in matters of succession and on the creation of a European Certificate of

are the ESCP and the EPO, which together with the Regulations on Service of Documents[24] and Taking of Evidence[25] are part of a larger constellation of instruments revised to more prominently incorporate digital communication.[26] I am focusing on the ESCP and the EPO because they are a clear effort by the EU to use digital technologies. It may be arguable how successful these efforts are, but they deserve their praise for being some of the first steps towards a more digitised European civil procedure. In addition, I focus on these two procedures because they are also the only procedures for which the Portal provides digital support to fill in the forms.

6.4.1 The European Small Claims Procedure (ESCP)

The ESCP creates a single uniform procedure in the EU for handling small claims of civil and commercial matter with a value of up to 5,000 Euros.[27] It was adopted by the European institutions in 2007 and amended in 2015. The aim of the ESCP is to facilitate access to courts for cross-border small claims and to reduce hurdles, such as divergent and complex procedures and differences in language. These hurdles made cross-border small claims immediately too expensive to litigate. Considering that for many small claims, litigation is the only dispute resolution form, high costs amount to a major hurdle to

---

Succession); mutual recognition of protection measures forms (concerning Regulation (EU) 606/2013 of the European Parliament and of the Council of 12 June 2013 on mutual recognition of protection measures in civil matters, and the related Commission Implementing Regulation (EU) 939/2014 of 2 September 2014 establishing the certificates referred to in Articles 5 and 14 of Regulation (EU) 606/2013 of the European Parliament and of the Council on mutual recognition of protection measures in civil matters).

[24] Regulation (EC) 1393/2007 of the European Parliament and of the Council of 13 November 2007 on the service in the Member States of judicial and extrajudicial documents in civil or commercial matters (service of documents), and repealing Council Regulation (EC) 1348/2000 [2007] OJ L324, 79–120. Amended by Regulation (EU) 517/2013 of 13 May 2013.

[25] Council Regulation (EC) 1206/2001 of 28 May 2001 on cooperation between the courts of the Member States in the taking of evidence in civil or commercial matters [2001] OJ L174, 1–24. Amended by Regulation (EC) 1103/2008 of The European Parliament and of The Council of 22 October 2008.

[26] X. E. Kramer, 'Access to Justice and Technology: Transforming the Face of Cross-Border Civil Litigation and Adjudication in the EU' in: Karim Benyekhlef, Jane Bailey, Jacquie Burkell and Fabien Gélinas (eds), *E-Access to Justice* (University of Ottawa Press 2016) 351–375.

[27] The ESCP applies to all Member States except for Denmark. Regulation (EC) 861/2007 of the European Parliament and of the Council of 11 July 2007 establishing a European Small Claims Procedure [2007] OJ L199, 1–22 as amended by Regulation (EU) 2015/2421.

access to justice. According to the ESCP, a claimant can use the procedure to send a form with the details of the case to the foreign court, which responds to the form and informs the defendant of the claim. The form is standard in all Member States, and as a result overcomes the previous divergent procedures and reduces language barriers. Moreover, filling in the form and sending it to the court does not require the presence of a lawyer, which often increases costs for many litigants. Overall, the ESCP's potential remains high even though it is not used frequently.[28] More importantly in view of the increasing presence of technology in our daily life and the increasing cross-border trade,[29] the e-Justice Portal offers the possibility to fill in the forms online. This way, a claimant can fill in the form online and send it together with the evidence to the competent court. The e-Justice Portal contains a wizard (a technical term for a guided electronic support) which can guide a claimant in filling in the form and prepare it for sending to the competent court. The help provided by the wizard is critical for many people unfamiliar with legal procedures. This does not mean, however, that the Portal sends the form to the competent court or that the form can be sent electronically to the court. In fact, 12 Member States have notified that their legislation does not allow the electronic submissions of the ESCP forms.[30] However, this may change with the approval of the proposed regulation on the digitisation of judicial cooperation as it will oblige public authorities and judicial institutions to accept these types of electronic communication.[31] Overall, the e-Justice Portal is still a good support tool for filling in the ESCP forms and identifying the correct court; the next step should be to send the forms directly from the portal. However, Member States should improve their legislation and set rules for accepting electronic submissions. As

---

[28] Rafał Mańko, 'European Small Claims Procedure: Legal analysis of the Commission's proposal to remedy weaknesses in the current system' (2014) European Parliamentary Research Service in-depth analysis, PE 542.137 https://www.europarl.europa.eu/RegData/etudes/IDAN/2014/542137/EPRS_IDA(2014)542137_REV1_EN.pdf accessed 07 May 2022. ECC-Net, *European Small Claims Procedure Report* (European Consumer Centres Network Report, 2012) 17-32 https://ec.europa.eu/info/sites/default/files/small_claims_international_claims_2012_en.pdf accessed 07 May 2022.

[29] Statistics from Eurostat show a constant increase in intra-EU export of goods. We may safely assume that part of this trade is small size trade that would create small value conflicts that would lead to small claims procedures. Eurostat statistics are available here: 'Intra-EU trade in goods – main features' (*Eurostat,* April 2021) https://ec.europa.eu/eurostat/statistics-explained/index.php?oldid=452727#Evolution_of_intra-EU_trade_in_goods accessed 07 May 2022.

[30] This has been identified as a detrimental point for the development of e-CODEX. See page 13 of the Study carried out within Work Package 3 of the e-CODEX project (e-CODEX D3.5/D3.7/D3.8 WP3 Final Report).

[31] Footnote 7.

it is often the case with digitising a process, it is not only a question of digitising a component, but the whole process should be digitised.

6.4.2 The European Order for Payment Procedure (EPO)

The EPO was established in 2006 and became applicable in 2007.[32] The aim of the Regulation was to simplify the procedures for obtaining an order for payment and for having one enforced in another Member State. It applies to civil and commercial matters and claims of a pecuniary nature. The order is granted in a one-sided procedure with only marginal review and can be declared enforceable if the defendant does not contest the order within 30 days. As in the case of the ESCP, the e-Justice Portal provides information on and forms for requesting an EPO.[33] The support provided should not be considered legal advice because it is focused on filling in the necessary form, but instead it should be considered as digital support. Reducing cost for obtaining an EPO improves the position of cross-border merchants. It removes the hurdles for finding redress even for small and medium enterprises involved in small claims.

6.5 E-CODEX

The e-justice Action Plan provides for an e-Justice Communication via Online Data Exchange, or e-CODEX. As the name suggests, e-CODEX aims at improving the communication between judicial authorities, legal practitioners, and citizens. It tries to do so by providing software that improves the connectivity between national systems. This way authorities, practitioners, and citizens can stay in their national digital environment, and communicate with another party across the border. In other words, unlike the Portal, e-CODEX is not a central system that collects and distributes information, but it is a nod used by national systems to communicate. This means that any participating

---

[32] Regulation (EU) 2015/2421 of the European Parliament and of the Council of 16 December 2015 amending Regulation (EC) No 861/2007 establishing a European Small Claims Procedure and Regulation (EC) No 1896/2006 creating a European order for payment procedure, *OJ L341,* 1-13.

[33] The Portal provides information on the EPO here: 'European payment order' (*European E-Justice,* 8 October 2021) https://e-justice.europa.eu/41/EN/european_payment_order accessed 07 May 2022, and additional information on the forms and how to fill them here: 'European Payment Order forms' (*European E-Justice,* 17 November 2021) https://e-justice.europa.eu/156/EN/european_payment_order_forms accessed 07 May 2022.

authority has nothing to change because e-CODEX is meant to be as little invasive as possible.

The history of e-CODEX can be traced back to December 2010 when its founding members met to discuss, develop, and test information exchange platforms. For the first time, e-CODEX was used in 2013 in a European Payment Order procedure. In this case, e-CODEX enabled secure communication between courts in Italy, Austria, and Germany. That was followed by successful pilots with the European Small Claims Procedure (2015), Business Registers (2015), Mutual Legal Assistance (2015), and Financial Payments (2016).

Currently, e-CODEX supports the EPO, the ESCP, and the interconnection of insolvency and business registers. The Service of Documents and the Taking of Evidence may be the next procedures to be supported by e-CODEX. In criminal law, e-CODEX supports the European Investigation Order (EIO) and the electronic evidence digital exchange system (e-EDES). A few other procedures may be supported in the upcoming years. The Commission considers e-CODEX a success. In fact, in December 2020, it proposed a regulation which would give to e-CODEX a better legal status and would hand it over to the European Agency for the Operational Management of large-scale IT systems in the Area of Freedom, Security and Justice (eu-LISA).[34] The proposed Regulation would make e-CODEX mandatory for all Member States and thus remedy the current voluntary, but uncertain, adoption of e-CODEX. The proposed regulation stipulates that eu-LISA should take over the management of e-CODEX by mid-2023.

The humble beginning of e-CODEX and its later success show how digitisation should unfold, with small but secure steps to bloom later. With time and more experience, projects can develop further and accept more participants, while increasing their scope. Large projects have many more possibilities to fail and often are difficult to manage. Hopefully, while e-CODEX is being

---

[34] Proposal for a Regulation of the European Parliament and of the Council on a computerised system for communication in cross-border civil and criminal proceedings (e-CODEX system), and amending Regulation (EU) 2018/1726, COM/2020/712 final. Eu-LISA is an agency tasked with developing and maintaining large IT projects for the EU. So far it operates many border electronic systems such as the Schengen Information System, the Visa Information System, and the European Travel and Information and Authorisation System. Moreover, eu-LISA is tasked with the research activities and with supporting pilot projects such as e-CODEX. The functioning of eu-LISA is regulated by Regulation (EU) 2018/1726 of the European Parliament and of the Council of 14 November 2018 on the European Union Agency for the Operational Management of Large-Scale IT Systems in the Area of Freedom, Security and Justice (eu-LISA), and amending Regulation (EC) 1987/2006 and Council Decision 2007/533/JHA and repealing Regulation (EU) 1077/2011 [2018] OJ L295 99–137.

consolidated under eu-LISA, all the involved parties are learning some of these lessons. E-CODEX, however, may also show a discrepancy. The Action Plans call for interoperability: in other words, Member States' digital systems should communicate with each other without intermediaries. But e-CODEX does exactly this. It serves as an intermediary to translate the languages of the different systems. Obviously, there is no single cure for all, and the central EU institutions are needed to coordinate legacy systems, but this should not be a trend or an easy way out.

6.6 EU JUSTICE SCOREBOARD

Since 2013, the EU has prepared an annual review of the judiciary in each Member State. This review is titled the EU Justice Scoreboard, and despite the misleading name is not meant to rank Member States or to declare a winner, but to compare Member States and hopefully to induce some healthy competition between them. The EU Justice Scoreboard 2021 is the latest addition to the series and of particular interest for this chapter because it contains information about court digitisation and technology implementation in courts and can be used to survey the level of penetration of technology in Member States' courts. Individual Member States provide most of the data for the Scoreboard, but they are not uniformly gathered. This is indicated in many figures in the Scoreboard. The consequence of this is that using the Scoreboard as a source of analysis is tricky in two ways. First, the Scoreboard is not intended to serve for ranking purposes. Thus, it tries its best to provide data, but it is not bothered by the absence of some. Second, considering that the source of the data and the way it is collected are not uniform, the Scoreboard is not a reliable source. Instead, it should be used as an indicator and its data should be cross-referenced with other sources.

Like its older versions, the 2021 EU Justice Scoreboard contains a section on the digitisation of courts. This section contains nine figures with details about the use of technology in courts. According to the data in the Scoreboard most Member States have some form of remote communication technology with their constituents. Although, the type of technology and the possibility of court constituents to access it is not very clear. Most advanced Member States have progressed well in the digitisation of court proceedings. Czechia, Estonia, Sweden, and Slovakia score very high on all the components of procedural rules allowing digital technology in courts. Remarkably, there is no East-West divide and no divide by economic development in the deployment of technology in courts. It seems the drive to adopt digitisation is internal and most probably complex. One component where Member States should have done better is the availability of online information about courts. This critique is only a quantitative one, because the figures of the Scoreboard say nothing about the quality of this information. The main point of this critique is that despite the 'maturity' of websites, courts find it hard to publish all the information available. Only six Member States have full points on this figure. The situation may be worse if we were to look at the quality of information. But in an age where online information is the only type of information available, this situation seems bad. And as said earlier in this chapter, developers should consider also cross-border users when designing their websites.

These two figures provide just a glimpse of the information contained in the Scoreboard. They tell about the adoption of technology and the information available online in the courts of EU Member States. While there are many excuses for not using technology in courts, there should be no excuse for not building websites rich in information and details. Cross-border litigants deserve better information in a way and language that they understand, and Member States should show their good will to provide this information. But the above are good examples of what the other figures tell. There are Member States that are spearheading the use of technologies and Member States that are lagging. This difference in technology adaptation speed is problematic for cross-border users as it reduces procedural predictability, offers a patchy landscape to investors, and threatens access to justice. The duty of the EU at this point is to provide incentives and examples of good practices for court digitisation and the Scoreboard should not be shy to do so.

6.7 ARTIFICIAL INTELLGENCE

In recent years, AI and distributed ledger technologies have provided solutions that increase efficiency and security in many areas of life. AI relies on massive amounts of data and algorithms to analyse inputs and related problems and provide fast and cheap solutions. Distributed ledger technologies share tiny bits of information among a large amount of nods, which then should all agree to assemble the whole information.[35] This distribution of information makes it impossible to alter the original information and thus is ideal to certify documents or encrypt them. Distributed ledger technologies serve as the backbone of cryptocurrencies or smart contracts. Today, these technologies are

[35] Imagine a chef wanting to protect a recipe from getting lost or changed. To protect his recipe, this chef divides it in ten pieces, keeps one for himself, and gives the other nine to nine other chefs. If he wants to read the recipe, he needs to call the chefs holding the other pieces, assemble the pieces together and read it. In addition, if he or another chef wants to change the recipe all the ten chefs should agree. In analogy to the distributed ledger technology, the nods are the chefs, and the information is the recipe. This is further complicated when encryption and thousands of users are added to the equation.

everywhere, from telephones, to cars, to weapons and hospital equipment. It is obvious that an early acceptance and investment in these types of technologies is important for developed nations and even more so for the EU, whose goal is to make Europe fit for the digital age.

With this goal in mind, the first step in addressing the need to boost and regulate AI was taken in 2018 when the Declaration on Cooperation on Artificial Intelligence was signed by many Member States. This document called for, among other things, ensuring a legal and ethical framework that would uphold legal rights and European values, but also support the development of AI.[36] In the same year the EU adopted the European AI Strategy.[37] In this document the EU made it clear again that it wants to develop AI systems, but at the same time it wants to protect the Union's values like those described in the Charter of Fundamental Rights of the EU. The strategy resonates the call of the 2018 Declaration and details what an ethical and legal framework on AI should entail. Among others, the personal data of citizens should be protected against misuse and meaningful information should be given when decisions are made by AI systems. Furthermore, and for the good of the Digital Single Market, high standards of liability rules should be maintained which should feed the other goal of building trust between AI products and users.

As part of the AI Strategy, the EU announced in March 2018 the creation of an AI Expert Group and a European AI Alliance. The aim of these initiatives was to gain as much expertise on matters related to AI and to hear from different stakeholders in developing strategies and legislation related to AI. This was followed by the creation of a High Level Expert Group on AI, whose mission is to address mid- and long-term challenges related to AI. As part of the efforts to build a political and economic platform for the development of AI, several institutions in the EU developed a Coordinated Plan on Artificial Intelligence.[38] As the name indicates, the Plan is intended as a to-do list for all the EU institutions. The final goal was to boost the technological and industrial AI capacity of the EU, prepare for the changes that AI may bring, and ensure an ethical and legal framework for the development of AI. Evidently, making

---

[36] European Commission, 'EU Member States sign up to cooperate on Artificial Intelligence' (*European Commission*, 10 April 2018) https://digital-strategy.ec.europa.eu/en/news/eu-member-states-sign-cooperate-artificial-intelligence accessed 07 May 2022.

[37] European Commission, 'Communication Artificial Intelligence for Europe' (*European Commission*, 25 April 2018) https://digital-strategy.ec.europa.eu/en/library/communication-artificial-intelligence-europe accessed 07 May 2022.

[38] European Commission, 'Coordinated Plan on Artificial Intelligence' (*European Commission*, 7 December 2018) https://digital-strategy.ec.europa.eu/en/library/coordinated-plan-artificial-intelligence accessed 07 May 2022.

the EU an AI powerhouse requires the development of a good legal framework. As such, ethics, civil liability, and data protection are of utmost importance, but the Plan calls also for the creation of regulatory sandboxes, which should allow companies to create and develop AI systems in controlled circumstances and under the supervision of authorities. AI and related technologies are new and both developers and regulators find it hard to predict how society and the economy will behave once a system is deployed. Ex ante regulation is hard and the best way to regulate a field where AI is introduced is by simply creating a regulatory sandbox.

In April 2019 the High Level Expert Group on AI presented the Ethics Guidelines for Trustworthy Artificial Intelligence.[39] The EU has focused a lot of attention on this issue and these guidelines are part of it. The Guidelines provide a list of seven requirements which an AI system should fulfil to be considered trustworthy. These requirements have to do with human agency and oversight, technical robustness and safety, privacy and data governance, transparency, diversity, non-discrimination and fairness, societal and environmental well-being, and accountability. As the Guidelines declare, the deployment of AI and its application are difficult to predict. Therefore, the Guidelines should be regarded as parameters, and the ethical concerns of an AI system should be considered in accordance with the field where it is applied. We can imagine that these Guidelines will have a considerable impact in the deployment of AI in courts, because they put humans at the centre of attention.

In June 2019 the High Level Expert Group published Policy and Investment Recommendations,[40] which was followed in July 2020 by the Sectoral Recommendations of Trustworthy AI.[41] Both documents detail per sector some of the elements that law- and policy makers should consider. One of the most important recommendations is to adopt a risk-based approach to regulation.

---

[39] European Commission, 'Ethics guidelines for trustworthy AI' (*European Commission*, 8 April 2019) https://digital-strategy.ec.europa.eu/en/library/ethics-guidelines-trustworthy-ai accessed 07 May 2022.

See also: European Commission, 'Communication: Building Trust in Human Centric Artificial Intelligence' (*European Commission*, 8 April 2019) https://digital-strategy.ec.europa.eu/en/library/communication-building-trust-human-centric-artificial-intelligence accessed 07 May 2022.

[40] European Commission, 'Policy and investment recommendations for trustworthy Artificial Intelligence' (*European Commission*, 26 June 2019) https://digital-strategy.ec.europa.eu/en/library/policy-and-investment-recommendations-trustworthy-artificial-intelligence accessed 07 May 2022.

[41] Pekka Ala-Pietilä, 'Sectorial considerations for Trustworthy AI – taking AI's context specificity into account' (*European Commission*, 23 July 2020) https://futurium.ec.europa.eu/en/european-ai-alliance/blog/sectorial-considerations-trustworthy-ai-taking-ais-context-specificity-account accessed 07 May 2022.

In other words, AI systems should be vetted on their impact and the risk they pose on humans and society. Those with unacceptable risk should be discouraged and unplugged. The assessment and the evaluation of these systems are left to the regulator based on the situation, but most importantly they call for continuous and ad hoc standards to be applied to specific situations. Courts for example should pay considerable attention to AI as a substitute for human staff. To help businesses and organisations, the Expert Group developed a webtool that developers can use to assess AI systems before deployment.[42] The webtool uses the ethics guidelines to provide an evaluation of the trustworthiness of an AI system and the potential problems that may emerge.

The latest step towards regulating AI is the proposal for a Regulation on Artificial Intelligence, dated April 2021.[43] The proposed Regulation aims at solving some of the problems that ethical guidelines could not solve. First, it aims at ensuring that AI systems in the Union are safe and do not threaten existing fundamental rights. Second, it tries to increase legal certainty to help investment and research on AI. Third, it tries to enhance an effective enforcement of existing laws on fundamental rights applicable on AI systems. Fourth, it tries to foster a common market for AI within the Union. To resolve the definitional problem related to AI as an emergent and dynamic technology, the Regulation considers AI as any software that uses one of the techniques or approaches listed in its first Annex. The idea is that the technologies listed in the Annex will be updated to keep up with scientific development, and that a broad and neutral definition better captures the dynamic nature of AI development. Article 5 of the proposed Regulation lists some AI practices that are prohibited. These prohibitions affect AI: that deploys subliminal techniques that may physically or mentally harm a person; that exploits vulnerabilities of a specific group of people causing them physical and mental harm; and that use some form of social scoring. Despite their good intentions, these prohibitions are broad and leave room for unequal application. For example, social media massively uses AI systems to generate or suggest content which tries to make people use these social platforms for longer. Inconsiderate use of social platforms has been suggested to cause psychological harm to many people, with children being more easily affected. Is the proposed regulation suggesting a ban on AI use in social media? I do not think so, but its wording

---

42 European Commission, 'Assessment List for Trustworthy Artificial Intelligence (ALTAI) for self-assessment' (*European Commission*, 17 July 2019) https://digital-strategy.ec.europa.eu/en/library/assessment-list-trustworthy-artificial-intelligence-altai-self-assessment accessed 07 May 2022.

43 Proposal for a Regulation of the European Parliament and of the Council Laying Down Harmonised Rules on Artificial Intelligence (Artificial Intelligence Act) and Amending Certain Union Legislative Acts, COM/2021/206 final.

may be interpreted as a yes by some governments and thus differences in application may arise. But if the intended outcome is to prohibit AI systems that cause psychological harm, why not ban social media that cause addiction, stress and trauma and their AI systems with this? There may be many answers to these issues, but they clearly illustrate how complex AI regulation is and how intricate AI use is.

Article 6 of the proposal defines high-risk AI systems and, as it was the case for general AI, the proposal gives a broad definition which refers to two annexes of the regulation. Annex II and Annex III will provide a list of applications and legislations that will define high-risk AI systems. The purpose for classifying high-risk systems is that they should obey a set of rules detailed in the Regulation. For this kind of system, it is necessary to have a risk management system and they should meet certain standards with regards to data usage, training, and management. Furthermore, risk management systems have and keep a particular documentation, and in addition to having a human oversight, they should be able to provide transparency and information about their operations to users. Clearly these requirements echo the Ethics Guidelines prepared by the High Experts Group on AI. And of course, high-risk systems are those where the guidelines are the most significant and applicable. In addition to these, providers of high-risk AI systems should follow a set of rules provided in the regulation. Again, these rules follow the logic of the Ethical Guidelines and seek to diminish the effects of high-risk AI by taking the 'side' of EU citizens rather than AI.

The proposed Regulation builds on these past activities. The main lesson derived from them is that AI is difficult to define because it is a realm characterised by rapid development, which require new definitions. Having difficulty in defining makes it difficult to regulate AI. Arguably the best approach is to define the limits of what is acceptable, for example fundamental EU values should not be violated. The Ethical Guidelines play an important role here. They have created the foundations upon which an AI legal framework can be developed. It prohibits systems that do not comply with EU values, tries to regulate high-risk AI, and for the rest takes a *laissez-faire* approach.

6.8 CONCLUDING REMARKS

Digitisation of justice is needed to both match the penetration of technology in society and to resolve some access to justice problems. Digitisation, however, needs permissive regulations to flourish and strict guidelines to protect fundamental rights. So far, the efforts of the EU to digitise justice have had the best intentions, but not the best outcomes. Member States have enjoyed the freedom to voluntarily join EU instruments and the freedom to adapt their legislation to the new digital technologies that the EU supports. The e-Justice

Portal, for example, can help EU citizens to electronically fill in the forms for the European Small Claims Procedure, but not all the Member States accept a digital submission. It goes without saying that digitisation is easier said than done. The legislative process in the EU is complex and it is made even harder by politics and principles that shift often. In addition, there is also the fear of the unknown, because while technology is promising, no one knows for certain how it will affect human behaviour. The complexities encountered with digitisation seem to have made the EU more cautious with regulating AI. It has so far created the Ethical Guidelines that should serve legislators to create new laws and policies. It uses broad definitions and flexible lists to regulate AI systems as much as possible yet falls short of being a legal framework delimiting the use of AI. Arguably the greatest lesson we can learn from the history of digitisation of justice in the EU is that it is never-ending.

7. AI and access to justice: An expansion of Adrian Zuckerman's findings

Nicolas Kyriakides, Anna Plevri and Yomna Zentani

7.1 INTRODUCTION

The integration of technology into the legal profession in a world driven by the fast-paced and tech-savvy is arguably inevitable as '[...] there is hardly a field of economic activity which has not been transformed by Artificial Intelligence'.[1] However, the legal sector appears to have been reluctant to adopt new technology, particularly in the form of artificial intelligence (AI) and Big Data processing.[2]

In light of this, the chapter aims at assessing the impact of the potential implementation of AI in the legal sector on access to justice. For this purpose, the chapter relies on the work by the eminent Adrian Zuckerman, Emeritus Professor of Civil Procedure at the University of Oxford; in particular, his recent paper entitled 'Artificial Intelligence – implications for the legal profession, adversarial process and rule of law'.[3] Zuckerman's influence on the study of civil procedure,[4] particularly through the reference of his works in the House of Lords and Court of Appeal and in foreign jurisdictions such as the Supreme Court of Canada, and his experience as an adviser to the Lord Woolf inquiry on access to justice, underline the importance of his work.[5] The following chapter seeks to explore and expand upon the findings made by Zuckerman,

1 Adrian Zuckerman, 'Artificial Intelligence – Implications for the Legal Profession, Adversarial Process and Rule of Law' (2020) 136 LQR 427.

2 Mark Cohen, 'Why is Law So Slow to Use Data?' (*Forbes*, 24 June 2019) https://www.forbes.com/sites/markcohen1/2019/06/24/why-is-law-so-slow-to-use-data/?sh=691f754db8eb accessed 30 May 2021.

3 Zuckerman, 'Artificial Intelligence' (n 1) 427.

4 Adrian Zuckerman, *Zuckerman on Civil Procedure: Principles of Practice* (4th edn, Sweet & Maxwell 2021).

5 Adrian Zuckerman, 'Biography' (*Adrian Zuckerman Civil Justice*) https://adrianzuckerman.co.uk/biography accessed 30 May 2021.

with particular attention to the risks associated with the implementation of AI in the judiciary, analysed through the lens of access to justice.

To expand on Zuckerman's findings, several key terms which will be used throughout the chapter must be considered and defined. We accept Zuckerman's wide-ranging definition of AI as 'the broader science of designing computers to act intelligently without necessarily being explicitly programmed to reach particular outcomes'.[6] Within this, Zuckerman identifies machine learning, defined as 'the use of data and algorithms to imitate the way that humans learn',[7] as a crucial element of AI and therein highlights a key issue: its inability to process or understand natural language.[8] However, Zuckerman also notes that this barrier is being eroded, citing Google's work on 'self-taught' or 'deep-learning' systems.[9]

Access to justice is a similarly broad concept. Garth and Cappelletti define access to justice as being based upon two pillars: that the legal system must be 'equally accessible to all' and that it must 'lead to results that are individually and socially just'.[10] These two principles may be subdivided into various aspects, including giving the general populace the opportunity and ability to have their voice heard, exercise their rights, challenge discrimination, and hold decision-makers accountable.[11] It is a fundamental aspect of the rule of law.[12]

The key advantages of the use of AI in the legal sector with regards to the umbrella of access to justice are the increased efficiency and associated reduction in costs, the predictability and consistency of judicial decisions, and the elimination of bias. These must be counterbalanced by the risks involved and other considerations, which include the loss of lawyers' skills, the importance of trust and public confidence in the judiciary, and a further discussion on the elimination of bias. After this review of the potential of AI and its associated risks, an outlook on the future of AI in the legal sector and some indication as

---

6 Zuckerman, 'Artificial Intelligence' (n 1) 428.

7 IBM Cloud Education, 'Machine Learning' (*IBM*, 15 July 2020) https://www.ibm.com/uk-en/cloud/learn/machine-learning accessed 29 June 2021.

8 Zuckerman, 'Artificial Intelligence' (n 1) 431.

9 Zuckerman, 'Artificial Intelligence' (n 1) 431; Jeff Dean and Andrew Ng, 'Using Large-scale Brain Simulations for Machine Learning and A.I.' (*Google Blog*, 26 June 2012) https://blog.google/technology/ai/using-large-scale-brain-simulations-for/ accessed 13 July 2021.

10 Bryant Garth, Mauro Cappelletti, 'Access to Justice: The Newest Wave in the Worldwide Movement to Make Rights Effective' (1978) *BuffLRev* 181, 182.

11 United Nations, 'Access to Justice' (*United Nations and the Rule of Law*) https://www.un.org/ruleoflaw/thematic-areas/access-to-justice-and-rule-of-law-institutions/access-to-justice/ accessed 30 May 2021.

12 Ibid.

to potential measures by which the risks of implementation may be mitigated will be given.

7.1.1 Zuckerman's Findings and the Scope of Discussion

Zuckerman explores the current use of technology in legal practice, including the use of computer applications by lawyers, as advocated for by Richard Susskind.[13] These are used primarily by lawyers themselves, as opposed to the judiciary. It is accepted that AI in these instances will have – and indeed has had – a major impact on the efficiency of the profession without substantial risks or downsides, particularly in areas such as document review and due diligence,[14] which are expensive processes and can result in delays.[15]

This increased efficiency is the economic driving force – led by both low-end and high-end consumers of legal services[16] – behind the ever greater implementation of technology in the legal sector: legal service providers are unlikely to tolerate costly human practices which are capable of being performed faster by machinery, for much lower cost.[17] The likely outcome encompasses decreased costs for clients, which will undoubtedly improve a key element of access to justice: making legal advice and representation more affordable.[18] It has been suggested that this will also assist in remedying the lack of public confidence in the justice system caused, in part, by the lack of affordable access to legal advice and representation.[19]

This chapter will primarily focus on the more controversial and disputed application of AI to the judiciary. Indeed, these are areas which Zuckerman also addresses, particularly with regard to the exercise of judicial discretion,[20] the nature of appeal,[21] and the public acceptance of the implementation of AI in

---

[13] Zuckerman, 'Artificial Intelligence' (n 1) 433; Richard Susskind, *Tomorrow's Lawyers: An Introduction to Your Future* (1st edn, OUP 2013) 82.

[14] Clive Freedman, 'Technology Assisted Review Approved For Use in English High Court Litigation' (2016) 13 *Digital Evidence and Electronic Signature Law Review* 139; Harry Surden, 'Machine Learning and Law' (2014) 89 *WashLRev* 87.

[15] Jane Donoghue, 'The Rise of Digital Justice: Courtroom Technology, Public Participation and Access to Justice' (2017) 80 MLR 955.

[16] Zuckerman, 'Artificial Intelligence' (n 1) 427.

[17] Barney Thompson, 'Lawyers look to AI to Cut Down on Disclosure Costs' *Financial Times* (London, 23 December 2018) https://www.ft.com/content/ad042a78-052f-11e9-9d01-cd4d49afbbe3 accessed 30 May 2021.

[18] Zuckerman, 'Artificial Intelligence' (n 1) 439.

[19] Raymond H. Brescia and others, 'Embracing Disruption: How Technological Change in the Delivery of Legal Services Can Improve Access to Justice' (2015) 78 *AltaLRev* 553.

[20] Zuckerman, 'Artificial Intelligence' (n 1) 438.

[21] Ibid., 445–446.

the judiciary.[22] A central part of the advantages of AI submitted by Zuckerman, even in applications within the judiciary, is that of consistency of judges and judicial decision-making.[23] He further submits that the judicial implementation of AI would erode the adversarial process irreparably.[24] These aspects, amongst others, are central to the following discussion.

Zuckerman's conclusions align, at least in part, with those presented in the following chapter. He praises the increased efficiency and potential cost savings of AI, whilst emphasising that there are substantial risks to the adoption of AI, particularly within the judiciary. Fundamentally, he submits that greater discourse and discussion are required,[25] and this chapter acts on this encouragement.

7.2 ADVANTAGES OF AI IMPLEMENTATION

This section will focus on the advantages of AI implementation and use by lawyers and in the judiciary. These advantages must be balanced against the risks and considerations, so as to assess the overall value of the implementation of AI.

7.2.1 Efficiency and Costs

A key aspect of access to justice is ensuring that those in need have access to legal advice and, if needed, representation at an affordable price. Litigation is notoriously expensive, and costs are often unpredictable, being predicated upon legal services charged at an hourly basis and cost-shifting rules – where the unsuccessful party may be ordered to pay the litigation costs of the successful party – present in many jurisdictions.[26] Notable drivers of costs at present are expensive procedures, such as disclosure in common law jurisdictions,[27] which AI may be able to handle far more efficiently and expediently – and therefore cost effectively – than a human lawyer. Indeed, Zuckerman highlights that 'Artificial Intelligence cost savings in legal services could make a transformative contribution to access to justice', citing present issues of unpredictable and disproportionate costs of legal representation.[28]

---

22 Ibid., 443–45.
23 Ibid., 439.
24 Ibid., 447–449.
25 Zuckerman, 'Artificial Intelligence' (n 2) 452–453.
26 Zuckerman, *Zuckerman on Civil Procedure* (n 4) 27.1.
27 Donoghue (n 15).
28 Zuckerman, 'Artificial Intelligence' (n 1) 439; Brescia and others (n 19).

This efficiency may be generated, for example, by the automation of the document review process in civil litigation. Therein, AI has transformed the cumbersome task of reviewing documents to a more streamlined and succinct process. The utilisation of predictive coding renders the disclosure process more efficient. In essence, AI reviews large datasets far more quickly – and potentially with greater accuracy – than is possible by humans. This occurs primarily in the form of Technology Assisted Review,[29] which uses 'predictive analytics' – essentially the extraction of information from existing datasets through a variety of techniques, such as machine learning – to identify patterns and predict outcomes.

With the aid of predictive coding, AI machinery is used to assist in the reviewing of documents with the help of subject-specific algorithms developed by subject matter experts. It has enabled litigators to identify the relevant information more quickly, without reviewing the full documentation. Given the advent of technology resulting in an increased volume of electronic documents, as opposed to paper, the traditional method of discovery in any case finds little utility in a predominantly digital world. As such, the main advantage of AI is its power to filter out large quantities of documents that are likely to be irrelevant, thereby preventing the human lawyer from wasting 'limited cognitive resources analysing them', particularly when the cost reduction in the document size is particularly large.[30]

Whilst one may question the reliability of AI in document review, AI disclosure in the US has been claimed to have a better track record than a human review of documents.[31] Grossman has highlighted that AI is not only more efficient but can also yield superior results as technology-assisted processes examine far more than the small fraction of documents which may be examined by human lawyers and does so in record times.[32]

AI may also be applied to legal research. Indeed, a study by the National Legal Research Group Inc, which examined how the CARA A.I. matter-based research system aided expert legal researchers, concluded that the tasks were completed 24.5 per cent faster than lawyers using traditional methods. This would be predicted to save the average lawyer approximately 132 to 210 hours annually.[33]

---

29 Freedman (n 14).

30 Surden (n 14).

31 Maura Grossman and Gordon V. Cormack, 'Technology-Assisted Review in E-Discovery Can be More Effective and More Efficient than Exhaustive Manual Review' (2011) 17 *Richmond Journal of Law and Technology* 1.

32 Ibid.

33 National Legal Research Group Inc, 'The real impact of using artificial intelligence in legal research' (*LawSites*, September 2018) https://www.lawsitesblog.com/wp

Another area of AI use in the legal sphere is the attempt to analyse and predict judicial outcomes and decisions. Algorithms by companies such as Ravel Law, Lex Machina, and Premonition Analytics use data to give insights into a given judge's patterns, abnormalities, rulings, and reversal rate. In essence, this enables one to predict judicial outcomes based on real data.[34] Whilst this is a relatively new and developing area of AI implementation, it has potential to increase access to justice by giving parties greater certainty by increasing the predictability of outcomes, which may in turn decrease the costs of litigation.

Ravel Law, an example primarily focused on US law, can predict outcomes based on relevant case law, the judge's previous rulings, and referenced language from over 400 federal and state courts.[35] The Judge Dashboard feature contains cases, citations, circuits, and decisions of a specific judge that is said to aid lawyers in understanding how a judge is likely to rule on a case. Lex Machina's timing analytics feature helps in predicting an estimated trial time of a case before a specific judge, whereas Premonition uses AI technology to predict a lawyer's success by analysing his win rate, the case duration, and type of claim as well as his pairing with a judge.[36]

These types of AI application will undoubtedly increase efficiency: both through the prediction of outcome providing better and more nuanced advice to clients on their chances of success in litigation, and through decreasing cost by eliminating the notoriously expensive time spent by lawyers on easily automated tasks such as document review. This will likely lead to a decrease in costs, and an increase in access to justice.

At present these services, particularly the predictive AI systems, are specialised and by their nature priced at a level which only the elite law firms of the world will likely be able to afford. It is therefore prudent to qualify the above advantages, as access to justice amongst those who suffer most from a lack of access – namely the poor and disadvantaged – will likely not benefit in the short term. However, as with all emerging technology, there is hope that

---

-content/uploads/sites/509/2018/09/The-Real-Impact-of-Using-Artificial-Intelligence-in-Legal-Research-FINAL2.pdf. accessed 30 May 2021.

34 S. Shin, 'How AI Enables Stronger Litigation' (*NU Property Casualty 360°*, 11 November 2019) https://www.propertycasualty360.com/2019/11/11/how-ai-can-help-you-be-a-better-litigator-414-166813/?slreturn=20201108022936 accessed 9 December 2020.

35 Daniel Faggella, 'AI in Law and Legal Practice – A Comprehensive View of 35 Current Applications' (*Emerj*, 14 March 2020) https://emerj.com/ai-sector-overviews/ai-in-law-legal-practice-current-applications/ accessed 14 July 2021.

36 Ibid.

prices will decrease and become more affordable in the long-term as the sector expands and competition between providers increases.

7.2.2 Predictability and Consistency of Decisions: The Judicial Application of AI

The judicial application of AI in adjudication offers the most tantalising potential benefits for access to justice: a vast increase in consistency and predictability of decisions, a far shorter adjudication time, and an associated erosion of the backlog of cases. As Zuckerman has emphasised, judicial decisions are influenced by a variety of human factors, including the judge's ability, knowledge, experience, moral inclinations, and political outlook.[37]

An AI judge, or even a human judge assisted by an AI system which highlights previous decisions on the same point of law, would be more consistent – and therefore more predictable – than a human judge, as an AI would not suffer from the same human factors. Indeed, its elimination of bias, explored further below, is also a key advantage.

The development and use of such systems have seemingly been slower than those in use by lawyers more generally, perhaps due to the implementation of AI into the judiciary depending primarily upon the willingness of the respective to introduce AI into court proceedings. Current laws in most jurisdictions do not allow for the use of AI in place of a human judge in adjudication, nor do they allow for the use of AI to assist human judges.[38] Nevertheless, as highlighted by Zuckerman, effective forms of machine adjudication, albeit in relatively simple and low-value disputes, have made headway in eBay and Amazon.[39] Whilst these cases are by their nature very often less complex and nuanced than those dealt with by public judges, they may eventually pave the way for the wider adoption of AI-based, or at the very least AI-assisted, adjudication.

Indeed, more advanced implementation may be seen in the AI-enabled Smart Courts of China, particularly in basic, non-complex, low-value contract and negligence disputes.[40] The purported aim of these measures is to 'promote

---

[37] Zuckerman, 'Artificial Intelligence' (n 1) 439.

[38] James Hope, 'Can a Robot Be an Arbitrator' in Axel Calissendorff and Patrik Schöldström (eds), *Stockholm Arbitration Yearbook* (Kluwer Law International 2019) 103, 104-111.

[39] Zuckerman, 'Artificial Intelligence' (n 1) 444; Frederick Wilmot-Smith, 'Justice eBay Style' (2019) 41 London Review of Books 27.

[40] Mimi Zou, '"Smart Courts" in China and the Future of Personal Injury Litigation' (2020) 2 *Journal of Personal Injury Law* 135, 137.

greater consistency of judgements [sic] across China, as well as mitigating potential gaps in judicial expertise'.[41]

If successful, these systems would greatly increase access to justice by decreasing the pressure on the judicial system. This pressure is felt strongly across the world and has recently been exacerbated by the COVID-19 pandemic.[42] Furthermore, if successful in mitigating gaps in judicial capacity, the use of AI in adjudication could have a revolutionary impact on access to justice in jurisdictions with a less well-established judiciary. However, for such progress to be made, a substantial shift in the laws regarding adjudication, and the risks, which are explored below, must be considered.

7.2.3 Bias and Machine Learning

Machine learning uses statistical analysis to identify patterns in datasets and may therefore consider factors which are statistically relevant, but morally reprehensible, in predictions or decision-making, such as race.[43] However, by introducing legislation which requires the AI system to disregard all such characteristics – including race, sex, and gender – the removal of bias can be achieved to a far greater extent than is presently possible with human judges. Indeed, as Zuckerman argues, it is easier to deal with algorithm bias than with human unconscious bias,[44] especially as psychological studies have shown that the average individual has an unconscious bias towards different social groups,[45] likely due to complex psychological processes.[46] AI could also help

---

[41] Ibid.

[42] House of Lords, Select Committee on the Constitution, *22nd Report of Session 2019 – 21: COVID-19 and the Courts* (2021) https://publications.parliament.uk/pa/ld5801/ldselect/ldconst/257/25702.htm accessed 30 May 2021; Steve Rubley, 'Battling Court Backlogs To Ensure Access to Justice for All' *New York Law Journal* (New York, 16 April 2021) https://www.law.com/newyorklawjournal/2021/04/16/battling-court-backlogs-to-ensure-access-to-justice-for-all/ accessed 30 May 2021; Pradeep Thakur, 'Backlog of 30-year-old Cases up by 61% in 2 years' *The Times of India* (Mumbai, 16 February 2021) https://timesofindia.indiatimes.com/india/backlog-of-30-year-old-cases-up-by-61-in-2-years/articleshow/80956134.cms accessed 30 May 2021.

[43] Zuckerman, 'Artificial Intelligence' (n 1) 437.

[44] Ibid.

[45] For example, see Anthony Greenwald and Mahzarin Banaji, 'Implicit Social Cognition: Attitudes, Self-Esteem, and Stereotypes' (1995) 102 *Psychological Review* 4; John Dovidio and others, 'On the Nature of Prejudice: Automatic and Controlled Processes' (1997) 33 *Journal of Experimental Social Psychology* 510.

[46] Charles Lawrence, 'The Id, the Ego and Equal Protection: Reckoning with Unconscious Racism' in K. Crenshaw and others (eds), *Critical Race Theory: The Key Writings That Formed The Movement* (The New Press 1995) 237.

eliminate any issue caused by the 'gambler's fallacy', which has been explored in the context of asylum and immigration decisions.[47]

Some have argued that computers and machines are able to '[...] entrench pre-existing inequalities while disguised as cost-effective innovation',[48] and have suggested that the development of AI contains a white, male bias as a result of programmers predominantly being white and male.[49] However, given the appropriate safety measures of ensuring that irrelevant characteristics are not considered by the AI – a fairly simple measure – this bias can be entirely avoided.

Bias in machine learning is primarily based on the datasets which are fed to the system,[50] rather than the programmers of said system. Thus, the finding of a white, male bias – if such is to be conclusively proven – is aside from the identity of the programmers and developers themselves. Indeed, when one considers the vast legal datasets which would be used for AI systems in a legal context, it is likely that bias stemming from an individual will largely be eliminated. However, systemic bias within a judicial system, which could be present in the data set, would be more difficult to eliminate entirely, especially in common law systems based on the doctrine of precedent.

The removal of bias is eminently in the interests of access to justice: it enables people to have the opportunity to seek justice and stand equally before the law, regardless of their individual characteristics. Indeed, the European Commission for the Efficiency of Justice has endorsed the use of machine learning to combat judicial bias.[51] However, the risks of this must also not be underestimated, as explored below.

---

47 Daniel Chen, Tobias Moskowitz and Kelly Shue, 'Decision-making under the gambler's fallacy: evidence from asylum judges, loan officers and baseball umpires' (2016) NBER Working Paper No. 22026.

48 Liberty, 'Liberty Report Exposes Police Forces' Use of Discriminatory Data to Predict Crime' (*Liberty Human Rights*, 4 February 2019) https://www.libertyhumanrights.org.uk/issue/liberty-report-exposes-police-forces-use-of-discriminatory-data-to-predict-crime/ accessed 30 May 2021.

49 Stack Overflow, Developer Survey Results 2017 https://insights.stackoverflow.com/survey/2017 accessed 30 May 2021; Aliya Ram, 'The Perils of AI bias' *Financial Times* (London, 10 April 2019) https://insights.stackoverflow.com/survey/2017#overview accessed 9 November 2020.

50 Sarah Gallo, 'Eliminating bias in AI with Implicit Bias Training' (*Training Industry*, 2 September 2020) https://trainingindustry.com/articles/diversity-equity-and-inclusion/eliminating-bias-in-ai-with-implicit-bias-training/ accessed 30 May 2021.

51 European Commission for the Efficiency of Justice (CEPEJ), *European Ethical Charter on the Use of Artificial Intelligence in Judicial Systems and their environment* (2018) 9.

7.3 RISKS AND CONSIDERATIONS: A CAUTIONARY TALE?

The following section seeks to expand the risks and considerations identified by Zuckerman and analyse them through the lens of access to justice, specifically in the context of AI implementation in the judiciary. Given the lack of extensive implementation of AI in the judiciary at present,[52] these are admittedly by their very nature hypothetical. These considerations primarily apply where, if it is possible, AI will pass tests of the types set out by Zuckerman.[53] These tests include one predicated upon indistinguishability: if AI judgments, based on identical litigation materials to those presented to human judges, produced judgments which could not be distinguished in a blind valuation, that would suggest that such AI judgments are acceptable.[54] This is in essence an application of the Turing test.[55]

7.3.1 Lawyers' Loss of Skills

Before delving into the risks and considerations that arise from the potential implementation of AI into the judiciary, it is prudent to briefly address a risk which Zuckerman identified regarding the use of AI in law more generally. The potential risk is that AI will not only decrease the number employed in the legal profession, but also erode the skills of those that do enter the profession, specifically in relation to the ability to scrutinise and respond to social injustice.

Zuckerman supports this by analogy to aeroplane pilots: increasing aeroplane automation has led pilots to gain less experience in flying aeroplanes and therefore struggle to respond to unexpected emergencies.[56] Viewed through the lens of access to justice, a serious decline in skills would also cause a decline in access to justice, as lawyers would inherently become less skilled and therefore less able to deal with the more complex issues presented to them by clients. Thus, the access to justice problem may eventually be shifted from primarily – and most strongly – affecting those engaged in low-value claims, to those seeking to resolve complex cases.

This argument, in our submission, is not wholly convincing when applied to the present uses of AI in the work of lawyers generally. Admittedly, lawyers

---

52 Zuckerman primarily identifies low-value disputes governed, e.g., by eBay and Amazon.

53 Zuckerman, 'Artificial Intelligence' (n 1) 442–443.

54 Ibid., 443.

55 Alan Turing, 'Computing Machinery and Intelligence' (1950) 59 *Mind* 433.

56 Zuckerman, 'Artificial Intelligence' (n 1) 441.

may become less adept at carrying the specific tasks carried out by the AI, but this is largely restricted to document review and due diligence. Thus, the lawyer's overall skill set will likely not be diminished; indeed, it is possible and desirable that the advent of AI in the legal profession will lead to more skilled, flexible, and creative lawyers who can focus their attention on matters to which AI at present is not well equipped to handle. The lack of direct experience in due diligence work will also likely not impact the quality of the judiciary of the future, where, as in common law jurisdictions, they are frequently recruited from the ranks of lawyers.

AI cannot replicate the type of abstract thinking required in many areas of legal practice, precisely because AI cannot understand natural language – it is unable to decipher the relationship between context and meaning in the way that humans can.[57] For example, AI has been of less use in practice areas such as Mergers and Acquisitions, where deals tend to be more nuanced and complex. Therefore, the advent of artificial technology can focus solicitors' efforts on higher-order legal skills, increasing the need for creative practitioners with advanced critical thinking abilities. This may also lead to an erosion – or at least a shift in focus – of law schools focusing on teaching the basic skills and knowledge required to provide advice on and solve simple legal problems and cases. Even after natural language processing is mastered, lawyers are likely to continue evaluating and critiquing how far the new technology is responding to the needs of justice.

Conversely, the loss of a trained, independent judiciary is far more serious and can heavily impact access to justice. Improving the efficiency and cost of legal services, as argued above, undoubtedly increases access to justice and the implementation of AI in legal firms is therefore commendable for such aspects as document review and due diligence. This, in our submission, outweighs the potential risk of a loss of legal skills highlighted by Zuckerman, if such a risk would even arise.

7.3.2 Trust and Public Confidence

An integral aspect of access to justice is public confidence and trust in lawyers, the judicial system, and the law. Without justice which is seen by the public at large to be fairly administered by a trusted system, the value of access to justice is greatly reduced. It is therefore central to the discussion of the implementation of AI in a legal context. Regarding the use of AI by lawyers generally, the increased efficiency of AI and the greater processing power of computers as

[57] Ibid., 431–432.

opposed to humans is likely to further trust and confidence in the profession. However, the implementation of AI in the judiciary is more complex.

Zuckerman recognises this risk, stating that 'public opinion may never accept complete AI takeover of adjudication because of a feeling that humans should have the last word on serious constitutional, moral or economic issues that affect the lives of many'.[58] Whilst he also identifies such advantages as consistency of decisions and economic benefits,[59] we submit that the risks of using AI in the judiciary outweigh these benefits.

Zuckerman identifies the automation of disputes on platforms such as eBay and Amazon as areas where public acceptance of an automated judgment is relatively high.[60] It is our submission that this is primarily due to the nature of these disputes: low-value and straightforward, which do not have feasible alternative options of recourse. In this context, the use of AI has also been trialled in Chinese courts in an effort to improve the consistency of decisions and mitigate gaps in judicial expertise.[61] However, these disputes are fundamentally different from the challenging disputes which will often proceed to litigation: the focus on low-value, straightforward disputes should be on settlement, in order to decrease the demand for courts and thereby increase access to justice.

The following subsections explore the various factors which fall under the umbrella of potentially negatively impacting trust and public confidence in the law and therefore access to justice.

7.3.2.1 Scope of judicial discretion and development of the law

A key aspect of an independent judiciary is their ability to scrutinise and respond to social injustice and changing social attitudes. This is most strongly noticeable in common law jurisdictions subject to the doctrine of precedence and 'judge-made' law. In addition, it is most pertinent in cases of judicial discretion in the broadest sense: the reaching of a decision when the law 'runs out',[62] encompassing general principles of law which lack precise definitions and are inherently context-specific, such as proportionality, reasonableness, and equity.

Judicial decision-making itself has been characterised as 'an area of daunting complexity, where highly sophisticated legal expertise merges with

---

58 Ibid., 444.
59 Ibid., 444–445.
60 Ibid., 443.
61 Zou (n 40) 137.
62 Zuckerman, 'Artificial Intelligence' (n 1) 438.

cognitive and emotional competence'.[63] The exercise of judicial discretion is not, as a layman may think, a mere exercise of judicial whim, but rather a form of structured discretion; it is thus not inconceivable that an algorithm will be able to respond to these challenges, but at present there is no such indication that this is possible.

AI fundamentally has no ability akin to this, for it is essentially a purely logical, algorithmic process which analyses and – at its best – interprets a wide range of legislation and previous decisions in seconds. However, it is not equipped with the kind of 'moral' or 'ethical' thought processes and considerations which judges employ in cases, especially those at the fringe or forefront of the law. Thus, it is inherently unsuitable to make such decisions, and this erosion of a key function of the judiciary will, in our submission, lead to an irreparable decline in trust and public opinion of the judiciary. Moreover, there is a danger that judges may feel limited by algorithmic constraints on their ability to make decisions freely and exercise their discretion, as has already been voiced as a concern with regard to the use of AI technologies in Chinese courts.[64] Admittedly, this argument is primarily tailored towards common law jurisdictions and is less applicable to their civil law counterparts.

One may suggest that one should distinguish between equitable standards or moral considerations, which might cause us to feel in certain ways and which are necessary in providing the law with normative content, and the application of the law based on emotions. Machines will never be able to process the latter, but they are already beginning to be able to process the former. It has already been found that, using a hybrid of supervised and unsupervised learning systems, algorithms can identify patterns such as equitable considerations as a form of rule-extraction.[65] Since AI might make more fine-grained distinctions than a human judge, it has been posited to potentially be more suited to deciding cases in a case-sensitive manner.[66]

Some have suggested that AI adjudication will strengthen the attraction of codified justice over equitable justice, leading to a self-reinforcing cycle: as AI makes codified justice more appealing, the advent of codified justice (through the introduction of machine-friendly laws)[67] will in turn make AI adjudication

---

[63] Giovanni Sartor and Karl Branting, 'Introduction: Judicial Applications of Artificial Intelligence' (2020) 6 *Artificial Intelligence and Law* 105.

[64] Zou (n 40) 138.

[65] Nikola Kasabov, 'Evolving Fuzzy Neural Networks for Supervised/Unsupervised Online Knowledge-Based Learning' (2001) 31 *IEEE Transactions on Systems, Man and Cybernetics* 902.

[66] Richard Re and Alicia Solow-Niederman, 'Developing Artificially Intelligent Justice' (2019) 22 *Stanford Technology Law Review* 242, 259.

[67] Zuckerman, 'Artificial Intelligence' (n 1) 434–435.

more appealing.[68] However, even if the issue of natural language processing is solved, this will likely lead to a dehumanisation of justice. Examples of where codified justice is inherently less appealing than equitable justice is in fringe or developing areas of law, as well as areas such as child custody, where the outcome is necessarily context-specific and previous decisions do not necessarily allow for the scope of judicial discretion required to create a just outcome. Without a just outcome – which does not necessarily entail a decision that will be consistent across scenarios with similar factual matrices – there cannot be access to justice.

Practical examples which may illustrate this point are the incorporation of events and the updating of values expressed through the law in the US Supreme Court in light of the 9/11 attacks and the publicised abuse at Abu Ghraib.[69] AI judges would not be able to incorporate and update the law to accommodate social, ethical, and moral factors influenced by such events, and there is a substantial issue of separation of powers if such tasks are left to the legislature and, potentially, the programmers of the AI systems.

Whilst it is arguable that this issue is counterbalanced by the predictability of legal outcome and consistency of decisions that have been identified above, this is unsatisfactory. Zuckerman appropriately points by analogy to the use of the Video Assistant Referee system in association football and the strict interpretation of the laws of the game to a standard some would consider unreasonable.[70] Indeed, it is likely that, given the vast amounts of data that AI is able to process and use as part of its decision-making, even if AI is able to incrementally adapt the law to modern society as judges are able to, AI would have to be increasingly consulted in order to predict the outcomes of proceedings. This stems primarily from the strict logical application of the law, which can be substantially removed from human expectations, and could thereby cause an erosion of personal autonomy.[71]

Machines cannot have as nuanced an understanding of subjective and situational factors, including modern social attitudes and policy concerns, that are so instructive to judges in the exercise of their discretion. As Zuckerman rightly emphasises,[72] this will likely lead to a distrust of the process of justice.[73]

---

[68] Re and Solow-Niederman (n 66) 261.

[69] Ibid., 269; Linda Greenhouse, 'The Supreme Court: Detainees; Access to Courts' *New York Times* (New York, 29 June 2004) https://www.nytimes.com/2004/06/29/us/the-supreme-court-detainees-access-to-courts.html accessed 30 May 2021.

[70] Zuckerman, 'Artificial Intelligence' (n 1) 450.

[71] Ibid.

[72] Ibid., 451.

[73] Frederick Wilmot-Smith, *Equal Justice* (Harvard University Press 2019) 1.

7.3.2.2 Issue of appeal

The issue of appeal was also highlighted as a key area of concern by Zuckerman.[74] Were an AI system of adjudication to be established, the system of appeal would inevitably be eroded. As Zuckerman has convincingly argued, it would make no sense for a separate AI to appeal an AI judgment, for 'there would be no point in using an inferior AI system at first instance, if better ones were available'.[75] Thus, human appeal of AI decisions is the only reasonable system of appeal.

On the face of it, human appeal of AI decisions is an attractive proposition. It would enable the judiciary to maintain its control over AI and to appropriately direct decisions on appeal. However, as Zuckerman notes, AI systems are vastly more powerful and can comprehend, analyse, and use a far greater amount of data than a human judge. Thus, there are two main issues from a technical standpoint: firstly, that human review could induce error; and secondly that the manner in which AI – using machine learning – reaches decisions is so complex as to be incomprehensible to a human audience.[76]

With regards to the former, a human review of an AI decision would require both parties to agree to submit the case to a human judge, due to some perceived error in the decision. Whilst this, by itself, is not a severe issue, it could lead to a lack of trust in the AI's capacity to make decisions and could lead to a rise in appeals sought. Moreover, when considered in conjunction with the latter issue, it is apparent that human review may be diminished and, in the long term, potentially unworkable. In response to this, there is a severe danger that AI systems will be programmed to deliver 'automated rationalisations' of decisions, which sound plausible to a human audience, but which do not reflect the AI's actual decision-making process.[77]

If there is no appeal process, then the courts would arguably suffer a crisis of legitimacy, which would cause public confidence to sink.[78] An essential part of public confidence in the judicial process is the adaption of the law to suit the individual circumstances of the case and the consideration and implementation of modern social attitudes and to give the losing party the opportunity to persuade a higher court that an error of law has been made. [79] Without a system of appeal, which can only be performed by human judges, confidence

---

[74] Zuckerman, 'Artificial Intelligence' (n 1) 445–446.

[75] Ibid., 445.

[76] Re and Solow-Niederman (n 66) 260.

[77] Ibid., 261.

[78] Tom Tyler, *Why People Obey the Law* (Princeton University Press 2006) 31–33; Zuckerman, 'Artificial Intelligence' (n 1) 451.

[79] Zuckerman, 'Artificial Intelligence' (n 1) 445; Joseph Raz, *The Authority of Law: Essays on Law and Morality* (OUP 1979) 180.

will therefore decrease, and access to justice will be hindered. Indeed, if such appeals are possible, notwithstanding the aforementioned difficulties, then appeals may be sought with an even higher frequency than at present, and any benefit in terms of efficiency would thereby be lost. Moreover, there exists an inherent danger in enabling machines to make binding legal decisions of influence without the possibility for human control.[80] These risks include the potential inability to properly consider social attitudes and elements of modern ethics and morality when applying historical judicial decisions or principles, particularly in common law jurisdictions. A binding decision without human control may not account for the wide discretion often given to judges, as for example in the application of equitable principles.

7.3.2.3 Adversarial system

Zuckerman argues persuasively that a judicial adoption of AI adjudication would likely lead to a collapse of the adversarial system,[81] and there is little further to add substantively. However, it is an interesting and important proposition from the perspective of access to justice and public confidence in the judicial system. If litigants are unable to have their day in court – an event which litigants often strive for, and the importance of which is recognised in the fundamental right to be heard[82] – then public confidence will likely fall.

Furthermore, the subjective, social, and in essence performative aspect of the court process and its value in the public representation of the process of justice will disappear. It is this aspect which, whilst perhaps not quantifiable, is often of substantial importance to the aggrieved parties. If parties, through the potential erosion of the adversarial system, do not feel that justice is achievable or that justice is not publicly seen to be performed, access to justice will be impaired. The loss of the adversarial system would also heavily impact the ability of the future judiciary: an important concern if, as above, they would be required to act as appellate judges for AI judgments.

In summary, the above factors would likely impact the public confidence and trust in the judicial process. This will inherently have a knock-on effect on access to justice, which will likely be significantly worsened. Whilst this may

---

80 Adesina Bello, 'Online Dispute Resolution Algorithm: The Artificial Intelligence Model as a Pinnacle' (2018) 84 *Arbitration* 159, 163; Arno Lodder and John Zeleznikow, *Enhanced Dispute Resolution Through the Use of Information Technology* (CUP 2010).

81 Zuckerman, 'Artificial Intelligence' (n 1) 447–449.

82 As exemplified, e.g., in Art 41(2)(a) of the Charter of Fundamental Rights of the EU, which states that the right to good administration (Art 41) includes: 'the right of every person to be heard, before any individual measure which would affect him or her adversely is taken'.

be felt more strongly in common law jurisdictions operating under a precedential system, its effects would also be felt in civil law jurisdictions, particularly in relation to appeal and the adversarial system.

7.3.3 Bias

The advantages of the ability of an AI system to eradicate any bias – conscious or unconscious – which may otherwise be present in human judges is commendable. However, the way in which an AI machine learning adjudicatory system would function would also thereby entail substantial changes to present legal norms.

If, as posited above, characteristics such as gender, sex, or race would not be taken into account by the algorithm, so too would the current protection of such protected characteristics in, for example, employment disputes or cases concerning anti-discrimination laws. It could also impact the operation of the family courts: an article published in 2006 found that 93 per cent of sole residence awards were made to mothers on the basis of their gender.[83] With an AI not taking these characteristics into account, the effect of a 'no bias' process and decisions could be widely felt.

It has also been suggested that gender bias in AI applications may 'have the potential of spreading and reinforcing harmful gender stereotypes [and] further stigmatising and marginalising women on a global scale'.[84] This view is predicated on AI datasets having gender biases:[85] however, as above, it must be a consideration of the legal datasets specifically that will be applied in order to determine whether such bias would also exist in the application of AI in the legal sector. Notwithstanding this, the emphases on the importance of developing pedagogy to advance the digital skills of women and young girls in these reports are essential to combatting this bias if it is also found in legal datasets.

It is difficult to determine whether the removal of bias would impact access to justice negatively. On the other hand, it is an admirable aim and one upon which the rule of law is predicated, through the key principle of equality before the law; on the other, the removal of the consideration of protected characteristics could cause substantial shifts in the present law – particularly in areas

---

83 Sandra Kielty, 'Similarities and Differences in the Experiences of Non-Resident Mothers and Non-Resident Fathers' (2006) 20 *International Journal of Law, Policy and the Family* 74.

84 United Nations Educational, Scientific and Cultural Organization (UNESCO), *Artificial Intelligence and Gender Equality: Key findings of UNESCO's Global Dialogue* (2020) 4.

85 United Nations Educational, Scientific and Cultural Organization (UNESCO), *I'd blush if I could: closing gender divides in digital skills through education* (2019).

of family law, for example – and therefore requires detailed consideration and a wholesale adoption may not be suitable. Again, this emphasises the need for the law – and its servants in the form of the judiciary – to remain human.

7.4 LOOKING AHEAD – THE FUTURE OF AI AND ACCESS TO JUSTICE

7.4.1 Disparity in Technology

The above discussion has examined AI in a rather abstracted and hypothetical way, concerned primarily with the impact of the adoption of AI in the judiciary. However, a key element which has not been considered thus far is the technological requirements for implementation.

Developed countries, whilst still having access to justice issues, are generally far further progressed and have the infrastructure to support the types of AI implementation considered here. On the other hand, although developing countries would benefit heavily from further technological innovations to ensure access to justice and mitigating the disparity in judicial ability is an honourable aim,[86] the resources and infrastructure needed for AI implementation and technological support are not within reach at present.[87]

Thus, even if AI can assist with improving access to justice in developed countries (if we are cautious in our assessment of the risks involved), it is unlikely to be of substantial assistance in the developing areas of the world, where access to justice is arguably poorest.[88] Technology, including AI, may assist to bridge the access to justice gaps, but one cannot solve access to justice solely with technological advancements.

[86] See, e.g., the use of AI-enabled Smart Courts in China: Zou (n 40) 135, 137.

[87] Nancy Siboe, 'Use of Artificial Intelligence by the Judiciary in the Face of COVID-19' *Oxford Human Rights Hub* (Oxford, 9th April 2020) https://ohrh.law.ox.ac.uk/use-of-artificial-intelligence-by-the-judiciary-in-the-face-of-covid-19/ accessed 30 May 2021.

[88] Alessandra Bergamin, '5 Billion People Around the World Lack Basic Access to Justice. These Organizations Are Out to Change That' *Ensia* (University of Minnesota, 9 January 2020) https://ensia.com/features/environmental-justice-access-to-justice-legal-empowerment/ accessed 30 June 2021; Kate Hodal, 'Poor Bear the Brunt as Global Injustice System Fails 5.1 Billion People – study' *Guardian* (29 April 2019) https://www.theguardian.com/global-development/2019/apr/29/global-justice-system-fails-5-billion-people-study accessed 30 June 2021.

7.4.2 Mitigation of Risks

If, as Zuckerman suggests, 'the use of technology in legal services is set to expand due to its undoubted advantages',[89] notwithstanding the risks considered above, it is prudent to suggest several approaches which may minimise or mitigate these risks.

The first approach concerns the use of AI and associated technologies by lawyers more generally. Regulations to control its expansion across different jurisdictions will likely arise as a result of increasing AI usage, but requirements to keep abreast of new developments in the technology itself would perhaps partially alleviate the issues, such as loss of skills, caused by the adoption of AI technology. Indeed, the American Bar Association's Model Rules of Professional Conduct already require that a lawyer should keep up to date with new developments in legal practice 'including the benefits and risks associated with relevant technology'.[90] Irrespective of whether similar provisions will be included in other jurisdictions and the Legal Professional Conduct Rules of EU Member States, the requirements of adaptability and lifelong learning will be retained by future lawyers. The education of future lawyers in AI and its uses has already begun, with new postgraduate courses on Law and Technology and changes in undergraduate syllabi beginning to appear.[91]

The second approach, and perhaps the most important with regard to the implementation of AI in the judiciary, is the need for strong, apposite legislation. As explored in the sections on bias, in order to improve access to justice it is advisable to require the AI systems to disregard individual protected characteristics, such as race, sex, or gender. This can be performed best through legislation, particularly as it is commercially unreasonable to require AI systems to be open-source as 'private companies regard their algorithm as key proprietary software that is protected'.[92] A report published by the European Commission for the Efficiency of Justice has also emphasised that it is insufficient to identify algorithm bias and take measures to limit it; rather, awareness of such issues must also be raised and pursued amongst stakeholders.[93]

---

[89] Zuckerman, 'Artificial Intelligence' (n 1) 453.

[90] ABA Model Rules of Professional Conduct, Rule 1.1.

[91] For example, at the University of Oxford, where the undergraduate Jurisprudence syllabus has been updated to include an option on 'Law, regulation and technology'.

[92] The Committee of Experts on internet intermediaries (MSI-NET), *Algorithms and Human Rights: Study on the human dimensions of automated data processing techniques and possible regulatory implications,* Council of Europe study DGI(2017)12, 38.

[93] European Commission for the Efficiency of Justice (CEPEJ), *European Ethical Charter on the Use of Artificial Intelligence in Judicial Systems and their environment* (2018) 9.

Whilst it is accepted that legislation is required for AI to be used in the judiciary, such legislation must restrict and confine the use of AI to, at most, ancillary use in order to preserve the adversarial system which Zuckerman rightly fears would be destroyed by a wholesale adoption of AI.[94] Zuckerman's comments on the encroaching nature of AI once introduced are pertinent here.[95] If such systems are introduced, Zuckerman's comments necessitate legislation that officially and exclusively restricts AI to ancillary use to prevent the replacement of the judiciary by AI in the future, given the adoption and implementation of AI in adjudication, even if only as an aid.

7.5 CONCLUSION

From the above, it is apparent that the implementation of AI in the judiciary is a controversial and complicated issue, which deserves further attention and discussion. It is accepted that the implementation of AI and associated technologies into the working lives of lawyers generally is a positive step which will assist in alleviating the oftentimes prohibitive cost of seeking legal advice and representation by increasing efficiency and unburdening lawyers, thereby inevitably assisting in advancing access to justice. AI's ability to combat and eliminate bias and improve the consistency of decisions is also admirable, albeit not without its issues.

However, the risks associated with the implementation of AI in the judicial sphere, including the issues of trust and public acceptance, appeal, discretion, and to some extent bias and its elimination, at present outweigh the advantages which may be gleaned from such implementation. This balancing exercise should be continually reviewed to determine what forms of implementation are appropriate, but there appear to be no solutions at present to Zuckerman's arguments relating to the demise of the adversarial system should AI be adopted as more than a merely ancillary tool.[96] In any event, it is submitted that strong legislation, particularly with regard to bias and strictly controlling the use of AI in the judiciary to ensure that it does not unduly encroach on the role of judges, is required in order to ensure effective implementation of any form.

The current discussion of AI implementation also does not sufficiently account for the issues of implementation in developing countries, where access to justice at present is often far worse than in developed countries. Furthermore, the impact of any AI implementation on alternative dispute resolution, such as arbitration and mediation, and their rising popularity, as well as any impacts on

94 Zuckerman, 'Artificial Intelligence' (n 1) 447–449.
95 Ibid., 447.
96 Ibid., 452.

criminal procedure, must also be considered to avoid the creation of a disparate and fragmented legal system.

The key aspect which must be advanced is access to justice in which the public rightly has trust and confidence. In some developing countries with justice systems rife with corruption and bias, an AI judiciary – or at the very least a human judiciary assisted by AI – may well be transformative in the field of access to justice. Nevertheless, the risks and considerations highlighted above must not be underestimated, nor will an AI system likely entirely solve the issues of corruption and bias. Some retention of the adversarial system is likely to be required and a complete adoption of AI courts is therefore unacceptable for serious civil litigation, although it is accepted that it may become the norm for low-value disputes[97] in the same way that machine adjudication by eBay and Amazon has become publicly accepted.

To conclude, Zuckerman's emphasis in the final paragraph of his paper on extracting the benefit of AI without 'undermining the foundations of our legal and social institutions' is key:[98] for as Nobel Peace Prize winner Christian Lous Lange has stated, '[t]echnology is a useful servant but a dangerous master'.[99] The time for judicial implementation of AI is not yet upon us and greater discourse on this topic alongside and intertwined with the development of ever-more advanced AI systems is necessary to ensure that access to justice – and the rule of law – is advanced throughout both the developed and developing world.

---

[97] Specifically, it has been suggested, for 'simple civil cases, possibly personal injury cases and certainly very simple contractual matters': Jemma Slingo referring to the prediction by Tania Sourdin in 'IBA 2020: Robots Don Black Cap for Lower Court Judges' *The Law Society Gazette* (9 November 2020) https://www.lawgazette.co.uk/news/iba-2020-robots-don-black-cap-for-lower-court-judges/5106337.article#:~:text=Lower%20court%20judges%20are%20likely,a%20'judge%20AI%20revolution accessed 30 May 2021.

[98] Zuckerman, 'Artificial Intelligence' (n 1) 453.

[99] Christian Lange, 'Internationalism' (*Nobel Lecture*, 1921) https://www.nobelprize.org/prizes/peace/1921/lange/lecture/ accessed 30 May 2021.

8. Automating due process – the promise and challenges of AI-based techniques in consumer online dispute resolution[1]

Martin Ebers

8.1 INTRODUCTION

8.1.1 Overview

Consumer Online Dispute Resolution (ODR) is becoming increasingly automated, especially in Alternative Dispute Resolution (ADR) schemes, which are replacing courts as the main redress providers in many areas. In the past, most solutions consisted of hand-coded systems relying on simple algorithms. More recent ODR systems are based on Artificial Intelligence (AI), in particular Machine Learning (ML) and Natural Language Processing (NLP), in order to structure communication, provide smart case management, gather information, diagnose problems, predict outcomes, influence negotiations, limit bias, reduce unrealistic settlement points and facilitate the resolution of the dispute. The use of AI-based techniques in Consumer ODR creates opportunities for consumers and redress systems in general, but also raises concerns in terms of fair trial rights and due process standards. Accordingly, this chapter presents a critical evaluation of AI systems in Consumer ODR, dealing especially with the extent to which AI systems can meet or violate due process standards and the question of whether there is a need to regulate the role of AI in Consumer ODR. Since AI systems are expected to become widespread mainly in the extra-judicial ADR area, but not in formal judicial proceedings,[2] this chapter focuses primarily on ADR out-of-court redress.

---

[1] This work was supported by a Center for Advanced Internet Studies (CAIS) grant.

[2] Cf also Council of the EU, Council Conclusions 'Access to Justice – Seizing the Opportunities of Digitalisation', Brussels, 8 October 2020, 11599/20, Nos. 33ff. Although the Council recognizes that AI has the potential to improve the functioning of justice systems, it underlines at the same time that its use must not interfere with the

The remainder of this chapter is structured as follows. Section 8.1 describes the general disruptive effects of technology on consumer redress and dispute resolution, as evidenced by the emergence of a large number of consumer disputes, but also by the rise of Consumer ODR, which offers a new set of AI-based tools and techniques for addressing conflict through the application of automated processes further discussed in section 8.2. Section 8.3 analyses the promise and challenges that AI brings to Consumer ODR. Section 8.4 specifically addresses the procedural and non-procedural safeguards of consumer due process and questions the applicability of the 'right to fair trial' to out-of-court ODR. The paper concludes in section 8.5 with a critical discussion of future directions of ODR, including the latest proposals of the European Commission on regulating AI systems and digital platforms.

8.1.2 Disruption of Consumer Redress by Technology

Technological disruption has been characterized as an external factor that pressures companies to innovate existing business models and value chains.[3] Additionally, disruptive technologies have often been described as the enablers of simplified, convenient and affordable products and services, which in turn are achieved through the creation of new business structures.[4] Technological advancements in the context of consumer protection are altering not only the ways consumers interact with businesses but also the ways they generate and even resolve disputes. The speed of the internet and the immediacy of transactions have empowered and boosted the confidence of consumers, and even simplified the business models for entering into transactions. However, the redress mechanisms offered by public or private actors to consumers have not evolved in a similarly progressive way.[5] Judicial means of resolving disputes are often inaccessible or suboptimal for consumer claims due to jurisdictional limitations, lengthy time frames and other procedural intricacies.

---

decision-making power of judges or judicial independence or infringe upon the right to a fair trial and effective remedy.

[3] Jaehun Lee, Taewon Suh, Daniel Roy and Mellisa Baucus, 'Emerging Technology and Business Model Innovation: The Case of Artificial Intelligence' (2019) 5(3) *Journal of Open Innovation: Technology Market and Complexity* 1–13 https://www.mdpi.com/500892 accessed 28 September 2021.

[4] Alessio Cozzolino, Gianmario Verona and Frank T. Rothaermel, 'Unpacking the Disruption Process: New Technology, Business Models, and Incumbent Adaptation' (2018) 55(7) *Journal of Management Studies* 1166–202 https://www.scheller.gatech.edu/directory/faculty/rothaermel/pubs/2018_JMS.pdf accessed 28 September 2021.

[5] Amy J. Schmitz and Colin Rule, *The New Handshake: Online Dispute Resolution and the Future of Consumer Protection* (American Bar Association Press 2017) 4.

The United Nations (UN) Guidelines for Consumer Protection of 1985 (UNGCP), as the first manifestation of international consensus in the development of consumer law along with other 'legitimate needs', also listed 'the availability of effective consumer redress' as one of the so-called seven consumer rights.[6] The ideological commitment of the UN to consumer protection was later influenced by the rise of e-commerce. Hence, the revised UNGCP of 2015 expanded the section on consumer redress, aiming to facilitate access to justice by transforming traditional redress mechanisms towards a broader access-to-justice paradigm, especially in the field of low-cost business-to-consumer (B2C) disputes.[7] This shift intends to give prominence to the development of alternative methods of resolving disputes over traditional judicial 'redress',[8] which, considering the linear, unadaptable and complex nature of court proceedings, is often thought to be a barrier to delivering 'expeditious, fair, transparent, inexpensive and accessible'[9] mechanisms of dispute resolution. However, UNGCP is not the only ideological commitment to consumer protection influenced by digitalization. The complexity of transforming and re-engineering courts has also encouraged European Union (EU) policymakers to think of non-judicial private dispute resolution schemes for consumer redress, leading inter alia to the adoption of the ADR Directive[10] and the ODR Regulation.[11]

---

[6] The United Nations General Assembly, Consumer protection: resolution/adopted by the General Assembly, 16 April 1985 (A/RES/39/248, UNGCP 1985) Section II, 3(f) https://undocs.org/en/A/RES/39/248 accessed 28 September 2021. The UNGCP 1985 was later expanded by the Economic and Social Council in resolution 1999/7 of 26 July 1999, and revised and adopted by the General Assembly in resolution 70/186 of 22 December 2015.

[7] Iris Benöhr, 'The United Nations Guidelines for Consumer Protection: Legal Implications and New Frontiers' (2020) 43 *Journal of Consumer Policy* 105–124.

[8] The United Nations Conference on Trade and Development (UNCTAD 2017), Manual on Consumer Protection (Geneva, United Nations 2017) 83–88, https://unctad.org/webflyer/manual-consumer-protection accessed 28 September 2021.

[9] The United Nations Conference on Trade and Development (UNCTAD 2016), Guidelines for Consumer Protection (New York and Geneva, United Nations 2016), Section V(F), para 37, 15 https://unctad.org/system/files/official-document/ditccplpmisc2016d1_en.pdf accessed 28 September 2021.

[10] Directive 2013/11/EU of the European Parliament and of the Council of 21 May 2013 on alternative dispute resolution for consumer disputes and amending Regulation (EC) No 2006/2004 and Directive 2009/22/EC (Directive on consumer ADR) [2013] OJ L 165/63.

[11] Regulation (EU) No 524/2013 of the European Parliament and of the Council of 21 May 2013 on online dispute resolution for consumer disputes and amending Regulation (EC) No 2006/2004 and Directive 2009/22/EC (Regulation on consumer ODR) [2013] OJ L 165/1.

8.1.3 ODR as a Disruptive Factor

ODR as a consumer-dispute-handling mechanism made its debut in the 1990s in parallel with the development and use of the World Wide Web, which increased online transactions and thereby disputes related to such transactions. The disruptive potential of ODR in the delivery of dispute resolution services has been classified by Rabinovich-Einy and Katsh[12] in terms of three main shifts, namely: (i) the shift from a physical environment to a virtual one; (ii) the shift from human intervention and decision-making to process automation; and (iii) the shift from a privacy-favorable setting to a data-driven environment. The second dimension – related to limiting human decision-making and empowering algorithmic systems – looks promising for reducing human bias[13] but casts doubt on the fairness of the process itself.[14]

One additional aspect of law disrupted by the emergence of ODR is the enforcement of decisions delivered by dispute resolution.[15] Modern forms of technology-driven private enforcement mechanisms go beyond the earlier models of private ADR, which still relied on state enforcement when necessary.

8.1.4 AI as a Disruptive Factor

As a conflict-handling mechanism that uses technology to facilitate the resolution of disputes,[16] ODR has shown potential to become one of the most targeted areas of AI-driven architectural and conceptual transformation.

First, AI as a tool has the potential to gradually develop ODR and help consumers and businesses to obtain the best possible results in solving industry-specific disputes. Second, in the most revolutionary scenario, autonomous AI-based ODR systems might convert from fictional hypotheses into the best practices required to handle consumer complaints. The ODR system of eBay is a prominent example of such a 'paradigmatic' system, as it 'goes beyond the use of individual tools'.[17] Unlike simple communication and case

---

[12] Orna Rabinovich-Einy and Ethan Katsh, 'A New Relationship between Public and Private Dispute Resolution: Lessons from Online Dispute Resolution' (2017) 32(4) *Ohio State Journal on Dispute Resolution* 695–723, 717.

[13] Ibid.

[14] Tal Z Zarsky, 'The Trouble with Algorithmic Decisions: An Analytic Road Map to Examine Efficiency and Fairness in Automated and Opaque Decision Making' (2012) 41(1) *Science, Technologies and Human Values* 118–32, 122–23.

[15] Riikka Koulu, *Law, Technology and Dispute Resolution, Privatisation of Coercion* (Taylor & Francis 2019).

[16] Ethan Katsh and Janet Rifkin, *Online Dispute Resolution: Resolving Conflicts in Cyberspace* (1st edn, Jossey-Bass 2001).

[17] Rabinovich-Einy and Katsh (n 12) 712.

management tools, the eBay system uses data to explore patterns of disputes and generates opportunities not only for solutions but also for conflict prevention.[18] Consequently, AI as an autonomous dispute resolution mechanism could severely disrupt the existing ODR schemes.

Overall, AI as a disruptive technological factor is capable of both the evolutionary sequential transition of ODR on the one hand, and a revolutionary 'turnaround' of the whole spectrum of consumer redress mechanisms on the other.[19] However, no technology can be disruptive without human activities, and AI as an external force of change is deeply social[20] in that the scale of its deployment in Consumer ODR will significantly depend on the actions of various stakeholders.

8.2 THE USE OF AI IN CONSUMER ODR

8.2.1 What is ODR?

ODR systems are constantly evolving. At a preliminary stage, the term ODR referred mostly to the usage of Information and Communications Technology (ICT) tools enabling parties to resolve their disputes. The United Nations Commission on International Trade Law (UNCITRAL) in its Technical Notes of 2017 on Online Dispute Resolution defined ODR as a 'mechanism for resolving disputes through the use of electronic communications and other information and communication technology'.[21] Hence, in light of this broad definition and the first generation of tools deployed, ODR has often been described as a mirrored version of ADR assisted principally with ICT tools.[22]

---

18 Steve Abernethy, 'Building Large-Scale Online Dispute Resolution and Trustmark Systems' (Proceedings of the United Nations Economic Commission for Europe (UNECE) Forum on ODR, Geneva, Switzerland, 30 June-1 July 2003) https://www.mediate.com/Integrating/docs/Abernethy.pdf accessed 28 September 2021.

19 On technological developments as disruptive forces see also Philip Boucher and others, European Parliamentary Research Service (EPRS), Disruption by Technology, PE 652.079, (2020) https://www.europarl.europa.eu/RegData/etudes/IDAN/2020/652079/EPRS_IDA(2020)652079_EN.pdf accessed 28 September 2021.

20 The social construction of technologies is further explained by Philip Boucher, EPRS, 'What if all technologies were inherently social?', PE 614.552, (2018) https://www.europarl.europa.eu/RegData/etudes/ATAG/2018/614552/EPRS_ATA(2018)614552_EN.pdf accessed 28 September 2021.

21 The United Nations, United Nations Commission on International Trade Law (UNCITRAL), *Technical Notes on Online Dispute Resolution section* (UNCITRAL Secretariat, 2017) Section V, para 24.

22 Gabrielle Kaufmann-Kohler and Thomas Schultz, *Online Dispute Resolution: Challenges for Contemporary Justice* (Kluwer Law International 2004) 5; Colin Rule, 'Is ODR ADR? A Response to Carrie-Menkel-Meadow' (2016) *International*

By contrast, the new generation of ODR systems holds immense potential to improve the dispute resolution experience through intelligent decision support systems, smart negotiation tools, automated resolution and ML. This new technological dimension of deploying ODR systems, which is largely based on AI techniques, will probably lead to totally new forms of dispute resolution. AI as an autonomous 'fourth party'[23] in ODR also shows the feasibility of slowly taking the place of the 'third party' and providing a comprehensive redress for consumers throughout the lifecycle of a dispute.

8.2.2 What is AI?

Despite the increased interest in AI, there is no consensus around its definition. According to some commentators, AI concerns 'the study of the design of intelligent agents'.[24] In the latter context, an intelligent agent is 'something that perceives and acts' and is capable of making rational decisions.[25] In the regulatory context, according to the European Commission's Communication on AI, the term AI 'refers to systems that display intelligent behavior by analyzing their environment and taking actions – with some degree of autonomy – to achieve specific goals'.[26]

Moreover, on 21 April 2021, the European Commission published a Proposal for an Artificial Intelligence Act (AIA-Proposal)[27] which represents a momentous step in its continuous strategy for AI aimed at putting European values at its centre. The AIA-Proposal suggests a future-proof definition of AI systems and defines them as: 'software that is developed with one or more of the techniques and approaches listed in Annex I and can, for a given set of human-defined objectives, generate outputs such as content, predictions, recommendations, or decisions influencing the environments they interact with'.[28] Annex I further lays down a list of AI techniques and approaches such

---

Journal on Online Dispute Resolution 8–11 http://www.colinrule.com/writing/ijodr.pdf accessed 28 September 2021.

23 The concept of technology as the 'fourth party' was originally introduced by Ethan Katsh and Janet Rifkin in their book *Online Dispute Resolution* (n 16) where they describe technology as the fourth party sitting at the dispute resolution table.

24 Peter Norvig and Stuart J Russell, *Artificial Intelligence: A Modern Approach* (3rd edn, Pearson Education Inc 2009) 2.

25 Ibid., 4.

26 European Commission, 'Communication on Artificial Intelligence for Europe', COM(2018) 237 final.

27 Proposal for Regulation of the European Parliament of the Council Laying Down Harmonised Rules on Artificial Intelligence (Artificial Intelligence Act) and Amending Certain Union Legislative Acts, COM(2021) 206 final.

28 Art 3(1) AIA-Proposal.

as ML, logic and knowledge-based and statistical. The decision for choosing such a broad definition might be justified by policy intentions to keep up with rapid developments in the field.

8.2.3 AI as a Tool for Communication and Case Management

If there is a conclusion that can be drawn today, it is that the technological functionalities of AI in Consumer ODR have not been fully exploited. Nevertheless, even the first generations of ODR mechanisms were technologically assisted by the functional capabilities of communication and case management. Zeleznikow identified these capabilities as crucial requisites for building a user-centric ODR system. According to him, an intelligent and user-centric ODR system ideally integrates the following six aspects: case management; triaging; advisory tools; communication tools; decision support tools; and drafting software.[29]

From a psychological point of view, communication is a cornerstone of the process of negotiation and dispute resolution. The reliance of globalized consumers located in different jurisdictions upon digital technologies has pushed ODR providers to integrate chatbots and other AI-based conversational interfaces in consumer dispute resolution. Thus, the use of conversational agents in ODR not only facilitates communication between disputants but also performs additional functions – for example, appeal drafting. One of the plausible examples of successfully deployed chatbots in ODR is 'DoNotPay', a system created by 19-year-old British programmer, Joshua Browder.[30] Users of the system who have created an account can communicate with a chatbot and ask questions about the parking ticket they want to appeal. The chatbot which also acts as an AI lawyer automatically generates appeals for users who may have a valid claim.

Smart case management systems can also motivate consumers to give preference to private ODR providers for redress. Such a system should have the functional capabilities of entering information, collecting relevant data and template-based initiation of disputes.[31] Users of these systems 'should be able to initiate the conflict, continuously access the data and be aware of timelines they need to meet, what documents are required at specific times,

[29] John Zeleznikow, 'Using Artificial Intelligence to provide Intelligent Dispute Resolution Support' (2021) 30 *Group Decision and Negotiation* 789–812.

[30] 'Appeal Parking Tickets in Any City, Contest California Parking Tickets' (*DoNotPay*) https://donotpay.com/learn/california-parking-tickets/ accessed 28 September 2021.

[31] Zeleznikow (n 29).

and the progress of the case'.[32] The broad architectural spectrum of AI-based case management includes e-filing, document repository, end-to-end case management systems and other tools. Modria is one of the ODR providers whose cloud-based, software-as-a-service (SaaS) platform – together with the modules of diagnosis, negotiation, mediation and arbitration – offers users case management and workflow systems that handle case intake, document generation, scheduling, reporting and status messaging.[33]

8.2.4 Information Gathering and Problem Analysis

Any rational approach to problem-solving requires information for understanding the problem that needs to be resolved. Information collection activities rely on input from third parties such as consumers and businesses; consequently, the efficiency of the dispute resolution outcome also depends on the critical skill of asking proper questions. The role of smart data collection in modern ODR schemes can be enhanced by interactive and self-administered interviewing systems.[34] For instance, the Ontology-driven Data Acquisition system (ODA)[35] which selects relevant questions depending on the disputants' responses combines two main components: (i) an ontological structure that is responsible for the modelling of juridical knowledge related to a specific domain and (ii) a logical engine aiming at exploring the ontological structure for producing questions and collecting responses to/from the dispute parties. Additionally, the use of such logical engines enables Consumer ODR to use context-sensitive adaptive questionnaires for information gathering and increase the overall user-friendliness of the system.

Apart from information gathering, problem diagnosis also plays a critical role in ODR. AI-based techniques for problem analysis enable early-stage

---

32 Ibid., 807.

33 'Modria is the Complete ODR Solution' (*Tyler Technologies*, 2007) https://www.tylertech.com/Products/Modria/Modria-Feature-Comparison-ChArtpdf accessed 28 September 2021.

34 Elisabetta Fersini and others, 'eMediation – Towards Smart Online Dispute Resolution' (2014) Proceedings of the International Conference on Knowledge Management and Information Sharing - KMIS 228–236 https://www.semanticscholar.org/paper/eMediation-Towards-Smart-Online-Dispute-Resolution-Fersini-Messina/778abbd180d8a43d3aa8afb19cbd30c60cad18ce accessed 28 September 2021.

35 Daniele Toti and others, 'Ontology-driven Data Acquisition: Intelligent Support to Legal ODR System' (2013) *Frontiers in Artificial Intelligence and Applications* 25–28 https://www.semanticscholar.org/paper/Ontology-driven-Data-Acquisition%3A-Intelligent-to-Arosio-Bagnara/b20911cfc24d134b6d828249d7eac74211c87c42 accessed 28 September 2021.

resolution of disputes even in the diagnosis phase.[36] It is also possible in the diagnosis phase to provide consumers with access to data related to resolutions achieved in similar kinds of cases. The latter will help users to build their expectations and even shape the so-called Zone of Potential Agreement (ZOPA).[37]

8.2.5 Negotiation Support and Blind-bidding Systems

The first generation of Negotiation Support Systems (NSSs), contrary to contemporary ones, did not explicitly use AI techniques and was mostly template-based. 'Split-up' was the first system that provided negotiation support based on ML.[38] The Split-up system was capable of advising users about the distribution of marital property as a consequence of separation in Australia and its initial goal was not negotiation support. However, when presenting the system to legal professionals, the developers found the Split-up design well-suited to supporting negotiation. In particular, the system can advise the parties about their respective Best Alternative to a Negotiated Agreement (BATNAs) and hence facilitate the dispute resolution.[39] Other ODR providers, namely FamilyWinner and AssetDivider, facilitate dispute resolution using decision analysis techniques and trade-off strategies.[40]

Some ODR providers are also offering blind-bidding processes where an automated algorithm evaluates bids from parties, assessing whether they are within a prescribed range to settle the case. In the field of ODR, blind-bidding systems are sometimes also referred to as expert systems.[41] However, unlike advanced expert systems, blind-bidding systems 'do not arrive at conclusions on the basis of reasoning with rules (as expert systems do), but merely apply a simple algorithm to determine whether offer and counter-offer are within a certain pre-defined range'.[42]

---

36 Colin Rule, 'Online Dispute Resolution and the Future of Justice' (2020) 16 *Annual Review of Law and Social Science* 277–292.

37 Ibid.

38 See Zeleznikow (n 29); John Zeleznikow 'The Split-Up Project: Induction, Context and Knowledge Discovery in Law' (2004) 3 *Law, Probability and Risk* 147–168.

39 Zeleznikow (n 29).

40 Brooke Abrahams, Emilia Bellucci and John Zeleznikow, 'Incorporating Fairness into Development of an Integrated Multi-agent Online Dispute Resolution Environment' (2012) 21(1) *Group Decision and Negotiation* 3–28.

41 Esther van den Heuvel, 'Online Dispute Resolution as a Solution to Cross-border Disputes. An Introduction to ODR (Master thesis, Utrecht University 2000) 8.

42 Arno R. Lodder and Ernest M. Thiessen, 'The Role of Artificial Intelligence in Online Dispute Resolution' (2003) Proceedings of the UNECE Forum on ODR 2003,

8.2.6 Argumentation Support Tools and Decision Support Systems

Just as legal argumentation is central to courtroom dispute settlement systems, it occupies a significant place in extra-judicial ADR and ODR. A dialogue system is an argumentation support tool which intends to help parties in ODR by improving the structure of the information exchanged between them.[43] In this system, statements made by parties in natural language are classified into three different categories: issues; supporting statements; and attacking statements.[44] The dialogue system can bring forward the statements of the complainant and the respondent in a structured and concise way. Such argumentation support tools might be helpful not only in dispute resolution but also in negotiations. However, the role of these tools in negotiation might be different insofar as the primary goal of the latter is to satisfy the interests of parties instead of just obtaining their positions.[45] Hence, 'successful negotiations with an argument support tool depend on parties approaching the task with the right attitude, i.e., attacking the problem rather than each other'.[46]

Decision Support Systems (DSS) involve two main types of systems: the first one that collects relevant information from raw data and the second one that is a complex system suggesting the best strategy for the fairest outcomes.[47] The tools used in DSS include rule-based reasoning, case-based reasoning and ML including neural networks.[48] Case-based reasoning, unlike rule-based reasoning, retrieves similar previous cases, identifies differences between the new case and previous case, transfers the retrieved case to the actual one and proposes the solution to the problem.[49] During the next phase of revision, the proposed solution is simulated or tested for success. If the test is passed suc-

---

1–18, 4 https://www.mediate.com/Integrating/docs/lodder_thiessen.pdf accessed 28 September 2021.

[43] Arno Lodder and Paul Huygen, 'eADR A Simple Tool to Structure the Information Exchange between Parties in Online Alternative Dispute Resolution' in Bart Verheij and others (eds), *Legal Knowledge and Information Systems. Jurix 2001: The Fourteenth Annual Conference* (IOS Press 2001) 117–129.

[44] Ibid.

[45] Lodder and Thiessen (n 42) 11.

[46] Ibid., 12.

[47] Davide Carneiro and others, 'Online Dispute Resolution: an Artificial Intelligence Perspective' (2014) 41(2) *Artificial Intelligence Review* 211–240.

[48] Arno R. Lodder and John Zeleznikow, 'Artificial Intelligence and Online Dispute Resolution' in M.A. Wahab, E. Katsh and D. Rainey (eds), *Online Dispute Resolution: Theory and Practice. A Treatise on Technology and Dispute Resolution* (Eleven International Publishing 2012) 73–94.

[49] Agnar Aamodt and Enric Plaza, 'Case-based Reasoning: Foundational Issues, Methodological Variations, and System Approaches' (1994) 7(1) *AI Communications* 39–59.

cessfully, the process of case-based reasoning concludes with the retainment phase, where the useful data from the problem case solution is indexed and included in the existing knowledge.[50]

In the field of ODR, DSS supports providers to analyse large volumes of information and hence improve the efficiency of dispute handling. The potential of DSS in the development of ODR is apparent. The functioning principles and goals of ODR, in turn, create new opportunities for the expansion of more user-centric DSS.

8.2.7 Evaluation

One of the key learnings from the overview of the promises of AI for consumers and providers in ODR is that current technology is not exploited as it could be. Indeed, from a large-scale perspective, the use of AI in ODR is still limited to simple IT applications developed for office automation, case management and databases or platforms for electronic document interchange. For instance, the European ODR platform has restricted technological design and merely represents a referral system that recommends a relevant dispute resolution body to the parties, automatically submits a consumer's complaint to the chosen dispute resolution body and under some circumstances allows both consumers and traders to access communications from the dispute resolution body via the platform. The techniques of AI – if deployed correctly – can make ODR much more effective than it is today. In particular, an AI-based ODR mechanism might be more consumer-centric, allowing vulnerable consumers to formulate and express their claims with simple objectives instead of explicit legal justifications.

8.3 THE PROMISE AND CHALLENGES OF AI IN CONSUMER ODR

8.3.1 Improving Efficiency, Effectiveness and Fairness

Many of the unique features of AI have often been considered as shortcomings in the process of consumer dispute handling. However, the overall rise in the use of algorithmic decision-making tools has altered that opinion. Nowadays, many characteristic functionalities of AI are regarded as potentially advantageous to Consumer ODR. Most notably, the technological capabilities of AI, if implemented properly, can improve the efficiency, effectiveness and fairness

---

50 Ibid.

of consumer redress as well as access to justice.[51] Moreover, the deployment of algorithmic automation in dispute resolution might also reduce errors, thereby improving the consistency of legal decision-making.[52]

Additionally, consumers as disputants who represent themselves in litigation 'often lack knowledge of legal issues or procedures and have difficulty negotiating good outcomes or presenting their case to a court or tribunal'.[53] Consequently, in dispute resolutions where decision-making can be considered a 'knowledge-manufacturing process', the use of DSS is most likely to help consumers to manage their knowledge.[54] DSS achieves this goal by strengthening consumers' competence both in representing and processing knowledge.[55]

Another additional benefit of AI in ODR can be found in the capabilities of ML and big data to jointly contribute to dispute prevention. Namely, data analysis and ML enable existing systems to 're-design for early dispute detection and handling which can reduce risk, liability, harm, inefficiency and injustice'.[56] The relevancy of the preventive function of AI in Consumer ODR is crucial due to the statistical trends related to the increasing number of transactions and the scale of dispute generation. Namely, in 2019 the worldwide B2C e-commerce sales approximated to 3.53 trillion US dollars and are predicted to grow to 6.54 trillion US dollars by 2022.[57]

Overall, the proper use of AI techniques in Consumer ODR has the potential to increase efficiency and participation.

---

[51] See Ronald W. Staudt, 'All the Wild Possibilities: Technology That Attacks Barriers to Access to Justice' (2009) 42(4) *Loyola of Los Angeles Law Review* 1117–1146; James E. Cabral and others, 'Using Technology to Enhance Access to Justice' (2012) 26(1) *Harvard Journal of Law & Technology* 243–323; Anjanette H. Raymond and Scott J. Shackelford, 'Technology, Ethics, and Access to Justice: Should an Algorithm Be Deciding Your Case?' (2015) 35(3) *Michigan Journal of International Law* 485–519.

[52] Bas van Zelst, *The end of justice(s): perspectives and thoughts on automation in dispute resolution* (Inaugural lecture, Maastricht University 2018) https://doi.org/10.26481/spe.20180608bz accessed 28 September 2021.

[53] John Zeleznikow, 'Can Artificial Intelligence and Online Dispute Resolution Enhance Efficiency And Effectiveness In Courts' (2017) 8(2) *International Journal for Court Administration* 30–45, 32.

[54] John Zeleznikow, 'Using Web-based Legal Decision Support Systems to Improve Access to Justice' (2002) 11(1) *Information and Communications Technology Law* 15–33, 17.

[55] Ibid.

[56] Leah Wing, 'Artificial Intelligence and Online Dispute Resolution Systems Design: Lack of/Access to Justice Magnified' (2017) 4(2) *International Journal of Online Dispute Resolution* 16–20, 18.

[57] Statistica, 'Retail e-commerce sales worldwide from 2014 to 2024' (Tugba Sabanoglu, Mar 26, 2021) https://www.statista.com/statistics/379046/worldwide-retail-e-commerce-sales/ accessed 28 September 2021.

8.3.2 Privacy and Security Concerns

One important issue that must be addressed when setting up AI-based ODR procedures is data protection and security. Compared to traditional dispute resolution, ODR as a data-driven and internet-reliant process raises additional data safety and confidentiality concerns. In particular, two main data safety and security dimensions can be identified in ODR: (i) external protection – aiming to protect private case information from external parties seeking to hack the system and obtain information and (ii) internal protection – aiming to protect private case information from unlawful disclosure or misuse by the system managers.[58] The increasing use of big data analytics has enhanced the issues of privacy and the protection from external threats and data security breaches. Data protection remains one of the most common concerns and the biggest obstacle preventing the wider adoption of ODR.

Another issue that needs to be addressed is the tension between transparency and confidentiality of ODR procedures.[59] Prospective disputants will most likely request information from ODR providers about how previous disputes were handled, what the outcomes were and what reasoning was used. On the one hand, ODR providers are bound to the principle of transparency when providing their services. On the other hand, the participants of a particular dispute want the ODR proceedings to be kept confidential. Accordingly, AI's capabilities to collect and generate new data further complicate the trade-off between confidentiality and transparency of ODR procedures.

8.3.3 Due Process – Fairness Concerns

The privatization of consumer redress and the proliferation of ODR-led justice institutions have already shown potential to decentralize justice systems. This shift from court-based adjudication of consumer disputes to private ODR mechanisms has resulted in the emergence of stateless justice[60] that poses challenges to due process and fair trial rights, which are exacerbated by the use of AI systems and other automation tools in the following ways:

---

[58] Carrie Shu Shang and Wenli Guo, 'The Rise of Online Dispute Resolution-Led Justice in China: An Initial Look' (2020) 1(2) *ANU Journal of Law and Technology* 25–42, 39.

[59] Anita Ramasastry, 'Government-to-Citizen Online Dispute Resolution: A Preliminary Inquiry' (2004) 79(1) *Washington Law Review* 159–174, 166.

[60] Pietro Ortolani, 'The Three Challenges of Stateless Justice' (2016) 7(3) *Journal of International Dispute Settlement* 596–627.

8.3.3.1 Loss of personal contact

AI-based ODR systems negatively affect the dynamics of traditional negotiation because they take place at a distance and in a virtual environment, rather than with face-to-face communication, which is vital for ADR, particularly in the context of mediation. ADR as a process is normally based on an informal, face-to-face discussion of the issues between the participants. Additionally, 'there is almost universal agreement that mediation is most effective if the parties to the dispute are physically present before the mediator'.[61]

Thus, the effectiveness of technologically advanced Consumer ODR might be challenged directly by the lack of an established relationship or personal connection between the disputants. The impersonality of AI-based ODR might also hinder the disputants from expressing feelings and emotions. Moreover, the transformation of the 'third party' into an intangible and algorithmic 'fourth party' in consumer ODR also decreases the potential of the process for building trust among the participants.

8.3.3.2 Power imbalances and information asymmetries

Two other common concerns related to the use of AI in ODR are power imbalances and information asymmetries,[62] which might be even more substantial in the context of consumer ODR, particularly in a scenario where a big company proposes to its users an AI-enhanced ODR tool that it has developed for resolving disputes between the company and its consumers. AI-driven big-data profiling techniques give companies the opportunity to gain superior knowledge about consumers' personal circumstances, behavioural patterns and personality, including future preferences. Based on these findings, companies can tailor their decisions in ways that maximize their expected utility.

Consumers, on the other hand, have no further insights into the internal use of AI systems in ODR proceedings. Usually, they are not even aware which technology is used and which predictions, recommendations or decisions have been personalized according to their profile. If, for example, an argumentation support tool or a DSS suggests a certain litigation strategy or recommends a certain decision, consumers are usually barred from understanding how this recommendation was achieved in the first place. This asymmetry arises not only because the algorithms used are well-guarded trade secrets, but also because the specific characteristics of many AI technologies – such as opacity

---

[61] William T D'Zurilla, 'Alternative Dispute Resolution' (1997) 45 *Los Angeles Business Journal* 352.

[62] Cf Giovanni Sartor, 'New aspects and challenges in consumer protection. Digital services and artificial intelligence', Study requested by the IMCO committee of the European Parliament, PE 648.790, April 2020.

('black box effect'), complexity, unpredictability and semi-autonomous behaviour – can make it impossible to understand the AI system's behaviour.

8.3.3.3 Risk of errors, bias and discrimination

Another common concern regarding ODR systems is that the results of algorithm-based decisions are not always accurate.[63] Coding errors and biases in algorithm-based decision-making mechanisms as well as biases in datasets can result in unfair and discriminatory outcomes.[64] Since AI systems do not understand the context of complex situations, their input data is the only context in which they operate; hence, if the data provided to train AI is incomplete or includes bias, then the output of AI can be expected to be incomplete and biased as well.

This problem will become perpetual if ODR providers start to use AI to determine results based on an analysis of similar cases which have been inaccurately grouped and indexed in the system. The effect of such bias can stretch to all the layers of ODR including procedures, predictions or decisions.

8.3.3.4 Risk of nudging and manipulation

Considering the digital architecture of ODR systems, the autonomy and self-determination of consumers can also be undermined by nudging and manipulation.[65] The term 'nudging' refers to 'the use of user-interface design elements to guide people's behavior in digital choice environments'[66] by the deliberate presentation of choices or organization of workflows.[67] Nudging

---

[63] See, e.g., Kiel Brennan-Marquez, 'Plausible Cause: Explanatory Standards in the Age of Powerful Machines' (2017) 70 *Vanderbilt Law Review* 1249–1301, 1255-57; Tal Z Zarsky, 'Transparent Predictions' (2013) 4 *University of Illinois Law Review* 1503–1569, 1506.

[64] See Janneke Gerards and Raphaële Xenidis, *Algorithmic discrimination in Europe: Challenges and opportunities for gender equality and non-discrimination law*, Special Report prepared for the European Commission (Publications Office of the European Union, 2021); Sam Corbett-Davies and others, 'Algorithm Decision Making and the Cost of Fairness' (Conference Paper, 23rd ACM SIGKDD International Conference, August 2017).

[65] See Ayelet Sela, 'E-Nudging Justice: The Role of Digital Choice Architecture in Online Courts' (2019) 2 *Journal of Dispute Resolution* 127–163. On choice architecture features see Richard H. Thaler and Cass R. Sunstein, *Nudge: Improving Decisions About Health, Wealth, And Happiness* (Penguin Books 2009) 85.

[66] Markus Weinmann, Christoph Schneider and Jan vom Brocke, 'Digital Nudging' (2016) 58 *Business & Information Systems Engineering* 433–436, 433.

[67] B.J. Fogg, Gregory Cuellar and David Danielson, 'Motivating, Influencing, and Persuading Users' in Andrew Sears and Julie A. Jacko (eds), *The Human-Computer Interaction Handbook: Fundamentals, Evolving Technologies, and Emerging Applications* (2nd edn, CRC Press 2007) 133–146.

(and also manipulation) is also present in ODR platforms. For example, AI-supported ODR architectures might influence consumers towards specific choices,[68] e.g., by presenting desired options as a preselected default (status quo bias), by adding unattractive options (decoy effect), by positioning an option earlier/later (primacy/recency effect), by positioning an option in the middle (middle option bias), by indicating a sum of money (anchoring effect) or by personalizing the choice environment for individual users according to group profiles. AI systems allow ODR platforms to 'dynamically tailor the choice architecture (including content, visualization, and procedure) in real time in order to increase its effectiveness on specific users with particular attributes'.[69]

Digital choice architectures and data-driven personalization can significantly improve the quality of services, but they also pose significant ethical risks, privacy issues and normative challenges.[70] Consequently, the question arises as to how providers of ODR schemes that are committed to values of due process, equality and neutrality can mitigate the risks of nudging and manipulation.

8.3.3.5 The 'black box' problem

According to the Stanford AI Index Report 2019, interpretability, explainability and transparency of AI systems alongside fairness are identified as the most regularly mentioned ethical challenges across 59 Ethical AI principles documents.[71] The field of Consumer ODR is no exception, as the so-called 'black box' problem can highly affect due process standards.

Broadly speaking, the black box phenomenon refers to scenarios in which we can see only input data and output data for AI systems without understanding exactly what happens in between. Only a few types of AI systems are directly interpretable for the user, such as decision trees or linear and logistic regression. By contrast, the vast majority of AI systems (support vector machines, ensemble tree methods such as random forests, gradient boosting machines

---

[68] In detail Sela (n 65) 139ff.

[69] Ibid., 155.

[70] See Ryan Calo, 'Digital Market Manipulation' (2014) 82(4) *The George Washington Law Review* 995–1051; Martin Ebers, 'Liability for Artificial Intelligence and EU Consumer Law' (2021) 12 *Journal of Intellectual Property, Information Technology and Electronic Commerce Law* 204–221, para 28ff.

[71] Raymond Perrault and others, *The AI Index 2019 Annual Report* (Stanford 2019) 149 https://hai.stanford.edu/sites/default/files/ai_index_2019_report.pdf accessed 28 September 2021.

and especially deep neural networks) show a degree of opacity that makes it hard to understand how AI decisions or predictions have been reached.[72]

Opaque AI systems can impair the right to due process and fair trial in various ways, depending on how they are used in an ODR procedure and for which purpose. According to Palmiotto,[73] opaque algorithms impact (i) the adversarial principle, when the parties cannot contradict the opponent's allegations; (ii) the equality of arms principle, when it creates a knowledge asymmetry between parties; (iii) the right to confrontation, when algorithms cannot be examined; and (iv) the right to have a reasoned decision, when algorithms do not explain or justify how a particular decision has been reached. Although these cases are more relevant in judiciary proceedings, the ideological spirit and universal nature of due process and fair trial principles are relevant for private ODR schemes as well.

8.3.4 Analysis

AI systems and data-driven personalization have the potential to significantly improve the efficiency, effectiveness and fairness of ODR schemes. At the same time, however, these systems as well as other forms of automation can undermine the fundamental principles of due process and fair trial, due to the previously discussed issues (loss of personal contact; new power and information asymmetries; risk of erroneous, biased or discriminatory outcomes; nudging and manipulation).

The stronger the shift from judicial proceedings to out-of-court ADR redress schemes and the more extensively digital technologies are used, the more pressing the question becomes of whether due process standards can be embedded in extra-judicial redress schemes. Accordingly, the following analysis addresses the procedural and non-procedural safeguards of consumer due process in out-of-court ODR disputes.

---

[72] For a comparison between the varying degrees of explainability of different AI systems see Bernhard Waltl and Roland Vogl, 'Explainable Artificial Intelligence – The New Frontier in Legal Informatics', Jusletter IT (22 February 2018) https://wwwmatthes.in.tum.de/file/13tkeaid0rhkz/Sebis-Public-Website/-/Explainable-Artificial-Intelligence-the-New-Frontier-in-Legal-Informatics/Wa18a.pdf accessed 28 September 2021.

[73] Francesca Palmiotto, 'The Black Box on Trial: The Impact of Algorithmic Opacity on Fair Trial Rights in Criminal Proceedings' in Martin Ebers and Marta Cantero (eds), *Algorithmic Governance and Governance of Algorithms* (Springer 2020) 49–70, 61.

8.4 PROCEDURAL SAFEGUARDS OF CONSUMER DUE PROCESS

8.4.1 Two-tier System in the EU

For efficient enforcement of consumer rights in the Member States, the European Union provides for the so-called 'EU enforcement toolbox' which combines a set of legislative and non-legislative tools. Consumer ADR and ODR systems are considered key components of that toolbox.[74] Both the ADR Directive and the ODR Regulation aim to facilitate out-of-court resolutions of consumer disputes with consumer-centric redress schemes. Amongst other goals, the creation of high-quality ADR entities, as one of the primary ambitions of the ADR Directive, also plays a crucial role in the proper functioning of the ODR platform – an interactive website providing a single point of entry for e-commerce disputes established under the ODR Regulation.[75]

One of the underlying intentions of the ADR Directive was to neutralize criticisms expressed towards ADR schemes lacking independence, accountability, and as such compromising due process standards.[76] For that reason, the ADR Directive promotes high-quality ADR entities through certification and monitoring schemes. To obtain a certification, ADR entities have to comply with the following binding quality principles established by the directive: accessibility, expertise, independence, impartiality, transparency, effectiveness, fairness, liberty and legality.[77] These requirements are 'binding quality requirements for ADR entities, the ADR procedures operated by them and – to a lesser degree – the substantive standards from which the outcome of the ADR procedure is derived'.[78] The broad spectrum of mandatory standards of compliance enshrined by the ADR Directive to some extent also attempts to translate and mirror the core elements of the right to a fair trial into ADR and ODR contexts.[79]

---

[74] European Commission, 'Report on the application of Directive 2013/11/EU on alternative dispute resolution for consumer disputes and Regulation (EU) No 524/2013 on online dispute resolution for consumer disputes', COM(2019) 425 final.

[75] Recital (12) ADR Directive.

[76] See Horst Eidenmüller and Martin Engel, 'Against False Settlement: Designing Efficient Consumer Rights Enforcement Systems in Europe' (2014) 29(2) *Ohio State Journal on Dispute Resolution* 261–298; Gerhard Wagner, 'Private Law Enforcement Through ADR: Wonder Drug or Snake Oil?' (2014) 51(1) *CMLRev* 165–194.

[77] Art 5–11 ADR Directive.

[78] European Commission (n 74) 3.

[79] Anne Kamphorst, 'The Right to a Fair Trial in Online Consumer Dispute Resolution' (2019) 8(5) *Journal of European Consumer and Market Law* 175–183.

However, the voluntary nature of certification allows non-certified ADR bodies to operate alongside certified ones across the EU Member States, which has resulted in the creation of a two-tier ADR landscape. The ADR Directive does not make the use of ADR mandatory in any economic sector. In other words, participation by businesses in ADR entities remains voluntary under the Directive.[80]

As the ADR Directive allows for both certified and non-certified ADR entities in EU Member States, the Directive tends to lead to inconsistent quality of ADR providers undermining at the same time the homogeneity of ADR sectors. Moreover, the protection offered by the ADR Directive does not apply to 'procedures before dispute resolution entities where the natural persons in charge of dispute resolution are employed or remunerated exclusively by the individual trader' nor to 'procedures before consumer complaint-handling systems operated by the trader'.[81] Thus, the wide variety of Consumer ODR bodies that provide AI-based ODR schemes for consumer redress are left outside the scope of the ADR Directive, which in turn might impair efficient enforcement of consumer rights and due process standards in various ways.

8.4.2 Safeguards under EU Primary and EU Secondary Law

Under certain conditions, out-of-court ODR proceedings are subject to judicial review based on the right to fair trial, which is enshrined, inter alia, in Article 6 European Convention on Human Rights (ECHR) and Article 47 Charter of Fundamental Rights of the European Union (EU-CFR).[82]

According to consistent case-law of both the European Court of Human Rights (ECtHR) and the Court of Justice of the European Union (CJEU), *mandatory* ADR procedures established by statute must be subject to judicial review. As the ECtHR already decided in *Albert and Le Compte v Belgium*[83] for administrative claims, out-of-court decision-making bodies do not have to

---

[80] On the other hand, the ADR Directive does not preempt Member States to make participation in an ADR process compulsory, as long as the right to access to justice is preserved (Art 1(2) ADR Directive), e.g., through an appellate or review process.

[81] Art 2(2)(a) and (b) ADR Directive. However, under Art 2(2)(a) ADR Directive the procedures exclusively paid for by traders can still be brought within the scope of ADR Directive when the member state allows it and extra measures are taken.

[82] The level of legal protection required by Art 47 EU-CFR goes beyond the level of protection required by the ECHR. cf Martin Ebers, *Rechte, Rechtsbehelfe und Sanktionen im Unionsprivatrecht* (Mohr Siebeck 2016) 253ff; Angela Ward, 'National and EC Remedies under the EU Treaty' in Catherine Barnard and Okeoghene Odudu (eds), *The Outer Limits of European Union Law* (Oregon 2009) 329–361, 329ff.

[83] *Albert and Le Compte v Belgium* App no 7299/75, 7496/76 (ECHR, 10 February 1983), para 29.

conform to the requirements of Article 6(1) ECHR, provided applicants have the possibility of appealing the decision to a court of law. In the same vein, the CJEU ruled in *Alassini*[84] that a mandatory out-of-court settlement procedure is compatible with the principle of effective judicial protection (Art 6 ECHR, Art 47 EU-CFR) only if 'the outcome of the settlement procedure is not binding on the parties concerned and thus does not prejudice their right to bring legal proceedings'.

Both courts also share the view that the right to access to court can be *waived by the parties* under certain conditions. The ECtHR accepts such a waiver[85] provided there is no coercion or constraint, and that the waiver is unequivocal and accompanied by 'minimum guarantees commensurate to its importance'.[86] A similar picture emerges in EU secondary law. According to Annex 1(q) Unfair Contract Terms Directive,[87] pre-formulated contract terms under which the business imposes arbitration proceedings on consumers are likely to be unfair and non-binding if they exclude or hinder the consumer's right to take legal action or to exercise a legal remedy.[88] Additionally, the CJEU clarified in *Asturcom Telecomunicaciones*[89] that, in connection with arbitration proceedings initiated by traders against consumers, there must be effective judicial control of arbitration awards in appeal and enforcement proceedings, which may lead to an obligation for the courts to assess of their own motion the unfairness of contract terms allowing the business to resort to arbitration.

In summary, this means that consumers are protected from (unfair) ODR out-of-court procedures at least to the extent that they must have the option of

---

84 Joined cases C-317/08, C-318/08, C-319/08 and C-320/08 *Rosalba Alassini and others* [2010] EU:C:2010:146, para 54. Additionally, the CJEU pointed out that mandatory ADR procedures (i) must not cause a substantial delay for the purposes of bringing legal proceedings, (ii) must suspend the period for the time-barring of claims, (iii) must not give rise to costs – or only very low costs – for the parties, and (iv) that electronic means must not be the only means by which the settlement procedure may be accessed.

85 See Lorna McGregor, 'Alternative Dispute Resolution and Human Rights: Developing a Rights-Based Approach through the ECHR' (2015) 26(3) EJIL 607–634, 617–18.

86 *Osmo Suovaniemi and others v Finland* App no 31737/96 (ECHR, 23 February 1999).

87 Council Directive 93/13/EEC of 5 April 1993 on unfair terms in consumer contracts [1993] OJ L 95/29.

88 See also CJEU, case C-342/13 *Katalin Sebestyén* [2014] EU:C:2014:1857, para 36; European Commission, 'Guidance on the interpretation and application of Council Directive 93/13/EEC on unfair terms in consumer contracts' [2019] OJ C 323/4, 62.

89 Case C-40/08 *Asturcom Telecomunicaciones* [2009] EU:C:2009:615; in detail Martin Ebers, 'From Océano to Asturcom: Mandatory Consumer Law, Ex Officio Application of Community Law and Res Judicata' (2010) 4 *ERPL* 823–845.

initiating ordinary court proceedings. The ODR procedure as such, however, is not subject to direct control according to the standards of Article 6 ECHR and Article 47 EU-CFR.

Admittedly, some scholars favour a direct horizontal effect of Article 47 EU-CFR for out-of-court procedures.[90] To support their claim, they state that the right to a fair trial should not only apply to expensive, hardly affordable court procedures but also to ODR out-of-court schemes, which are not only more economical for consumers and traders, but also require less funding than court systems.

At the end of the day, there is little reason to adopt the view that the fundamental right to a fair trial is directly applicable in private ODR schemes. Articles 6 ECHR and 47 EU-CFR grant the right to a fair trial only before a 'tribunal', whereas privately adjudicating ODR bodies cannot be considered as tribunals, because their jurisdiction is based on a civil contract.[91] Moreover, the traditional scope of fundamental rights is the vertical relationship between the state and citizens. Accordingly, most scholars are (still) of the opinion that fundamental rights do not apply directly to private parties.[92] This interpretation is confirmed by case-law. Although the CJEU decided in a number of judgments that some of the provisions of the EU-CFR might have horizontal direct effect,[93] such an effect has only been recognized in traditional court proceedings. Consequently, both the ECtHR and the CJEU emphasize that no direct review of out-of-court proceedings arises from the right to fair trial, but only the consumer's right to appeal to the ordinary courts following ADR proceedings.[94]

---

[90] Kamphorst (n 79).

[91] Consequently, arbitrational tribunals cannot initiate preliminary ruling procedures before the CJEU; see CJEU, case 102/81 *Nordsee Deutsche Hochseefischerei* [1982] EU:C:1982:107; case C-125/04 *Guy Denuit und Betty Cordenier* [2005] EU:C:2005:69.

[92] cf Olha Cherednychenko, *Fundamental Rights, Contract Law and the Protection of the Weaker Party* (Sellier European Law Publishers 2007); Jörg Neuner (ed), *Grundrechte und Privatrecht aus rechtsvergleichender Sicht* (Mohr Siebeck 2007); Gert Brüggemeier, Aurelia Colombi Ciacchi and Giovanni Comandé (eds), *Fundamental Rights and Private Law in the European Union*, vol 1: *A Comparative Overview* (Cambridge University Press 2010).

[93] cf especially case C-414/16 *Egenberger* EU:C:2018:257. For an overview of CJEU case-law see Sacha Prechal, 'Horizontal Direct Effect of the Charter of Fundamental Rights of the EU' [2020] 66 Revista de Derecho Comunitario Europeo 407–426. For a discussion of CJEU case-law on fundamental freedoms see Ebers (n 82) 498–521.

[94] See n 83ff.

8.4.3 Other Safeguards

The rapid growth of private ODR schemes also triggered some other international and self-regulatory initiatives[95] such as codes of conduct, trust marks, other sector-specific standards and feedback systems.[96]

A good example of a non-state tool containing rules governing online-procedures for resolving disputes is the Uniform Domain Name Resolution Policy (UDRP) established by the Corporation for Assigned Names and Numbers (ICANN)[97] and recommended by the World Intellectual Property Organization (WIPO)[98] for resolving disputes over the registration and use of an internet domain name between the registrar body and domain-name holder as customer. ICANN's resolution policy sets up a quasi-autonomous international dispute-resolution regime 'consisting of judicial, arbitral and ministerial components, which, in the aggregate, form an apparatus with jurisdiction to adjudicate and enforce'.[99]

Particularly noteworthy are also the already mentioned UNCITRAL Technical Notes for Online Dispute Resolution, which are designed for the resolution of low-value, high-volume cross-border transactions conducted in whole or in part by the use of electronic communication,[100] including B2B and B2C transactions.[101] Originally, the responsible UNCITRAL Working Group III was to prepare not only Technical Notes, but also Rules covering inter alia the accreditation of ODR providers and third-party neutrals and

---

[95] A list of ODR standards, principles and guidelines is provided by the National Center for Technology and Dispute Resolution (NCTDR) on its webpage http://odr.info/standards/ accessed 28 September 2021.

[96] Feedback systems have the potential to contribute enhanced fair trial standards insofar as they create an incentive that encourages appropriate behaviour and compliance with outcomes.

[97] Corporation for Assigned Names and Numbers (ICANN), The Uniform Domain Name Resolution Policy (UDRP) https://www.icann.org/resources/pages/policy-2012-02-25-en accessed 28 September 2021.

[98] World Intellectual Property Organization (WIPO), WIPO Guide to the Uniform Domain Name Dispute Resolution Policy (UDRP) https://www.wipo.int/amc/en/domains/guide/ accessed 28 September 2021.

[99] Joachim Zekoll, 'Online Dispute Resolution: Justice without the State?' [2014] Research Paper Series No 2014-02, Max Planck Institute for European Legal History, 18, 1-19.

[100] Draft Preamble of the UNCITRAL Technical Notes for Online Dispute Resolution (n 20).

[101] The Notes do not distinguish between business and consumers; instead, they simply refer to parties. Thereto Pablo Cortés, *The Law of Consumer Redress in an Evolving Digital Market* (Cambridge University Press 2018) 183.

substantive legal principles for resolving disputes.[102] However, due to a lack of consensus, the deliberations and decisions of the Working Group did not result in ODR Rules, but instead in Technical Notes, which are descriptive and non-binding.[103]

Other initiatives have also been unsuccessful to date. Although there have been several other attempts to formulate formal standards,[104] no enforceable governance frameworks for ODR have yet emerged.

8.5 FUTURE DIRECTIONS OF CONSUMER ODR

The preceding analysis shows that the use of AI systems in ODR proceedings is far from being unproblematic, since their uncontrolled use can undermine due process requirements. So far, neither EU primary nor EU secondary law provides a well-established legal basis for a right to fair trial in private ODR schemes. Quite the contrary: the miscellany of self-regulatory procedures and standards generated by diverse Consumer ODR bodies obscures consumers from understanding their due process rights in AI-led proceedings and makes it difficult to acknowledge the safeguards involved under each scheme.

Admittedly, there is sufficient evidence to recognize minimum fair trial standards in ODR proceedings, especially when AI systems are used. Accordingly, this chapter closes with a critical discussion of future directions of ODR, including the latest proposals of the European Commission on regulating AI systems and digital platforms.

8.5.1 The European Commission's Proposal for an Artificial Intelligence Act

On April 21, 2021, the European Commission presented its long-awaited proposal for a Regulation laying down harmonized rules on AI, the so-called Artificial Intelligence Act (AIA-Proposal).[105] The new rules would apply

---

[102] Ibid., 182.

[103] As to the reasons see Constantina Sampani, 'Online Dispute Resolution in e-commerce: Is Consensus in Regulation UNCITRAL's Utopian Idea or a Realistic Ambition?' (2021) *Information & Communications Technology Law* 235–254.

[104] See, e.g., Council of Europe, Guidelines of the Committee of Ministers of the Council of Europe on online dispute resolution mechanisms in civil and administrative court proceedings, CM(2021)36add4-final https://search.coe.int/cm/Pages/result_details.aspx?ObjectId=0900001680a2cf96 accessed 28 September 2021; ABA, Recommended Best Practices for Online Dispute Resolution Service Providers https://www.americanbar.org/content/dam/aba/administrative/dispute_resolution/dispute_resolution/best_practices_final_102802.pdf accessed 28 September 2021.

[105] See n 27.

directly to both public and private actors inside and outside the EU as long as the AI system is placed on the Union market or its use affects people located in the EU (Art 2(1) AIA-Proposal).

Whereas certain AI systems and practices are directly prohibited (Art 5 AIA-Proposal), most emphasis is put on high-risk AI systems. According to Article 6 AIA-Proposal, an AI system is classified as high-risk if it is intended to be used as a safety component of a product (Annex II AIA-Proposal) or if it is a stand-alone AI system listed in Annex III AIA-Proposal. High-risk AI systems must comply with the mandatory requirements set out in Articles 8–15 AIA-Proposal regarding the quality of data sets used; technical documentation and record-keeping; transparency and the provision of information to users; human oversight; and robustness, accuracy and cybersecurity.

The AIA-Proposal has been criticized by consumer associations for being weak on consumer protection as it focuses on 'a very limited range of AI uses and issues'.[106] Indeed, despite the innovative risk-based structure, the proposal appears to have some remarkable gaps. First of all, the AIA-Proposal neither includes specific consumer rights – such as a right to contest an algorithmic decision and obtain human oversight – nor remedies in case something goes wrong.[107] The proposal is also silent on effective complaint procedures. Additionally, the proposal ignores the factual reality created by the privatization of consumer adjudication. The draft regulates the use of AI systems in dispute resolution for ordinary court proceedings only, but not for private ODR schemes. According to Annex III No. 8(a) AIA-Proposal only AI systems 'intended to assist a judicial authority in researching and interpreting facts and the law and in applying the law to a concrete set of facts' are classified as 'high-risk' AI systems.

Consequently, no specific requirements are imposed for out-of-court consumer ODR using AI systems.

8.5.2 The European Commission's Proposal for a Digital Services Act

Interesting policy trends relating to the privatization of judicial redress and the outsourcing of decision-making powers can be identified in the field of digital services – namely in the European Commission's proposal for a Digital

---

[106] BEUC, 'EU proposal for artificial intelligence law is weak on consumer protection' (Press Release, 21 April2021) https://www.beuc.eu/publications/eu-proposal-artificial-intelligence-law-weak-consumer-protection/html accessed 28 September 2021.

[107] Ibid.

Services Act (DSA-Proposal)[108] published on 15 December 2020 – in order to update the existing rules on platform responsibilities in the provision of digital services.[109]

Article 17 DSA-Proposal requires online platforms to provide all recipients of services[110] access to an effective internal complaint-handling system,[111] which enables complaints to be lodged electronically and free of charge against certain decisions taken by the online platform on the grounds that the information provided by the recipients is illegal content or incompatible with its terms and conditions. Moreover, Article 18 DSA-Proposal gives recipients the right to select certified out-of-court dispute settlement bodies to appeal against decisions delivered by the internal complaint-handling system.

The proposal does not clearly define the relationship between the platform's in-house dispute handling mechanism (Art 17 DSA-Proposal) and external ADR procedures (Art 18 DSA-Proposal), especially whether these mechanisms should be provided as alternatives. Furthermore, Article 17(5) DSA-Proposal prohibits online platforms from designing their internal decision-making schemes based solely on automated means, which in turn limits the usability of AI for the digital consumer redress and their content management. However, as far as platforms are not obliged to disclose the rules of the procedure, Article 17 DSA-Proposal is still inadequate to ensure the transparency of the internal complaint-handling procedure,[112] especially in the scenario where AI techniques are partially deployed. At the same time, the DSA-Proposal prohibits fully automated decisions only for internal complaint-handling systems, but not for external out-of-court dispute settlements.[113] Another contradictory aspect is that the certification standards of ADR entities under

[108] Proposal for a Regulation of the European Parliament and of the Council on a Single Market For Digital Services (Digital Services Act) and amending Directive 2000/31/EC, COM(2020) 825 final.

[109] For a critical assessment of the DSA-Proposal, see Caroline Cauffman and Catalina Goanta, 'A New Order: The Digital Services Act and Consumer Protection' (2021) *European Journal of Risk Regulation* 1–17.

[110] According to Art 2(b) DSA-Proposal, the concept of the 'recipient of the service' covers any natural or legal person who uses the relevant intermediary service. Therefore, recipients can be both traders and consumers.

[111] It is mandatory for the platforms to have an internal complaint-handling system except when they qualify as micro or small enterprises within the meaning of the Annex to Recommendation 2003/361/EC (Arts 16 and 17).

[112] See BEUC, The Digital Services Act Proposal, Position Paper BEUC-X-2021-032, 09/04/2021, 22 https://www.beuc.eu/publications/beuc-x-2021-032_the_digital_services_act_proposal.pdf accessed 28 September 2021.

[113] Accordingly, external out-of-court dispute procedures are only subject to Art 22 GDPR which indeed prohibits fully automated decisions in para 1 but at the same time provides for numerous exceptions in para 2.

the DSA-Proposal are lower than the requirements established under the ADR Directive.[114] Such a regulatory fragmentation of certification standards could further weaken the uniformity of consumer due process enforcement.

8.5.3 Outlook

We are witnessing a major revolution in the ways in which consumer disputes are handled. One of the most significant trends in the field of consumer redress is the ongoing shift from public systems of adjudication to various private Consumer ODR schemes. The use of AI-based techniques in out-of-court proceedings not only reinforces this trend, but also raises concern as to whether fair trial rights and due process standards can be ensured. At present, there are no overarching enforceable governance frameworks for private ODR schemes to substantiate and enforce due process rights. The existing self-regulatory standards adopted by the private sector are equally non-systematic and fragmented. Thus, it is complicated for consumers to appreciate the mechanisms and safeguards involved under various schemes. Regardless of the growing body of research, the protection of consumer-specific due process rights in AI-based private Consumer ODR schemes has mostly remained peripheral.

Pablo Cortés[115] suggested over a decade ago that European policymakers should take the necessary steps to introduce regulatory measures in order to ensure fair and efficient ODR, considering not only the use of mandatory ODR clauses and enforceable ODR decisions of accredited ODR providers, but also procedural standards for extra-judicial ODR. Such standards could, as other commentators have pointed out,[116] be based on a proportionate model in which due process standards depend on the value and complexity of the dispute.[117]

Indeed, for the homogeneous enforcement of consumer rights in the era of AI, it would be advisable to have at least some kind of categorization of ODR systems and corresponding standards, established through the development of uniform criteria that ensure consumers' right to a fair trial in all privately operated (including AI-based) out-of-court dispute resolution systems. The EU legal framework based on the ADR Directive and the ODR Regulation as components of the 'EU enforcement toolbox' partially addresses due process

---

114 BEUC (n 112) 22.

115 Pablo Cortés, *Online Dispute Resolution for Consumers in the European Union* (Routledge 2011) 191–206.

116 Julia Hörnle, *Cross-Border Internet Dispute Resolution* (Cambridge University Press 2009) 217–219.

117 See also Cortés (n 101) 181, pointing out that ensuring due process for private ODR rules inevitably creates tension between efficiency and fairness, since legal formalities have a knock-on effect on the cost and time of the dispute resolution process.

concerns; however, these legal tools appear to be largely outdated as they do not adequately address the lacunae created by the algorithmic automation.

9. E-negotiation in the EU: Current experiences, challenges, and new scenarios[1]

Marco Giacalone and Seyedeh Sajedeh Salehi

9.1 INTRODUCTION

Historically, there is a large body of published studies focusing on the concept of 'negotiation', per se, in various disciplines.[2] Over recent decades a considerable amount of literature has been published on e-negotiation. Among all the existing literature, the majority of scholarly opinions can be found in the fields of behavioural sciences,[3] computer science, and law. In each field

---

[1] Disclaimer: This work is the result of conducting research as part of the NEMESIS project (co-funded by the EU H2020 under Grant Agreement no. 890793). The content of this chapter represents the views of the authors only and is their sole responsibility. The European Commission does not accept any responsibility for use that may be made of the information it contains.

[2] See e.g. Max H. Bazerman and others, 'Negotiation' (2000) 51 *Annual Review of Psychology* 279; Dean G. Pruitt, *Negotiation Behavior* (Academic Press 2013); Deborah F. Shmueli, Sandra Kaufman, and Connie Ozawa, 'Mining Negotiation Theory for Planning Insights' (2008) 27 *Journal of Planning Education and Research* 359; Randall G. Rogan, Mitchelle R. Hammer, and Clinton R. van Zandt, *Dynamic Processes of Crisis Negotiation: Theory, Research, and Practice* (ABC-CLIO 1997); Gregory Kersten and Hsiangchu Lai, 'Negotiation Support and E-Negotiation Systems' in Frada Burstein and Clyde W. Holsapple (eds), *Handbook on Decision Support Systems 1: Basic Themes* (Springer 2008); Coelho Helder and Fernando Lopes, *Negotiation and Argumentation in Multi-Agent Systems: Fundamentals, Theories, Systems and Applications* (Science Publishers 2014); Charles B. Craver, *Effective Legal Negotiation and Settlement* (LexisNexis 2012); Carrie J. Menkel-Meadow, 'Legal Negotiation: A Study of Strategies in Search of a Theory Review Essay' (1983) *American Bar Foundation Research Journal* 905; Carrie J. Menkel-Meadow, 'Chronicling the Complexification of Negotiation Theory and Practice' (2009) 25 *Negotiation Journal* 415.

[3] By behavioural sciences we refer to a wide range of disciplines, including psychology, social psychology, sociology, and behavioural economics.

of study, scholars have tried to define the concept of e-negotiation based on different elements, such as the nature of disputed subject-matter, the type of procedure, and means to conduct e-negotiation as well as the purpose of conducting e-negotiation. Due to the use of divergent elements, the definition of e-negotiation varies in the literature of these disciplines leading to terminological confusion. Moreover, in conducting CREA (Conflict Resolution with Equitative Algorithms) and NEMESIS (Negotiation and Mediation Sensible Issues' Solutions) projects, the authors worked in close collaboration with research groups composed of computer scientists and behavioural economists, to design an e-negotiation software for resolving civil disputes.[4] As jurists, we found that there is an insufficient degree of common understanding of 'e-negotiation' among legal scholars on the one hand, and computer and behavioural scientists on the other.[5] Thus, as the main focus of this study is 'e-negotiation' within these two contexts, it is essential to provide a clear conceptual explanation of this term that helps to better understand the discussions in sections 9.2 and 9.3 of this chapter. The present chapter also aims at exploring the application of e-negotiation – as part of the Online Dispute Resolution (ODR) regime in general – for resolving civil disputes in various jurisdictions. The main objective behind the latter is to better assess the existing best practices in implementing e-negotiation for resolving civil disputes in the EU. Against this backdrop, the first section discusses the existing definitions of e-negotiation in behavioural and computer science on the one hand, and legal context on the other, to have a clear understanding of their implications. The second section explores the use of e-negotiation by the existing prominent ODR service providers in and outside the EU. Further, the authors critically analyse the EU ODR platform and its function in relation to the practice of

---

4 In CREA (co-funded by the EU Justice program 2014–2020 under grant agreement no.766463) and NEMESIS (co-funded by the EU H2020 under grant agreement no. 890793) projects, we examined the application of advanced e-negotiation models for resolving civil disputes in EU. See Marco Giacalone and Sajedeh Salehi, 'CREA: An Introduction to Conflict Resolution with Equitative Algorithms' in Francesco Romeo, Marco Dall'Aglio, and Marco Giacalone (eds) *Algorithmic Conflict Resolution – The CREA Platform* (Giappichelli Torino 2019) 21.

5 The first author's note: A prominent example of using the term e-negotiation in different contexts was clearly seen in my case study experience – during the exploitation of the NEMESIS project – with a team of computer scientists working in a legal tech company that provides e-negotiation services. One of the significant findings that emerged from this case study was that while I referred to e-negotiation as a method for resolving disputes, these experts addressed – and used – e-negotiation only in the context of concluding online contracts. This contextual difference – that led to initial confusion among us – was the main reason to develop a discussion on e-negotiation concept definition in computational science, behavioural sciences, and law in this research.

e-negotiation for settling business-to-consumer disputes. Finally, the third section focuses on the lessons learnt from the application of e-negotiation for civil dispute resolution in EU and provides several important implications for the future of improvement in citizens' access to justice through the application of effective e-negotiation models.

9.1.1 Concept Definition: E-negotiation

In studying the concept of 'e-negotiation' in behavioural sciences, computer science, and law, scholars support the conclusion that the purpose of negotiation is to reach a mutual agreement. However, the approach and direction taken by these studies, on the one hand, and the application of e-negotiation on the other, manifests itself in different structures. For instance, while in behavioural sciences literature the focus is primarily put on the psychological and behavioural characteristics of the parties involved in the course of negotiation, on the contrary, computer scientists consider negotiation in the context of its application in concluding contracts between software agents in automated negotiation processes. Nonetheless, legal literature mostly analyses the notion of e-negotiation within the framework of dispute resolution. These contextual differences can cause confusion on some occasions, especially when the term negotiation is used in layman's terms or in public speeches, without referring to the particular context in which the term is used.[6] On this account, the main purpose of this section is to provide a clear distinction between the use of e-negotiation in the fields of behavioural sciences and computer science as against its use in legal literature.

9.1.2 Behavioural Sciences and Computational Studies

The study of negotiation in behavioural sciences is not a recent phenomenon.[7] Compared to computational sciences and law, there exists much wider knowledge of the concept of negotiation in behavioural sciences.[8] The most

---

[6] As happened to the authors in several interdisciplinary projects such as CREA and NEMESIS.

[7] See e.g. Jeffery Z. Rubin and Bert R. Brown, *The Social Psychology of Bargaining and Negotiation* (New York: Academic 1975); Debra L. Shapiro and Ann von Glinow, 'Negotiation in Multicultural Teams: New World, Old Theories?' (1999) 29 *The Academy of Management Review* 578; Roy J. Lewicki and Neil Stark, 'What is Ethically Appropriate In Negotiations: An Empirical Examination of Bargaining Tactics' (1996) 9 *Social Justice Resolution* 69.

[8] Turan Nazli and others, 'Toward a Unified Negotiation Framework: Leveraging Strengths in Behavioral and Computational Communities' in Katia Sycara, Michele

common definition of negotiation that has been used by many scholars in their research refers to negotiation as 'a form of conflict behaviour, which occurs when two or more parties try to resolve a divergence of interest by means of conversation'.[9]

This broad and general definition indicates that while negotiation is perceived as a common human behaviour, it can also be considered as one of the most complicated human activities.[10] In the majority of published scholarly literature on negotiation in behavioural sciences, this concept has been substantially explored in close relation to fairness, ethics, and values that play significant roles in any negotiation process.[11] Given the extensive literature on negotiation in various behavioural sciences, contrary to our expectations, there are only few studies – compared to computer science and law – that have explicitly defined the concept of 'e-negotiation'.[12] Therefore, the latter concept remains a poorly defined term in behavioural sciences literature. One of the rare theoretical and empirical studies on the use of electronically mediated negotiations was carried out by Moore et al. in 1999.[13] Despite their research lacking a specific definition of e-negotiation, it however refers to the two fundamental pillars of an electronically conducted negotiation. According to Moore et al., each e-negotiation necessarily involves a process of solution generation and decision-making.[14] It may be viewed that their study has analysed the implementation of a basic form of e-negotiation (via e-mail) from the conflict resolution perspective, which is similar to the legal approach towards e-negotiation.

Regarding the notion of e-negotiation[15] in computer science literature, it has been more than two decades since a significant amount of research has focused

---

Gelfand, and Alisson Abbe (eds) *Models for Intercultural Collaboration and Negotiation. Advances in Group Decision and Negotiation* (Springer 2013).

[9] Pruitt Dean G. and Sung Hee Kim, *Social Conflict: Escalation, Stalemate, and Settlement* (3rd edn, McGraw-Hill 2004); Katia Sycara, Gelfand Michelle and Alisson Abbe A, *Models for Intercultural Collaboration and Negotiation* (Springer 2013); Thompson Leigh L. *Negotiation Theory and Research* (Psychology Press 2006).

[10] Roy J. Lewicki, Daniel J. McAllister and Robert J. Bies, 'Trust and Distrust: New Relationships and Realities' (1998) 23 *AMR Journal* 438.

[11] Bazerman and others (n 2) 287.

[12] In the behavioural sciences, the definition of 'negotiation' is often used to define 'e-negotiation' as well.

[13] Don Moore and others, 'Long and Short Routes to Success in Electronically Mediated Negotiations: Group Affiliations and Good Vibrations' (1999) 77 *Organizational Behavior and Human Decision Processes* 22.

[14] Ibid., 24.

[15] There are other terms ie automated negotiation and/or computational negotiations, that computer scientists use to refer to e-negotiation. See Fernando Lopes, 'Computational Negotiation' in Coelho Helder and Fernando Lopes (eds), *Negotiation*

on studying this concept.[16] The major focus of the existing literature has heavily relied upon examining the e-negotiation from mathematics, game-theory, and economic viewpoints. For providing a more concrete and in-depth analysis of e-negotiation, it is essential to reflect that these computational perspectives have also considered this concept in connection with behavioural sciences.

Given that, compared to the behavioural sciences literature – that are more focused on e-negotiation from individual's perspective – computer scientists have shown more interest in considering this concept from the standpoint of automated and decision-support systems. In this sense, an e-negotiation system has been defined as a software that deploys the Internet-based communication technologies through a web to facilitate, host, support (and automate) tasks and activities carried out by negotiators and/or any third-party in the course of negotiation.[17] As Kersten and Lai (2008) noted, taking into account the e-negotiation system as a software which is employed and/or integrated as part of a web, the scope of negotiation can be widely extended to any other software – e.g. e-mail and videoconference – with the potential to be used as a means of communication by negotiators.[18]

In a comprehensive study conducted by Braun et al. in 2006 on methods and models of e-negotiation systems and the software used for this purpose, they adopted a similar approach – in defining e-negotiation – to behavioural sciences.[19] In this study, e-negotiation was referred to as 'a decentralized

---

and Argumentation in Multi-Agent Systems: Fundamentals, Theories, Systems and Applications (Science Publishers 2014).

[16] See e.g. Peter Braun and others, 'E-Negotiation Systems and Software Agents: Methods, Models, and Applications' in Jatinder ND Gupta, Guisseppi A Forgionne and Manuel Mora T. (eds), *Intelligent Decision-making Support Systems: Foundations, Applications and Challenges* (Springer 2006); Peyman Faratin, 'Automated Service Negotiation Between Autonomous Computational Agents' (Thesis, Queen Mary University of London 2000); David Kinny, Michael Georgeff and Anand Rao, 'A Methodology and Modelling Technique for Systems of BDI Agents' in Walter Van de Velde and John W Perram (eds), *Agents Breaking Away* (Springer 1996).

[17] Kersten and Lai (n 2) 554.

[18] This approach was already supported by some other scholars. See e.g. Alain Pekkar Lempereur, 'Innovation in Teaching Negotiation: Towards a Relevant Use of Multimedia Tools' (2004) 9 *International Negotiation* 141; Don A. Moore and others, 'Long and Short Routes to Success in Electronically Mediated Negotiations: Group Affiliations and Good Vibrations. Organ Behaviour Human Decision Process' (1999) 77 *Organizational Behaviour and Human Decision Processes* 22; Yufei Yuan, Milena Head, Mei Du, 'The Effects of Multimedia Communication on Web-based Negotiation' (2003) 12 *Group Decision Negotiation* 89; N.R. Jennings and others, 'Automated Negotiations: Prospects, Methods and Challenges' (2001) 10 *Group Decision Negotiation* 199.

[19] Braun and others (n 16) 271.

decision-making process used to search for and arrive at an agreement that satisfies the requirements of two or more parties in the presence of limited common knowledge and conflicting preferences'.[20]

Overall, in computer science-related literature the definitions of e-negotiation have clear similarities with the ones provided in behavioural sciences. In both disciplines, the scholars have taken ex-ante approaches in studying the concept of e-negotiation[21] either in terms of concluding a contract or examining the psychological aspects of human behaviour in negotiation.[22] The definition of e-negotiation in computational studies, to a great extent, is unified in a sense that most of such interpretations refer to e-negotiation as a process in which the principal focus is put on employing software, web, and support systems to establish an automated negotiation. Nonetheless, perhaps the main issue with most of these descriptions in computational studies is the lack of adequate emphasis on significance of the human-characteristics – i.e. emotions, values, and cultural factors – in e-negotiations.[23]

9.1.3 Legal Literature

Awareness of the concept of 'e-negotiation' among legal scholars is not a recent phenomenon. Within the last two decades the notion of 'e-negotiation' – as part of the ODR regime in general – has received an extensive amount of scholarly attention in the legal sphere.[24] However, we believe that the conceptual definition of e-negotiation provided by Ethan Katsh and Janet Rifkin (2001) still pioneers among the existing literature on ODR.[25] They referred to this phenomenon as a 'fourth party' that facilitates a dispute resolution process

---

20 Ibid.

21 In the present study, the terms ex-ante and ex-post – in the e-negotiation concept definition – are used to refer to pre- and post-dispute contexts, respectively.

22 See for more information (on the ex-ante and ex-post approaches to negotiation) Noriyuki Yanagawa and Mariko Watanabe, 'Ex Ante Bargaining and Ex Post Enforcement in Trade Credit Supply: Theory and Evidence from China' (2013) *Journal of the Institute of Developing Economies JETRO*.

23 Nazli and others (n 8).

24 Sometimes referred to as 'dyadic negotiation'. See Carrie J. Menkel-Meadow, 'Mediation, Arbitration, and Alternative Dispute Resolution (ADR)' (Social Science Research Network 2015) SSRN Scholarly Paper ID 2608140 https://papers.ssrn.com/abstract=2608140 accessed 29 April 2021; John Lande, 'A Framework for Advancing Negotiation Theory: Implications from a Study of How Lawyers Reach Agreement in Pretrial Litigation' (2014) 16 *Cardozo Journal of Conflict Resolution* 1.

25 Ethan Katsh and Janet Rifkin, *Online Dispute Resolution: Resolving Conflicts in Cyberspace* (Jossey-Bass 2001). See also Pablo Cortes, 'A European Legal Perspective on Consumer Online Dispute Resolution' (2009) *Computer Telecommunications Law Review* 1.

for the other three parties with the assistance of the necessary information and communication technological (ICT) tools. Considering ICT as the fourth party at the negotiation table like a 'friendly and patient robot', the first two parties – that are negotiators – are the two disputants while the third party is the human facilitator. The fourth party (automated negotiation system) embodies a range of facilities in the same manner that the third party does.[26] It is to be noted that in the last few years a growing body of legal literature are emphasizing the use of e-negotiation in a broader context with the capacity to cover both litigious (court-related proceedings) and non-litigious processes (i.e. any alternative model of dispute resolution).[27] In particular, e-negotiation systems may help in organizing information, sending automatic responses, and modifying written communications in a more polite and constructive manner (i.e. blocking foul language). They may also monitor performance, schedule meetings, clarify interests, and prioritize them for the parties to increase transparency and efficiency of dispute resolution procedure.[28] Moreover, these systems enable the involved parties to meet online and work in a shared and protected environment, to get direct access to the databases with precedents, to retrieve and manage key documents, and more importantly to organize old meetings through voice and video-conferencing with the possibility to use auto-translation services where appropriate.[29]

E-negotiation systems may be divided into the two main sub-categories namely, assisted negotiation and automated negotiation. Nonetheless, it may sometimes involve a combination of these two methods. In an assisted negotiation process, parties voluntarily get involved in the negotiation aiming at resolving the incurred issue with the help of a third party. Despite the engagement of the third party, the disputants reach agreement without any external entity empowered to make a decision against their will. In this process, the parties are provided – by the service provider – with a range of facilities, such as a secure platform, communication means, and a possible cloud documents storage.

---

26 Alan Gaitenby, 'The Fourth Party Rises: Evolving Environments of Online Dispute Resolution' (2006) 38 *University of Toledo Law Review* 101.

27 Orna Rabinovich-Einy and Ethan Katsh, 'Artificial Intelligence and the Future of Dispute Resolution: The Age of AI-DR' in Mohamed Abdel Wahab, Daniel Rainey and Ethan Katsh (eds), *Online Dispute Resolution: Theory and Practice* (Eleven International Publishing, 2021).

28 Katsh and Rifkin (n 25) 6.

29 Ibid.

In general, the most significant advantages of the assisted negotiation systems can be observed in their informality, simplicity, and user-friendliness.[30] One of the most renowned models of assisted negotiation systems is eBay[31] which in collaboration with SquareTrade[32] – an ODR service provider – enables a significant number of eBay customers to use an assisted negotiation system for resolving disputes with traders.

In an automated negotiation process, ICT tools take over the negotiation by assisting parties to negotiate online through a process called 'blind-bidding'. Blind-bidding is known as a negotiation procedure that is designed to determine economic settlements for claims in which liability is not challenged.[33] The 'automated' characteristic of these systems – which eliminates the necessity for the involvement of a human third-party – makes the e-negotiation system notably simple and straightforward without any necessity for further assistance to the negotiators. Commonly, automated negotiation involves two parties: a) the party who makes the offer or the side who is going to pay, and b) the demanding party or the one who is seeking payment. Ordinarily, in a multi-user blind-bidding negotiation, in order to enhance the efficiency of process, the system imposes a time-limit on the entire parties to avoid the endless negotiation process among them and keep the flow of negotiations on the right track or end the process. One considerable example of using automated negotiation systems is Fair Outcomes Inc., which according to Lodder and Zeleznikow (2010) has taken an effective strategy in conducting e-negotiation.[34] This company provides its users with access to several proprietary systems that are grounded in mathematical algorithmic theories of fair division based on the model of Brams' algorithms of fair division.[35]

As we have seen, unlike computer and behavioural scientists, jurists have taken an ex-post approach towards e-negotiation. In a legal framework, e-negotiation – where all its major elements including disputants,

---

30 Paul Motion, *Article 17 ECD: Encouragement of Alternative Dispute Resolution. Online Dispute Resolution: A View from Scotland* (Hart Publishing 2005).

31 E-bay https://www.ebay.com accessed 25 April 2021.

32 SquareTrade www.squaretrade.com accessed 25 April 2021.

33 Robert Forsythe, Isaac R.M. and Thomas Palfrey, 'Theories and Tests of "Blind Bidding" in Sealed-Bid Auctions' (1989) 20 *The RAND Journal of Economics* 214.

34 Arno R. Lodder and John Zeleznikow, *Enhanced Dispute Resolution Through the Use of Information Technology Law and Technology, Science, Communication* (Cambridge University Press 2010) 91. See also Marco Giacalone and Sajedeh Salehi, 'Online Dispute Resolution: The Perspective of Service Providers' in Francesco Romeo, Marco Dall'Aglio and Marco Giacalone (eds) *Algorithmic Conflict Resolution* (Giappichelli Torino 2019).

35 Steven J. Brams and Alan D. Taylor, *Fair Division: From Cake-Cutting to Dispute Resolution* (Cambridge: Cambridge University Press 1996) 30.

a neutral third party, and technology as the fourth element are present – is utilised to resolve a dispute. Further, in cases of applying advanced forms of e-negotiation, the ICT as one of the major components of the process can assist the parties in analysing legal issues and decision-making by replacing the human third-party.[36] As Thiessen (2012) emphasized, application of advanced e-negotiation provides the parties with an opportunity to have access to a neutral, super intelligent, and secure platform that assists them in reaching an agreement in an expedited and cost-effective manner.[37]

9.1.4 E-negotiation: A Worldwide Perspective

At present, e-negotiation is used across the world as a model of online dispute resolution. There are several advantages – i.e. cost-effectiveness, expedition, convenience, and simplification – making e-negotiation attractive for resolving civil disputes between counterparts. Despite these advantages in using e-negotiation to resolve disputes, one should bear in mind that not all e-negotiation service providers have succeeded in offering an efficient e-negotiation service to their users. The following section investigates into some of the most commonly used e-negotiation services – either offered by public and/or private service providers – around the world,[38] analysing their strengths and the major grounds of their failures, where appropriate.

9.2 E-NEGOTIATION: EXAMPLES OF BEST PRACTICES

9.2.1 Smartsettle – Canada

The Canadian-based e-negotiation service provider was developed by Ernest Thiessen in association with his company iCan Systems Inc.[39] Smartsettle

---

36 Pablo Cortes, *The Law of Consumer Redress in an Evolving Digital Market: Upgrading from Alternative to Online Dispute Resolution* (Cambridge University Press 2017) 47.

37 Ernest Thiessen, Bruce Hiebert, and Paul Miniato, 'ODR and eNegotiation' in Muhammad Abdel Wahab, Ethan Katsh, and Daniel Rainey (eds) *Online Dispute Resolution: Theory and Practice* (Eleven International Publishing 2012).

38 These services were selected based on criteria i.e. their extensive use by individuals for civil dispute resolution and offering a complete online platform that supports the whole negotiation process from intake to conclusion. This approach has been adopted by Bellucci and Zeleznikow (2018). See Emilia Bellucci and John Zeleznikow, 'How Online Negotiation Support Systems Empower People to Engage in Mediation: The Provision of Important Trade-off Advice' (2018) 5 *IJODR* 94, 95.

39 SmartSettle www.smartsettle.com/smartsettle-infinity accessed 25 April 2021.

enables its users to engage in an e-negotiation process on a secure virtual platform. There are several offered packages for using e-negotiation systems that a potential user can choose from based on some criteria, such as type and value of the issue to be negotiated, also the number of parties involved in this process. For high-value cases, where several parties with many issues are involved, the offered e-negotiation system is the Smartsettle Infinity.[40] The Smartsettle Infinity – in the capacity of a multi-interest negotiation tool – is claimed to be a technically comprehensive and advanced e-negotiation system, which is particularly designed to deal with sophisticated negotiation procedures among unlimited number of parties and issues to swiftly optimise solutions.[41] This program uses a blind-bidding mechanism to enable negotiators to rate their preferences based on the importance that they attach to the issue at stake. For instance, in concluding an agreement among various shareholders, the blind-bidding model used in the Smartsettle Infinity demands each party to explicitly indicate the amount of money they intend to receive. Subsequently, either side of the e-negotiation process receives suggestions – based on their preferences – from the algorithmic system. The party is free to accept or reject the offer at any time. Currently, Smartsettle Infinity is claimed to be the world's most advanced e-negotiation system.[42] Despite this, to further evaluate the effectiveness of this tool, future studies are recommended to provide more concrete and thorough analysis.

9.2.2 The Civil Resolution Tribunal – Canada

The Canadian Civil Resolution Tribunal (CRT)[43] was primarily developed in 2011 as an alternative to the existing traditional courts in British Colombia, Canada.[44] The CRT, which is also the first of its kind in the entire world, uses e-negotiation as part of a combined dispute resolution process.[45] Currently, the CRT has jurisdiction over the majority of low threshold claims that fall under $5,000;[46] specific types of traffic injuries disputes; strata property (regardless of the amount of the claim); and disputes related to societies and cooperative

---

40 Ibid.

41 Rabonovich-Einy and Katsh (n 27).

42 See Cortes (n 36).

43 Civil Resolution Tribunal https://civilresolutionbc.ca accessed 29 April 2021.

44 Anjanette H. Raymond and Scott J. Shackelford, 'Technology, Ethics, and Access to Justice: Should an Algorithm be Deciding your Case?' (2014) 35 *Michigan Journal of International Law* 485, 505.

45 Shannon Salter S. and Darin Thompson, 'Public-Centred Civil Justice Redesign: A Case Study of the British Columbia Civil Resolution Tribunal' (2017) *Social Science Research Network* 114.

46 Canadian dollar (CAD).

associations of any amount.[47] The CRT uses a multi-tier model of ODR to provide a more convenient, cost-effective, and facilitated access to justice for citizens.[48] While the first phase refers to the use of a solution explorer by the applicant, the second phase relates to the e-negotiation between the parties involved in a dispute. This design, with the aim to shift from an adversarial to an amicable approach towards resolving the dispute, provides the parties with an opportunity to have an interest-based e-negotiation. This approach assists the parties to put more emphasis on identifying their common grounds through direct communications with each other and reach a possible agreement.[49]

In case the applicant is not able to find the answer to his/her issues in the solution explorer, s/he can begin with the negotiation. The CRT e-negotiation is optimized by a constructed direct party-to-party negotiation and emphasizes the collaboration among the parties. On the one hand, such a non-adversarial collaborative e-negotiation process facilitates a more amicable, cheaper, and quicker dispute resolution experience for the users. While the CRT e-negotiation model supports the parties through the provision of specific templates to be used for producing statements and arguments, the process is subject to short and strict timelines. During the entire e-negotiation procedure, the CRT's least intervention is limited to monitoring the communications exchanged between the parties to ensure that no one is subjected to abuse or harassment during the communications. It is noteworthy that the parties may fail to reach an agreement in the CRT e-negotiation phase; however, they have at least obtained more knowledge about each other's preferences and the existing opportunities up-front the next level, namely adjudication.

9.2.3 Family_Winner and AssetDivider[50] – Australia

Family_Winner[51] was developed by Zeleznikow and Bellucci, in 2003, as a computerized program enabling its users to find the best possible ways of

47 See Civil Resolution Tribunal (n 43).

48 See Salter and Thompson (n 45) 116.

49 Ibid.

50 The first developments in using decision-support systems in the context of dispute resolution in Australia were through the efforts of Zeleznikow and Stranieri within their 'Split-Up' project. See Andrew Stranieri and others, 'A Hybrid Rule – Neural Approach for the Automation of Legal Reasoning in the Discretionary Domain of Family Law in Australia' (1999) 7 *Artificial Intelligence and Law* 153.

51 See Emilia Bellucci and John Zeleznikow, 'Developing Negotiation Decision Support Systems That Support Mediators: A Case Study of the Family-Winner System' (2006) 13 *Journal of Artificial Intelligence and Law* 233.

attaining their goals through a decision support system.[52] The advice given by this Australian model of e-negotiation was mostly predicated on the Nash's equilibrium of optimal negotiations,[53] by deploying a range of game theory strategies to provide the best possible suggestions for the parties on how to distribute the items based on the value of the relevant ratings (according to parties' preferences).[54] To ensure a fair division of property, Family_Winner used the point-allocation model of the 'Adjusted Winner' theory.[55] Family_Winner was applied to divorce-related issues – that fall under the scope of the Australian Family Law[56] – and for matters that are concerned with asset division procedures.[57] Despite the evaluation of Family_Winner by legal practitioners and mediators as a model of negotiation decision support system with great potential, there were some serious concerns indicating that this system has not adequately focused on the issue of justice (e.g. the necessity to consider the needs of children in negotiations between divorcing couples).[58]

The feedback obtained from the Family_Winner enabled Bellucci and Zeleznikow to develop a new system called AssetDivider, in 2008. In the newly designed model, the limitations of its predecessor were removed to improve the efficiency of the new model. AssetDivider is also greatly focused on the parties' interests and mutual gains (based upon a trade-off strategy) in lieu of emphasizing only the parties' self-interest.[59] Through listing a disputed item, it will be allocated to the disputant that has valued it more through the rating system. Upon the completion of items allocation, the parties are provided with information about the realistic financial obligations on items considering their current and future financial status.[60] In general, as stated by AssetDivider's developers, this system can be most useful as a preparatory supportive tool prior to the real negotiation process. The parties can greatly benefit from this model to clearly determine their priorities and preferences in the asset division process – having a safe financial security for the future –

---

52 John Zeleznikow, 'Can Artificial Intelligence and Online Dispute Resolution Enhance Efficiency and Effectiveness in Courts' (2017) 8 *IJCA* 30, 41.

53 John Nash, 'Two-Person Cooperative Games' (1953) 21 *Econometrica* 128.

54 Zeleznikow (n 52).

55 Brams and Taylor (n 35).

56 Bellucci and Zeleznikow believed that the Family_Winner was not a domain dependent instrument. See Bellucci and Zeleznikow (n 51) 236.

57 Zeleznikow (n 52).

58 Ibid.

59 Emilia Bellucci, 'Software Developed for Use in Family Mediation-AssetDivider' (2009) 482 *CEUR Workshop Proceedings* 56.

60 Bellucci and Zeleznikow (n 38) 95–6.

on the one hand, and to identify the issues that may prevent the parties from achieving a mutual satisfactory agreement on the other.[61]

9.2.4 Resolver – The United Kingdom

Resolver[62] is a platform which was officially launched in 2014 for providing consumers and traders with an opportunity to resolve the conflict through a complete e-negotiation procedure. This digital platform and the offered services enable consumers to get access to an easy model of complaint resolution to seek justice directly from the business counterparty. Resolver entails a full list of e-mail contacts of the complaint departments or any customer service-related section of thousands of major companies in the UK. It facilitates an environment for the parties to have an opportunity for discussing the incurred issues in a structured and transparent manner. The consumer can file his/her complaint with the intended company through filling in an online form. In filling in this form, the consumer is assisted by having access to templates containing standard phrases for drafting the complaint. The users can even insert emoticons to better express their emotions during communications. Upon completion of the form, it is then directly sent to the relevant customer service or complaint department of that particular company. The trader can respond to the Resolver e-mail address to keep the record of the exchange of messages in the platform's case file for further communications between the parties. Users are notified through their e-mail about any responses from the counterparty and are prompted to escalate when responses are not received. If the trader does not respond to the complaint in a reasonable period, the consumer can escalate his/her case to the relevant ombudsman, adjudicators, or choose using any other dispute resolution method. At present, Resolver can be used in a wide category of industries, such as finance, telecom, transport, and travel. This service is free of charge for consumers and businesses who would like to use this intermediary digital platform to resolve their disputes.

9.3 E-NEGOTIATION IN THE EU

Previous sections discussed the world best practices of e-negotiations. In this part, we will focus on some of the main present and past e-negotiation models across the EU that provide their users with an opportunity to engage in direct e-negotiation for the purpose of settling disputes. The use of e-negotiation in the EU – compared to Canada and Australia – is limited. Nevertheless,

61 Ibid., 101.

62 The Resolver https://www.resolver.co.uk accessed 29 April 2021.

it remains imperative to study and analyse the existing European models to understand the opportunities and challenges in developing advanced models of e-negotiation systems at the Union level.

9.3.1 Rechtwijzer and Uitelkaar.nl[63] – The Netherlands

Rechtwijzer[64] was established with the intention of not only reducing the costs of civil proceedings considerably, but also improving access to justice for citizens in the Netherlands. [65] This service was presented in two versions. In 2007, the Dutch Legal Aid Board[66] designed Rechtwijzer 1.0 platform with the purpose of aiding citizens to find a lawyer and/or judicial support. This directory was further developed in 2014 as Rechtwijzer 2.0 by the Dutch Ministry of Justice and Security[67] in collaboration with The Hague Institute for the Innovation of Law (HiiL)[68] and Modria.[69] The fundamental objective of the updated version was to assist citizens to resolve different types of disputes through a multi-tiered and facilitated process – e.g. diagnosing the issue and providing a secure and reliable virtual environment for conducting direct negotiation with the counterparty – on a coherent online platform.

This platform facilitated engaging in an asynchronous – and fully confidential – dialogue for disputants based on their given answers during the Questions and Answers session.[70] Rechtwijzer 2.0 platform initially began with settling matrimonial disputes, including divorce[71] and other ancillary matters (e.g. child custody and maintenance allowance).[72] This competency was then extended to other types of conflicts, such as landlord-tenant issues

---

63 See Laura Kistemaker, 'Rechtwijzer and Uitelkaar.nl. Dutch Experiences with ODR for Divorce' (2021) *Family Court Review* 4.

64 Rechtwijzer literally refers to 'conflict resolution guide'.

65 Kistemaker (n 63).

66 In Dutch *'Raad voor Rechtsbijstand'*.

67 Government of the Netherlands https://www.government.nl/ministries/ministry-of-justice-and-security accessed 25 April 2021.

68 The Hague Institute for Innovation of Law https://www.hill.org/project/rechtwijzer accessed 29 April 2021.

69 Modria is a well-established ODR platform run by the US-based TylerTech Inc. See https://www.tylertech.com/products/Modria accessed 25 April 2021.

70 The diagnosis, information provision, and the dialogue between the parties on the platform were gratuitous; however, the applicants were charged for submitting a case and/or the third-party involvement during the process. See Cortes (n 36) 54.

71 Dory Reiling, 'Beyond Court Digitalization with Online Dispute Resolution' (2017) Social Science Research Network 2017, SSRN Scholarly Paper ID 2999333 https://papers.ssrn.com/abstract=2999333 accessed 28 April 2021.

72 David John Harvey, *Collisions in the Digital Paradigm: Law and Rule-making in the Internet Age* (Bloomsbury Publishing 2017).

and employment disputes. In case the negotiation fails to settle the dispute, the parties can escalate the issue to mediation and/or arbitration. Although the platform was designed in a concrete and transparent structure, it failed to attract citizens' interest to favour it over the traditional means of access to justice. Ergo, in early 2017, Rechtwijzer 2.0 was terminated by the collaborating partners. The major reason behind this failure can be mainly found in the shortfall of the government funding to support the project. Some scholars also believed that Rechtwijzer 2.0 was not given enough time – considering the time required for raising citizens' awareness and time-consuming nature of family disputes – to prove its potential as it only functioned for three years.[73] Despite the closure of Rechtwijzer, an alternative platform was established as part of a developed programme by the legal tech company Justice42 in collaboration with HiiL. This new platform which is called Uitelkaar.nl[74] remains exclusively limited to the divorce market in the Netherlands.

Uitelkaar.nl services are fee-based and the applicant pays a fixed rate based on the selected module designed for divorce and/or parenting.[75] By using Uitelkaar.nl, the parties can directly discuss their interests, indicate their preferences, and finally write down the concluded agreement between themselves. This ODR platform provides couples with an opportunity to discuss their issues in a structured method to amicably reach an agreement. As Kistemaker (2021) points out there is evidence that supports that this platform has functioned successfully in meeting its core objective of providing an effective model of e-negotiation process.[76] One of the novelties of Uitelkaar.nl is the use of a 'case manager' during negotiations between the parties. In this system, the lawyers' involvement has been limited to reviewing a concluded agreement and/or providing necessary advice on a specific subject-matter for the disputants. However, the case manager – who is in fact a paralegal acting as a personal coach for each individual case – plays an essential role throughout the negotiation process by conducting a variety of administrative tasks and providing basic legal assistance to ensure the process moves in a correct direction and leads to a legally enforceable agreement.[77] Based on the collected surveys for the period of 2017–2019, the majority of the users emphasized the effective role of the 'case manager' within the conflict resolution process.[78]

---

73 Roger Smith, 'The decline and fall (and potential resurgence) of the Rechtwijzer' (Legal Voice UK, 12 September 2017) http://legalvoice.org.uk/decline-fall-potential-resurgence-rechtwijzer accessed 24 April 2021.

74 Uitelkaar.nl https://uitelkaar.nl accessed 30 April 2021.

75 Ibid.

76 Kistemaker (n 63).

77 Ibid., 5.

78 Ibid., 6–7.

In summary, the preliminary findings show that the Uitelkaar.nl platform certainly offers new opportunities to its users to experience a more cost-effective, expedited, and amicable dispute resolution for their divorce-related conflicts. Nonetheless, further research and investigations are necessary to analyse whether this model of e-negotiation has been successful in accomplishing its main objectives.

9.3.2 Youstice[79] – Slovakia

Youstice is an ODR service provider based in Slovakia that was founded in 2014 with the principal objective to handle large volumes of low-value consumer complaints about online or offline purchases of goods and services. Youstice enables its consumer and business users to experience a simple ODR process through using various methods. For instance, the applicant has access to a list of common issues and possible redresses and a list of ODR service providers with direct access to the profiles of the accredited ADR experts. Nonetheless, one of the most significant features of this ODR platform refers to the application of a two-level dispute resolution model,[80] namely negotiation and referral to an ADR expert, that can be conducted within the Youstice's smart web platform. E-negotiation takes place as the initial phase of dispute resolution between consumer and trader. This structured or asynchronous dialogue can take place within a limited area on the platform. All these communications can be conducted in the languages of the parties with the possibility of using simultaneous translation.[81] The majority of disputes are resolved at the negotiation level.[82] Nevertheless, if the parties fail to reach an agreement, each side can advance to the second phase of dispute resolution and submit the application to an accredited ODR entity chosen from the available list on the Youstice's website. The use of the facilitated negotiation level is free of charge for consumers,[83] and Youstice funds itself from the retailers who pre-register and display the Youstice logo on their marketing.

---

[79] Youstice www.youstice.com accessed 25 April 2021.

[80] Cortes (n 36) 54–5.

[81] Colin Rule, 'ODR News April 2014' (2014) 1 *International Journal of Online Dispute Resolution* 97.

[82] 'MEET JUSTICE - Online Dispute Resolution' http://www.odreurope.com/meet-justice accessed 20 April 2021.

[83] In the second phase where the parties submit the unresolved case to an accredited ODR entity, the third-party (ODR service provider) fee applies. See Cortes (n 36) 55.

9.3.3 EU ODR Platform: A Cross-border Model of E-negotiation

9.3.3.1 Establishment and function

The EU Online Dispute Resolution platform[84] was established in compliance with Regulation (EU) No 524/2013 on online dispute resolution for consumer disputes (the EU ODR Regulation).[85] Pursuant to Article 2 of the Regulation, the major objective of creating the EU ODR platform (the Platform) is to facilitate the use of effective, low-cost, expedited, and fair out-of-court ODR mechanisms for resolving disputes between consumers and traders at the Union level. Therefore, since early 2016 the Platform has been functioning as a central access point to connect EU consumers and EU-based traders with the registered competent ADR bodies to settle their disputes. It is, however, necessary to point out that according to Article 2 of the ODR Regulation, the Platform can only be used in cases of – domestic and/or cross-border – disputes stemming from online purchases of goods and services.[86]

The ODR Regulation has mandated each Member State to designate and announce the name and contact details of – at least – one ODR contact point (i.e. European Consumer Centre Network bodies or any other association body) to the European Commission. Any of the introduced contact points must have necessarily at least two ODR advisers to support and assist the parties in the process of resolving disputes related to a complaint submitted to the Platform.[87]

This ODR procedure consists of four main phases to initiate a complaint. Firstly, the consumer (or the consumer representative) should contact the trader by filling in the online complaint form that is accessible through the website of the Platform.[88] This form is available in all the EU official languages and users are able to benefit from a translation tool – integrated in the system – to convert the exchanged messages and texts into the language of

---

[84] See the Platform at https://ec.europa.eu/consumers/odr/main/?event=main.complaints.screeningphase accessed 25 April 2021.

[85] Regulation (EU) No 524/2013 of the European Parliament and of the Council of 21 May 2013 on online dispute resolution for consumer disputes and amending Regulation (EC) No 2006/2004 and Directive 2009/22/EC (Regulation on consumer ODR).

[86] Pablo Cortes, *The New Regulatory Framework for Consumer Dispute Resolution* (Oxford University Press 2016) 5.

[87] Art 7, the EU ODR Regulation.

[88] 'Online Dispute Resolution' (*European Commission*) https://ec.europa.eu/consumers/odr/main/?consumer-question3=N&complaintType=1&event=main.complaints.new accessed 25 April 2021.

the receiving party.[89] In this sense, as language differences is one of the main barriers to effective access to justice for consumers in the EU,[90] we believe that offering consumers free translation is a considerable step towards facilitating access to justice for them.

Next, upon submission of the complaint form, the trader will receive an e-mail that contains a link to be directed to the Platform.[91] Once the trader has been notified about the complaint and its supporting information – bearing in mind that there is no obligation to accept the consumer's invitation for taking part in the ADR process – three possible scenarios can be imagined: 1) to directly contact the consumer to resolve the dispute through negotiation; 2) to agree with the consumer on having one of the approved ADR bodies get involved and help settling the dispute, and paying the settlement fees to the ADR entity; or 3) to avoid responding to the consumer's complaint that closes the case within 30 calendar days after submission of the complaint.[92] In the latter circumstance, Article 9(8) of the ODR Regulation provides that the complainant party shall be informed by the Platform about the right to contact an ODR adviser to obtain information related to other available remedies for seeking justice.

If the parties agreed on an approved ADR body to assist them resolving their dispute, the Platform will automatically send the information and details of the case to the selected ADR entity. The ADR body then assesses the dispute and should respond to the parties without delay to inform them whether it will handle the complaint. If the dispute resolution body refuses to deal with the case and the parties do not agree on another ADR entity, the file will be closed, and the complainant will be treated under the provisions of Article 9(8) to contact an ODR adviser. On the other hand, where the ADR entity has agreed to handle the case, it is not obligatory to conduct the dispute resolution process on the Platform. As a result, if necessary, the neutral third party can invite the parties to an external platform to proceed with the settlement.

Finally, the ADR body should take its final decision within a maximum of 90 calendar days from the date it has received the complete complaint file.[93]

---

[89] Emma Van Gelder and Alexandre Biard, 'The Online Dispute Resolution Platform after One Year of Operation: A Work in Progress with Promising Potential' (2018) Social Science Research Network 2018, SSRN Scholarly Paper ID 3169254:5 https://papers.ssrn.com/abstract=3169254 accessed 25 April 2021.

[90] Elena Ontanu and Ekaterina Pannebakker, 'Tackling Language Obstacles in Cross-Border Litigation: The European Order for Payment and the European Small Claims Procedure Approach' (2013) 5(3) *Erasmus Law Review* 169.

[91] Art 9(3), the EU ODR Regulation.

[92] Cortes (n 86) 121. See also Van Gelder and Biard (n 89).

[93] Art 8 of the Directive 2013/11/EU of the European Parliament and of the Council of 21 May 2013 on alternative dispute resolution for consumer disputes and amend-

It is noteworthy that the ADR entity shall transmit all the information concerning the date of receipt of the complaint file, the subject-matter of the case, the closing date of the dispute resolution process, and finally the result of the procedure to the Platform.[94]

9.3.3.2 Assessment and future implications

Despite the features and function of the Platform that were previously discussed, the central concern remains the extent to which this online tool has achieved success in providing consumers with an effective, fair, expedited, and low-cost access to justice for their claims. One of the most considerable impacts of launching the Platform can be observed in the context of raising awareness about the use of ODR methods for resolving consumer-to-business disputes. Consumer awareness has been considered as a critical key element in the success of an ODR establishment.[95]

In this regard, the data published by the EU Commission within the third statistical report on the function of the Platform covers significant information regarding its use by consumers within the entire period of 2019.[96] According to this report, in 2019, approximately 2.8 million visits have been registered for the Platform, which compared to the registered figures for 2018 where 5 million people[97] visited the Platform, the number of visits has been drastically decreased. The main cause for this considerable reduction may be connected to the offered 'self-test' process by the system. Consequently, during the self-test process many consumers found that the use of the Platform is not the most appropriate redressal mechanism to resolve their dispute with their counterpart, leading to a significant decrease in the number of filed complaints with the Platform.[98]

---

ing Regulation (EC) No 2006/2004 and Directive 2009/22/EC (Directive on consumer ADR).

94 Art 10, the EU ODR Regulation.

95 Maria Jose Schmidt-Kessen, Rafaela Nogueira, and Marta Cantero Gamito, 'Success or Failure? Effectiveness of Consumer ODR Platforms in Brazil and in the EU' (2020) 43 *Journal of Consumer Policy* 659, 668.

96 European Commission, *The 3rd Statistical Report of the European Commission on the Functioning of the European ODR Platform* (December 2020) https://ec.europa.eu/info/sites/info/files/odr_report_2020_clean_final.pdf accessed 25 April 2021.

97 European Commission, *The 2nd Statistical Report of the European Commission on the Functioning of the European ODR Platform*, (December 2018) https://ec.europa.eu/info/sites/info/files/2nd_report_on_the_functioning_of_the_odr_platform_3.pdf accessed 25 April 2021.

98 The self-test option enables the complainants to identify the most appropriate dispute resolution method for their issues with the trader. See *The 3rd Statistical Report* (n 96).

In our viewpoint, the main shortcoming refers to the fact that the Platform only functions as a referral point that connects the disputants to a neutral third-party. Despite this, the tool has the potential to function as an independent e-negotiation system to be used by disputants as a well-established and stand-alone dispute resolver tool. The present chapter favours the approach that proffers the Platform should be developed into a two-tiered procedure. Accordingly, in the first stage this tool plays the role of a third party in e-negotiation procedures providing consumers and traders with an opportunity to directly negotiate their issues without any external intervention. At this level, the parties should have the possibility for recording all the exchanged communications and information between them.[99] If the direct negotiation between the disputants fails and they cannot reach a settlement, the dispute can be escalated to the next level; namely agreeing on an approved ADR entity amongst the list available on the Platform. At this phase, the ADR body enters the negotiation process as the fourth party and assists the disputants to reach an agreement. The final issue refers to limiting the use of the Platform to disputes that arise out of e-commerce transactions. As a result, offline transactions remain ineligible to benefit from this instrument. We believe that the Platform must be also made available to disputes arising from offline transactions to meet the needs of more consumers and traders for settling their disputes in a more cost-effective and expedited way.

In summary, the establishment of the EU ODR platform has increased the consumers and businesses' awareness of out-of-court forms of dispute resolution, particularly e-negotiation. However, future improvements are crucial in order to further develop this system from a mere referral point to a two-tiered independent, trustworthy, and efficient e-negotiation tool with the potential to conduct the entire negotiation process between consumers and traders on this forum.

9.3.4 Lessons Learnt and Ways Forward

The devoted efforts into developing advanced models of e-negotiation systems across the EU have remained limited to local tests at national levels. The findings of this chapter manifest that – so far – the only model of cross-border e-negotiation at the Union level is the EU ODR Platform. However, this tool only functions as an intermediary platform that offers considerably basic e-negotiation services to consumers and business. Analysing successful experiences from common law countries such as Canada, Australia, and the UK in using advanced models of e-negotiation for resolving civil disputes proves

[99] This approach has been adopted by Cortes in (n 86) 136–7.

the potential of these tech-driven models to ameliorate effective access to justice for citizens. At the EU level, in a civil law context, considering there are 27 Member States with different and sophisticated civil procedural rules, extremely lengthy court proceedings, and high costs for consumers manifest for a necessity to follow the common law experiences in developing the application of amicable, simplified, and user-friendly systems for resolving civil disputes. Although the substantial differences between common law and civil law jurisdictions have affected their approaches towards integrating ODR into their legal systems,[100] we still believe that the experiences of common law countries in application of e-negotiation are useful for civil law systems in (at least) three major themes: methodology, design, and system implementation. An e-negotiation system has the potential for protecting EU citizens and granting effective remedies to improve individuals' access to justice for their disputes and, in particular, maintaining the immense advantage of consumer trust in the EU internal market.

During this research, we understood that the first and the most significant obstacle refers to the existing inadequate awareness among consumers and traders about the benefits of using e-negotiation. The low degree of citizens' awareness of an ODR system most probably results in its failure.[101] Therefore, we recommend that policy makers invest in appropriate measures for raising citizens' awareness of the existence as well as benefits of using e-negotiation for resolving their disputes.

The second major impeding factor refers to the lack of public and also private funding available to e-negotiation system developers. It is critical to financially foster feasible projects for developing e-negotiation systems. The financial support will enable interested and qualified stakeholders to conduct the relevant need-assessment and capacity-building research for designing and testing effective models of e-negotiations. Next, the present lack of court-annexed ODR system – i.e. in encouraging disputants to exhaust e-negotiation prior to commencement of the court proceedings – can be also considered as a challenge for increasing the use of these systems by citizens. For instance, the successful inclusion of ODR as part of the litigation proceedings in India has resulted in increased use of out-of-court dispute resolution

---

[100] Civil law countries – compared to common law jurisdictions – have taken a less lenient approach towards introducing ODR into their legal systems. The main reason, according to Dory Reiling, is to be found in the requirements for making significant changes into procedural and legal frameworks of civil law legal systems. See Julia Hornle and Matthew Hewitson, 'Technical Study on Online Dispute Resolution Mechanisms' (2018) European Committee on Legal Cooperation (CDCJ 5) 44, 115.

[101] Schmidt-Kessen, Nogueira, and Cantero Gamito (n 95) 668.

models by citizens and has released the courts from a huge workload.[102] Another advantage of implementing court-annexed ODR grounds in enhancing individuals' trust and more willingness from disputants to try the amicable and non-litigious dispute resolution models. One should, however, note that the state's support in encouraging also facilitating the use of such systems plays a pivotal role in advancing the application of e-negotiation.

Eventually, to ensure that end-users get access to an effective and secure e-negotiation model, it is necessary for the service providers to sufficiently engage in constant monitoring, assessment, and improvement of the technological systems used for services offered to their users. These tasks can be either carried out based on self-built improvement processes or via periodic and systematic developers' intervention.[103] In this spirit, one should note that the application of e-negotiation is no longer limited to simply using e-mails or videoconferences by negotiators to reach a settlement. In the recent years, the legal-tech companies have benefited from applying algorithms in designing more sophisticated systems of e-negotiation to increase the effectiveness of such models of dispute resolutions. At the Union level, over the last decade several projects have been carried out by academics in order to design automated negotiation systems with the potential to be used for resolving cross-border civil claims. One of these EU-based schemes is the CREA project that was launched in 2017 by a group of legal scholars in close collaboration with behavioural economists and computer scientists. The CREA project thoroughly examined the possibility of implementing advanced negotiation systems – based on game-theory algorithms – in cases of transnational asset divisions in divorce and inheritance-related conflicts in seven EU jurisdictions.[104] The CREA project also established a 'European Common Ground of Available Rights (ECGARs)' by extracting the similarities – in the rules of asset division in divorce and inheritance – among the laws of the involved Member States, and incorporated this data into the CREA Software.[105] Nonetheless, considering that the CREA is a recent e-negotiation model,

---

[102] Chitranjali Negi, 'Concept Online Dispute Resolution in India' (2015) Social Science Research Network, SSRN Scholarly Paper ID 2596267 https://papers.ssrn.com/abstract=2596267 accessed 27 April 2021.

[103] John Zeleznikow, 'The Split-up Project: Induction, Context and Knowledge Discovery in Law' (2004) 3 *Law, Probability and Risk* 147.

[104] These Member States included Belgium, France, Italy, Slovenia, Croatia, Greece, and Lithuania. See Giacalone and Salehi (n 4).

[105] See for more information on the ECGARs Marco Giacalone and Sajedeh Salehi, 'Conflict Resolution with Equitative Algorithms – A tool to establish a European Common Ground of Available Rights' in Silvio Martuccelli, Francesco Romeo, and Marco Giacalone (eds), *The European Common Ground of Available Rights* (Scientifica Napoli 2019) 111.

further research is certainly needed to fully evaluate the extent to which this instrument has proven successful in achieving its core objectives, and enabling its users to reach an agreement via using an amicable e-negotiation procedure.

9.4 CONCLUSION

The objective of the current chapter was to explore the concept of e-negotiation and its existing applications for resolving civil disputes in the EU and beyond. For that purpose, we initially discussed the concept of e-negotiation in behavioural sciences and computer studies against the backdrop of legal literature. It was understood that the main common feature among all these fields is in considering e-negotiation as an applicable method for reaching a mutual agreement between parties using ICT tools. The major differences, however, arise in the approach taken by computer and behavioural scientists that explore e-negotiation mostly from an ex-ante perspective, while jurists adopt a more ex-post approach to e-negotiation in the context of dispute resolution. As the first study of its type, we pointed out the existing gap in a common understanding of the notion of 'e-negotiation' and the context of its application among legal scholars on the one hand, and computer and behavioural scientists on the other. Thence, the insights gained from the first part of this chapter can contribute to filling this gap and facilitate cross-disciplinary dialogues among jurists and other scientists, especially when they need to work together.[106]

This chapter also assessed several widely used e-negotiation systems around the world, discussing their strengths and weaknesses. At the EU level, we referred to the EU ODR Platform as a system that, despite its current limited capacity, has the potential to offer a successful model of an EU e-negotiation system. This Platform, certainly, can be valuable in promoting cross-border access to justice – particularly for vulnerable groups – through facilitating e-negotiations between consumers and traders on a single platform. Overall, the findings of this study indicate that learning from the best global practices and tackling the existing obstacles in the EU can help to establish an effective e-negotiation model for resolving civil disputes as a means to improve citizens' access to justice.

---

[106] As happened to the authors in several interdisciplinary projects such as CREA and NEMESIS.

10. Unpacking content moderation: The rise of social media platforms as online civil courts

Catalina Goanta and Pietro Ortolani

10.1 INTRODUCTION

In today's data-driven economy, social media platforms enable an ever-growing range of interactions. As a consequence, users have been increasingly generating 'content', such as tweets, Facebook posts, or Instagram images. Unavoidably, such interaction (which is often global in scale) also generates disputes. For example, social media content can infringe copyright, constitute an unfair commercial practice, or violate privacy. Social media platforms allow users to 'report' content, i.e., to file complaints. Through these reporting mechanisms, users request the platforms to take action, and 'moderate' the content. Moderation typically amounts to removing the content, making it inaccessible, and/or suspending or terminating the accounts of those who posted the content. The purpose of this chapter is to analyse content moderation in relation to the dispute resolution architectures currently being built by social media platforms. By moderating content, social media platforms operate as veritable online courts.

In the past years, content governance has found itself high on the agenda of many social media platforms. Platforms have been developing private infrastructures intended to enhance self-regulation (e.g., Facebook Oversight Board; Twitch Safety Council),[1] or to ensure compliance with mandatory norms (e.g., the EU Audiovisual Media Services Directive).[2] Through these initiatives, platforms attempt to show their willingness to create or adhere to

---

[1] 'Facebook Oversight Board' https://oversightboard.com accessed 29 April 2021; 'Introducing the Twitch Safety Advisory Council' (*Twitch*, 14 May 2020) www.blog.twitch.tv/en/2020/05/14/introducing-the-twitch-safety-advisory-council/ accessed 29 April 2021.

[2] Directive 2010/13/EU of the European Parliament and of the Council of 10 March 2010 on the coordination of certain provisions laid down by law, regulation or

rules that ought to protect public interest. However, these very platforms are essentially private entities, not designed to uphold fundamental rights in the same way as sovereign States. To a certain extent, this explains why platforms such as Facebook, Instagram, TikTok or Twitter prioritize certain forms of content moderation over others. In other words, platforms decide which rights should be protected (either algorithmically, or through human moderation), and which rights remain without a remedy. As an illustration, copyright or terrorist activity on social media is often algorithmically screened and taken down in case of infringement, whereas content affecting consumers (e.g., the non-disclosure of advertising)[3] beyond criminal activities (e.g., illegal sales) is not. These preliminary observations show how uneven and fragmented the current landscape of content moderation is. As a consequence, it is necessary to scrutinize the phenomenon, assessing how, and to what extent, social media platforms contribute to the protection of different types of rights.

As already mentioned, when users have problems with the content they encounter, they can report it to the platform. In limited instances, the platform operates as a mediator; for instance, to comply with the US Digital Millennium Copyright Act,[4] Youtube allows users to negotiate remedies such as sharing revenue in the case of so-called Content ID claims. In the vast majority of cases, however, platforms act as adjudicators. On the one hand, this phenomenon can enhance access to justice, allowing an efficient resolution of low-value, high-frequency disputes that cannot be realistically dealt with by individual courts. On the other hand, however, the way in which platforms currently perform these functions raises significant worries; at the moment, access to justice depends on private, largely automated decision-making processes established by platforms, lacking transparency and legitimacy.

The remainder of the chapter proceeds as follows. Section 10.2 lays down the theoretical framework, explaining why content moderation should be understood as a form of digital dispute resolution, and how social media platforms have progressively embraced their role as private adjudicators. This section includes an empirical overview of the reporting mechanisms of four social media platforms (Facebook, TikTok, Twitch and Twitter). In section 10.3, we explore the current shortcomings of content moderation, pointing out three problems which currently affect the transparency and legitimacy

---

administrative action in Member States concerning the provision of audiovisual media services [2010] OJ L 95 (Audiovisual Media Services Directive).

[3] The use of 'advertorials' constitutes an unfair commercial practice, pursuant to point 11 of Annex I to Directive 2005/29/EC of the European Parliament and of the Council of 11 May 2005 concerning unfair business-to-consumer commercial practices in the internal market, [2005] OJ L 149 (Unfair Commercial Practices Directive).

[4] Digital Millennium Copyright Act of 1998.

of the dispute resolution activities carried out by platforms through content moderation. In section 10.4, we analyse Facebook's recent decision to institute a quasi-judicial body, the Oversight Board, to deal with delicate and significant content moderation disputes. Section 10.5 explores the possible future regulation of content moderation, with specific reference to the European Union and the proposal for a Digital Services Act (hereinafter, DSA). Finally, section 10.6 presents some conclusions.

10.2 CONTENT MODERATION AS CONFLICT RESOLUTION

Social media platforms have undergone numerous iterations, which resulted in fundamental changes as to user demographics, business models, and range of interactions. If, in its early days, Facebook had the aim of connecting people studying at the same university,[5] its goals and uses gradually shifted towards content monetization. In 2021, Facebook also displays a marketplace connecting buyers and sellers,[6] an 'ad library' allowing businesses to promote sponsored content into users' news feeds,[7] as well as considerable volumes of undisclosed advertisement taking the form of goods or services endorsed by influencers,[8] just to give a few examples of some defining characteristics. The same trends can be observed for other social media platforms as well.

In this landscape, an increasing variety of behaviours and interactions is channelled into content. Given the increasing complexity of the range of activities that users carry out through platforms, the past years were marked by mounting concern regarding platform governance, with a particular focus on content moderation policies. What should be allowed on platforms, and what should be taken down? Legal scholarship focusing on freedom of expression, intermediary liability, hate speech and democracy, among others, has thoroughly reflected upon the different facets of content moderation, at the crossroads between private ordering and public regulation.[9]

---

[5] C McFadden, 'A Brief History of Facebook, Its Major Milestones' (*Interesting Engineering,* 2020) www.interestingengineering.com/history-of-facebook accessed 29 April 2021.

[6] 'Facebook Marketplace' www.facebook.com/marketplace/ accessed 29 April 2021.

[7] 'Facebook Ad Archive' www.facebook.com/ads/library/ accessed 29 April 2021.

[8] See for instance C Goanta and S Ranchordás (eds), *The Regulation of Social Media Influencers* (Edward Elgar 2020).

[9] J M Balkin, 'The Future of Free Expression in a Digital Age Free Speech and Press in the Digital Age' (2008) 36 *Pepperdine Law Review* 427; A Heldt, 'Borderline Speech: Caught in a Free Speech Limbo?' (2020) *Internet Policy Review* www

Social media are, to a certain extent, a breeding ground for conflict. Research done at the intersection of social science and computer science reveals that user-defined communities will inevitably experience conflict. To be sure, this is not an exclusive feature of the online realm; however, empirical research confirms that online communities typically entail a significant degree of conflict and, as such, generate the need for conflict resolution. In a study looking at 40 months of Reddit comments and posts, Kumar et al. show that '1% of all communities initiate 74% of all conflicts' ('wars' or 'raids') on this social media platform.[10] As a consequence, when social media platforms make binding decisions on content moderation, they unavoidably profile themselves as engaging in private dispute resolution, deciding on a wide range of delicate disputes where free speech must be balanced against other rights and values.[11] For instance, the Facebook Oversight Board has recently decided on whether former US President Donald Trump should be allowed back to the platform.[12] In light of this, it is necessary to take a closer look at social media content moderation through the 'lens' of dispute resolution.

10.2.1 Dealing with Conflicts on Social Media Platforms

The role of platforms as dispute resolution service providers has been inspired by eBay's early model of online dispute resolution, which relied on a combination of reputation mechanisms, evidence submission and automated remedies,[13] which in turn encouraged mediation experiments such as those

---

.policyreview.info/articles/news/borderline-speech-caught-free-speech-limbo/1510 accessed 29 April 2021.

[10] S Kumar, W L Hamilton, J Leskovec and D Jurafsky, 'Community Interaction and Conflict on the Web' *The Web Conference* (2018) https://snap.stanford.edu/conflict/ accessed 29 April 2021.

[11] K Klonick, 'The New Governors: The People, Rules, and Processes Governing Online Speech' (2018) 131 *Harvard Law Review* 1598–1670; O Pollicino and M Bassini, 'Free Speech, Defamation and the Limits to Freedom of Expression in the EU: A Comparative Analysis' in A Savin and J Trzaskowski (eds), *Research Handbook on EU Internet Law* (Edward Elgar 2014) 508–542.

[12] Oversight Board, Case decision 2021-001-FB-FBR. See also L Gradoni, 'Constitutional Review via Facebook's Oversight Board: How platform governance had its Marbury v Madison' (*Verfassungsblog,* 2021) https://verfassungsblog.de/fob-marbury-v-madison/ accessed 25 June 2021; K Klonick, 'The Facebook Oversight Board: Creating an Independent Institution to Adjudicate Online Free Expression' (2020) 129 *Yale Law Journal* 2318–2499; E Douek, 'Facebook's Oversight Board: Move Fast with Stable Infrastructure and Humility' (2019) 21 *North Carolina Journal of Law & Technology* 1.

[13] L Mommers, 'Visualization of Dispute Resolution: Establishing Trust by Recycling Reputation' (2006) 15 *Information and Communications Technology Law*

conducted by Katsh et al.[14] Other platforms, such as Wikipedia, developed an equally acclaimed dispute resolution approach combining mediation, arbitration, and negotiation.[15] It would be beyond the scope of this chapter to assess what the added value of these dispute resolution mechanisms may be, with reference to the specific platform within which they are embedded, and the type of activities carried out on each platform. For the purposes of this chapter, suffice it to note that approaches to dispute resolution vary significantly across platforms. In fact, not all platforms deemed it necessary to design dispute resolution mechanisms; sharing economy platforms, in particular, have for a long time refused to resolve disputes among users. This has been the case for ride-sharing platform Uber, which at the time of writing still does not feature any formal dispute resolution centre. Airbnb initially adopted the same approach, but then introduced a 'Resolution Center' (in the words of the platform itself) which uses existing reservations logged by users as the starting point for two particular actions: requesting and sending money.[16] Overall, according to the legal scholarship on ODR and the sharing economy, the dispute resolution role of platforms such as Uber or Airbnb remains fluid and a 'work in progress'.[17] By contrast, social media platforms have recently adopted a more explicit role as adjudicators, most likely in the light of all the attention received by content governance in public policy around the world.

An example of the progressive 'judicialization' of social media platforms is the aforementioned Facebook Oversight Board, whose structures clearly resemble that of a judicial authority. This body will be analysed more thoroughly in section 4. A variation of this model is the Twitch Safety Advisory

175, 180. See also N Solovay and C K Reed, *The Internet and Dispute Resolution: Untangling the Web* (Law Journal Press 2003); R Koulu, *Law, Technology and Dispute Resolution* (Routledge 2018); L Edwards and C Wilson, 'Redress and Alternative Dispute Resolution in EU Cross-Border E-Commerce Transactions' (2007) 21 *International Review of Law Computers & Technology* 315, 326.

14 E Katsh, J Rifkin and A Gaitenby, 'E-Commerce, E-Disputes, and E-Dispute Resolution: In the Shadow of eBay Law' (2000) 15 *Ohio State Journal on Dispute Resolution* 705.

15 D A Hoffman and S K Mehra, 'Wikitruth through Wikiorder' (2009) 59 *Emory LJ* 151; O Rabinovich-Einy and E Katsh, 'Digital Justice: Reshaping Boundaries in an Online Dispute Resolution Environment' (2014) 1 *International Journal of Online Dispute Resolution* 5.

16 Airbnb Resolutions, https://www.airbnb.com/resolutions accessed 29 April 2021.

17 H Scheiwe Kulp and A L Kool, 'You Help Me, He Helps You: Dispute Systems Design in the Sharing Economy' (2015) 48 *Washington University Journal of Law & Policy Introduction* 179. See also M Cantero Gamito, 'Regulation.com. Self-Regulation and Contract Governance in the Platform Economy: A Research Agenda' (2017) 9 *European Journal of Legal Studies* 53.

Council, looking to advise Twitch on content moderation policies. Moreover, even in platforms (like Twitter) that have not instituted such a court-like body (yet), there is an increasing acknowledgement that content moderation requires conflict-resolving decisions, with important repercussions on freedom of expression. These decisions are normally taken through a combination of algorithms, which detect certain categories of content, and human moderators.

These, however, are rather new developments. In an initial phase, platforms refrained from developing dispute resolution infrastructures. As earlier iterations of social networks were generally user-defined, moderation of speech was left up to the communities built around the platforms, as an inherent characteristic of new, digital public spaces. More recently, platform governance has increasingly eroded the power of users in shaping their own participatory space, given the continuous automation of processes that will be discussed in further detail in the following section.[18]

Before looking at how platforms currently deal with users and conflicts, it is important to sketch a basic taxonomy of the possible conflicts that may come into play, in the context of content moderation. Departing from a broad understanding of 'conflict', as an expression of disagreement which may have legal repercussions, it is useful to distinguish among three main categories of conflicts:

(i) *Conflicts between users and the platform*: users disagree with platform actions (e.g., taking down their content) or policies (e.g., nudity policies).

(ii) *Conflicts between different users*: users disagree between themselves, whether bilaterally (e.g., making disparaging or misleading statements about a business competitor, posting content that violates another user's trademarks or other IP rights, or violating another user's consumer rights)[19] or multilaterally (e.g., 'cancel culture' practices, whereby an ad-hoc swarm of social media users deliberately attack another user's reputation).[20]

---

[18] C Goanta and J Spanakis, 'Influencers and Social Media Recommender Systems: Unfair Commercial Practices in EU and US Law' (TTLF Working Papers No. 54/2020) www.law.stanford.edu/publications/no-54-influencers-and-social-media-recommender-systems-unfair-commercial-practices-in-eu-and-us-law/ accessed 29 April 2021; J G Webster, 'User Information Regimes: How Social Media Shape Patterns of Consumption' (2010) 104 *Northwestern University Law Review* 593, 604.

[19] Paolo Cavaliere, 'Glawischnig-Piesczek v. Facebook on the Expanding Scope of Internet Service Providers' Monitoring Obligations' (2019) 5 *European Data Protection Law Review* 573.

[20] N K Carr, 'How Can We End #CancelCulture - Tort Liability or Thumper's Rule?' (2020) 28 *Catholic University Journal of Law and Technology* 133.

(iii) *Conflicts involving third parties*: content posted on social media platforms may infringe the rights of non-users, for reasons analogous to those considered under (ii) above. Non-users, however, find themselves in a different situation, as they may be unable to activate the content moderation procedures of the platform.

While the mapping of stakeholders, interests and potential clashes which may escalate into conflicts can always be undertaken more systematically, this basic taxonomy fleshes out a crucial characteristic of this ecosystem: platforms are often parties to conflicts arising out of their private ordering. This raises considerable concerns relating to transparency and impartiality. From this perspective, social media platforms are the regulators, judges and enforcers of content moderation. Users present their case through procedures designed by the platform, limited by the goals of the platform, and often inaccessible to non-users.[21]

In sum, content moderation has an intrinsic dispute resolution dimension. On the one hand, platform-administered content moderation procedures are not the only avenue of redress: in the examples mentioned above, disputes arising out of violations of copyright, consumer or competition law may be brought before the competent national court(s), or resolved through a variety of 'traditional' ADR mechanisms. On the other hand, however, this is often unlikely to happen in practice. Many parties will not pursue any of those avenues, due to costs and other bottlenecks. For many categories of disputes, especially when the economic value is relatively limited, plaintiffs will remain inactive.[22] Content moderation procedures, by contrast, are relatively simple to initiate and, most importantly, virtually costless. In practice, thus, social media platforms may be the only authority before which these disputes are brought for resolution. To be sure, it would be misleading to claim that content moderation on social media platforms should be exclusively understood as a form of private dispute resolution; the governance aspect of the phenomenon is obviously crucial and should not be disregarded. However, dispute resolution is one of the facets of content moderation, and a non-negligible one.

---

21 For example, Facebook does not provide customer support via telephone: S John, 'How to contact Facebook for problems with your account and other issues' (*Business Insider,* 2019) www.businessinsider.nl/how-to-contact-facebook-problems-with-account-other-issues?international=true&r=US accessed 29 April 2021.

22 F Weber, '"A chain reaction" or the Necessity of Collective Actions for Consumers in Cartel Cases' (2018) 25 *Maastricht Journal of European and Comparative Law* 208; M Ioannidou, 'Compensatory Collective Redress for Low Value Consumer Claims in the EU: A Reality Check' (2019) 27 *European Review of Private Law* 1367.

Understanding content moderation as a form of dispute resolution may be useful both at the descriptive and at the normative level. Descriptively, it is possible to highlight similarities and differences between content moderation and other dispute resolution mechanisms (such as court litigation, or arbitration), which procedural lawyers are more familiar with. Such an approach can help understand to what extent current content moderation procedures offer sufficient due process guarantees, and how they perform these dispute resolution functions. Prescriptively, a procedural viewpoint can help determine whether content moderation is in need of reform. As already mentioned, for many categories of parties, platforms may be the only viable dispute resolution forum. Therefore, if platforms do not offer an avenue of redress, those parties will not be able to obtain the enforcement of the rights which, on paper, they would be entitled to. In certain cases, the question whether the 'law in the books' coincides with the 'law in action' may largely depend on whether social media platforms offer an effective possibility of redress through content moderation. Inasmuch as content moderation procedures constitute a sort of informal procedural law-making, parties left without redress may in practice have no right at all (*nullum jus sine actione*).

10.2.2 An Empirical Incursion into Social Media Reporting Systems

So far, we explored the topic of content moderation from a broad perspective of conflict resolution, in a theoretical sense. To further flesh out the issues that content moderation poses to platform governance and legal compliance, this section reports the findings of an empirical exercise, focusing on what we identify as 'actionable content' on the mobile applications of four social media platforms namely, Facebook, TikTok, Twitch, and Twitter. These platforms were selected due to a combination of factors based on their size, novelty and platform affordances.

Actionable content reflects the procedural grounds on which platforms allow users to report content. They can equally be referred to as 'platform affordances' in the context of social science research.[23] We systematically explored actionable content on the four selected platforms, in order to make an overview of existing labels used in these environments. We use observations gathered during November 2020[24] through a combination of digital ethnogra-

[23] See for instance B Rieder and J Hofmann, 'Towards Platform Observability' (2020) 9(4) *Internet Policy Review* https://policyreview.info/articles/analysis/towards-platform-observability accessed 22 June 2021.

[24] As platform affordances are constantly upgraded, we decided to focus on a given moment in time, instead of systematically observing changes across a more extensive period.

phy and walk-through methods, extensively used in communication studies and sociology, among other fields.[25] To report on these observations, in what follows, we will focus on two main points: (i) the availability of reporting affordances; (ii) the reporting labels attributed by platforms to actionable content. While platforms may also add relevant references to content moderation in community guidelines, it is important to note that our analysis focuses on describing the reporting mechanisms, which is an understudied aspect of content moderation by social media platforms.

10.2.2.1 The availability of reporting affordances

On their mobile applications, all four platforms provide reporting support, which can be engaged through as little as one click (or tap). Twitter and Facebook users can report posts by clicking the 'More options' button, which is placed on the upper right corner of each post to indicate additional actions which can be taken to engage with that content. TikTok offers the report feature under its 'Share' button. Unlike the other three platforms, which allow users to report specific posts made by another user, Twitch focuses exclusively on reporting users instead of posts, although the options of doing so indirectly reflect content reports as well.[26] To do so, users must engage with the 'Options' button found on the top right corner of a live stream.

While report buttons can be engaged with only one action, the way in which they are designed raises two questions. First, there is an issue of access: are these buttons easy to find for users who want to report potential content conflicts? This is a matter for further behavioural research at the intersection of computer-human interaction and website design. Second, there is a question of perception: platform interfaces shape the way in which users perceive available actions. If sharing and reporting content are placed under the same menu, the way in which users relate to and use reporting mechanisms may be affected. For instance, TikTok's 'Share' button is sometimes visible as an arrow, and sometimes as the WhatsApp icon, in order to communicate the desirability of sharing that content on other media. In other words, TikTok has adopted a much different approach in content dissemination than other platforms, as it facilitates the sharing of content for instance on WhatsApp. Users can thus send TikTok links to one another in order to increase traffic to the (web)app. If reports are available under this particular button, but users are nudged more towards sharing than towards filing complaints, it can be argued

---

[25] S Bishop, 'Influencer Management Tools: Algorithmic Cultures, Brand Safety, and Bias' (2021) *Social Media + Society*.

[26] This is possible on Facebook, Twitter and TikTok as well, but with slight variations which are not covered by this empirical exercise.

that the design of this button is a dark pattern. A dark pattern is an interface design choice that may result in nudging users into behaviour patterns which are against their interests.[27] This conclusion, unfortunately, cannot be clearly drawn without additional behavioural research, which is necessary to reveal whether interface design is used in a way that is conducive to a constructive use of these reporting mechanisms.

10.2.2.2 The reporting labels attributed by platforms to actionable content

The content labels used by the four social media platforms under scrutiny for reporting purposes differ widely in granularity. We report on the main categories of actionable content, which we clustered according to very broad legal features. This resulted into six main clusters, as indicated in Table 10.1 below. Several observations can be made on the basis of this overview. First, it is noteworthy that most of the content which the four platforms allow users to report is labelled around content restrictions which seem to have a criminal nature, and which is likely to be prohibited under the law of most countries where the platforms operate. Examples include content relating to terrorism or jeopardizing minor safety. Hate speech is featured in this cluster as well, although national legal systems will most likely translate hate speech into a broader array of crimes, such as incitement to hatred, insult and/or defamation. Second, three out of the four platforms have separate support centres for intellectual property infringements. This often entails submitting reports which allow users to provide more evidence (e.g., screenshots), but which may also require a certain capacity to submit the complaint (e.g., being the holder of an intellectual property right). Third, when comparing the different clusters of actionable content in the light of platform affordances, Twitch stands out with its approach of focusing on reporting users, rather than content. From this perspective, Twitch does not police individual content, but user behaviour. If this behaviour is reported on the grounds allowed for by the platform, this can have repercussions for the user, which can include temporary or permanent banning.

All in all, reporting mechanisms as the ones briefly investigated in this section show that platforms have an inherent hierarchy of actionable content, which is determined according to internal policies relating to legal compliance.

[27] K B Cornelius, 'Zombie Contracts, Dark Patterns of Design, and "documentisation"' (2019) 8(2) *Internet Policy Review* https://policyreview.info/articles/analysis/zombie-contracts-dark-patterns-design-and-documentisation accessed 22 June 2021. See also A Mathur, M Kshirsagar and J Mayer, 'What Makes a Dark Pattern... Dark?: Design Attributes, Normative Considerations, and Measurement Methods' (2021) *CHI '21: Proceedings of the 2021 CHI Conference on Human Factors in Computing Systems* 1–18.

Table 10.1 Actionable content on Facebook, TikTok, Twitch and Twitter

Actionable content cluster	**Facebook**	**TikTok**	**Twitch**	**Twitter**
Criminal	• Nudity • Violence • Hate speech • Harassment • Terrorism • Mocking victims • Bullying • Child abuse • Promoting drug use • Non-consensual intimate images	• Dangerous organizations and individuals • Harassment or bullying • Minor safety • Violent and graphic content • Animal cruelty • Hate speech • Pornography and nudity	• Violence or threats to harm • Harassment • Impersonation • Sexually explicit or sexually suggestive content • Sexual violence or exploitation • Extreme violence, gore, or other obscene content • Terrorism or acts of mass violence	• Suspicious or spam • Abusive or harmful • It displays a sensitive photo or video
Consumer	• Fraud or scam • Unauthorized sales	• Illegal activities and regulated goods • Misleading information	• Spam, scam/malicious content • Prohibited game	
Intellectual property	• Intellectual property	• Separate form	• Separate form	• Separate form
Personhood			• Underaged user	
Procedural			• Bits acceptable use policy violation[a] • Other terms of service violation • Site suspension evasion • Chat ban evasion	
Other	• False news • Spam • Suicide or self-injury	• Suicide, self-harm and dangerous acts • Spam • Others	• Self-harm • Offensive username • Miscategorized content or other category violation • Cheating in online game	• Suspicious or spam • Self-harm or suicide

Note: [a] 'Bits' are virtual tokens which can be purchased on Twitch and spent on live streams by transferring them to favourite streamers.

By emphasizing intellectual property infringements, or content of a potentially criminal nature, platforms inadvertently show what mandatory legal norms they choose to prioritize in their content moderation approaches. Conversely, platforms choose not to engage with mandatory rules which may come from other fields of law, such as consumer protection. While in the European Union it is generally accepted that users who monetize content on social media must disclose sponsored posts,[28] and content monetization is skyrocketing, none of the investigated platforms had any actionable content label for non-disclosed advertising. In addition, the architecture of reporting mechanisms can also shed light on the reason why these mechanisms do or do not exist. On Twitch, user reporting, coupled with sanctions relating to account access if violations are determined to have occurred, supports the platform in policing content which goes against policy guidelines. We argue that reporting mechanisms are not primarily used to give users access to platform justice, but rather to channel the policy areas on which platforms want to take measures. One benefit of doing so is to use reporting mechanisms to crowdsource content labelling, which can be further used in the various content recognition models deployed internally.

10.3 THREE ISSUES WITH CONTENT MODERATION

As illustrated in the previous section, social media platforms allow users to file complaints about the content that is present on the platform. In doing so, platforms can potentially contribute to the effective protection of rights, and the enforcement of the law. However, in practice, these goals are pursued in an uneven an imbalanced fashion. While platforms generally provide an avenue of redress against content that would be qualified in several legal systems as criminally relevant, the same does not hold true for other fields of law, such as consumer protection law, as our empirical analysis shows. Just to give a practical example, on many social media platforms, content is 'monetized' according to a business model where famous users ('influencers') advertise products, without disclosing that they are indeed conducting advertisement. As already mentioned, this practice is incompatible with EU consumer law; for this reason, if platforms allowed users to report this type of content, they could meaningfully contribute to the enforcement of consumer law, making good on their own legal obligations to engage in such disclosures of advertisement.[29] However, as illustrated, many platforms do not offer this possibility to users. Platforms, hence, seem to ignore this type of business-to-consumer (B2C)

---

[28] C Riefa and L Clausen, 'Towards Fairness in Digital Influencers' Marketing Practices' (2019) 8 *Journal of European Consumer and Market Law* 64.

[29] Ibid.

disputes, in spite of a growing body of transnational standardization, soft law and jurisprudence, all pointing in the same direction – that disclosing advertising on social media is a matter of consumer protection, and therefore (in some jurisdictions) a hard, mandatory limit to the contractual freedom enjoyed within a platform's private ordering.

Furthermore, platform infrastructure – in other words, the code on which each platform rests – creates semi-automated procedures which may limit the usefulness (or even fairness or legality) of reporting mechanisms. In many social media platforms, if a user reports content with the wrong label (i.e., choosing the wrong option out of the menu that the platform offers), this will lead to an unsuccessful report. What is more, the general terms and conditions of many social media platforms make no disclosure in this respect. Such a strict and opaque approach has a significant negative impact on the overall fairness of content moderation as a form of dispute resolution. To start with, the procedural frameworks used by social media platforms already limit the choice of a user in reporting content, which must be fitted within a closed number of often ill-designed categories. In addition, if the existing categories are not used properly, this deprives the user of any access to a potential remedy. It is crucial to consider the consequence of such automatism, in order to grasp the shortcomings of current content moderation practices from the perspective of dispute resolution. While the latter is supposed to be user-centric, and focused on remedying harms, content moderation in its current state is not even a matter of bilateral B2C customer care. Instead, what transpires when looking at the categories of actionable content is that reporting may very well be a techno-social process of crowdsourcing algorithmic progress, in such a way as to facilitate the evasion of liability by platforms as intermediaries. In other words, there is a significant risk that, instead of valuing the users' input in identifying unlawful content and providing effective redress, platforms mainly use the input of users to train their algorithms, and at the same time to preserve their immunity as mere hosts of user-generated information.[30] This leads to a situation where there is an appearance that platforms are trying to solve user conflicts, when in fact, other factors may play a role in the practice of implementing content moderation approaches.

Lastly, an emerging issue is to what extent reporting mechanisms enabled by platforms are still based on the 'notice and take-down' dynamic, and to what extent they are shifting towards a 'notice and other action' model, in

---

[30] See Art 14 of Directive 2000/31/EC of the European Parliament and of the Council of 8 June 2000 on certain legal aspects of information society services, in particular electronic commerce, in the Internal Market [2000] OJ L 178 (E-Commerce Directive).

the light of new European reforms. This will be further explored in section 10.5. The question, here, is what type of measure social media platforms should take, and whether the 'take-down' of the content is always an adequate remedy. In its general terms, Facebook makes the following specification: 'We also can remove or restrict access to your content, services or information if we determine that doing so is reasonably necessary to avoid or mitigate adverse legal or regulatory impacts to Facebook.'[31] While the removal of content is a rather clear measure, the same does not hold true for the restriction of access. When visiting a social media platform, the content we see is selected and curated by a so-called 'recommender system', which should present us with the most relevant information, given our data and past behaviour on the platform.[32] Recommender systems, hence, are the backbone of information diffusion on social media platforms. An interesting question, then, is whether platforms should also allow different forms of redress, by adapting their recommender systems, so that for instance a certain piece of content does not circulate to the point of becoming 'viral'. In principle, such a gradation of remedies could play an important role, allowing platforms to strike an adequate balance between freedom of expression and the protection of other rights and values.[33] However, recommender systems are opaque, and operate according to parameters that remain generally undisclosed, and are practically impossible to reverse-engineer. As a result, the current reality of content moderation lacks transparency and accountability. For instance, users on social media platforms may receive a so-called 'shadow ban', i.e., a measure whereby their profile or content is made less visible on the platform, but the affected user receives no notification or warning that they have been banned.

In the current landscape of content moderation, platforms are faced with increasing pressure to control content generated by its users. In doing so, the three issues of content moderation explored in this section (selective reporting mechanisms, their limited scope and algorithmic opacity) raise concerns relating to the actions platforms undertake to give users access to viable private remedies and procedures that do not affect their access to justice. Needless

[31] 'Facebook Terms' https://www.facebook.com/terms.php accessed 29 April 2021.

[32] P Covington, J Adams and E Sargin, 'Deep Neural Networks for YouTube Recommendations' (*Proceedings of the 10th ACM Conference on Recommender Systems* 2016) www.dl.acm.org/citation.cfm?id=2959190 accessed 29 April 2021; N Tintarev and J Masthoff, 'Explaining Recommendations: Design and Evaluation' in F Ricci, L Rokach and B Shapira (eds), *Recommender Systems Handbook* (Springer 2015) 382.

[33] E Goldman, 'Content Moderation Remedies' (2021) *Michigan Technology Law Review*, forthcoming.

to say, such an untransparent way of dealing with content-related disputes is incompatible with legitimate and accountable dispute resolution.

10.4 PLATFORMS EMBRACING THEIR ADJUDICATIVE FUNCTION: THE CASE OF THE OVERSIGHT BOARD

Social media platforms are embracing the dispute resolution dimension of content moderation in their public relations strategies, acknowledging (with varying degrees of openness) how content moderation constitutes a form of private adjudication. The most explicit example is the one of Facebook, with the institution of the Oversight Board, since no other social media platform has gone so far in mimicking an independent, precedent-creating institution which is supposed to rule on content moderation matters. In November 2018, Mark Zuckerberg announced Facebook's intention to 'create a new way for people to appeal content decisions to an independent body, whose decisions would be transparent and binding'.[34] Against that background, Facebook launched a public consultation process with a variety of stakeholders.[35] The results of the consultation fed into the design of this new body,[36] which was officially announced in September 2019 with the publication of a 'Charter', setting out inter alia the composition of the Board, its procedures, and its governance. This document, starting from its very title, explicitly confirms Facebook's ambition to create a court-like structure, borrowing from the experience (and the symbolic power) of both national and international courts. The Oversight Board Charter (hereafter 'Charter') has been rightly defined as a 'constitution-like document'[37] and can be understood as one of the steps of 'self-constitutionalization' of the platform.[38] Observing the phenomenon through the lens of dispute resolution, the Board can be understood as an example of transnational procedural law-making, whereby Facebook expressly acknowledges the adjudicative dimension of content moderation, and the need for adequate due process guarantees. For decades, procedural lawyers have highlighted how, by

---

[34] 'A Blueprint for Content Governance and Enforcement' www.facebook.com/notes/mark-zuckerberg/a-blueprint-for-content-governance-and-enforcement/10156443129621634/?hc_location=ufi accessed 29 April 2021.

[35] Brent Harris, 'Getting Input on an Oversight Board' (Facebook, 1 April 2019) http://about.fb.com/news/2019/04/input-on-an-oversight-board/ accessed 29 April 2021.

[36] Klonick (n 12).

[37] Ibid., 2457–8.

[38] G Teubner, 'Self-Constitutionalizing TNCs? On the Linkage of "Private" and "Public" Corporate Codes of Conduct' (2011) 18 *Indiana Journal of Global Legal Studies* 617.

looking at the procedures of the courts of a given State, we can gain insights as to how that State organizes its own authority, and what 'ideal of officialdom' it embraces.[39] Also from this point of view, then, a close look at the procedural dimension of content moderation can be meaningful; inasmuch as social media platforms emerge as repositories of power and as quasi-sovereign entities, the procedures they create can help us grasp their understanding of their own authority.

The Oversight Board, which is currently composed of 20 Members, can be seized in two main ways. First, the Board can review Facebook's content moderation decisions, on the request of one or more users. If a certain content has been taken down by Facebook, the user that posted the content may ask the Oversight Board to review the decision, and order that the content be reinstated on the platform. Alongside the initiative of users, Facebook itself may submit requests for review to the Board.[40] In both instances, the basis of decision making is supposed to be 'Facebook's content policies and values'.[41] Drawing an analogy with litigation in civil and commercial matters, the users' initiative may be understood as a form of private enforcement of such 'policies and values', while Facebook's own referrals constitute an example of public enforcement. Needless to say, the substantive rules to be enforced here would not be provisions of national law, but 'policies and values' that legally bind the users inasmuch as they are enshrined in Facebook's terms and conditions. In its first decisions, however, the Oversight Board has interpreted its mandate broadly, and made references to international human rights law as a normative standard against which the legality of these policies and values should be assessed.[42] To date, hence, it remains unclear to what extent content moderation at the Oversight Board will remain confined within the boundaries of Facebook's own internal rules and guidelines.

According to the Charter, 'the board has the discretion to choose which requests it will review and decide upon',[43] and should select the cases that have 'the greatest potential to guide future decisions and policies'.[44] This mechanism of case selection resembles the certiorari process, whereby the US Supreme Court selects a small number of cases out of all petitions, generally

39 M Damaška, *The Faces of Justice and State Authority: A Comparative Approach to the Legal Process* (Yale University Press 1986).

40 Art 2(1) Oversight Board Charter.

41 Art 2(2) Oversight Board Charter.

42 See Gradoni (n 12) with reference to Case Decision 2020-004-IG-UA, where the Oversight Board relied on the International Covenant on Civil and Political Rights (ICCPR) and the UN Guiding Principles on Business and Human Rights (UNGPs).

43 Art 2(1) Oversight Board Charter.

44 Ibid.

focusing on disputes which raise important legal questions, and can contribute to the development of a certain area of law. Furthermore, Facebook's ability to request from the Board guidance as to 'future decisions and policies'[45] echoes the role played by certain domestic and international courts in the context of preliminary ruling procedures. Such a discretion also entails that, as already mentioned, certain parties will obtain adequate redress through content moderation, while others will face the choice between bringing their case elsewhere, or factually giving up on their legal entitlements.

Each selected case is assigned to a panel of five members, assisted by a case manager. The procedure is rather inquisitorial: the Board receives information from Facebook itself, and can 'gather additional information, including through subject matter experts, research requests or translation services'.[46] The involvement of private parties, by contrast, is limited: according to the Charter, 'the posting person or the reporting person will have the opportunity to submit relevant and informed written statements to the Board'.[47] In other words, the party seeking review will be allowed to make written submissions and to present documentary evidence, but will generally not be invited to an oral hearing. In a nutshell, the Board procedure resembles that of many continental European constitutional courts, with a prevalence of written over oral submission, a limited role for the disputing parties, and an emphasis on the development of the law for the future (rather than the resolution of a specific dispute).

The Board's decisions 'include a determination on the content, as well as a corresponding plain language explanation of the board's rationale'. The Board may also decide to include in the decision a 'policy advisory statement, which will be taken into consideration by Facebook to guide its future policy development'.[48] This reinforces the conclusion that one of Facebook's primary reasons-for-action, when instituting the Board, was the need to develop a consistent body of precedent, to guide and justify future content moderation decisions and policies.[49] It remains to be seen to what extent Facebook will maintain its willingness to adhere to that case-law and whether the Board ends up reshaping the platform's policies in a substantial and invasive way. For the time being, the cases decided by the Board are not sufficient to make long-term predictions as to the Board's standpoint vis-à-vis Facebook.

The Board's decisions are public, and archived in a publicly accessible database, so as to ensure a strong persuasive (if not outright binding) precedential

45 Ibid.
46 Art 3(3) Oversight Board Charter.
47 Art 3(3) Oversight Board Charter.
48 Art 3(4) Oversight Board Charter.
49 Klonick (n 12).

value.[50] The Charter declares the binding nature of the Board's decisions, and Facebook's obligation to implement them promptly.[51]

10.5 INJECTING LEGITIMACY FROM WITHOUT: THE DIGITAL SERVICES ACT (DSA) PROPOSAL

In its current state, content moderation on social media platforms can be analysed from the perspective of dispute resolution, existing at the crossroads between two normative tensions. The first tension concerns the decision-making basis, i.e., the substantive standards that platforms use, to determine whether a certain content should be taken down, or otherwise restricted. On the one hand, the relationship between platforms and users remains, to date, mainly a matter of contract law, so that platforms will normally seek a decision-making basis in their own terms and conditions, claiming the faculty to moderate content which does not comply with the obligations that the users contractually undertake. On the other hand, however, contract law does not exist in a vacuum, but within a broader framework of (national and supranational) law. The latter may sometimes restrict freedom of contract, typically to ensure the enforcement of mandatory provision of law, and to avoid violations of public policy. In the case of content moderation, this entails that the law may occasionally require the removal of illegal content, despite the fact that the content is not incompatible with the platform's terms and conditions. Conversely, the law may sometimes regard a content moderation decision as an excessive limitation of a user's fundamental rights (such as freedom of expression), despite the fact that the decision was taken in accordance with contractual terms and conditions that the user agreed to.

The second tension happens at the boundaries between platform self-regulation, and regulation at the national and supranational level. On the one hand, developments such as Facebook's decision to create the Oversight Board suggest a willingness on the side of the platforms to introduce further self-regulation and procedural guarantees in the field of content moderation (although the reasons for such willingness remain, to date, unclear).[52] On the other hand, however, calls for more public regulation of content moderation are intensifying on both sides of the North Atlantic. This tension is, in and of itself, nothing new or specific to content moderation: whenever a form of private, out-of-court dispute resolution emerges and gains traction, the question unavoidably arises whether and to what extent sovereign entities should

50 Art 3(6) Oversight Board Charter.
51 Art 4 Oversight Board Charter.
52 Klonick (n 12).

impose a ‘judicialization’ of that dispute resolution mechanism. This typically results in the injection of due process guarantees from without, through mandatory provisions of procedural law. In this vein, van Loo proposes that the procedural regulation of platforms should build on past experiences, namely on the regulation of other private dispute resolution schemes, such as credit card chargebacks.[53]

Understanding the two aforementioned tensions (between contract and mandatory law, and between self- and public regulation) is useful to contextualize the EU proposal for a new Digital Services Act (hereinafter, DSA). The DSA is the most important reform in platform governance which will shape the future of European regulation on the matter during the next decades. Moreover, as it will be explored in this section, the DSA proposes extensive dispute resolution obligations for digital platforms.

On 15 December 2020, the European Commission published a proposal for a new ‘Regulation on a Single Market For Digital Services’,[54] commonly referred to as DSA. The proposed instrument, which forms part of European Digital Strategy *Shaping Europe's Digital Future*, aims to overhaul the EU legislative framework concerning digital services and online communications, largely developed before the emergence of online platforms and social media. If the DSA proposal will be adopted, EU law will set forth a comprehensive set of rules on content moderation, applicable to social media platforms as well as other online intermediaries.

10.5.1 Content Moderation under the DSA: Distinctions and Purposes

The DSA proposal acknowledges that content moderation may serve two distinct purposes: the enforcement of a platform's terms and conditions (when the content is incompatible with the users' contractual obligations), or the enforcement of (national and/or EU) law (when the content is unlawful). The DSA proposal also acknowledges that content moderation can interfere with the principle of freedom of expression, and that sufficient guarantees must be put in place to ensure that the latter is respected.[55]

The DSA proposal is based on two key distinctions:

(a) The distinction between the moderation of ‘unlawful’ content (i.e., content that is incompatible with mandatory provisions of national or EU

---

[53] R Van Loo, ‘Federal Rules of Platform Procedure’ (2020) 88 *University of Chicago Law Review* 1.

[54] COM(2020) 825 final, 2020/0361(COD).

[55] Recital 22 and Art 12(2) DSA.

law), and the moderation of content that is legal but in violation of the platform's terms and conditions;

(b) The distinction between moderation performed on the platform's own initiative, and moderation requested by a user through one of the notification systems described above (labelled by the DSA proposal as 'notice and action mechanisms').[56]

The DSA does not regulate the procedures of the national judicial or administrative authorities that may be seized with a content moderation case: in accordance with the principle of procedural autonomy of the Member States, it is up to the latter to provide procedures that enable complainants (in our example, the consumer) to seek the removal or restriction of illegal content, as long as those procedures comply with the general principles of equivalence and effectiveness. By contrast, if the complainant triggers the available notice and action mechanism, the DSA sets forth an articulate body of procedural rules and guarantees.

10.5.2 Notice and Action Mechanisms

Pursuant to Article 14 of the DSA proposal, platforms must 'put mechanisms in place to allow any individual or entity to notify them of the presence on their service of specific items of information that the individual or entity considers to be illegal content'. Moreover, Article 14 requires that the mechanisms at hand be available to 'any individual or entity', thus including non-users (i.e., parties that have no account on the platform). Nevertheless, not all notices are 'born equal' under the DSA: according to Article 19, certain entities can be granted the status of 'trusted flaggers', and the platform will then be obliged to process and decide upon the notice of trusted flaggers 'with priority and without delay'.[57]

Furthermore, Article 14 requires that these mechanisms 'be easy to access, user-friendly, and allow for the submission of notices exclusively by electronic means'. While compliance with the last requirement is easy to assess, criteria such as ease of access and user-friendliness seem to be intrinsically subjective, and not easily enforceable. At first glance, therefore, there seems to be a risk that different platforms will interpret these requirements in different ways, ultimately resulting in procedural fragmentation. Article 34 of the DSA proposal, however, tries to limit this risk, by encouraging voluntary standardization across platforms. This approach seems to strike an adequate balance between

---

56 Art 14 DSA.
57 Art 19(1) DSA.

the desirability that platforms shape their own procedures and update them without unnecessary constraints, on the one hand, and the need for procedural uniformity and predictability, on the other hand. While it is obviously too early to predict whether such standardization will indeed occur, it is worth mentioning that encouraging precedents exists: in the field of international arbitration, for instance, arbitral institutions around the world have progressively converged towards a certain procedural model, borrowing from each other's experiences until a relatively uniform and predictable procedure emerged, while at the same time preserving sufficient space for flexibility.

Article 14(2) streamlines the submission of notices, specifying which elements should be included. The requirement that notices be 'precise' and 'adequately substantiated' ensures that the platform will have sufficient information to determine whether a certain content is unlawful and will be able to comply with the obligations that derive from the notice. After the notice, the platform must send the complainant a notification of receipt, and process the notice 'in a timely, diligent and objective manner'.[58] At this stage, the platform is free to determine whether the notice should be processed by a human, or by a machine; however, if the platform uses 'automated means', this must be disclosed to the complainant.[59] The platform must notify its decision to the individual or entity that has made the notice. That party must also be informed on the redress possibility in respect of the decision.[60]

The DSA imposes a set of procedural guarantees on the platform, in cases where the latter decides to remove or disable access to a certain content, irrespective of whether the decision was initiated through a notice and action mechanism or not, and of whether the platform deemed the content to be unlawful, or incompatible with its own terms and conditions. The platform is obliged to provide a 'clear and specific statement of reasons'[61] to the user that posted the content. Pursuant to Article 15, the statement must explain whether the content has been removed, or access to it has been disabled. In the latter case, the platform must also disclose 'the territorial scope of the disabling of access'. Second, the platform must indicate 'the facts and circumstances relied on in taking the decision'. Among these, the platform must disclose whether the decision originated from a notice, within the meaning of Article 14. Third, the platform must disclose whether the decision was made through 'automated means', including whether a machine detected or identified the content. Fourth, the platform must indicate what legal or contractual ground

58 Art 14(6) DSA.
59 Art 14(6) DSA.
60 Art 14(5) DSA.
61 Art 15 DSA.

it relies on. If the content was deemed to be illegal, the platform must explain why the content is considered to run counter to the legal ground identified by the platform. Conversely, if the content is deemed to be incompatible with the platform's terms and conditions, the platform must indicate the contractual ground it relies upon and explain why the content is considered to be incompatible with that ground. Fifth, the statement must indicate the redress possibilities available to the user. In this respect, three main avenues are possible, the platform's internal complaint-handing mechanisms, out-of-court dispute settlement, and judicial redress. The next section will focus on the first avenue, as it directly concerns the adjudicative role of platforms. First, however, a further obligation must be pointed out. Article 15(4) requires that the platform to 'publish the decisions and the statements of reasons, referred to in paragraph 1, in a publicly accessible database managed by the Commission'. Not only does this enhance platform accountability by enabling external scrutiny, but in addition, the consolidation of a body of precedent encourages consistency not only within each platform, but also across them. From this point of view, the policy goals of the DSA are akin to those of Facebook with the institution of the Oversight Board, which also aims at ensuring more predictability and consistency of outcomes.

10.5.3 Internal Complaint Handling

Article 17 obliges platforms to put in place an 'effective internal complaint-handing system'. This system should be available to users for at least six months, following a decision finding that a certain content is illegal, or incompatible with the platform's terms and conditions. More specifically, the platform may have decided not only to remove or disable access to the content, but also to suspend or terminate the provision of the service to the user, and either suspend or terminate the user's account, or both. In all of these cases, the user must be able to access a 'user-friendly' complaint-handing mechanism, which must 'enable and facilitate the submission of sufficiently precise and adequately substantiated complaints'.[62] Article 17 contains some binding provisions, dictating how the complaint-handing system should be organized by the platform. First, decision-making at this stage cannot be entirely automated; while the initial content moderation decision could be made by a machine (as long as it complies with the requirements of Art 15), this appellate stage necessarily requires human intervention. Furthermore, the provision requires that complaints be handled 'in a timely, diligent and objec-

[62] Art 17(2) DSA.

tive manner'.[63] The DSA proposal does not expound on the standard of review that the platform should adopt; however, the decision should be 'reversed', if the complaint 'contains sufficient grounds' to conclude that the content was not illegal or incompatible with the platform's terms and conditions. In other words, whether the decision will be reversed depends on how convincing and well-illustrated the complaint is, while the platform does not have a duty to carry out any independent fact-finding. As a consequence, the platform may refuse to reverse a content moderation decision because the complaint does not sufficiently elaborate on the grounds it relies upon. The complaint-handing mechanism of Article 17, hence, should be seen not as a *de novo* assessment of the case, but as a review, which the platform will only carry out if and inasmuch as an adequately substantiated complaint has been brought. Conversely, the platform may refuse to reconsider whether the content is illegal or incompatible with its own terms and conditions, if the complainant failed to specify while he/she filed the complaint.

In light of the above, it is in the interest of a complainant to provide a sufficiently detailed overview of the grounds on which the complaint is based. In practice, the platform's interface will play a crucial role, taking into account the fact that the complainant is unlikely to have legal representation at this stage. As described above, the interface can facilitate or hinder the filing of the complaint, thus ensuring 'access to justice by design'. Ease of use, transparency, predictability and granularity should be key goals for platforms, when designing their complaint-handling systems. Standardization would be a significant added value: if different platforms offered comparable complaint-handing mechanisms, this could significantly facilitate the filing of sufficiently substantiated complaints. From this point of view, Article 34 comes across as a missed opportunity, as it encourages the standardization of the submission of notices under Article 14, but not of the submission of complaints under Article 17. This is all the truer, considering that the industry itself is currently attempting such standardization. The Oversight Board, for instance, has been designed as to be potentially adopted and used by platforms other than Facebook and Instagram in the future. As noted by Klonick, this is reflected by the language of the Oversight Board Charter, which is intentionally vague, so as allow other platforms to submit themselves to the Board's decision-making.[64]

---

63 Art 17(3) DSA.
64 Klonick (n 12) 2475-6.

10.5.4 Beyond Platform Procedure: Out-of-court Dispute Settlement and Court Litigation

Complainants have the right to bring their case outside platforms. In this respect, two main avenues must be considered, out-of-court dispute settlement and court litigation. The DSA partially regulates both avenues.

The DSA mainly conceives of out-of-court dispute settlement as an extrajudicial appellate mechanism, available to parties whose complaints have been declined by the platform's internal complaint-handling system. Article 18 enables the national Digital Services Coordinators of each Member State to certify dispute settlement bodies established on the territory of the Member State in question. Additionally, Member States also have the possibility of directly setting up a dispute settlement body, which would then operate alongside the other certified bodies. A complainant can select any certified body, whose decision will be binding on the platform. Platforms have a duty to cooperate with the body in good faith, and promptly implement the body's decisions.

As for court litigation, in accordance with the principle of procedural autonomy of the Member States, the DSA does not regulate the procedures through which national courts resolve content moderation-related disputes. However, the DSA does regulate certain aspects concerning the enforcement of court decisions in the field of content moderation. More specifically, pursuant to Article 8(1), Member State courts can issue 'orders to act against illegal content'. Article 8 indicates the minimum elements that such orders must contain, so that platforms can understand what implementing measures are required, and act accordingly.

A particularly interesting aspect is the territorial scope of court orders. According to Article 8(2)(b), the territorial scope of the order should 'not exceed what is strictly necessary to achieve (the order's) objective'. Therefore, while violations of EU law would generally warrant an EU-wide removal of illegal content, content that is declared incompatible with national provisions of law will generally only be removed within the territory of the relevant Member State. The rationale of Article 8(2)(b) is to ensure that national and EU law will not be applied extraterritorially. Member State courts, hence, are indirectly discouraged from requiring worldwide action against content that may not be illegal outside the EU, or outside a single Member State. At the same time, this regulatory framework can lead to striking practical results. While illegal content may remain visible and accessible outside the territory of a certain Member State (or of the EU), content that is incompatible with the platform's terms and conditions will normally be removed by the platform with worldwide effects.

10.6 CONCLUSION

In this chapter, we have analysed the dispute resolution dimension of content moderation on social media. We have observed how social media platforms unavoidably perform certain dispute resolution functions, when taking decisions with respect to content. We also offered empirical insights from a study on the actionable content mechanisms offered by four social media platforms. From this point of view, content moderation can effectively contribute to the enforcement of substantive law, making sure that the parties' rights are actually translated into practice. We have observed how social media platforms have initially resisted such a dispute resolution role but have recently come to accept it. Despite this progressive acceptance, however, the reality of content moderation is far from satisfactory. Despite the current shortcomings, it is interesting to notice how social media platforms increasingly accept their role as adjudicators, and sometimes even set up court-like structures, such as the Oversight Board. In the future, due process guarantees may be injected by way of regulation. In the EU, the current DSA proposal has the potential to reshape content moderation as a form of digital dispute resolution.

11. Access to digital justice: In search of an effective remedy for removing unlawful online content

Naomi Appelman, Joanna van Duin, Ronan Fahy, Joris van Hoboken, Natali Helberger and Brahim Zarouali

11.1 INTRODUCING THE PROBLEM: INADEQUATE REMEDIES FOR REMOVING UNLAWFUL ONLINE CONTENT

11.1.1 A New Challenge to the Civil Justice System

Engaging in online communication has become a prerequisite for participation in modern cultural, social, and professional life.[1] Inevitably, this also means people are more likely to be confronted with content that is harmful to them or to others and, insofar as it can be qualified as unlawful, should not be allowed to remain online. The publication and dissemination of unlawful online content, and especially the lack of effective remedies to stop this, has proven to be a persistent policy problem in the European Union (EU), for which a solution is both urgently needed and hard to find.[2] Unlawful online content poses a new challenge to the civil justice system at the crossroads with online speech

[1] José van Dijck, Thomas Poell, and Martijn de Waal, *The Platform Society: Public Values in a Connective World* (Oxford University Press 2018); Julie E. Cohen, *Between Truth and Power: The Legal Constructions of Informational Capitalism* (Oxford University Press 2019).

[2] Commission Recommendation on measures to effectively tackle illegal content online C(2018) 1177 final (March 1, 2018); European Commission, Digital Services Act package: deepening the Internal Market and clarifying responsibilities for digital services, Ref. Ares(2020)287768, (4 June 2020); Council of Europe Committee of Experts of freedom of Expression and Digital Technologies, Guidance note on best practices towards effective legal and procedural frameworks for self-regulatory and co-regulatory mechanisms of content moderation, MSI-DIG(2021)04 (18 March 2021).

regulation. More often than not, injured individuals fail to find an avenue to get unlawful content removed and are effectively denied access to justice.[3] For example, the content might have been posted anonymously, the platform is unwilling to take it down or the content has already spread to a larger audience.

This chapter focuses on the removal of unlawful content that causes personal harm and, as such, falls within the scope of Article 8 of the European Convention on Human Rights (ECHR). Article 8 ECHR protects the fundamental right to respect for private and family life. Importantly, this includes one's reputation, privacy and personal data.[4] The protection of Article 8 ECHR only extends to attacks on personal honour and reputation that 'attain a certain level of seriousness' and that hampers one's enjoyment of the right to a private life.[5] Consequently, in the context of this chapter unlawful content refers to content that interferes with an individual's right to a private life (Art 8 ECHR) to such an extent that the right to the freedom of expression (Art 10 ECHR) of the perpetrator should be restricted and the content should be removed. Examples include cyberbullying, the publication of credit card details or other privacy-sensitive information, and the dissemination of sexual images without consent. Crucially, unlawful content should be distinguished from harmful content; the former violates a legal norm (such as slander), where the latter is considered to be socially undesirable yet not necessarily in violation of a legal norm (such as disinformation).

The type of unlawful content that is central to this chapter may affect the people involved deeply and personally, which stresses the importance of enabling them to get it offline as soon as possible. The opportunity to do so directly touches on the fundamental right to a fair trial and an effective remedy, i.e. a means of recourse to address a rights violation (Arts 6 and 13 ECHR and Art 47 of the EU Charter of Fundamental Rights). Despite the high stakes, there is a general consensus that within the legal framework of the EU citizens are insufficiently protected against unlawful online content; more specifically, the available remedies and procedures for quickly getting it removed are inade-

[3] For examples from the Dutch context see: Jan-Dirk Verhey, 'Vrouw daagt Facebook om seksvideo' *AD* (Rotterdam, 1 June 2015); Juliët Boogaard, 'De vrouw die jou haar naaktfoto's wil verkopen, die is nep' *NRC Handelsblad* (Amsterdam, 14 June 2021); Rosa Oosterhoff, 'Privéadressen zzp'ers openbaar: "Lijkt alsof eerst je leven op het spel moet staan voordat er iets gebeurt"' *NH Nieuws* (Amsterdam, 12 June 2021).

[4] *Springer v Germany* App 39954/08 (ECHR, 7 February 2012) [83].

[5] *Pihl v Sweden* App 74742/14 (ECHR, 7 February 2017) [24].

quate.[6] Many European countries have struggled with the search for solutions,[7] and the regulation of unlawful online content has been a priority on the EU regulatory agenda for years.[8] Offering effective remedies that reconcile sufficient procedural safeguards and protection of the freedom of expression with the speed and vast spread of online communication as well as the mediating role of internet services has proven to be exceedingly difficult.

11.1.2 Combining Two Perspectives

The central problem this chapter addresses is the lack of effective remedies for individuals who are confronted with allegedly unlawful online content. It explores two questions. First, in what respect existing procedural routes fail to provide a solution, and second, by what means the gap in legal protection could be addressed? To answer these questions the chapter will take the Netherlands as a concrete example to understand how the obstacles that people face play out in practice. After all, the available procedural options in a concrete case are dependent on the specific national context as EU competencies only reach so far.[9] To analyse *why* it is so difficult to offer adequate remedies, the chapter combines the perspectives of access to justice and online speech regulation. In doing so, the chapter will place the challenges identified in the Dutch context in the broader EU legal framework and discuss relevant developments such as the proposed EU Digital Services Act (DSA).[10]

---

[6] See, Proposal for a regulation COM(2020) 825 final on a Single Market For Digital Services (Digital Services Act and amending Directive 2000/31/EC [2020]; MSI-DIG(2021)04 *supra* n 2; Ref. Ares(2020)287768 *supra* n 2.

[7] See UK Draft Online Safety Bill (May 2021); Germany Netzwerkdurchsetzungsgesetz vom 1 September 2017 (BGBl. I S. 3352); France LOI n° 2020-766 du 24 juin 2020 visant à lutter contre les contenus haineux sur internet.

[8] European Commission Communication on Tackling Illegal Content Online COM(2017) 555 final (September 28, 2017); EU Code of Conduct on Countering Illegal Hate Speech Online (30 June 2016); European Commission Communication on Shaping Europe's Digital Future COM/2020/67 final (19 February 2020); C(2018) 1177 *supra* n 3; Ares(2020)287768 *supra* n 2; MSI-DIG(2021)04 *supra* n 2.

[9] On the concept of national procedural autonomy of the EU Member States, see e.g., W. van Gerven, 'Of Rights, Remedies and Procedures' (2000) 37 *CMLRev* 501; J.T. Nowak, 'Considerations on the Impact of EU Law on National Civil Procedure', in V. Lazic and S. Stuij, *International Dispute Resolution*, (TMC Asser Press 2018) 1–41; J.M.L. van Duin, 'Effective Judicial Protection in Consumer Litigation. Article 47 of the EU Charter in Practice' (Intersentia 2021, forthcoming).

[10] 2020/0361(COD) *supra* n 6.

The chapter is based on a study conducted for the Dutch government into the need for a legal remedy to quickly take down unlawful online content.[11] The aim of the study was to identify bottlenecks in current procedures and to gauge the societal need for procedural innovation. As we will argue in this chapter, however, the underlying premise that there could be a uniform (procedural) solution is flawed. The problem cannot be solved (only) by simplifying or speeding up the process or by regulating dominant social media companies with extended due diligence obligations. Instead, the problem must be reframed and recognised for what it is, i.e., multi-faceted and heterogeneous. A systemic outlook is required that accounts for the conflicting fundamental rights at stake, as well as the tension between different institutional and procedural safeguards. In particular, strengthening the protection of internet users' Article 8 ECHR rights will inevitably have an impact upon other users' rights to freedom of expression (Art 10 ECHR) as well as, possibly, their rights of defence (Art 6 ECHR).

First, we will focus on the specific Dutch context and briefly outline the scope, methodology and outcomes of our study (section 11.2). Then, we will analyse our findings against the background of the broader debates on online speech (and platform) regulation as well as access to (civil) justice (sections 11.3 and 11.4). We will discuss the wider EU regulatory context to gain better insight into the problem, in light of the open and decentralised structure of the internet and the increasingly dominant position of a few social media platforms (section 11.3). We will also connect our findings to the broader debate on access to justice, to show in what way the problem stands out (section 11.4). When these two perspectives are combined, a trade-off emerges between various safeguards on the one hand and accessibility, scalability and speed on the other (section 11.5). As our analysis reveals, there is no single procedure that can properly balance all the divergent rights and interests concerned with content moderation in the online environment. Therefore, we conclude with a call for a problem-oriented approach, where the removal of unlawful online content is seen as a collection of related specific issues that require a tailored solution.

---

[11] Joris van Hoboken, Naomi Appelman, Anna van Duin, Tom Blom, Brahim Zarouali, Michelle Seel, Elisabetta Stringhi, Natali Helberger, Ronan O Fathaigh, 'Voorziening voor verzoeken tot snelle verwijdering van onrechtmatige online content' (A report for the Wetenschappelijk Onderzoek- en Documentatiecentrum, 2020). The full report – including the annexes referred to in this chapter – can be consulted via https://www.rijksoverheid.nl/documenten/rapporten/2020/11/30/tk-bijlage-aanbieding-wodc-onderzoek-voorziening-voor-verzoeken-tot-snelle-verwijdering-van-onrechtmatige-online-content accessed 2 April 2022.

11.2 MAPPING THE PROBLEM IN THE DUTCH CONTEXT

11.2.1 Survey and Expert Interviews

In the Netherlands, the difficulty of removing unlawful content was placed on the political agenda after a petition was signed by 135,000 citizens to act against cyberbullying.[12] A call was made for the introduction of a simple, quick and cheap procedure for the removal of unlawful content, which led to the abovementioned study we conducted for the Dutch government.[13] This section will briefly outline the scope, methodology and outcomes of this study. As indicated, the specific focus of the study, as well as this chapter, is on Article 8 ECHR and all unlawful content that falls within its range.

To map the problem in the Dutch context, our study consisted of a representative survey, a series of expert interviews, and a legal analysis. In February 2020 the survey was conducted with a representative sample of the Dutch population.[14] The survey had three parts. The first part aimed to identify people's experience with various forms of harmful content and the type of internet service used. The second part focused on Notice and Takedown and complaint procedures offered by internet services themselves. The third part dealt with people's considerations whether to take legal action or not. In May and June 2020 semi-structured interviews were held with experts from different fields. An expert workshop was organised to validate the findings and discuss potential solutions.[15] Parallel, a legal analysis of the different (extra)legal routes available to deal with unlawful online content was conducted in civil, administrative, and criminal law. This chapter will be limited to the findings in respect of civil justice.

Both the survey and the expert interviews confirmed that the difficulty of getting unlawful online content removed is widely seen as a societal problem which warrants government intervention.[16] Not only is it considered important

---

[12] *Kamerstukken II* 2018/19, 34602, 2.

[13] Van Hoboken et al 2020 *supra* n 11.

[14] The survey was conducted at CentERdata's LISS panel (n=1576). For survey questions and full research results see van Hoboken et al. 2020 Annex V and Annex VI *supra* n 11.

[15] Including experts from civil society, the judiciary, lawyers, academics and the government. For a full list of names and affiliations see: van Hoboken et al 2020 Annex IV *supra* n 11.

[16] States have a positive obligation to guarantee the effective enjoyment of the right to privacy and to provide effective remedies to address rights violations: see e.g., *K.U. v Finland* App 41288/15 (ECHR, 2 December 2008) [79]; *Mosley/United Kingdom* App

and urgent to find a solution, it is also an epitome of regulatory challenges in the digital age. Notably, due to the specific focus on Article 8 ECHR, i.e., unlawful content that affects people in their personal capacity, the type of harm this unlawful content creates can be immensely damaging for one's private life. Our survey results reveal that people consider the publication of privacy-sensitive information as well as private images without consent as the most problematic. Moreover, it turns out that 15 per cent of the Dutch population, a significant minority, has personal experience with online content they experience as harmful. However, strikingly, the available means of recourse are often not utilized. Only 1.4 per cent of the population have considered taking legal action. This appears to be partly due to the perceived length, complexity, and costs of a legal procedure, as well as a lack of knowledge of the applicable rules. Another major obstacle concerns the (im)possibility for injured individuals to find the appropriate actor to address.[17] We will take a closer look at these obstacles in the next subsection and get back to them in sections 11.3 and 11.4. The survey results, in particular, will be revisited in respect of access to justice (section 11.4).

11.2.2 Obstacles for Removing Unlawful Online Content

The expert interviews together with the survey gave considerable insight into why it is so difficult to get unlawful content offline. The obstacles people may encounter can be brought down to seven main categories:[18] the type of internet service, recurring content, an unknown or unreachable counterparty, the type of content, a lack of specialised knowledge, personal circumstances, and (other) barriers to access to court, which encompass length, complexity, and costs.

First, the type of internet service through which the content is made available can be decisive for the way in which, or even whether, unlawful content can be removed. For example, and as will be discussed in detail in section 11.3, certain services, such as hosting providers, are liable if they do not remove unlawful content whereas electronic communication services are often technically not able to do so.[19] Second, the category of recurring content refers to the notion that when a specific platform or hosting provider removes unlawful content, there is no guarantee it will not resurface on another platform. This

---

48009/08 (ECHT, 10 May 2011) [71]; *Khadija Ismayilova/Azerbaijan* App 30778/15 (ECHR, 10 October 2019) ECLI:CE:ECHR:2019:0110JUD006528613[115].

[17] Van Hoboken et al 2020 figure 3 p 31 *supra* n 11.

[18] Ibid., para 2E p 34.

[19] Art 14 e-Commerce Directive [2000] OJ L178, 17 July 2000, 1–16; European Electronic Communication Code [2018] *OJ L* 321/36.

obstacle is directly related to the decentral and at the same time international nature of online communication. Third, getting the content removed can also be hampered greatly by the fact that the party who has posted it is unknown or unreachable, e.g., because they are anonymous or in another jurisdiction (outside the EU). As will be discussed in section 11.3, these three obstacles are directly connected to debates in EU speech regulation.

Fourth, some content is more easily removed than others. There is a wide variety of content that can be qualified as unlawful. Different types of content fall under different legal regimes and entail a different burden of proof or level of scrutiny. For example, the unlawfulness of an insulting comment is usually more difficult to establish than a case of image-based sexual abuse. Fifth, the rules governing the removal of unlawful content are particularly complex on different levels; the type of internet service, the grounds for unlawfulness and the legal and factual position of the counterparty can all differ, not to mention the potential applicability of foreign laws. Navigating this complex landscape requires specialised knowledge usually reserved to media or privacy lawyers. But even they are not always able to retrieve the necessary data to use as evidence or to identify the counterparty. This creates a considerable obstacle for injured individuals, namely, to determine how and where to seek help. A sixth significant obstacle can be found in an individual's personal environment. Examples include shame and fear of social repercussions, gender-related insults, or underage children needing assistance from their guardians. These factors are individual- or group-specific and are therefore mentioned separately from other obstacles generally associated with access to court, the seventh and final category (see further section 11.4).

It diverges per case and per person which obstacles may arise. This demonstrates that getting unlawful content removed is a heterogeneous problem. It becomes even more complex when a systemic view is adopted and other factors come into play, in particular scalability of procedural routes for removal (see section 11.3.3). As we will see in the following section, the first three categories of obstacles are related to online speech regulation at large and stem from the decentral and open structure of the internet. Any solution will have to directly engage with this broader context to offer an effective remedy. The last four obstacles are related to the debate on access to justice in a broad sense. Sections 11.3 and 11.4 will engage with these broader debates. The results of our empirical study of the Netherlands are placed in the context of online speech regulation at EU level (section 11.3), and subsequently connected to access to justice and the specific procedural landscape of the Netherlands (section 11.4).

11.3 THE PROBLEM SEEN FROM THE PERSPECTIVE OF ONLINE SPEECH REGULATION

11.3.1 Policy Debates at EU Level

The question why it is so hard for people to quickly have unlawful content taken offline must primarily be understood in the specific context of online communication. As will be discussed, the options people have and the obstacles they face are directly informed by issues related to the very structure of internet-based communication, as well as the legal and policy debate on online speech regulation and intermediary liability. Indeed, the European Court of Human Rights (ECtHR) has recognised the 'dangers' that arise from online communication, including that illegal content can be disseminated 'like never before', 'worldwide, in a matter of seconds' and 'remain persistently available online'.[20] The policy debate and the associated scholarship on online speech regulation can thus help to explain where the obstacles people face stem from and why these obstacles are so difficult to tackle.

The emergence of dominant social media companies, the role of digital platforms in facilitating abusive speech, and their unilateral power over content moderation online, have placed them at the centre of scholarly and regulatory discussion at EU level. In this debate, the focus is on holding platforms responsible for combating harmful content[21] or curbing their power over online speech.[22] The European Commission (EC) has been actively making policy on illegal content, while ensuring the protection of fundamental rights – in particular the freedom of expression and the right to a private life – in the online environment.[23] In both its 2017 Communication on Tackling Illegal Content Online and the 2018 Recommendation on Measures to Effectively Tackle Illegal Content Online, the EC recognised the serious harm illegal content can do and called upon online platforms to improve their policies and active enforcement without resorting to over-removals which, on the flip side,

---

20 *Delfi AS v Estonia* App no 64569/09 (ECHR, 16 June 2015) [110].

21 Philip M. Napoli, *Social Media and the Public Interest: Media Regulation in the Disinformation Age* (Columbia University Press, 2019); Tarleton Gillespie, *Custodians of the Internet: Platforms, Content Moderation, and the Hidden Decisions that Shape Social Media* (Yale University Press, 2018).

22 Nicolas P. Suzor, *Lawless: The Secret Rules that Govern Our Digital Lives* (Cambridge University Press, 2019); Jack Balkin, 'Free Speech is a Triangle' (2018) 188 *Columbia Law Review*.

23 2020/0361(COD) *supra* n 6; COM(2017) 555 final *supra* n 8; COM/2020/67 final *supra* n 8; C(2018) 1177 *supra* n 2; Ares(2020)287768 *supra* n 2; EU Code of Conduct on Countering Illegal Hate Speech Online.

can seriously impair the freedom of expression.[24] Further, the EC implemented legislation delineating the responsibilities of platforms with regard to specific unlawful content such as of a terrorist nature or constituting an IP infringement.[25] Finally, and as will be discussed below in section 11.4.3, the DSA proposal both codifies and sets out new norms that directly impact people's ability to get unlawful content removed.[26] Additionally, in 2021 the Committee of Ministers of the Council of Europe issued a Recommendation focusing on the role of internet intermediaries in combating unlawful online content.[27] More specifically, the Recommendation sets out how fundamental rights protected in the ECHR are implicated in content moderation practices and outlines co- and self-regulatory approaches to combating unlawful content online.

11.3.2 Open and Decentralised Structure of the Internet

The first three categories of obstacles identified through our survey and the expert interviews – the type of internet service, recurring content, and an unreachable counterparty – can be apprehended by looking at online speech regulation debates. Specifically, the open and decentralised structure of the internet and online communication is a material factor in the difficulty of removing content.[28] This makes it hard for injured individuals to find the appropriate actor to address, let alone to achieve take-down and stay-down.[29] Even if content is taken down from one website, it may reappear elsewhere. With information stored on servers around the globe, content can be transferred easily from website to website. Traditionally, this structure is celebrated as democratising public debate and beneficial to the freedom of speech, as it creates relatively low barriers to entry and there is often no editorial control

---

24 COM(2017) 555 final *supra* n 8; C(2018) 1177 final *supra* n 2.

25 Regulation (EU) 2021/784 on addressing the dissemination of terrorist content online [2020] OJ L172/79; Directive (EU) 2019/790 on copyright and related rights in the Digital Single Market and amending Directives 96/9/EC and 2001/29/EC [2019] OJ L 130/92; Directive (EU) 2010/13 on the coordination of certain provisions laid down by law, regulation or administrative action in Member States concerning the provision of audiovisual media services [2018] OJ L303/69.

26 DSA COM(2020) 825 final *supra* n 6.

27 MSI-DIG(2021)04 *supra* n 2.

28 Christina Angelopoulos and Stijn Smet 'Notice-and-Fair-Balance: How to Reach a Compromise between Fundamental Rights in European Intermediary Liability' (2016) *Journal of Media Law* 283; Van Hoboken et al. (2020) *supra* n 11 p 37.

29 Here, 'take-down' refers to taking specific content offline and 'stay-down' refers to ensuring that specific content does not reappear and, rather, permanently stays offline. See further: Angelopoulos and Smet (n 28).

over online publication.[30] However, for a person trying to remove a specific piece of content it poses considerable challenges. Not only do they need to track all the places where the content pops up, it is possible that legal steps have to be taken against every platform or website separately.

Moreover, the procedural options available to an individual can be limited when the counterparty (i.e., the person posting the unlawful content) is located in another jurisdiction or is wholly unknown. This makes access to justice all the more complicated as well (see further section 11.4). A degree of anonymity is seen as crucial for the effective exercise of freedom of expression online and instrumental in protecting privacy.[31] Yet, it is also one of the reasons that the legal process of tracing someone's identity through hosting providers or internet service intermediaries is very laborious and time intensive.[32] When the counterparty is unknown or unreachable, injured individuals have no other option than addressing the hosting provider involved. As a consequence, they are either dependent on the cooperation of this hosting provider or they have to sue them. In either case, the risk of recurring content is significant as the original party that posted the content is not directly addressed in the process.

Perhaps most crucial for the speed of removal is the type of internet service on which the content is placed. As mentioned, the EU regulatory debate regarding online speech regulation has focused mainly on the role of the large social media platforms. However, a pivotal factor to take into consideration is the broad spectrum of different types of intermediaries of which social media platforms are only one.[33] They can fall under very different legal regimes where the responsibilities and possibilities with respect to removing unlawful content differ considerably. For example, online communication services such as WhatsApp or Signal may not be able to remove unlawful content from their private messaging services due to telecommunications regulation or

---

[30] Elettra Bietti, *A Genealogy of Digital Platform Regulation* [2021] forthcoming; Jonathan Zittrain, 'A History of Online Gatekeeping' (2006) 19 *Harvard Journal of Law & Technology* 253–467.

[31] See Wolfgang Benedek and Matthias C. Ketteman 'Freedom of Expression and the Internet' [2013] study for the Council of Europe; Cf. La Rue F. (16 May 2011), Report of the Special Rapporteur on the promotion and protection of the right to freedom of opinion and expression, UN Doc. A/HRC/17/27, para 84.

[32] Case C-582/14 *Breyer v Germany* [2016] ECLI:EU:C:2016:779; for the Dutch context see: HR 25 november 2005, ECLI:NL:HR:2005:AU4019, NJ 2009/550, m.nt. P.B. Hugenholtz onder NJ 2009/551 (Lycos/ [...]).

[33] Joris van Hoboken, João Pedro Quintais, Joost Poort and Nico van Eijk, 'Hosting Intermediary Services and Illegal Content Online: An Analysis of the Scope of Article 14 ECD in light of developments in the online service landscape' [2018] Content & Technology (Study for the European Commission DG Communications Networks).

encryption methods.[34] By contrast, other intermediaries that qualify as hosting providers are subject to a conditional liability and can be held liable if they do not remove unlawful content promptly once they become aware of it.[35] This category of hosting providers will be the focus of this chapter.

In the EU, the term 'hosting provider' is a legal category that refers to a type of internet service that allows people to upload information which it will store ('host') for them. Examples include big transnational social media such as Facebook, Twitter or TikTok, which enable people to post their own content on the platform. Importantly, however, it also includes smaller or independent websites with comment sections or bulletin boards that have a much smaller user base and less means. The ECtHR has summarised the legal position of this diffuse category of hosting providers by stating that they 'should not be held responsible for content emanating from third parties unless they failed to act expeditiously in removing or disabling access to it once they became aware of its illegality'.[36] This conditional liability for unlawful content has resulted in many hosting providers implementing a so-called Notice and Takedown procedure, where they remove ('take down') content after a user has notified them of the unlawful nature of that content ('notice').[37]

11.3.3 Notice and Takedown and the Central Role of Hosting Providers

At first sight, Notice and Takedown might sound like a suitable solution to the challenges posed by unlawful content. There are nevertheless concerns from the perspective of access to justice, particularly due to a lack of procedural safeguards – as will become apparent in section 11.4.

The central mediating role played by hosting providers also brings out a tension between getting unlawful content offline as fast and efficiently as possible and protecting the freedom of expression. As hosting providers are the ones storing the content and making it available to others, they are in a prime position to check and control this content, thereby preventing the dissemination of unlawful content. The EU is increasingly using this central position by transferring responsibility to hosting providers for combatting specific forms

---

[34] Directive (EC) 2002/58/EC of 12 July 2002 concerning the processing of personal data and the protection of privacy in the electronic communications sector [2002] OJ L201/37; Directive (EC) 2018/1972 of 11 December 2018 establishing the European Electronic Communication Code [2018] OJ L321/36.

[35] Art 14 Directive (EC) 2000/31 on certain legal aspects of information society services, in particular electronic commerce, in the Internal Market [2000].

[36] *Tamiz v the United Kingdom* App 3877/14 (ECHR, 19 September 2017) [84].

[37] Aleksandra Kuczerawy, 'Private Enforcement of Public Policy: Freedom of Expression in the Era of Online Gatekeeping' (PhD Thesis, University of Gent 2018).

of unlawful content, such as IP infringements or terrorist content, to hosting providers.[38] However, this also means hosting providers are in a position to remove *lawful* content and limit people's freedom of expression. As such, the regulatory challenge is to both incentivise hosting providers to swiftly remove unlawful content and not stimulate them from unduly limiting people's freedom of expression online. The ECtHR is acutely concerned with avoiding a 'chilling effect' on freedom of expression online, and has found that imposing too-strict forms of liability over online publications will have 'foreseeable negative consequences on the flow of information on the Internet'.[39] Indeed, the Council of Europe's Committee of Ministers has also warned against States imposing 'disproportionate' regulatory frameworks on platforms which are 'likely to lead to the restriction of lawful content and to have a chilling effect on the right to freedom of expression'.[40]

Additionally, within the category of hosting providers there is still a large variety that greatly impacts the effectiveness of Notice and Takedown procedures in enabling an individual to get unlawful content removed quickly. For example, the scale and reach as well as the cooperativeness of the hosting provider can be determining factors in the speed and efficiency with which content can be removed. Large social media platforms such as Facebook and Twitter have established elaborate Notice and Takedown procedures for people to request the removal of specific content.[41] Even though these procedures can still be criticised from a freedom of expression perspective,[42] getting

---

[38] See n 25.

[39] *Magyar Jeti Zrt v Hungary* App 11257/16 (ECHR, 4 December 2018) [83]. *See also*, Ronan O Fathaigh, 'The Chilling Effect of Liability for Online Reader Comments' (2017) 22 *European Human Rights Law Review* 387.

[40] Recommendation of the Committee of Ministers to Member States on the roles and responsibilities of internet intermediaries, CM/Rec (2018) 2 (March 7, 2018) para 1.3.6.

[41] For a discussion see: Kate Klonick, 'The Facebook Oversight Board: Creating an Independent Institution to Adjudicate Online Free Expression' (2020) 129 *Yale Law Journal*; Evelyn Douek, 'Facebook's "Oversight Board:" Move Fast with Stable Infrastructure and Humility' (2019) 21 *North Carolina Journal of Law & Technology*; Robyn Caplan, 'The Artisan and the Decision Factory: The organizational Dynamics of Private Speech Governance' in Lucy Bernholz, Hélène Landemore and Rob Reich (eds) *Digital Technology and Democratic Theory* (University of Chicago Press, 2021).

[42] Content is often removed based on the terms and conditions offered by the platforms themselves that do not necessarily conform to freedom of expression standards. For a discussion see: Molly K. Land, 'Regulating Private Harms Online: Content Regulation Under Human Rights Law', in Rikke Frank Jørgensen (ed), *Human Rights in the Age of Platforms* (MIT Press 2019) 285; Suzor (2019) *supra* n 22; Aleksandra Kuczerawy, 'Intermediary Liability and Freedom of Expression: Recent Developments in the EU Notice and Action Initiative' (2015) 31 *Computer Law & Security Review*.

content removed from smaller independently hosted websites can be much more challenging. This is especially the case when a hosting provider is not willing to cooperate or even has the hosting of unlawful content as its business model, such as websites where involuntarily nude images are shared.[43] When the hosting provider refuses to comply or actively tries to obstruct an attempt to get content removed, the only remaining option is to turn to the courts. Simultaneously, however, content on the large social media platforms can potentially spread much faster and wider. As such, the hosting provider can be a decisive factor in the ease and speed of removal and the extent of the harm caused by the unlawful content.

Further, a more systemic challenge is posed by the vast quantity of content shared online. For example, YouTube claims more than 500 hours of content are uploaded to its platform every minute.[44] Any procedure designed to offer adequate access to justice for people confronted by unlawful online content needs to accommodate this enormous scale. Operating at such scale clearly causes tension with due process demands on a procedure to remove unlawful content. As such, unlawful online content poses a large challenge to the capacity of the traditional civil justice system.

This overview of the EU context already reveals the complexity of removing unlawful online content. Our findings on the Netherlands discussed in section 11.2 cannot be viewed in isolation; they must be seen from the broader perspective of online speech regulation. Still, to understand the specific challenges and obstacles an individual might face when confronted with unlawful content online, another perspective is needed. The problem must be connected to access to justice debates as well, where the procedural landscape and its limitations can be taken into account. We have identified various procedures that are available under Dutch law, including the Notice and Takedown procedures offered by online platforms (currently on the basis of self-regulation).[45] As will be discussed in the following section, none of these procedures can fully address all seven obstacles identified in our study and at the same time reconcile sufficient safeguards with the need for speed, scalability and accessibility.

---

[43] For example www.vagina.nl, a website that is currently being sued in a collective action in the Netherlands by Stichting Stop Online Shaming: https://stoponlineshaming.org accessed 2 April 2022. See also van Hoboken et al. (2020) *supra* note 11 p 61.

[44] See https://blog.youtube/press/ for more information see the YouTube transparency reports at: https://transparencyreport.google.com/youtube-policy/removals?hl=en accessed 2 April 2022.

[45] The seven procedures examined in the report are the ordinary civil procedure, summary civil proceedings, application procedure, ex parte procedure, complaint at DPA, exercising individual GDPR rights and the Notice and Takedown procedure.

11.4 THE PROBLEM SEEN FROM THE PERSPECTIVE OF ACCESS TO JUSTICE

11.4.1 Need for Speed

The question of what constitutes an effective procedure to quickly remove unlawful online content is inextricably linked to the broader debate on access to justice. Our study affirms that a lack of knowledge or (financial) means, as well as other personal circumstances, may prevent or deter people from taking legal action. These issues are well-known in the context of access to justice and certainly not unique for the removal of unlawful online content. However, what makes the problem particularly pressing is the need for speed as well as the sheer volume of cases, which, combined with issues arising in the context of online speech regulation (see section 11.3), make it particularly difficult to find a solution.

Earlier research that has been done in the Netherlands showed that people's needs and motives for (not) going to court may differ according to different target groups and the type of legal problems they encounter. The availability of economic and socio-psychological resources also plays a role. People always make a cost-benefit trade-off to some extent: the seriousness of the problem, the (financial) interest involved and the expected outcome influence the decision whether or not to take further steps.[46] Research by the European Parliament shows that in general EU citizens consider costs, (lack of) access to legal assistance, the length of proceedings and the enforcement of court decisions as major obstacles.[47] Furthermore, the complexity of legislation can form a barrier.[48] This is all the more true in cross-border cases, where citizens may have to deal with the law of another jurisdiction. There are also considerable differences between people in terms of their ability to act independently, which can lead to inequality.[49] In a study from 2004, the Dutch Council for Social

---

[46] M.J. ter Voert and M.S. Hoekstra, *Geschilbeslechtingdelta 2019. Over verloop en afloop van (potentieel) juridische problemen van burgers*, 15–16.

[47] European Parliament, 'Effective Access to Justice' (2017), https://www.europarl.europa.eu/thinktank/en/document.html?reference=IPOL_STU(2017)596818, accessed 2 April 2022, pp 10–11.

[48] FRA (European Union Agency for Fundamental Rights), *Access to justice in Europe: an overview of challenges and opportunities* (Publications Office of the European Union 2011), http://fra.europa.eu accessed 2 April 2022, 38.

[49] For example, elderly people with a lower level of education may not possess the digital skills to find legal information online; see n 87 and 88 of van Hoboken et al. 2020 (n 11). E. Bauw et al., *Naar een nabijheid rechter? Een onderzoek naar de inpasbaarheid van de vrederechter in België en Frankrijk in het Nederlandse Rechtsbestel* (Utrecht: Universiteit Utrecht-Montaigne Centrum voor Rechtsstaat en Rechtspleging

Development noted that the problem is not so much the supply of information, but a lack of knowledge or skills to be able to make effective use of it at an early stage. The inaccessibility experienced by people thus becomes a real obstacle.[50] This requires a comprehensive and proactive approach to access to information, help and advice, whereby people are helped at an early stage.[51]

The four remaining categories of obstacles identified in our study – the type of content at issue, a lack of specialised knowledge, personal circumstances, and (other) barriers to access to court – all relate to access to justice in a broad sense. Expert interviews confirm that a lack of access to legal information and advice is one of the prime hurdles. This is not only the case with the removal of illegal online content, but with all kinds of legal problems that people face. With online content, however, the time factor weighs extra heavily. The longer harmful content stays online, the greater the personal and or social impact because it can spread very quickly.

11.4.2 The Dutch Procedural Landscape

There are various types of court proceedings available under Dutch law that, in theory, suffice for the purposes of obtaining a decision that certain content is unlawful and must be removed. However, only a fraction of cases concerning the removal of unlawful online content are brought before the courts. As mentioned in section 11.2, the main deterring factors appear to be the length, complexity, and costs of court proceedings. Ordinary court proceedings (in first instance) last between six to nine months on average and are therefore not suitable if time is of the essence. Summary proceedings could provide a way to obtain an injunction more rapidly, but it is still a matter of weeks rather than days – unless the claimant can convince the court that the situation is not only urgent but must be resolved urgently. Both types of proceedings require that the counterparty is known and summoned to appear in order to be heard before the court.

2019) 57; Wetenschappelijke Raad voor het Regeringsbeleid, *Weten is nog geen doen: een realistisch perspectief op zelfredzaamheid* (Den Haag: WRR 2017); College voor de Rechten van de Mens, *Jaarlijkse rapportage mensenrechten in Nederland. (*Toegang tot het recht 2018) 47.

[50] J.M. Barendrecht and Y.P. Kamminga, Toegang tot het recht: de lasten van een uitweg (RMO-advies; 32), Den Haag: RMO December 2004. See also OECD, Understanding effective access to justice, OECD Conference Centre, Paris 4 November 2016, OECD.org, 5.

[51] R. Macdonald, 'Access to Civil Justice', in *The Oxford Handbook of Empirical Research* (Oxford University Press 2012).

A complicating factor is that the legal landscape is scattered and therefore particularly difficult to navigate, as observed in section 11.2. As indicated, there is a wide variety of unlawful content that falls within the scope of Article 8 ECHR but it is governed under different regimes. For privacy infringements, for instance, the applicable legal framework is different than for defamation. Importantly, the associated harm and reasons for fast removal may differ, as well as the difficulty in establishing a specific type of unlawfulness. This can create a mismatch between the need of an individual to get content removed as fast as possible due to the harm caused or the risk that the content will spread, and the need for a thorough substantive assessment leading up to a judicial decision.

None of the types of civil proceedings we have analysed – ordinary court proceedings, summary proceedings, and a special *ex parte* procedure for violations of IP rights[52] – are fully adequate in terms of costs, length and complexity. Only the *ex parte* procedure could be considered fast enough, but at present it does not apply to the removal of online content and it is questionable whether it would address all other obstacles. For instance, it still requires specialist knowledge, and it is not possible in the Netherlands to bring proceedings against an anonymous party. It is unclear what role internet services should fulfil in this respect, e.g., whether they should disclose the personal details of the party that has posted the content (see section 11.2 above).

More importantly, the *ex parte* procedure does not fully account for the freedom of speech, because the counterparty is not heard before an order is given and the court's assessment is preliminary. In the context of defamatory statements related to elections, the ECtHR has held that 'as desirable as the expeditious examination of such disputes may be, it should not result in the undue curtailment of the procedural guarantees afforded to the parties', in particular the defendants.[53] Similarly, in cases concerning the removal of unlawful online content, the defendant should always have a possibility to contest the removal. Widening the scope of the *ex parte* procedure would not only require a special justification. It is also not immediately obvious whether it should be extended to cases where the unlawfulness cannot be established upfront and it requires a more elaborate assessment. Apart from this, scalability is an issue here as well, which brings us back to the promise of (out-of-court) Notice and Takedown procedures.

---

[52] Arts 3:396 and 6:167 BW, 6:196c jo. 3:15d BW, 35 Uitvoeringswet AVG, 1019e Rv.

[53] *Kwiecién v Poland* App 51744/99 (ECHR 9 January 2007) [55].

11.4.3 Notice and Takedown, Accessibility and Procedural Safeguards

Notice and Takedown procedures are relatively accessible as there are no monetary costs tied to the procedure, there is no mandatory legal representation, and the procedure is relatively simple. Notably, the ECtHR has concluded that a notice-and-action mechanism which guarantees 'effective procedures allowing for rapid response' can be an 'appropriate tool' and 'viable avenue' for protecting Article 8 ECHR rights.[54] However, our survey showed that more than a third of the Dutch population is wholly unfamiliar or not very familiar with these Notice and Takedown procedures, indicating that many people might not be able to find them accessible. Further, the process and decision are left entirely up to the hosting provider in question and are currently very opaque.[55] This opacity is mainly due to the fact that the current regulatory framework does not mandate any transparency as to how these procedures work and on the actual decision-making process.[56] For example, it can be wholly unclear whether a notification is decided on by a human content moderator, an automated system or a combination of both.[57]

Whilst the Notice and Takedown procedures offered by the hosting providers themselves are clearly equipped to remove unlawful online content quickly and at scale, it is far from ideal for both the injured individual (whose request for takedown might unduly be denied) as well as the alleged wrongdoer (whose content might unduly be removed). As the process is entirely left to the hosting provider, there are neither institutional safeguards that ensure the application of the law, nor procedural safeguards that guarantee due process, including the right to be heard.[58] A truly 'effective' remedy also encompasses the latter, especially where conflicting fundamental rights – Articles 8 and 10

---

[54] *Magyar Tartalomszolgáltatók Egyesülete and Index.hu Zrt v* Hungary App 22947/13 (ECHR, 2 February 2016) [91].

[55] Aleksandra Kuczerawy, 'Private Enforcement of Public Policy: Freedom of Expression in the Era of Online Gatekeeping' (PhD Thesis, University of Gent 2018); Kate Klonick, 'The New Governors: The People, Rules and Processes Governing Online Speech' 131 *HarvLRev* 1598.

[56] The proposed Digital Services Act (*supra* n 3) tries to ameliorate this situation, see e.g., Arts 12, 13, 20(4), 23, 29.

[57] See e.g., Tarleton Gillespie, 'Content Moderation, AI, and the Question of Scale' (2020) 7 *Big Data and Society* 2.

[58] The proposed Digital Services Act (*supra* n 3) tries to ameliorate this situation with, e.g., codification of the notice and takedown procedure (Art 14), the requirement to inform and explain when a user's content is taken down (Art 15) and an internal complaint procedure for online platforms (Art 17).

ECHR – are at stake.[59] A focus on the position of the injured individual is too one-sided; the other party's right to freedom of expression and a fair trial must also be taken into account, especially where the unlawfulness of the content is contested and cannot be established upfront. This emphasises the importance of contestation and developing procedures which force hosting providers to consider all interests involved.[60]

The accessibility and scalability of Notice and Takedown procedures explain the focus of the policy debate on regulating the position of hosting providers. The most ambitious regulatory effort in this regard has been the proposed DSA. In taking a tiered approach, the DSA aims to codify the existing Notice and Takedown procedures for all hosting providers (Art 14), implement a complaints procedure for online platforms (Art 17) and mandate avenues for users to out-of-court dispute settlement procedures for disputes based on the complaints procedure (Art 18). Additionally, the DSA creates several transparency obligations for hosting providers (e.g., Art 12) and online platforms (e.g., Art 23). As such, the DSA can go some way in strengthening the procedural safeguards that currently lack in the Notice and Takedown procedures and offering a more reliable procedure for people to get unlawful content removed. For example, based on the DSA, users will have the right to be properly informed of a decision following their complaint or notice, and people will have the possibility to appeal a decision following a complaint. However, far from all obstacles are addressed in this piece of legislation. Depending on the effectiveness of the eventual implementation and enforcement, a user can still be very much dependent on the willingness of a particular hosting provider to cooperate. Additionally, the obstacles related to recurring content or perpetrators who are unreachable or unknown remain unresolved (see section 11.3 above).

Our survey further indicates that reporting possibilities (including Notice and Takedown) being easy to find are considered to be the most important feature.[61] Indeed, this underlines the importance of providing clear and accessible information to people who are confronted with unlawful online content, in particular as regards the parties to address and what steps to follow in order to gather evidence and substantiate a request for removal. Increased participation online may lead to new problems but can also contribute to a new solution. In

---

[59] See *Mosley v United Kingdom* App 48009/08 (ECHR,10 May 2011) [129]; *Lingens v Austria* App 9815/82 (ECHR, 8 July 1986) [46].

[60] Similarly see Caplan 2021 *supra* n 41; Jillian C. York, 'Silicon Values: The Future of Free Speech under Surveillance Capitalism' (Verso 2021); Susan J. Brison and Katharine Gelber (eds) *Free Speech in the Digital Age* (Oxford University Press 2019).

[61] Van Hoboken et al. 2020 figure 5a p 56 (n 11).

the Dutch context, there is already a wealth of information available on various websites, offering practical tips and tools. They are often specifically tailored to data protection issues or content that could also be labelled as a criminal offence.[62] However, people do not think in 'legal categories'; therefore, we submit that, rather than procedural innovation, a 'roadmap' is needed that directs people towards Notice and Takedown first, with court proceedings as a last resort. We will elaborate in the final section of this chapter.

11.5 A LAYERED APPROACH TO REMOVING UNLAWFUL CONTENT ONLINE

When the problem of removing unlawful online content is connected to both the broader European discussions on online speech regulation and the ongoing debates on access to justice, the heterogeneity of the problem becomes clearly visible. The different tensions identified in this chapter explain why existing procedural routes fail to provide a solution. There is not a single (judicial or extrajudicial) procedure that reconciles sufficient safeguards with the need for speed, scalability and accessibility. Crucially, a trade-off will always have to be made between these different elements.

At present, the Dutch civil justice system does not seem to be sufficiently equipped to deal with this trade-off. Accessibility provides the main challenge, whilst ensuring due process and protecting the freedom of expression remain difficult to control when content moderation is left to internet services alone. Interestingly, this is where the perspectives of online speech regulation and access to justice come together: how can 'digital justice' be served in an effective way, with due regard for fundamental rights? The right to a fair trial and the freedom of expression demand that the position of all relevant actors is taken into account. But if the procedure is not fast enough, the harm done continues or increases and the content may spread elsewhere. This is also where a tension emerges between a pragmatic turn, seeing citizens primarily as 'users' of the civil justice system and pushing for extrajudicial solutions, and a view on courts as 'keepers' of procedural and substantive safeguards, in particular in light of the freedom of speech.

The obstacles related to access to court cannot be addressed in isolation, just as it is not possible to design one uniform procedure for all types and varieties

---

62 See e.g., Bits of Freedom, 'Tips en Tools', https://www.bitsoffreedom.nl/tips-en-tools; Autoriteit Persoonsgegevens, 'Voorbeeldbrief Privacyrechten', https://autoriteitpersoonsgegevens.nl/nl/zelf-doen/voorbeeldbrieven-privacyrechten; Politie.nl, 'Naaktfoto's gelekt', https://www.politie.nl/themas/naaktfotos-gelekt.html; Vraag het de politie, 'Pesten & Online', https://www.vraaghetdepolitie.nl/pesten-en-online, all accessed 2 April 2022.

of unlawful online content that properly balances the divergent rights and interests involved. Therefore, procedural innovation is not the (only) answer. Some of the obstacles identified in our study are intrinsic to the structure of the internet, in particular the issues of recurring content and the counterparty being unreachable or unknown, i.e., anonymous. These can only partly be solved by imposing more responsibilities on hosting providers in respect of Notice and Takedown procedures. However, that there is no uniform solution does not mean there is nothing to be done. We propose to take a problem-oriented approach, where the removal of unlawful online content is seen not as a single problem but rather a collection of related specific issues that require a tailored solution. Most importantly, citizens who seek a remedy in their individual case need easy access to information and assistance on whom to address and which routes to follow, in- and out-of-court. As observed in section 11.4, this could be done in the form of an online 'roadmap' that includes a step-by-step plan with different modalities or an 'escalation model', according to, for instance, the type of content at issue and the actors involved. The bigger the impact on someone's personal life, the higher the urgency. Another, more overarching solution is to improve and promote the use of a central contact point where injured parties can go for further advice, insofar as they are able to find their way and overcome personal obstacles to ask for help. Such contact points already exist in the Dutch context[63] but are scattered along the type of content at issue and may not be as easy to find. Our study provides a steppingstone for more empirical research into people's needs and perceptions in respect of 'access to digital justice'. Understanding the problem is an important first step; the search for an effective remedy continues.

[63] See e.g., Meldknop.nl, veiliginternetten.nl, landelijk meldpunt internetoplichting or meldpunt internetdiscriminatie.

PART III

Collectivising and monetising civil litigation

12. Dutch collective actions and the rise of entrepreneurial actors: Navigating between access to justice and a claim culture

Ilja Tillema

12.1 INTRODUCTION

Since 1994, Dutch foundations and associations (hereafter: representative organizations) can bring a collective action for injunctive or declaratory relief in the interest of others;[1] 25 years later, after years of debate, the collective action for damages act – abbreviated as WAMCA – was published.[2] As a result, since January 2020, representative organizations are also allowed to claim *for damages* in a collective action. Meanwhile, and gradually, collective actions have involved representative organizations and/or third-party litigation funders that also have an own interest in the action: a share of the proceeds in case of success. To what extent have such entrepreneurial actors contributed to access to justice, and will this contribution intensify with the arrival of the WAMCA? This chapter addresses these questions, in particular by looking back on the developments and the experiences gained in the past decades.[3]

1 Pursuant to s 3:305a *Burgerlijk Wetboek* (the Dutch Civil Code; abbreviated as 'BW').

2 *Wet Afwikkeling Massaschade in Collectieve Acties* (Act on Collective Damages Claims). See *Stb.* 2019, 130; *Stb.* 2019, 447. For an – informal – English translation, see www.rechtspraak.nl/SiteCollectionDocuments/New-dutch-legislation-on-collective-actions.pdf accessed 31 July 2021.

3 Parts of this publication, in particular sections 12.2 and 12.3, in content are largely based on the research conducted for Ilja Tillema, *Entrepreneurial Mass Litigation: Balancing the Building Blocks* (doctoral thesis, Eleven Publishing 2019), and section 12.4.1 is a follow-up on part of an earlier study: Ilja Tillema, 'Entrepreneurial Motives in Dutch Collective Redress: Adding Fuel to a "Compensation Culture"?' in Willem H. van Boom (ed), *Litigation, Costs, Funding and Behaviour: Implications for the Law* (Routledge 2017) paras 4.1–4.3.

The chapter is structured as follows. In section 12.2, I sketch the development of the collective action acts, within the broader context of Dutch collective redress. Section 12.3 describes the development of the market for entrepreneurial parties, and their potential contribution to access to justice. Section 12.4 presents data on collective actions and the actors involved, including the first WAMCA data, and the lessons learned so far. I provide a brief outlook on future issues in section 12.5, also in light of the new EU Representative Actions Directive.[4] The chapter closes with concluding remarks in section 12.6.

12.2 THE DEVELOPMENT OF THE LEGAL FRAMEWORK FOR COLLECTIVE ACTION

Over the past decades, collective redress in the Netherlands has developed by way of two general civil law mechanisms that have been designed specifically for judicial collective redress: collective action (s 3:305a BW) and collective settlement (ss 7:907–910 BW). In addition, in particular in cartel damages claims, collective redress has been obtained by aggregating claims through assignment.[5] Hereafter, I will focus on the collective action route.[6] It has evolved along the following lines.

Although there are earlier traces, it was not until the 1970s that the discussion on collective actions really took off.[7] From then onwards, Dutch case law and doctrine started to unfold the concept of collective actions by represent-

---

4 Directive of the European Parliament and of the Council (EU) 2020/1828 of 25 November 2020 on representative actions for the protection of the collective interests of consumers and repealing Directive 2009/22/EC [2020] OJ L409/1 (Representative Actions Directive).

5 See, for instance, Rb Amsterdam 15 May 2021, ECLI:NL:RBAMS:2021:3574 on the trucks cartel; Rb Rotterdam 23 June 2021, ECLI:NL:RBROT:2021:6635 on the elevators and escalators cartel; Hof Amsterdam 6 July 2021, ECLI:NL:GHAMS:2021:1940 on the air cargo cartel.

6 For an overview of the other mechanisms see Tillema, *Entrepreneurial Mass Litigation* (n 3) para 6.5. For a recent publication on the collective action and settlement regulation, see also Ianika N. Tzankova and Xandra E. Kramer, 'From Injunction and Settlement to Action: Collective Redress and Funding in the Netherlands' in Alan Uzelac and Stefaan Voet (eds), *Class Actions in Europe: Holy Grail or a Wrong Trail?* (Springer 2021) 97–130.

7 On the 1937 act on collective agreements, pursuant to which a union can bring a claim on behalf of employees, see N. Frenk, *Kollektieve akties in het privaatrecht* (Kluwer 1994) 105ff; on incidental case law, see M.J.P. Verburgh, *Privaatrecht en kollektief belang. Verdediging van kollektieve belangen via de burgerlijke rechter* (Tjeenk Willink 1975).

ative organizations, and since 1980 – in line with European developments[8] – various pieces of legislation authorized such organizations to bring claims in the interest of others.[9] Gradually, the idea gained ground that certain parties should have capacity to litigate in order to protect the interest of others without having to enter into specific powers of attorney or comparable arrangements. The growing body of legislative mechanisms correlated with jurisprudential developments. Towards the 1970s, published case law from lower courts showed an increase in cases in the areas of labour, consumer, competition, and environmental law that concerned a wider 'audience' than just the litigating parties. In 1983, the Supreme Court first gave standing to an association that represented other persons' interests.[10] Although it constructed standing on the association's own interest, the court ruled that in the interest of due process it would be inefficient to require aggrieved parties to bring their claim individually. Yet, in this first stage of Dutch collective redress, bringing a claim as a representative organization was a risky endeavour, as the courts were still hesitant to allow them to have standing. To some extent, this improved after a landmark ruling in 1986, brought by three environmental organizations on the dumping of dredged material.[11] For the first time, the Dutch Supreme Court held that, under certain conditions, foundations or associations could bring a collective action to obtain injunctive or declaratory relief in the interest of others without having an own interest – even without a specific regulation that allowed them such power. The Supreme Court considered that the environment concerned many diffuse as well as unspecified individuals' interests, and that the bundling of such interests by a representative organization would provide efficient legal protection.

In 1994, the case law was codified with the introduction of the general collective action in section 3:305a BW, and the legislator revoked the defragmented legislation to avoid discussions on the applicable legal framework. It was incited by the growing awareness that individual litigation in mass harm situations, specifically in public interest matters, was incidental at most, and thus, substantive laws were not (sufficiently) enforced. Individuals were either not prepared to or incapable of seeking redress, because their interests were insufficient or the litigation costs were too high. The legislator presumed that

---

[8] See, in particular, Council Directive 84/450/EEC of 10 September 1984 relating to the approximation of the laws, regulations and administrative provisions of the Member States concerning misleading advertising [1984] OJ L250/17, inspired by the German Unterlassungsklage.

[9] For instance, the *Wet misleidende reclame* included the possibility for consumer organizations to apply for an order to stop or rectify misleading advertising.

[10] HR 1 July 1983, NJ 1984, 360 (*LSV*).

[11] HR 27 June 1986, NJ 1987, 743 (*De Nieuwe Meer*).

such thresholds for having access to justice would not exist, or to a lesser extent, for representative organizations.[12] Hence, since 1994, a representative organization has the authority to bring a collective action to court. It may concern any type of civil claim, and must represent the similar interests of other persons. With this collective action, injunctive or declaratory relief could be obtained; until 2020 (see hereafter), the procedure rejected the possibility of claiming compensatory relief. Such collective action would require – possibly complicated – individual assessment for which the action was not deemed suitable, whereas compensation could also be achieved through a voluntary settlement or individual action following the declaratory judgment.[13]

In practice, however, the need for compensatory collective redress remained. This need turned into legislation due to the DES case, which concerned pharmaceutical product liability claims. After years of litigation, the victims' representative had reached an amicable settlement with the liable parties. In order to both compensate the victims and obtain finality, the parties wished to have the settlement declared binding. This led to the introduction of the WCAM in 2005.[14] In short, this procedure provides for one or more representative organizations, on the one hand, and the alleged liable party or parties, on the other, to submit a joint application to the Amsterdam Court of Appeal requesting it to declare legally binding a settlement that contains rights to compensation for the class members.

In the following years, additional measures were implemented to further improve private enforcement in mass harm situations. The main innovation was that, as of July 2012, a district or an appellate court can refer a preliminary question to the Dutch Supreme Court, on its own initiative or at the request of one of the parties.[15] It can do so if the answer is necessary to come to a decision, and is of direct importance to either a mass dispute or to the resolution of numerous other, factually similar civil disputes.

---

[12] See, for instance, Kamerstukken II 1975/76, 13611 (3) 8; Kamerstukken II 1991/92, 22486 (3) 2.

[13] Kamerstukken II 1991/92, 22486 (2) 30; Kamerstukken II 1991/92, 22486 (3) 29ff; Kamerstukken II 1993/94, 22486 (15).

[14] *Wet Collectieve Afhandeling Massaschade* (Collective Mass Claims Settlement Act); *Kamerstukken II* 2003/04, 29414. See also, for instance, Willem H. van Boom, 'Collective Settlement of Mass Claims in The Netherlands' in Matthias Casper and others (eds), *Auf dem Weg zu einer europaischen Sammelklage?* (Sellier 2009) 171–192; Ianika Tzankova and Daan Lunsingh Scheurleer, 'The Netherlands' in Deborah R. Hensler, Christopher Hodges and Magdalena Tulibacka, *The Globalization of Class Actions* (SAGE Publications 2009) 149–160.

[15] Ss 392–394 *Wetboek van Burgerlijke Rechtsvordering* (the Dutch Code of Civil Procedure; abbreviated as 'Rv'); *Kamerstukken II* 2010/11, 32612.

Nevertheless, the debate on collective redress continued. The main concern was to bridge the gap between the collective action and WCAM for those situations in which the (alleged) liable party is not willing to negotiate. This prolongs the settlement of mass damage because class members still need to bring individual actions after a declaratory judgment. Therefore, in November 2011, the possibility to collectively claim for damages was proposed by a member of the Dutch Parliament.[16] After years of debate and revisions, the renewed collective action act, WAMCA, entered into effect in January 2020.[17] As mentioned, it expands the collective action under section 3:305a BW to actions for damages. As in the WCAM, the act allows for (abstract) damage scheduling, either as part of a judgment or a court-approved collective settlement, under which approach individual compensation is tied to the particular subclass to which the class member belongs.[18] Hence, individual matters such as causation and quantum might be taken into account to a certain extent only. A collective settlement remains the preferred route to obtain collective redress.[19] The act stimulates this by improving the quality of the representative parties (stricter rules on their governance, funding, and representativeness),[20] coordination (judicial case management, and the appointment of an exclusive representative organization),[21] and the finality of a settlement agreement or judgment (opt-out technique). To enable a settlement, the court can also refer a preliminary question to the Supreme Court.[22] To approve a settlement, the court follows the same criteria as those under the WCAM: it assesses whether the interests of the class members are sufficiently guaranteed, in particular whether the amount of the compensation awarded is reasonable.[23] If the settlement is declared binding, all individuals affected by the mass damage event are bound, unless they opt out within a certain period (of at least three months) following the announcement of the order.[24] If parties do not settle, the action results in a judgment that has binding effect on all class members who have not opted out after the admissibility phase.

---

16 Kamerstukken II 2011/12, 33000-XIII (14).
17 n 2.
18 S 1018i Rv; *Kamerstukken II* 2016/17, 34608 (3) 50–53.
19 Kamerstukken II 2016/17, 34608 (3) 4.
20 See ss 12.3.1 and 12.4.3.
21 See ss 12.4.2 and 12.4.3.
22 Pursuant to the aforementioned ss 392–394 Rv.
23 Ss 1018h (2) Rv jo 7:907 (3) BW.
24 Ss 1018f (1) Rv and 1018h (5) Rv, as amended in *Kamerstukken II* 2017/18, 34608 (7).

12.3 FUNDING COLLECTIVE ACTIONS AS A BUSINESS MODEL

12.3.1 The Rise and Regulation of Entrepreneurial Parties

As follows from the previous section, ineffective access to justice has been one of the main drivers of the emergence of the collective action acts. However, the operation of such mechanism depends on the initiative of representative organizations. Bringing a collective action can be a costly and risky endeavour, given its complexity, scale, and duration. Hence, organizations are not always able or willing to undertake action. In recent years, entrepreneurial parties have started to fill this gap, driven by the prospect of a potentially sizeable return on investment. For even if the individual claims of class members are negatively valued, mass damage events are likely to constitute a high positive-value claim. In return for investing in such action, the entrepreneurial party can obtain part of the proceeds if the action is successful. This can be arranged through a contingency fee (alike) contract with individual class members, and/or as part of the settlement agreement with the party that was held liable. The *Fortis/Ageas* settlement illustrates such arrangement, as well as the substantial proceeds that can be made as a return on the investment.[25] As part of the €1.3 billion settlement agreement that followed years of securities litigation concerning the Fortis collapse in 2007/08, four representative organizations received €45 million from Ageas (Fortis' successor). In addition, three of them received another – projected – €80 million, following the result-based arrangements they had entered into with individual class members. On a settlement award of €1.3 billion such total could be considered relatively modest (10 per cent). In view of the estimated costs of around €30 million, however, in absolute terms such pay-out is hardly a gratuity, even though a settlement of this size obviously is not an everyday occurrence.

For years, entrepreneurial parties were free to choose their business model and funding arrangement as they were unregulated by law or professional rules, other than general civil and corporate law. This has changed in the past decade.[26] First, as a result of criticism about the performance of certain (board members of) representative organizations, the Claim Code was issued:

---

[25] Hof Amsterdam 13 July 2018, ECLI:NL:GHAMS:2018:2422, paras 5.14–15. See also section 12.4.3.

[26] See also Ianika N. Tzankova, 'Funding of Mass Disputes: Lessons from the Netherlands' (2012) 8 *Journal of Law, Economics & Policy* 549; Tzankova and Kramer (n 6); Xandra Kramer and Ilja Tillema, 'The Funding of Collective Redress by Entrepreneurial Parties: The EU and Dutch Context' [2020] 2(2) Revista Ítalo-Española de Derecho Procesal 165.

a self-regulatory initiative on good governance that came into effect in 2011, and was revised in 2019.[27] It lays down general provisions that aim to give represented parties more clarity and guarantees on the organizations that act on their behalf. The code is based on the principle of 'comply or explain', and consists of seven principles and explanatory notes on, inter alia, the composition, task, and remuneration of the representative organizations' (supervisory) board, and since 2019, on third-party litigation funding. Neither the representative organization nor its (in)direct stakeholders should pursue profit, but the organization is allowed to be compensated for expenses incurred or services provided. This may include a reasonable uplift for future actions and/or the investment made. If the organization is backed by a third-party funder, this should be publicly disclosed, as well as the outlines of the funding arrangement. Furthermore, the funder should be financially sound, may not influence the organization's litigation decisions, nor otherwise create a conflict of interests. Although the Claim Code does not include sanctions for non-compliance, courts can take this into consideration: since its establishment, the code has been used as a guideline for courts to assess a representative organization's admissibility.[28] This admissibility test, laid down in section 3:305a (2) and (3) BW, also aims to prevent unethical or abusive practices. After having been upgraded in 2013, a representative organization will not obtain standing if its claim does not sufficiently guarantee the interests of the class members.[29] Since 2020, the WAMCA lays down further restrictions, concerning the organization's governance, funding, and representativeness. The court has the authority to assess the organization's financial means, experience, and expertise, its measures to enable class members to monitor or control its decisions, and to request the disclosure of its annual account and report. These strict requirements can be disregarded if they are deemed to be disproportionate, for instance, for representative organizations with a public interest motive.

The entrepreneurial party can be the representative organization itself or, more likely, a third-party litigation funder that backs the organization. Often, the representative organization is founded for a particular mass damage event, possibly in cooperation with a law firm and/or a litigation funder. Either way, the entrepreneurial party provides or endorses a platform to assemble

---

[27] See https://warehouse.budh.nl/system/assets/uploads/001/111/662/23f4d501a23fc1e779865e822c7cc0c5a1b30345/Claimcode_2019_9789462906082_original.pdf accessed 31 July 2021.

[28] See, for instance, Jim van Mourik and Eddy Bauw, 'De Claimcode van 2011 tot 2019' in A.H. van Delden and others (eds), *Claimcode 2019* (Boomjuridisch 2019) 25–70.

[29] See *Kamerstukken II* 2011/12, 33126 (3) 4–5; *Kamerstukken II* 2012/13, 33126 (7) 10ff.

class members and increase leverage to pursue collective redress, in order to, eventually, share in the proceeds of the action. It is these parties that incited the aforementioned regulation and that are referred to when statements are used such as 'the proliferation of claim foundations, compensation culture, and entrepreneurial lawyering'.[30] They are said to mainly look after their own interests rather than those of the aggrieved parties, and some of them have indeed displayed undue behaviour.[31] Indeed, the own, commercial interest of the entrepreneurial party adds an extra layer to a collective action, and might incentivize unethical or abusive behaviour. At the same time, the funding of collective actions by entrepreneurial parties can play a pivotal role in improving access to justice. This brings me to taking a closer look into the potential contribution of entrepreneurial parties.[32]

12.3.2 Improving Access to Justice or Inciting a Compensation Culture?

When an entrepreneurial party is involved, it bears the costs and risks of the class members and, in case of third-party funding, their representative organization. They no longer have to pre-finance litigation costs or run the risk of having to pay (a part of) the adverse costs. This way, entrepreneurial parties facilitate or improve access to justice. This also addresses psychological barriers to effectuate individual claims, as their presence might solve class members' (or their representative's) rational apathy and risk aversion.[33] Entrepreneurial parties thus can serve various types of parties: the one that lacks financial resources to engage in litigation, the one that is risk averse,

---

[30] See, for instance, Kamerstukken II 2011/12, 33126 (3) 5; Jan Kleinnijenhuis, 'Nieuwe wet tegen malafide claimclubs' Trouw (Amsterdam, 8 December 2012); Jesse Frederik, 'Waarom wij de Amerikaanse claimcultuur moeten importeren' De Correspondent (Amsterdam, 10 June 2014); Camil Driessen, 'Valt er hier nog wat te claimen?' NRC (Amsterdam, 10 October 2015); André de Vos, 'Elke klacht zijn eigen claim' *FD* (Amsterdam, 30 September 2016); Bart Mos, 'Deur op kier voor Amerikaanse claimcultuur' *De Telegraaf* (Amsterdam, 4 March 2019).

[31] The most notorious example is provided by *Stichting Loterijverlies*, whose founder and sole board member was replaced by the court after having been accused of, among others, illegally funnelling part of the foundation's funds into private accounts. See Hof Amsterdam 31 January 2017, ECLI:NL:GHAMS:2017:210.

[32] Hereafter, I focus on the contribution of entrepreneurial parties in light of access to justice. On other potential benefits and drawbacks that are related to entrepreneurial mass litigation, see Tillema, *Entrepreneurial Mass Litigation* (n 3) ch 3.

[33] See, for instance, Louis Vischer and Tom Schepens, 'A Law and Economics Approach to Cost Shifting, Fee Arrangements and Legal Expense Insurance' in Mark Tuil and Louis Visscher (eds), *New Trends in Financing Civil Litigation in Europe: A Legal, Empirical and Economic Analysis* (Edward Elgar 2011) 7.

and/or does not want to see the litigation costs on the balance sheet, and/or the one that fears retaliation or has hopes of engaging in future business with the alleged wrongdoer. Moreover, depending on the construction, the parties do not have to invest effort and time, or might appreciate more hands on deck.[34]

By reducing financial obstacles, entrepreneurial parties can also help to resolve the free-rider problem. This problem can negatively affect the operation of collective actions.[35] Free-riders are passive class members that do not (financially) contribute to the action yet do benefit from the result thereof. Such benefit can be the evidence or information gathered in the proceedings, the judgment – that has some effect of precedence – or the settlement award. The free-rider problem makes it difficult for representative organizations to distribute the costs among class members, which might even lead to an action not being initiated. Moreover, active claimants' support might be necessary to provide evidence to underpin the action, to monitor the representative's actions, and to create its representativeness. The cure that entrepreneurial parties can provide is twofold. First, they reduce the (financial) threshold for individuals to participate, and therewith incentivize them to do so rather than await the action of others. Second, even when the contingency fee provides an insufficient incentive to participate, the entrepreneurial party might create or engage in a remuneration construction that does not require a contractual relationship with class members, as the *Fortis/Ageas* settlement agreement illustrates.[36]

Finally, active entrepreneurial parties address information deficiencies that obstruct access to justice: a lack of information on and knowledge of – the infringement of – rights. They invest time and energy in searching for and assessing potential infringements. If an action is initiated, they provide information about the wrongful behaviour and the available remedy through various channels and assemble and organize class members.[37]

---

[34] Nick Rowles-Davies, *Third Party Litigation Funding* (Oxford University Press 2014) 12–19.

[35] See, for instance, Roger Van den Bergh and Louis Visscher, 'The Preventive Function of Collective Actions for Damages in Consumer Law' (2008) *Erasmus Law Review* 5; Sonja Keske, Andrea Renda and Roger Van den Bergh, 'Financing and Group Litigation' in Mark Tuil and Louis Visscher (eds), *New Trends in Financing Civil Litigation in Europe: A Legal, Empirical and Economic Analysis* (Edward Elgar 2011) 60; Roger Van den Bergh, 'Private Enforcement of European Competition Law and the Persistent Collective Action Problem' (2013) 20 *Maastricht Journal of European and Comparative Law* 24ff.

[36] See section 12.3.1.

[37] See, for instance, Rowles-Davies (n 34) 150–151; Bentham Europe, 'Submission to the Ministry of Security and Justice: Dutch Draft Bill on Redress of Mass Damage in

On the other hand, entrepreneurial parties are said to create or sustain a compensation or claim culture. Urban legends regarding the McCoffee spill case and a microwaved poodle aside, it is cases such as the following that have incited opposition against entrepreneurial mass litigation:

> Recently, Ferrero U.S.A. settled lawsuits brought by two moms who said they were deceived by health claims made on jars of the chocolate hazelnut spread Nutella. Yes, if you bought Nutella thinking it was spinach in a jar – actually even if you bought it because you find it delicious – you are a winner.[38]

European opponents label cases such as these as 'American situations'; an ominous motto to oppose the introduction of certain American elements into European legal systems.[39] One of the situations the expression refers to is the alleged American compensation culture, which is boosted by entrepreneurial parties. Not uncommonly, however, the opponents fail to underpin such statement or omit additional facts. Furthermore, such opposition poses the question of how to label, for instance, political or regulatory activities aimed at banning any reference to meat on the packaging of vegetarian meat replacements.[40] European situations? Obviously, beneath the surface of empty rhetoric might lie serious issues. Although compensation culture is a rather ambiguous phenomenon, the main concern seems to be that entrepreneurial parties increase the number of claims and the amount of damages, or engage in abusive or unethical behaviour, such as pursuing frivolous claims.[41] These effects might increase courts' workload, deteriorate a jurisdiction's business climate, reduce trust in its judicial and legal system, and impose disproportion-

---

a Collective Action' (*Internetconsultatie*, October 2014) 4 www.internetconsultatie.nl/motiedijksma/reacties accessed 31 July 2021.

[38] David Segal, 'A Rising Tide Against Class-Action Suits' *The* New York Times (New York, 5 May 2012), as quoted by Richard Marcus, 'America's Dynamic and Extensive Experience with Collective Litigation' in Christopher Hodges and Astrid Stadler (eds), Resolving Mass Disputes: ADR and Settlement of Mass Claims (Edward Elgar 2013) 170.

[39] See, for instance, some contributions in Burkhard Hess and others, *Evaluation of Contributions to the Public Consultation and Hearing: 'Towards a Coherent European Approach to Collective Redress'* (Universität Heidelberg 2011).

[40] See, for instance, the editorial 'Das Aus für die vegane Currywurst' *Zeit Online* (28 December 2016) www.zeit.de/gesellschaft/zeitgeschehen/2016-12/agrarminister-christian-schmidt-kennzeichnung-vegetarische-produkte accessed 31 July 2021; Kamerstukken II 2016/17, 2017Z00040; 'NL: NVWA Project misleidende etikettering' (*NVC Nederlands Verpakkingscentrum*, 26 October 2017) www.nvc.nl/news/item/nl-nvwa-project-misleidende-etikettering/ accessed 31 July 2021.

[41] See, for instance, Kevin Williams, 'State of Fear: Britain's 'Compensation Culture' Reviewed' (2005) 25 Legal Studies 499; J. Hand, 'The Compensation Culture: Cliché or Cause for Concern' (2010) 37 Journal of Law and Society 569.

ate costs on industry: the fear of litigation might lead to defensive behaviour, high insurance costs, harm competitive behaviour, and/or negatively impact innovation. Furthermore, the costs of litigation and/or compensation might be redistributed.

In general, '[b]asic economics dictates that if the costs of litigation are reduced, there will be more of it'.[42] Entrepreneurial parties do not necessarily reduce costs, but facilitate access to justice by taking over the pre-financing of costs and the cost risk which, as mentioned, reduces the threshold for a claimant to pursue his claim. This is why, generally, contingency fees are said to increase litigation.[43] Logic dictates that the same applies to entrepreneurial parties in *mass* litigation, where the potential to increase the volume of litigation is amplified by the fact that entrepreneurial parties might actively search for claims, raise publicity, and approach class members.[44] On the other hand, the boost in litigation might be mitigated by the fact that entrepreneurial parties will only take on quality claims, filter out unmeritorious ones, rather settle than litigate, and pursue only those claims of a particular type and value.[45] Moreover, an increase in mass litigation might go hand in hand with a decrease in regular litigation.[46] An increase in mass litigation might furthermore be unrelated to the activity of entrepreneurs but caused by other factors, such as a financial scandal or crisis. There is some empirical evidence, but depending on aspects such as the type of case, claimant, fee, and – possibly – jurisdiction it either underpins or refutes the intuition or theory that (various types of) private litigation funding increase (mass) litigation volume.[47]

---

42 Cento Veljanovski, 'Third-Party Litigation Funding in Europe' (2012) 8 *Journal of Law, Economics and Policy* 405, 438.

43 Visscher and Schepens (n 33) 17.

44 Veljanovski (n 42) 440.

45 See, for instance, Veljanovski (n 42) 420, 439–441; Rowles-Davies (n 34) 108–111, 116–117; Joanna M. Shepherd, 'Ideal Versus Reality in Third-Party Litigation Financing' (2012) 8 *Journal of Law, Economics and Policy* 593, 595.

46 Marc Galanter, 'The Vanishing Trial: An Examination of Trials and Related Matters in Federal and State Courts' (2004) 1 *Journal of Empirical Legal Studies* 459.

47 See, for instance, Nicholas M. Pace, *Class Actions in the USA: An Overview of the Process and the Empirical Literature* (RAND 2007) 46–48; Paul Fenn and Neil Rickman, 'The Empirical Analysis of Litigation Funding', in Mark Tuil and Louis Visscher (eds), *New Trends in Financing Civil Litigation in Europe: A Legal, Empirical and Economic Analysis* (Edward Elgar 2011) 131–148; Vicky Waye and Vince Morabito, 'Financial Arrangements with Litigation Funders and Law Firms in Australian Class Actions' in Willem H. van Boom (ed), *Litigation, Costs, Funding and Behaviour: Implications for the Law* (Routledge 2017) 155–200; David S. Abrams and Daniel L. Chen, 'A Market for Justice: A First Empirical Look at Third Party Litigation Funding' (2013) 15 *University of Pennsylvania Journal of Business Law* 1075; Vince Morabito, 'An Empirical Study of Australia's Class Action Regimes, Fifth Report: The

In short, the extent to which entrepreneurial parties indeed increase mass litigation depends on several variables, and is difficult to (in)validate.[48] This brings me back to the Dutch situation. In the following, I will assess to what extent entrepreneurial actors, so far, have contributed to access to justice.

12.4 DEVELOPMENTS IN THE MARKET AND JURISPRUDENCE

12.4.1 Dataset I: Collective Action Judgments from 1999 to 2019

Since the introduction of section 3:305a BW, representative organizations frequently bring collective actions. To address the question of whether entrepreneurial motives have contributed to an increase in the number of claims, I have expanded a case law study on collective action judgments that I undertook in 2016, by adding data from 2016 to 2019.[49] I have compiled all collective action judgments in first instance courts from 1999 to 2019 that have been published in the Dutch court database (*rechtspraak.nl*).[50] In total, I have found and analysed 387 unique judgments, supplemented with publicly available information on the cases and/or representative organizations. It is important to note that the consulted database is said to contain most judgments, but it might not list all existing case law.[51] Either way, the sample does reveal indicative trend lines, and enables tentative conclusions to be drawn.

For the analysis, I have categorized the different types of organizations based on the type of interest that they protect. First, there is the representative organization that pursues a public interest, such as the enforcement of environmental law or fundamental rights. The second group concerns those that

---

First Twenty-Five Years of Class Actions in Australia' (20 July 2017) http://ssrn.com/abstract=3005901 accessed 31 July 2021.

[48] Visscher and Schepens (n 33) 18; Michael Faure, Fokke Fernhout and Niels Philipsen, 'No Cure, No Pay and Contingency Fees' in Mark Tuil and Louis Visscher (eds), *New Trends in Financing Civil Litigation in Europe: A Legal, Empirical and Economic Analysis* (Edward Elgar 2011) 41; Jef De Mot, Michael Faure and Louis Visscher, 'Third Party Financing and its Alternatives: An Economic Appraisal' in Willem H. van Boom (ed), *Litigation, Costs, Funding and Behaviour: Implications for the Law* (Routledge 2017) 46.

[49] For the previous study, see Tillema, 'Entrepreneurial Motives in Dutch Collective Redress' (n 3) paras 4.1–4.3.

[50] The database is in operation since 1999. I conducted the search by using the following keywords: '3:305a', '305a', and '*collectieve actie*'. The dataset includes judgments in collective actions in summary proceedings; see also section 12.4.2.

[51] For the selection criteria, see 'Selectiecriteria' (*Rechtspraak.nl*) www.rechtspraak.nl/Uitspraken-en-nieuws/Uitspraken/Paginas/Selectiecriteria.aspx accessed 31 July 2021.

protect a – more – private interest, such as those of consumers, employees or personal injury victims. The third category contains representative organizations that also protect a private interest, but a professional one, such as trade associations or employers. These three types of organizations mainly operate by charging membership fees, contributions, and/or receiving donations. The fourth and last category of representative organizations might cover all these interests, and in addition, they have an own interest in the outcome of the litigation due to the contingency fee (alike) arrangement.

Figure 12.1 below presents the number of collective actions and the distribution of the four types of representative organizations. The black line on top depicts the total number of actions, those below subdivide this number between the four types of organizations that were responsible for bringing the actions.

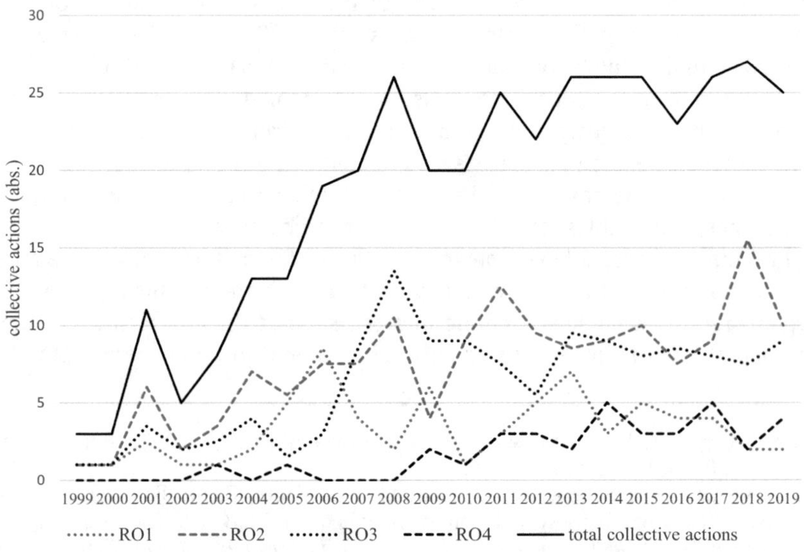

Figure 12.1 Number of collective action judgments in first instance courts per type of representative organization (1999-2019) (n=387)

Compared to the data from 1999 to 2015, the new data present no major divergence. On the whole, I can restate my finding that the graph depicts an upward trend of collective actions that have been dealt with by the Dutch courts, and that the initiators responsible for bringing most cases are those that represent the interests of 'weaker' parties, such as consumers and employees (RO2s), and cases in which business interests were dealt with, such as those of trade associations (RO3s). The Dutch trade union confederation *FNV* (qualified as RO2) is responsible for bringing most actions: 17 per cent (66 out of 387 actions). The data back the claim that, in total, there is an increased enforcement of mass wrongdoings. However, in a little over a decade, the number of collective actions has not fluctuated much and seems to remain modest, with an average of 24 actions a year. On average, 12 per cent of these actions is instigated by entrepreneurial organizations (RO4).[52] The number of their actions starts to gradually climb from 2008 onwards, but remains (well) under the level of the number of cases brought by the other representative organizations.

Zooming in on the type of cases that the entrepreneurial parties bring, it is manifest that they are mainly involved in financial products litigation, including securities: this category makes up 63 per cent of their actions (22 out of 35). The remaining actions that were brought by an entrepreneurial party concern (other types of) consumer law (7), personal injury (4) and privacy (2). The relatively large number of financial products' litigation, however, is somewhat distorted by competing collective actions: actions that concern the same mass damage event, but which are brought by different representative organizations in separate collective actions. Nevertheless, the finding is backed by the type of WCAM settlements that have been declared binding since 2005. Out of the eight mass damage events, seven fall within this category, and in five of the subsequent collective settlements, entrepreneurial parties were involved.[53]

It will be interesting to observe whether, and, if so, to what extent the number of actions (brought by entrepreneurial parties) will shift with the legislative amendment of 2020. Will it cause a major landslide? As a first glance, I have examined the 2020 data, which I will present in the following section.

12.4.2 Dataset II: WAMCA Cases from 2020

The data presented in this section have been assembled from two databases: the one used in the previous section plus the new central register for collective actions.[54] The latter has been established as part of the WAMCA, which requires registration of the writ of summons.[55] Hence, the register contains all collective actions that have been filed in 2020. Except for one type: collective actions in summary proceedings. These actions, given their urgency, are not

---

52 Measured as of 2009; in total 33 out of 266 actions.

53 See Tillema, 'Entrepreneurial Motives in Dutch Collective Redress' (n 3) para 4.4, to which the *Fortis/Ageas* settlement has been added since.

54 See 'Centraal register voor collectieve vorderingen' (*Rechtspraak.nl*) www.rechtspraak.nl/Registers/centraal-register-voor-collectieve-vorderingen accessed 31 July 2021.

55 S 1018c (2) Rv.

expected to be centrally registered.[56] As to maintain a level of comparability with the previous dataset, I have assembled these actions via the route followed in the previous section. Thus, the data presented in this section concern collective actions that were brought in 2020, and, therefore, follow the WAMCA rules.

In 2020, 24 collective actions were filed. This number equals the average from dataset I. This is somewhat surprising; I expected the number to drop a little in the first year due to cold feet and/or start-up issues. The WAMCA has made various rules stricter, and, therefore, the complexity and costs of bringing a collective action have increased. Seemingly, however, the new rules have not much affected access to justice in this sense. Obviously, I do not know the dark number: maybe this factor has indeed played a role and the number would have been higher had it not. Another novelty that could have caused a (slight) downward trend in the number of actions, but seemingly has not, is that as of 2020, competing parties might still initiate separate claims that concern the same mass damage event, but this can no longer lead to separate, competing collective actions. For under the WAMCA, if more than one organization files a claim, the court will appoint the most suitable one as the exclusive representative.[57] This party becomes the lead claimant that, in principle, is the one that conducts the litigation.

Out of the 24 collective actions in 2020, four involved entrepreneurial parties. This, too, is in line with the trend, the number remains within the bandwidth as presented in Figure 12.1 above. In one out of those four actions, a competing entrepreneurial party brought a separate claim under the WAMCA. This case (a diesel affair case against – in essence – Daimler) now awaits the appointment of the exclusive representative organization.

Obviously, with a single year as a reference it is unwise to make any projections, but so far, there is no indication that the outcome of the analysis for 2021 will be radically different: by the end of July, 16 collective actions were filed, three of which were brought by an entrepreneurial party.

12.4.3 Some Additional Observations

The previous data hint that the contribution of entrepreneurial parties, so far, has remained modest. In this section, I highlight some additional observations as to the contribution to access to justice by these parties.

First, entrepreneurial parties have contributed to the development of a 'plaintiff bar', in particular in financial products litigation. As mentioned in

---

56 S 1018b (1) Rv.

57 S 1018e (1) Rv. See also section 12.4.3.

section 12.3.2, these parties might very well not forego litigation due to financial or psychological restrictions. Furthermore, the availability of funding and professional players adds muscle to the already countervailing power of a class that challenges a powerful defendant. This all levels the playing field between the opponents in litigation, thereby creating equality of arms. When faced with a financially sound and professionally equipped opponent, defendants might refrain from engaging in strategical conduct to subdue, intimidate or outspend claimants.[58]

Fortification of the claimant side is also noticeable in emerging cooperative initiatives. Entrepreneurial parties operate alongside, and may compete with, each other or the more traditional ones, but cooperation is taking place as well. This was already visible in WCAM settlements, where different types of representative organizations successfully have joined forces in the past.[59] Such cooperation is now also starting to take place in collective actions. For instance, the *Consumentenbond*, the Dutch consumer organization that was founded in 1953, has entered into a joint venture with an entrepreneurial party, *Consumentenclaim*, and their actions also involve third-party litigation funders.[60] This bundling of different types of experience and expertise could not only reinforce an action in particular, and access to justice in general, but it could also prevent abusive behaviour, as they monitor each other in order to protect their respective reputations. As one court stated, a longstanding organization such as the *Consumentenbond* is expected to adequately represent the interest of consumers, whether or not they cooperate with an entrepreneurial party.[61] I suspect it will not want to lose such reputation. The cooperation also aligns with the aim of appointing an exclusive representative organization: eliminating the practice of competing collective actions as they increase costs for parties and society.[62]

I have also tried to gain information on the percentages charged by entrepreneurial parties. A first observation is that this information is not always clear or made – publicly – accessible. Some organizations state on their website that their action is 'free of charge', neglecting to mention – immediately, and/or

---

[58] cf Stephen C Yeazell, 'Getting What We Asked For, Getting What We Paid For, and Not Liking What We Got: The Vanishing Civil Trial' (2004) 1 *Journal of Economics, Law and Policy* 943, 955.

[59] See, for instance, Tzankova (n 26); Tillema, 'Entrepreneurial Motives in Dutch Collective Redress' (n 3) para 4.4.

[60] See www.claimservice.nl/over-ons/ accessed 31 July 2021, and the collective action against TikTok, in which Consumentenbond Claimservice cooperates with Stichting Take Back Your Privacy, which cooperation is financially backed by BPGL Funding. See www.stichtingtakebackyourprivacy.nl/faqs/ accessed 31 July 2021.

[61] Rb Amsterdam 29 maart 2018, ECLI:NL:RBAMS:2018:1682, para 4.7.

[62] *Kamerstukken* 2016/17 34608 (3) 6, 14 and 42ff.

in clear terms – that a percentage will be deducted from either the individual proceeds or collective settlement (on the issue of transparency, see also hereafter). Where available, the data indicate that the percentages vary from 5 to 30 per cent. Some organizations charge an additional sign-in participation fee.[63] Others charge a percentage that is inversely proportional to the chosen sign-in fee.[64] Some parties, over time, reduce their percentage, as they also receive remuneration as part of the collective settlement.[65] Furthermore, some price competition is noticeable, in competing collective actions that revolve around the same mass harm event. For instance, in the so-called *woekerpolis* affair (financial products litigation), six competing organizations charged a percentage varying from 5 to 17.5 per cent. So some elements of a competitive market exist, which might lead to more choice and a better deal for class members and/or representative organizations that are in need of litigation funding, and class members with a strong claim should be readily able to find someone to facilitate the pursuit thereof.[66] However, it is questionable whether class members can compare the return value (quality of services) for the advertised percentages, and the variety of entrepreneurial parties operating in the market might not be big enough to generate competitive rates.[67] The rule of appointing an exclusive representative organization might add an element to improve competition, as the court must take into consideration the size of the represented class, the amount in dispute, as well as the other and previous activities that the candidate has undertaken for the represented type of class members or collective redress in general.[68] It remains to be seen whether this rule indeed improves competition or, eventually, causes a decline in the number of competing parties, reducing or even negating any positive effects.

---

[63] See, for instance, www.loterijverlies.nl/kosten accessed 31 July 2021.

[64] See, for instance, www.woekerpolis.nl/lidmaatschap accessed 31 July 2021; www.brandstofverlies.nl/kosten accessed 31 July 2021.

[65] See, for instance, Hof Amsterdam 13 July 2018, ECLI:NL:GHAMS:2018:2422 (*Fortis/Ageas*), paras 5.36 and 5.38.

[66] cf Keske, Renda and Van den Bergh (n 35) 71; Van den Bergh (n 35) 30; Abrams and Chen (n 47) 1079; Stephen Friel, Jonathan Barnes and Alex Hickson, 'England & Wales' in Stephen Friel and Jonathan Barnes (eds), *Litigation Funding 2020* (Law Business Research 2019) 27.

[67] cf Waye and Morabito (n 47) 164; Deborah R. Hensler, 'Financing Civil Litigation: the US Perspective' in Mark Tuil and Louis Visscher (eds), *New Trends in Financing Civil Litigation in Europe: A Legal, Empirical and Economic Analysis* (Edward Elgar 2011) 152–153.

[68] S 1018e (1) Rv. cf John C. Coffee Jr, 'Accountability and Competition in Securities Class Actions: Why Exit Works Better Than Voice' (2008) 30 *Cardozo Law Review* 407; Hensler (n 67) 161.

A final observation concerns the stricter rules on admissibility. In 2017, I noted that standing in court was obtained relatively easily.[69] This has changed in the past years; courts seem to have grown in their task of assessing – the stricter rules on – admissibility.[70] A lack of transparency such as described above will therefore most likely belong to the past.[71] Moreover, with the WAMCA, even more aspects of the representative organization's business model are assessed in the (separate) admissibility phase – to prevent abuse, as mentioned, not to discourage (entrepreneurial) representative organizations from entering the market. The representative organization must now provide information, publicly, on the financial contribution they charge, and – if so asked by the court – their financial capacity, and the particularities of the funding construction.[72] Moreover, the court can now – albeit marginally – assess the reasonableness of the potential proceeds that the organization will gain in case of success.[73] As mentioned in section 12.3.1, the recovery of costs 'and something' has turned into an important method of funding some organizations' activities, as well as allowed them to establish a war chest for future actions. Before, this was not generally part of the court's assessment.[74] In a landmark ruling regarding the *Fortis/Ageas* settlement, the Amsterdam Court of Appeal first held that its assessment of the settlement's reasonableness should always include that of the organization(s)' remuneration, regardless of whether the remuneration is awarded to an entrepreneurial or a non-profit entity.[75] To help the court do so, parties should be transparent on the fee provisions in the settlement documents and their business model in general. This judgment has sharpened the rules for (entrepreneurial) representative parties, which are now also part of the WAMCA. Although the judicial assessment of the remuneration in collective actions remains uncharted territory, and, therefore, challenging, it seems that the new rules on governance, representativeness, and funding will lead to a thorough judicial supervision of representative

---

[69] Tillema, 'Entrepreneurial Motives in Dutch Collective Redress' (n 3) para 4.3.2.

[70] See, similarly, Van Mourik and Bauw (n 28); Tzankova and Kramer (n 6).

[71] See, for instance, Rb Oost-Brabant 20 July 2016, ECLI:NL:RBOBR:2016:3892.

[72] S 3:305a (2) BW, *Kamerstukken II* 2017/18, 34608 (6) 10-12, 25-27, 29; *Kamerstukken II* 2017/18, 34608 (9) 10; *Kamerstukken II* 2017/18, 34608 (10) 1. See also Claim Code, Principe III para 7.

[73] *Kamerstukken II* 2016/17, 34608 (3) 11-12; *Kamerstukken II* 2016/17, 34608 (6) 25. See, similarly, Rb Zeeland-West-Brabant 10 August 2016, ECLI:NL:RBZWB:2016:5217.

[74] See, for instance, Ianika Tzankova and Deborah Hensler, 'Collective Settlements in the Netherlands: Some Empirical Observations' in Christopher Hodges and Astrid Stadler (eds), Resolving Mass Disputes: ADR and Settlement of Mass Claims (Edward Elgar 2013) 100ff.

[75] Hof Amsterdam 13 July 2018, ECLI:NL:GHAMS:2018:2422.

organizations. This is crucial to an effective and trustworthy collective action system.[76]

12.5 THE WAY FORWARD: THE DEBATE CONTINUES

So far, the contribution of entrepreneurial parties remains noticeable yet modest, and the new rules have not raised apparent thresholds for having access to justice. A mix of representative organizations coexists, at times competing, at times cooperating. Nevertheless, the situation is anything but stationary. In the years to come, the WAMCA will continue to present challenges to parties, courts, and the legislator. How will unappointed organizations behave once their competitor has been named exclusive representative, and how will courts deal with this issue, also in light of the new rule that allows for full indemnification of a successful (exclusive) representative organization's litigation costs?[77] How will this affect litigation costs and compensation in general? Will representative organizations continue to coexist or will the entrepreneurial ones eventually outweigh the more traditional organizations? Et cetera! Given the lingering risks, the large societal impact of collective actions, and the important, yet complex new judicial role, the legislator remains vigilant. It is monitoring the developments, and has already scheduled an evaluation to take place in 2025.[78]

Also, the Dutch developments cannot be detached from the European debate on representative actions.[79] This debate has led to the 2013 Recommendations, a first horizontal European approach to collective redress,[80] and, more recently, to the Representative Actions Directive.[81] The latter requires Member States to implement a(n additional) procedure for representative actions that allow for, inter alia, collective compensatory measures in situations of domestic or cross-border mass harm. The topic of third-party litigation funding and

---

76 cf Theodore Eisenberg, Geoffrey Miller and Roy Germano, 'Attorney's Fees in Class Actions: 2009–2013' (2017) 92 *New York University Law Review* 938.

77 S 1018l (2) Rv.

78 See *Kamerstukken II* 2017/18, 34608 (7) s IV.

79 See, more elaborately, Tzankova and Kramer (n 6); Kramer and Tillema (n 26).

80 Commission Recommendation 2013/396/EU of 11 June 2013 on common principles for injunctive and compensatory collective redress mechanisms in the Member States concerning violations of rights granted under Union Law [2013] OJ L201/60; Commission, 'Towards A European Horizontal Framework For Collective Redress' (Communication) COM(2013) 401 final.

81 Alexandre Biard and Xandra Kramer, 'The EU Directive on Representative Actions for Consumers: A Milestone or Another Missed Opportunity?' [2019] 27 Zeitschrift für Europäsisches Privatrecht 249.

related forms of entrepreneurial lawyering has also been added to this agenda. Whereas the Recommendation viewed the topic with caution,[82] the Directive acknowledges its potential contribution to access to justice, and supports third-party funding, albeit under certain conditions. In short, it requires Member States to ensure that entities are transparent about their funding source in general, that the funder cannot unduly influence the entity's litigation decisions, is not a competitor of or dependent on the defendant, and that (other) conflicts of interest are prevented. Courts or administrative authorities should be empowered to assess compliance with these requirements. The topic will remain food for further political debate on the legal, ethical, and economic aspects of the matter.[83]

12.6 CLOSING REMARKS

The collective settlement of mass claims is growing into an important area of Dutch private law. In the past decade, entrepreneurial parties have entered this arena. For some, this has incited the fear of triggering an 'American-style compensation culture', in which commerce-driven parties primarily pursue their own interests, potentially harming those of (absent) group members, defendants, and/or society at large. At the same time, funding is said to play a pivotal role in collective actions, and entrepreneurial parties can solve the enforcement gap by improving access to justice. This has left the legislator and judiciary with the daunting task of navigating between the potential benefits and drawbacks. In this chapter, I have zoomed in on some of those challenges. So far, there is no real evidence that the (slow) rise in the number of collective actions is related to entrepreneurial lawyering. Furthermore, so far, opening the action for claims for damages has neither hampered access to justice nor fueled excessive litigation. The new legislation and growing body of case law on collective actions further demonstrate that a stricter approach is beginning to take shape in the Netherlands, in line with the European developments. The chapter has also shown that courts will continue to face challenges in the assessment of the business model of representative organizations, and that the political debate on entrepreneurial parties will continue. To maintain an effective and

---

[82] Recommendations 30 and 32 state that Member States, in general, should not permit contingency fees or third-party litigation funding, unless such funding is regulated by a public authority to ensure the interests of the parties. See also Communication, COM(2013) 401 final, 3, 8–9, and 15.

[83] See also the recently published EPRS report: Jérôme Saulnier, Klaus Müller and Ivona Koronthalyova, 'Responsible Private Funding of Litigation: European Added Value Assessment' (European Parliament Research Service, March 2021); Tzankova and Kramer (n 6) para 5.

trustworthy collective action system, it is essential to combine transparency and accountability with the sustainability of entrepreneurial parties. In this balancing act, which is shaped by factors such as the type of claim, damage, and class member, both sides of the coin need to be addressed. Unavoidably, incidents will occur in this process, which might require (further) regulation, the fine-tuning thereof or control thereon. Incidents do not only affect a particular case, but also feed the mistrust on entrepreneurial parties in particular, or collective actions in general. Yet, it is equally important to not let black sheep cloud the bigger picture and push the advantages to the background.

13. German collective actions – is litigation funding in a dead end?

Astrid Stadler

13.1 INTRODUCTION

Funding is a key issue in collective redress, and particularly third-party funding (TPF) plays an important role in high-value cases. Nevertheless, there is no legal framework for TPF in Germany, and case law is not in favour of TPF either as will be shown below. This chapter explains recent court decisions on funding issues and analyses their background. In addition, it presents the German legislature's latest draft on a reform of the German Legal Services Act and its cautious attempt to allow contingency fees for lawyers.

The discussion draws on several fundamental factors: Germany has a fairly efficient legal aid system compared to other countries. It is available for consumer associations, but rarely used as the risk of adverse cost orders is not covered. Funding by lawyers based on contingency fee arrangements is also not available under current German law. Contingency fees were banned until a 2006 decision of the Federal Constitutional Court set aside the strict prohibition and argued that access to justice may require contingency fee arrangements if claimants have no other way to hedge their procedural risk.[1] Since then, a circumspect regulation has been in place which allows success fees for lawyers under extraordinary circumstances.[2]

However, meanwhile a new market for debt collecting companies emerged. Cartel Damage Claims (CDC) was one of the first companies operating in the field of competition law with a business model based on the assignment of claims resulting from mass harm events. They started to offer enforcement of the claims in exchange for a success fee. Due to the lack of group or class actions mechanisms in Germany, several legal technology companies and

---

1 BVerfG 1 BvR 2576/04, BeckRS 2007, 21754.

2 See the former versions of Federal Lawyers' Act (*Bundesrechtsanwaltsordnung*) s 49(b)(2); Act on the Renumeration of Lawyers (*Rechtsanwaltsvergütungsgesetz*) s 4(a).

platforms also began to specialize in this field and to aggregate claims on a large scale by assignment. They are particularly important not only in the enforcement of damages claims in the Volkswagen emissions scandal and in consumer law in general, but also in Europe-wide cartel damages cases such as Air Cargo, Hydrogen Peroxide, Lifts and Escalators, Sodium Chlorate, Paraffin Wax and Trucks.

These new players in the legal services market took benefit from Germany's prohibition on contingency fees for lawyers, that does not apply to debt collection companies or special purpose vehicles, often called 'claims vehicles'. This obvious mismatch has inevitably resulted in a legal and political conflict between lawyers, the legal technology sector, and debt collectors. To provide a level playing field, policy makers decided to liberalize contingency fees for lawyers, but they were encountering resistance from lawyers' interest groups. These groups fear the commercialization of the profession and instead prefer an almost complete ban on the debt collecting activities of legal technology firms and special purpose vehicles. Their fear that the commercial interest of lawyers might prevail over professional ethics and result in a 'litigation industry' is in accordance with the traditional resistance against US-style contingency fees in Europe, particularly in Germany.

The European Directive on representative actions in the collective interest of consumers (hereinafter, the 'Directive') reflects a similar attitude and fails to address the funding issue properly.[3] It gives legal standing only to consumer associations that are not profit oriented. Even German consumer associations, which are better off than many others in Europe because they receive considerable public funding and membership fees, have limited budgets for litigation and can afford only a small number of legal proceedings per year. It is therefore not a realistic starting point of the Directive that non-profit consumer associations will be able to deal with most or even a considerable number of mass harm events in consumer law without additional funding.

In an early draft of the Directive, the EU Commission had suggested that Member States must provide adequate financial support for consumer associations.[4] Unsurprisingly, that proposal did not survive the legislative process

---

[3] Directive (EU) 2020/1828 on representative actions for the protection of the collective interest of consumers and repealing Directive 2009/227EC [2002] OJ L409/1.

[4] Art 15 read in a former version as follows: 'Member States shall take the necessary measures to ensure that procedural costs related to representative actions do not constitute financial obstacles for qualified entities to effectively exercise the right to seek the measures referred to in Articles 5 and 6, such as limiting applicable court or administrative fees, granting them access to legal aid where necessary, or by providing them with public funding for this purpose.' cf Interinstitutional File 2018/0089 (COD) of 28 November 2019.

as it was rejected by the Member States. Article 20 of the Directive now only requires the Member States to take measures to ensure that the costs of the proceedings related to representative action do not prevent qualified entities from effectively exercising their right to seek the measures referred to in Article 7. Article 20 para 2 lists public funding for qualified entities as a non-binding example. Moreover, the Directive does not ban TPF but requires Member States to ensure that there are no conflicts of interests and that economic interests in the outcome of the representative action do not divert the action 'away from the protection of the collective interests of consumers'. As will be shown later in this chapter, this is an argument which can easily be (mis-)used against TPF in many cases.

13.2 LEGAL COSTS AND TYPES OF THIRD-PARTY FUNDING

13.2.1 Allocation of Costs Between the Parties

The need for TPF depends on the forum's system of procedural costs, court fees, lawyers' fees, and cost-shifting rules which determine the procedural risk for claimants. German civil procedure law allocates costs between the parties following the loser-pays principle. Court fees and lawyers' fees are based on fixed statutory tariffs depending on the amount in controversy in the individual case. Lawyers are free to enter into agreements with their clients that allow an hourly fee for the lawyer's remuneration, but there is no shiftability of costs based on hourly fees and work done. Adverse cost orders can only result in the reimbursement of the statutory tariff fees. It is therefore a definite advantage of the German system that claimants and defendants can easily predict their financial exposure. Everyone who considers filing an action can use one of the online calculation tools to estimate the procedural costs for all instances and the potential reimbursement to the opponent.[5] Tariff-based systems also facilitate the availability of legal expenses insurance.[6]

[5] See e.g., 'DAV-Prozesskostenrechner' (*Anwaltsblatt*) https://anwaltsblatt.anwaltverein.de/de/apps/prozesskostenrechner accessed 29 March 2021; 'Prozesskostenrechner' (*Roland Prozessfinanz*) https://www.der-prozesskostenrechner.de accessed 29 March 2021.

[6] Chris Hodges, Stefan Vogenauer, and Magdalena Tulibacka (eds), *The Costs and Funding of Civil Litigation* (Hart 2010) 78.

13.2.2 Adequate Remuneration for Lawyers in Collective Actions

Despite the advantages of tariff-based lawyers' fees, the disadvantages of the strictly fee-based system can be illustrated by the German *Musterfeststellungsklage* filed by the vzbv (*Verbraucherzentrale Bundesverband*) – the German umbrella organization of consumer associations – against Volkswagen AG in the Volkswagen emissions scandal. On 1 November 2018, a new procedural instrument came into force in Germany: the representative action for declaratory relief in the interest of consumers (*Musterfeststellungsklage*, hereinafter, 'MFK proceedings'). MFK proceedings are actions not for damages but only for declaratory relief. If the representative action is successful, consumers, in a second step, must file individual actions for the enforcement of their damages' claims. To benefit from the outcome of the MFK proceedings, consumers simply need to register their claims informally.

The same day the new rules came into force, the vzbv filed the first action to obtain a declaratory judgment on Volkswagen's tort liability in the emissions scandal. Within a few days, more than 440,000 consumers registered their claims. However, shortly before the Federal High Court was expected to render a landmark decision in the emissions scandal in another – individual – action on 25 May 2020, the MFK proceedings ended abruptly in February 2020 after only two court hearings. Vzbv and Volkswagen, under considerable time pressure, negotiated an agreement to conclude the MFK proceedings and to avoid the unknown consequences of the expected Federal High Court decision. In an out-of-court settlement, they agreed on a framework for individual settlements between Volkswagen and a portion of the registered consumers. Volkswagen agreed to offer individual settlements to approximately 260,000 of the registered consumers, and in exchange, vzbv agreed to withdraw the entire MFK action.

Vzbv, although representing consumers' interests, did not participate in the further process of carrying out the individual settlements, and Volkswagen was under no obligation to render account of the process or to provide transparency. Finally, more than 92 per cent of the 260,000 diesel car owners accepted the settlement and thus avoided the risk of a court decision.[7] On 25 May 2020, the Federal High Court (*Bundesgerichtshof*) decided in its landmark decision that Volkswagen was liable under tort law to pay full compensation to all purchasers of the respective diesel vehicles.[8] The settlement offers were of

---

[7] Günter Hirsch, 'Die Abwicklung des VW-Vergleichs im Ombudsverfahren' [2020] Verbraucher und Recht 454, 456.

[8] BGH, 25.05.2020 - VI ZR 252/19.

course below the full compensation, but consumers had to choose between partial compensation and the risk of receiving no compensation at all should the Federal High Court deny liability.

Interestingly, the parties of the MFK action did not use the settlement mechanism provided by the MFK rules of the German Civil Procedure Code (ss 605–613) but decided in favour of an out-of-court settlement. Thus, the statutory mechanisms to safeguard the interests of the registered consumers did not apply. There was, for example, no need for court approval of the settlement terms, nor did all the registered consumers have the opportunity to decide whether they wanted to accept the settlement. Section 611 of the German Civil Procedure Code provides opt-out proceedings for consumers after service of process of the court-approved settlement. If more than 30 per cent opt out, the whole settlement fails, according to section 611 para 5, and the MFK proceedings must continue. The non-application of section 611 in the *Volkswagen* case thus makes a considerable difference: with the out-of-court settlement to which section 611 does not apply, only the 260,000 registered consumers who did in fact receive a settlement offer could decide whether to accept it or not. The rest of the 440,000 registered consumers,[9] among which there were numerous fake claims,[10] neither received a settlement offer nor had the opportunity to opt out and thus overthrow the whole settlement.[11]

---

9 Among those registered consumers who did not receive a settlement offer from Volkswagen were all foreign consumers. This was because a decision in the MFK proceedings would probably not have had a binding effect for them. According to the vzbv's explicit statement of claim, the MFK proceedings were to assess Volkswagen's liability only based on German tort law. It is likely that domestic tort law would apply to the claims of consumers residing outside Germany, according to Art 4 of the Rome II Regulation. Thus, they would not have derived any benefit from a declaratory judgment against Volkswagen based on German law, and their registration, although formally correct, could create no binding effect for a judgment. As the prospects to benefit from the MFK proceedings were low, Volkswagen insisted on excluding these foreign consumers from their settlement offer. See Astrid Stadler, 'Grenzüberschreitende Wirkung von Vergleichen und Urteilen im Musterfeststellungsverfahren' [2020] Neue Juristische Wochenschrift 265. Meanwhile, another MFK action has been filed against Volkswagen in the interest of Italian buyers of Volkswagen diesel cars.

10 Registration requires only a formal check, and nobody examined whether the particular consumer really had a claim against Volkswagen or even bought one of the diesel vehicles subject to the litigation. Persons applying for registration therefore often gave fake names, such as Donald Duck, and the total number of registrations was higher than the number of meritorious claims.

11 For a critical review of the settlement, see Astrid Stadler, 'Pyrrhussieg für den Verbraucherschutz – vzbv umgeht durch Vereinbarung mit VW gesetzliche Sicherungsmechanismen' [2020] Verbraucher und Recht 163. In a reply the vzbz legal department defended the strategy, see Jutta Gurkmann and Ronny Jahn,

But how is all this related to the remuneration of lawyers? The answer is simple: a settlement is the only way for the claimant's lawyer to receive adequate remuneration – if he or she is a skilful negotiator. An out-of-court settlement which is not subject to scrutiny by the court or the registered consumers is even better. In the *Volkswagen* case, the law firm representing vzbv failed in their first attempt to negotiate remuneration of approximately 50 million euros. According to the final settlement, they received 500,000 euros from the defendant.[12] Without any settlement, the statutory fee vzbv's lawyers would have been entitled to amounted to some 8,000 euros. The reason for this amazingly low fee is a statutory cap on the amount in controversy for MFK proceedings.

Specifically, irrespective of the real amount at stake, the maximum amount on which court and lawyers' fee calculations may be based is 250,000 euros (s 48 para 1 sentence 1 of the Court Fees Act; s 23 of the Act on the Remuneration of Lawyers). The cap was intended to lower the procedural risk for consumer associations that have legal standing to bring an MFK action. Policy makers, however, did not realize or neglected the fact that no law firm can handle these complex cases for such ridiculous remuneration. The cap of fees also triggers a problem of equality of arms because defendants will of course always be able and willing to pay their lawyers by the hour and thus ignore the cap. Regarding its binding effect for all registered consumers, it is extremely important for them to defend an MFK action, and they will spare no effort to do so.

Consequently, the German legislature, probably unintentionally, imported the principal-agent conflicts typical in US class actions to the German system. Lawyers of the representative entity have a significant interest in not striving for a court decision but to accept almost any settlement offer from the defendant's side as long as they are entitled to more than 8,000 euros. In general, one must be aware of the fact that both extremely low and extremely high lawyers' fees, such as contingency fees, might have a considerable impact on procedural strategy and can create the wrong incentives for a settlement.

13.2.3 Options for Litigation Funding

If we look at the broader picture of litigation funding, there are several options available in Germany. Before-the-event (BTE) insurance is popular among

'Außergerichtlicher Vergleich im Rahmen einer Musterfeststellungsklage' [2020] Verbraucher und Recht 243.

[12] Pia Lorenz, 'Was VW sich die Abwicklungshoheit kosten lässt' (*Legal Tribune Online*, 28 February 2020) https://www.lto.de/recht/hintergruende/h/abgasskandal-musterfeststellungsklage-olg-braunschweig-vw-vzbv-vergleich-vereinbarungen-anwaltskosten/ accessed 29 March 2021.

German private households, but it is not available for companies or representative entities such as consumer associations. Several insurance companies also offer after-the-event (ATE) insurance based on a thorough assessment of the individual case, its chances of success, and the defendant's ability to meet adverse cost orders. ATE is a growing global market with a focus on commercial litigation for high-value cases and cases in which there is no competition with BTE legal expenses insurance.[13] ATE appears in many formats and covers the traditional two-party litigation setting as well as collective-redress litigation. Usually, ATE insurance funders do not play an active role in the proceedings and do not act as claimants based on an assignment of the claim or the claims. German consumer associations have used ATE insurance, but landmark decisions of the Federal High Court in 2018 and 2019 have largely put an end to this practice (see section 13.3).

Another option for funding litigation is special purpose vehicles and legal technology companies, which take up not only smaller claims based on a success fee but also large-scale damages claims in cartel cases.[14] Legal technology companies operate on a cost-efficient basis by aggregating claims of similar type eligible for software-based administration and acquisition via internet platforms. The claims may arise from a mass harm event or from a series of violations of consumer law, tenancy law, air passenger rights, and so on. They offer a complete package of legal services to risk-adverse claimants who are not eligible for legal aid or a contingency fee arrangement, and they pursue claims in their own name. To provide risk-free litigation for the assignors, these companies often cooperate with external third-party funders.

As these claim vehicles provide not only funding but also legal services in terms of claims assessment, out-of-court negotiations with the debtor, and so forth, they must be registered according to the German Legal Services Act. The Legal Services Act intends to protect courts and the public against unqualified providers of legal services and thus, at least de facto, provides a monopoly for lawyers by prohibiting the provision of legal services by non-lawyers. Since a 2008 reform of the Act, there have been several exceptions in place

---

[13] For details, see Ilja Tillema, *Entrepreneurial Mass Litigation – Balancing the Building Blocks* (11th Int Pub, Erasmus University Rotterdam 2019) 125. See also Astrid Stadler, 'Funding of Mass Claims in Germany – Caught Between a Rock and a Hard Place?' in Willem van Boom (ed), *Litigation, Costs, Funding and Behaviour – Implications for the Law* (Taylor & Francis 2016) 201.

[14] Besides CDC, there are e.g., special purpose vehicles (DB Competition Claims; DB Barnsdale) established by the Deutsche Bahn AG, which is often a victim of price-fixing cartels. The special purpose vehicles were established to pursue the cartel tort claims of not only Deutsche Bahn AG and its subsidiaries but also of other assignors.

subject to approval by the governing authority and to formal registration. For registration, debt collection companies must provide proof of their basic legal knowledge and indemnity insurance. Registration is, however, no safe harbour. There are other pitfalls to be aware of (see section 13.4).

13.3 AFTER-THE-EVENT INSURANCE

In the absence of a legal framework for TPF in Germany, there is also no prohibition of TPF. Claimants[15] are free to cooperate with commercial litigation funders, and the contract terms are subject to general contract rules and restrictions. If, for example, the success fee is too high, it can be considered usury (s 138 para 2 of the German Civil Code) or *contra bonos mores* (s 138 para 1 of the German Civil Code), but success fees of 30–35 per cent that are customary in the particular market are without problems. Nevertheless, in 2018, the Federal High Court imposed clear restrictions for consumer associations' use of commercial TPF.[16]

In the 2018 case, a consumer association had brought an action for skimming off illegally gained profit from the defendant based on section 10 of the Unfair Competition Act. The defendant was one of the biggest telecommunication providers in Germany. Since 2012, it had overcharged customers when returning debit notes and issuing reminders to pay debts. In previous proceedings, courts had declared the defendant's related standard contract terms invalid. Despite an injunction to stop the illegal practice, the defendant continued to charge the high fees. The company even paid an administrative fine imposed for the violation of the injunction, as it was more lucrative to collect the illegal fees, which aggregated to a total of 10 million euros.[17]

Section 10 of the Unfair Competition Act, enacted in 2005, gives legal standing to consumer associations to initiate disgorgement proceedings. Traders that have violated consumer protection law and have thus harmed a great number of consumers (suffering small amounts of individual loss) are liable for paying the illegally gained profit to the Federal Budget. Such disgorgement proceedings involve a high risk for the representative entities, which do not benefit from a successful action but have to pay considerable procedural costs out of their low budgets when they lose the case. An amount in controversy of 10 million Euros involves a procedural risk for a litigation over all three instances of approximately 1.16 million euros, and the plaintive consumer association

---

[15] Defendants do not often use TPF.

[16] BGH, 13.09.2018 - I ZR 26/17, BeckRS 2018, 24788, DE:BGH:2018:130918UIZR26.17.0.

[17] Michael Loschelder, 'Prozessfinanzierung bei Gewinnabschöpfung' [2018] Gewerblicher Rechtsschutz und Urheberrecht in der Praxis 534.

had entered into a TPF agreement with a commercial litigation funder because their own budget would not have allowed them to take such a risk. The success fee agreed upon was 30 per cent. As the amount claimed from the defendant was to be paid to the Federal Budget, the Federal authority responsible for the administration of the money (*Bundesamt für Justiz*) had been asked for their consent and had agreed to the funder's success fee.

The Federal High Court, in a rather surprising and very much criticized decision, held that by using TPF, the consumer association misused its legal standing to bring an action for skimming off illegally gained profit.[18] It argued that when enacting section 10 of the Unfair Competition Act, the legislature was aware of the funding problems of the representative entities having legal standing to bring these cases and had accepted that only a few actions would be filed (which became reality). The Court did not consider the consent of the *Bundesamt für Justiz*, and even challenged its correctness, and based its decision on a violation of good faith and fair dealing, by arguing that the primary purpose of the action was no longer the protection of consumer rights but the gaining of profit for the funder.[19] As the legislature had accepted that consumer associations will not be able to afford many disgorgement proceedings, they should not be allowed to solve the problem by using TPF. Consumer associations would thus give up their freedom to decide which actions can be filed and could only pursue cases approved by funders.

The decision was heavily criticized by academics and lawyers, particularly for its effect of preventing the use of section 10 of the Unfair Competition Act and consequently frustrating consumer associations' efforts to protect consumers against illegal practices.[20] The Federal High Court nevertheless confirmed its decision in 2019[21] and ignored a decision of the Court of Appeals Schleswig,[22] which had strongly argued against the 2018 judgment. The decisions reflect a strong aversion to entrepreneurial litigation. If the legislature does not step in, consumer associations are no longer in the position to bring

---

[18] BGH, 13.09.2018 - I ZR 26/17, BeckRS 2018, 24788, DE:BGH:2018:130918UIZR26.17.0.

[19] Ibid., fn 18 [37].

[20] See, e.g., Loschelder (n 17); Axel Halfmeier, 'Rechtsmissbrauch durch Prozessfinanzierung bei Gewinnabschöpfungsklage' [2019] 1 Wirtschafts- und Bankrecht 27; Astrid Stadler, 'Sittenwidrigkeit der Prozessfinanzierung eines gemeinnützigen Verbraucherschutzverbandes' [2019] Juristenzeitung 203. One positive commentator even welcomed the end of the funding business model: Helmut Köhler, 'Gewerblich finanzierte Gewinnabschöpfungsprozesse: Ende eines Geschäftsmodell' [2019] Wettbewerb in Recht und Praxis 139.

[21] BGH, 09.05.2019 - I ZR 205/17, GRUR 2019, 850, DE:BGH:2019:090519UIZR205.17.0.

[22] OLG Schleswig, 14.02.2019 - 2 U 4/18, Verbraucher und Recht 2019, 270.

actions under section 10 of the Unfair Competition Act. Even though the court's arguments follow from the particular circumstances of the enactment of section 10 of the Act, there is a high likelihood or risk that courts will apply this line of argument to other types of funded actions brought by representative entities in the interest of consumers.

The future and effectiveness of representative actions under Directive 2020/1828 will strongly depend on the availability of TPF. When implementing the Directive, the German legislature needs to clarify that qualified entities are allowed to cooperate with commercial funders as a matter of principle.

13.4 THIRD-PARTY FUNDING BY DEBT COLLECTION COMPANIES

13.4.1 Assignments Invalid According to Substantive Law

The business model of debt collection companies or claim vehicles has been put to the test before German courts in recent years. It suffered a first, significant drawback in the cement cartel litigation, when in 2013 and 2015 German courts held that assignments to CDC were void. CDC is a Belgian company that specializes in the enforcement of damage claims arising from cartel infringements and is registered as a legal service provider in Germany. The Düsseldorf District Court (2013)[23] and the Düsseldorf Court of Appeals[24] (2015) held that assignments of claims to CDC were *contra bonos mores* (s 138 of the German Civil Code) and hence null and void.

The findings were based on older case law, according to which it makes a difference whether a company simply buys a claim and becomes the new owner of the claim, taking the full risk of enforcement, or whether the assignment is only for the purpose of a debt collecting process and the assignor remains the true owner of the claim from an economic perspective. CDC's business model does not include a 'real purchase' of claims. Cartel victims make an assignment of accounts receivable for collection, and CDC agrees to pay 67–70 per cent of the damages awards to the assignors. If the assignee is only the 'legal owner' of the claim, but from an economic perspective it is still the assignor, the assignments are subject to strict control by courts to avoid abuse.

---

[23] LG Düsseldorf, 17.12.2013 - 37 O 200/09 (Kart) U., BeckRS 2013, 22380, DE: LGD:2013:1217.37O200.09KART.U.00.

[24] OLG Düsseldorf, 18.02.2015 - VI-U (Kart) 3/14, BeckRS 2015, 5317, DE: OLGD:2015:0218.VI.U.KART3.14.00.

German courts consider it, for example, generally illegal for an assignor to simply use an assignment to a 'poor' claimant party to shift the risk of reimbursement of litigation cost to the defendant. When the cement cartel litigation started, CDC as an assignee was not financially equipped to fully bear the litigation risk. The Düsseldorf courts emphasized that thus the defendants ran the risk of not being able to recover adverse costs should the action be dismissed. In arguing so, they considered only the situation of CDC at the beginning of the litigation and ignored the fact that almost ten years later, at the time of the decision in the first instance, the financial situation of CDC had improved considerably, and CDC was able to meet the adverse cost order. The court nevertheless identified an unjustified shift of the cost risk to the defendants and completely left aside the efficiency and cost advantages of bundling the claims for both parties. The decision was particularly debateable against the background of German civil procedure rules which do not require plaintiffs to provide security for costs and thus accept that defendants have no 'right to a solvent plaintiff'.[25] For the assignors, these findings were extremely burdensome because part of their claims were statute-barred because the assignment was null and void, and thus the action filed by the wrong claimant did not stop the limitation period from running.

The irony of the cement cartel litigation in Germany is that courts in all instances had dealt with CDC's action over more than ten years without even touching upon the merits of the case and the key issues of competition law and quantification of damages. Because of the applicability of section 138 of the German Civil Code, claims vehicles which operate based on the assignment model must take care to either provide security of costs on a 'voluntary' basis to avoid assignments being void or to cooperate with third-party funders to cover the risk of adverse cost orders.

13.4.2 Assignments Violating the Legal Services Act

13.4.2.1 Market for legal services

More than ten years later, the assignment model of legal technology companies and claim vehicles has again become the target of defendants in actions arising from the Volkswagen emissions scandal (namely the actions of myRight) and several cartel damages actions, particularly in the truck cartel. The attacks against the business model reflect a common interest of defendants and lawyers who realize that legal technology firms and special purpose vehicles increasingly attract 'big cases' and may pull the rug from under lawyers' feet.

---

25 For a more detailed analysis of the case, see Tillema (n 13) 141 fn 10.

The provision of legal services by debt collection companies has changed considerably over the decades. Once, these companies offered services for companies unwilling to pursue individual claims on their own, and the activities of these companies were strictly limited to out-of-court activities, including judicial default actions (*Mahnverfahren*) and enforcement proceedings. In recent years, new fields of law have become attractive for commercial debt collection: the aggregation of claims in cartel cases, following the pioneer CDC, by which claimants benefit from TPF and from synergies for the quantification of damages. In a second step, legal technology companies entered the market offering risk-free enforcement of aggregated claims in mass harm situations from which largely identical damages arise, albeit dispersed on a large scale.

Synergetic effects follow from the homogeneous nature of the claims and because they allow a software-based collection and administration via internet platforms. The two trends have in common that companies offer a fully integrated approach which includes court proceedings in which the companies can act in their own name based on the assignments. Due to the lack of procedural instruments for pooling claims, claim vehicles aggregate claims based on substantive law. What initially seemed unproblematic under the Legal Services Act, which exclusively applies to out-of-court activities, became an increasingly worrisome thorn in the legal professions' flesh and caught the attention of lawyers' interest groups.

13.4.2.2 Scope of application of Legal Services Act

Although claim vehicles are formally registered under the Legal Services Act, defendants have argued that debt collection companies may offer only out-of-court services and violate the Legal Services Act if it is clearly their strategy from the very beginning to also act as claimants in court proceedings.[26] Although accepted by some courts, the argument does not carry much weight, as there is a clear distinction between out-of-court legal services governed by the Legal Services Act and activities before courts, to which the Civil Procedure Code exclusively applies and which does not restrict the filing of actions based on an assignment of claims.[27] Whenever claim vehicles initiate

---

26 Some District Courts followed that line of argument: LG München I, 07.02.2020 - 37 O 18934/17, DE:LGMUEN1:2020:0207.37O18934.17.0A - *Financialright Claims GmbH*; LG Hannover, 04.05.2020 - 18 O 50/16 - *Cartel Damage Claims* (Sugar Cartel case); LG Hannover, 01.02.2021 - 18 O 34/17 - *Cartel Damage Claims* (Sugar Cartel case). Others explicitly rejected the argument: LG Braunschweig, 23.12.2019 - 3 O 5657/18 - *myRight (Dieselgate)*.

27 LG München I, 07.02.2020 - 37 O 18934/17, ibid.; LG Hannover, 01.02.2021 - 18 O 34/17, ibid.

court proceedings, their service is no longer within the scope of the Legal Services Act and therefore cannot violate this Act. It is also not practical to require out-of-court activities in many cases. Volkswagen and most defendants in recent cartel cases made it clear from the outset that they are not willing to settle the cases but that they insist on court decisions. Why should claim vehicles, nevertheless, be obliged to offer settlement negotiations just to prove that they do not exclusively have court proceedings in mind?[28]

13.4.2.3 Conflicts of interest

Another argument of defendants which had the desired effect before some courts claims a violation of section 4 of the Legal Services Act. Generally, section 4 of the Legal Services Act is a rule which intends to protect persons seeking legal advice against conflicts of interest that may arise for the service provider. Such conflicts are similar to principal-agent conflicts, which we are familiar with from US class action, and they may emerge when service providers enter into conflicting contractual agreements. Defendants and some lower courts have identified such conflicts based on two main lines of argument:[29] if debt collection companies like myRight use external third-party funders, they might have to run with the hare and hunt with the hounds. MyRight as an assignee and claimant party might accept an early settlement offer by the defendant based on a cost-benefit equation to avoid additional costs to be paid by the funder. At the same time, the assignors expect full compensation of their harm and every procedural effort it takes to obtain it.

Although, in theory, one may construe such conflicts, one must keep in mind that all participants, assignors, assignee, and funder, have the same basic interest: obtaining as much money as possible from the defendant. There is almost no contractual relationship without conflicting interests to some extent.[30] Without the full-service approach of claim vehicles, many assignors, particularly consumers, would refrain from enforcing their damages claims in the first place.

---

28 In the same way: LG Braunschweig, 23.12.2019 - 3 O 5657/18 (n 26).

29 LG München I, 07.02.2020 - 37 O 18934/17 (n 26); LG Ingolstadt, 07.08.2020 - 41 O 1745/18, BeckRS 2020, 18773, DE:LGINGOL:2020:0807.41O1745.18.0A; LG Hannover, 04.05.2020 - 18 O 50/16 (n 26); LG Hannover, 01.02.2021 - 18 O 34/17 (n 26). In contrast, LG Braunschweig, 23.12.2019 - 3 O 5657/18 (n 26) did not see a conflict of interests.

30 Alexander Morell, 'Keine Kooperation ohne Konflikt' [2019] Juristenzeitung 809; also confirmed meanwhile by BGH, 13.7.2021, II ZR 84/20, ECLI:DE:BGH:2021:130721UIIZR84.20.0.

13.4.2.4 Aggregation of claims

Another potential conflict of interest was said to derive from the bundling of claims in a single proceeding. Defendants and courts argued that the aggregation of claims which are not completely identical, and which have different prospects for success might be settled by the assignee in a mass settlement that ignores these differences. Consequently, 'bad' claims will be attended to at the expense of 'good' ones. Such a reasoning fails to consider that assignors are often aware of this effect and have accepted it because the numerous advantages of aggregating claims outweigh the risk of conflicts of interest.

Particularly in cartel damages cases, assignors are often large- and medium-sized companies which make an informed choice. They cooperate with claims vehicles because the assignees will analyse data and documents and because the likelihood of proving the market-wide effects of cartels and for the quantification of damages is better when more data provided by the assignors are available for economic experts. Moreover, procedural costs are lower and the prospects for a settlement usually better when the defendant has the opportunity to resolve numerous claims. It is therefore pivotal to capture the whole picture and to not focus on potential conflicts of interest with limited effects.

13.4.2.5 Position of Federal High Court

Regional courts which accepted the defendants' arguments and dismissed claims were anxious to explain why they did not follow a 2019 landmark decision of the Federal High Court.[31] The Court had explicitly advocated a liberal interpretation of the Legal Services Act and an open-minded understanding of debt collection services, considering that the market for legal services is changing rapidly and that restrictions imposed may violate the fundamental rights of assignors and legal service providers. In a series of subsequent cases, the Court confirmed its findings.[32]

Nevertheless, several questions regarding potential conflicts of interest addressed in section 4 of the Legal Services Act remain unanswered because they were irrelevant to the case considered by the Federal High Court. Though

---

[31] BGH, 27. 11. 2019 – VIII ZR 285/18, BeckRS 2019, 30591 [141], DE:BGH:2019:271119UVIIIZR285.18.0; for a commentary, see Astrid Stadler, 'Grenzen der Inkassozession nach dem Rechtsdienstleistungsgesetz' [2020] Juristenzeitung 321.

[32] BGH, 06.05.2020 - VIII ZR 120/19, DE:BGH:2020:060520UVIIIZR120.19.0; BGH, 27.05.2020 - VIII ZR 45/19, BeckRS 2020, 11014, DE:BGH:2020:270520UVIIIZR45.19.0; BGH, 27.05.2020 - VIII ZR 121/19, DE:BGH:2020:270520UVIIIZR121.19.0; BGH, 27.05.2020 - VIII ZR 128/19, DE:BGH:2020:270520UVIIIZR128.19.0; BGH, 27.05.2020 - VIII ZR 129/19, DE:BGH:2020:270520UVIIIZR129.19.0.

the Court held that debt collection companies are allowed to offer litigation funding themselves, it did not address situations in which they cooperate with an external commercial funder. Section 4 of the Legal Services Act requires that the conflict arises due to the existence of different contracts from which contradictory obligations may result for the legal service provider and will thus not apply if litigation funding is a fully integrated part of a single contract between the provider and the assignor. If, however, external funders become involved, the situation might be different, particularly if a third-party funder claims to have some influence on the proceedings, for example, the right to approve or reject settlements. Where courts have assumed a violation of section 4 of the Legal Services Act, they considered the assignments invalid, which has severe consequences for the assignors if the action (by the assignee) was filed to stop the limitation period from running. It remains to be seen whether upper courts will overturn these decisions.

13.4.3 Liberalization of Legal Services

In this rather unclear situation, in November 2020, the German legislature published a tentative draft of a reform of the Legal Services Act and of some fundamental principles of professional rules for lawyers.[33] In January 2021, the legislative process began with a slightly changed version of the draft.[34] The basic idea is, as mentioned above, to allow contingency fee arrangements for lawyers in some situations to provide a level playing field with debt collection companies. The draft suggests that lawyers should be allowed to take over procedural risks and to operate based on contingency fee arrangements if, in case of court proceedings, the amount in controversy is not more than 2,000 euros. For lawyers' out-of-court activities, there is no cap. Thus, lawyers can now aggregate small claims and enforce them based on a success fee.

There was a lively debate on whether the option is economically attractive for lawyers and, from a more fundamental perspective, whether lawyers should be allowed at all to have an economic interest in the outcome of the litigation, albeit a rather limited one. It became, however, clear that policy makers are not willing to completely ban legal services provided by debt collection companies and claims vehicles. The only question to be answered is still how to define

---

[33] Federal Ministry of Justice and Consumer Protection, 'Entwurf eines Gesetzes zur Förderung verbrauchergerechter Angebote im Rechtsdienstleistungsmarkt' (Bundesministeriums der Justiz und für Verbraucherschutz, 12 November 2020) https://www.bmjv.de/SharedDocs/Gesetzgebungsverfahren/Dokumente/RefE_Rechtsdienstleister.pdf accessed 29 March 2021.

[34] The final version of the new law is available at: Bundesgesetzblatt BGBI.2021 I, 3416.

'debt collection' and what type of cases should be exclusively for lawyers. The Federal High Court refrained from providing a generally applicable definition of 'legal services' because the market is changing rapidly and, in the first draft, policy makers agreed that it seems wise to not hamper further developments in the legal services market by enacting a rather narrow definition. Nevertheless, the draft of January 2021 attempts to limit at least debt collection services to some core activities.

The new law further provides a shift from the prohibition of the provision of legal services by non-lawyers to an information model. New rules will require legal service providers to inform consumers who seek their advice and services inter alia about third-party funding and its implications, alternative methods of enforcing consumer claims without having to pay a success fee, and, if applicable, about the aggregation of claims in court proceedings. Moreover, to provide more legal certainty for legal service providers and their clients, the role of administrative authorities is strengthened. Based on documents and information to be submitted by applicants, they now have to check whether the business model is in line with the Legal Services Act or suitable in terms of conflicts of interest. Once the application has been approved and applicants have been registered as legal service providers, civil courts are expected to accept these businesses' business models unless they have changed since registration.

13.5 SUMMARY

Traditional concepts of funding such as BTE insurance do not provide solutions in mass litigation. At present, the framework for funding mass claims in Germany is still difficult. Contingency fee arrangements with lawyers are now available due to a paradigm shift by policy makers, but the practical implications are not yet clear. Market conditions for commercial third-party funders are somewhat difficult. Some landmark decisions have restricted the availability of TPF for consumer associations, thus putting the effective enforcement of consumer rights at risk. Some lower courts have also denied the aggregation of claims by claims vehicles and declared the assignments invalid due to violations of the Legal Services Act. A tentative draft from the federal government for a reform the Legal Services Act may result in a remedy for some problems.

In the long term, there is definitely a need for not only a liberal framework legislation on TPF but also for the establishment of an access-to-justice fund for representative actions under the new Directive 2020/1828.[35] Third-party

---

[35] Such a fund has been suggested by numerous authors in the past; see Gerhard Wagner, *Verhandlungen des 66. DJT*, vol II (CH Beck Munich 2006) A 14. See

funders are unwilling to take all cases, and consumer associations do not have the budgets to pursue all mass harm events without additional funding sources.

also Hans-W. Micklitz and Astrid Stadler, *Unrechtsgewinnabschöpfung* (Nomos 2003) 129; Hans-W. Micklitz and Astrid Stadler, *Das Verbandsklagerecht in der Informations- und Dienstleistungsgesellschaft* (Gutachten BMVEL 2005) 1142; Stefaan Voet, 'Cultural Dimensions of Group Litigation: The Belgian Case' (2013) 41 *Georgia Journal of International and Comparative Law* 433, 469; Jenny Buchner, Kollektiver Rechtsschutz für Verbraucher in Europa (Vandenhoeck & Ruprecht 2015) 202; Astrid Stadler, 'Kollektiver Rechtsschutz Quo Vadis?' [2018] Juristenzeitung 793, 801–802; Caroline Meller-Hannich, *Gutachten 72. DJT* (CH Beck Munich 2018) A 60, A 88; Karl-Heinz Fezer, 'Zweckgebundene Verwendung von Unrechtserlösen und Kartellbußen zur Finanzierung der Verbraucherarbeit' (*KOPS*, 27 February 2019) https://kops.uni-konstanz.de/handle/123456789/23103 accessed 29 March 2021.

14. Transparency and oversight of class actions funding in Canada[1]

Catherine Piché

14.1 INTRODUCTION

Bentham once said that restrictions against litigation funding are a 'barbarous precaution' born out of a 'barbarous age'.[2] Must litigation funding be moderated, controlled, or approved judicially? Which kind and form of financing of litigation, whether individual or collective, is acceptable, and beneficial to group members? How is such financing provided in a collective litigation context? Is a public form of financing preferable to well-structured and controlled forms of private financing?

In the past few decades, the volume of class action litigation has steadily risen around the world, such that significant amounts of capital are required to prosecute these actions, provide access to justice, and provide equal opportunities to plaintiffs and defendants. In Canada, class actions are financed either privately by plaintiff firms, by the class members themselves by way of an indemnity by plaintiff's counsel, through assistance from third-party financiers, and/or through public funding. Third-party litigation funding, while considered somewhat controversial, exists and has led to private funding agreements that have been judicially approved. There is, nonetheless, a legitimate concern that without regulation, such funding may subvert the public policy purposes of the class action and core values of our legal system such as client confidentiality, the preservation of attorney–client privilege, and the attorney duties to remain independent and avoid conflicts of interest.

This chapter will address both public and private forms and modalities of financing class action litigation in Canada. After highlighting the relevant

---

[1] The following article has inspired us in writing the present chapter: Catherine Piché, 'Public Financiers as Overseers of Class Proceedings' (2016) 12:3 *NYU JL & Bus* 779.

[2] Jeremy Bentham, *The Works of Jeremy Bentham*, vol 3, part 1 (ed Bowring, William Tait 1843).

economical considerations and enablers in class action litigation, the chapter discusses the private funding of class actions in Canada, including its rationale and mechanisms, and public funding entities in the Canadian provinces of Quebec and Ontario. Ultimately, the chapter argues that financing class actions publicly through assistance by entities such as the Canadian province of Quebec's *Fonds d'aide aux actions collectives* (the assistance fund for class action lawsuits; hereafter the 'Fonds') is a most appropriate and effective way to finance class action litigation, whenever available, and that the *Fonds* is effective as a class litigation funding mechanism and independent oversight body.

14.2 CLASS ACTIONS IN CANADA

14.2.1 Overview of Available Collective Redress Mechanisms

Quebec's class actions provisions in the Code of Civil Procedure (hereafter 'CCP'),[3] similar to other legislation adopted throughout Canada[4] and US Rule 23 of the Federal Rules of Civil Procedure (hereafter 'Rule 23'),[5] enable a person who is a member of a class of persons to sue, without a mandate, on behalf of all the members of the class and to represent the class.[6] Quebec, a primarily civilian jurisdiction, with a hybrid procedural law, was the first Canadian province to introduce class action legislation in 1978.[7] Quebec class

---

[3] Code of Civil Procedure, CQLR, c C-25.01, arts 571–604. The New Code has come into force on 1 January 2016 and seeks to make the civil justice system more accessible, while protecting the rights of all parties to state their claims before a court.

[4] See, e.g., Ontario Class Proceedings Act, SO 1992, c 6, s 2(1) (hereafter 'Ont CPA'); British Columbia Class Proceedings Act, RSBC 1996, c 50, s 2(1). It is worth noting that Canada' legislative competence is distributed between the federal government and the provincial (and territorial) governments. All questions of private law and of civil procedure are exercised by the provinces. The Canadian Constitution determines the powers of the federal and provincial governments, The territories exercise powers delegated from the federal government, and those powers are harmonious with those constitutionally granted to the provinces.

[5] Federal Rules of Civil Procedure (hereafter 'FRCP') 23.

[6] Statutory authority for class action proceedings in Quebec is codified in the Quebec CCP in arts 571 to 604 CCP

[7] An Act Respecting the Class Action, SQ 1978, c 8 (hereafter 'ARCA'), enacting ss 999–1052 CCP. For a further discussion of the history of the Canadian class action, see: Shain Finn, *Class Actions in Quebec: Notes for Non-Residents* (Carswell 2014); Andrew Borrel, 'The Evolving Evidentiary Standard for Certification in Canada' (2005) 26:6 *Class Action Rep* 3; Garry D. Watson, 'Class Actions: The Canadian Experience' (2001) 11 *Duke J Comp & Intl L* 269; W.A. Bogart, 'Questioning Litigation's Role – Courts and Class Actions in Canada' (1986–87) 62 *Ind L J* 665; Williams, 'Consumer

action law was enacted 'with policy objectives of promoting and favouring access to justice, and more efficiently enforcing social and remedial legislation', as a 'measure intended to advance a public interest agenda, along with labour reform and consumer protection statutes'.[8] Importantly, preoccupied by the accessibility of the class action as a procedural tool for litigants regardless of their resources,[9] the Quebec legislator established a governmental agency for the distribution of public funds to potential class action representatives: the *Fonds d'aide aux actions collectives.*[10]

In the rest of Canada, class action reform followed in 1982, with the publication of the *Ontario Law Reform Commission Report on Class Actions.*[11] The impetus for modern class action legislation in Canada effectively arose out of the recognition by the Supreme Court of Canada in *Naken*[12] that the previous rules of court for representative proceedings were inadequate, and that a 'comprehensive legislative scheme for the institution and conduct of class actions' was needed. Since then, all of the Canadian provinces except one (Prince Edward Island), and including the Federal Court of Canada, gradually enacted class proceedings statutes.[13] The legislative schemes adopted across Canada drew on US rules and class action experience, but with a more liberal approach to certification.

In 2001, a trilogy of Supreme Court of Canada class action cases officially recognized the critical importance of class actions in Canada.[14] In another 2013

Class Actions in Canada – Some Proposals for Reform' (1975) 13 *Osgoode Hall L J* 1; John A. Kazanjian, 'Class Actions in Canada' (1973) 11 *Osgoode Hall L J* 397. Also see generally on the Canadian class action settlement law, Catherine Piché, *Fairness in Class Action Settlements* (Carswell 2012).

8 Catherine Piché, 'The Cultural Analysis of Class Action Law' (2009) 2 *Journal of Civil Law Studies* 101, 118; also see Pierre-Claude Lafond, 'Le recours collectif: entre la commodité procédurale et la justice sociale' [1998–99] 29 Revue de Droit Université Sherbrooke 3, 24 (explaining how the procedure was adopted at a time of great social change).

9 Yves Lauzon, 'Le recours collectif Québécois: description et bilan' (1984) 9 *Canadian Business Law Journal* 324, 335.

10 The *Fonds* has become the *Fonds d'aide aux actions collectives* with the New Code, and as per the Act Respecting the Fonds d'aide aux Actions Collectives, ch F-3.2.0.1.1, sanctioned on 1 April 2016.

11 Ontario Law Reform Commission, Ministry of the Attorney General, *Report on Class Actions* (1982).

12 *Naken v General Motors of Canada Ltd* [1983] 1 SCR 72 (SCC).

13 See notably: Class Proceedings Act, 1992, SO 1992, c 6 (province of Ontario); Class Proceedings Act, RSBC 1996, c 50 (province of British Columbia); Part 5.1 of the Federal Courts Rules.

14 *Western Canadian Shopping Centres v Dutton* [2001] 2 SCR 534 (*Dutton*); *Hollick v Toronto (City)* [2001] 3 SCR 158 (*Hollick*); *Rumley v BC* [2001] 3 SCR 184.

trilogy of class action cases, Canada's highest court confirmed that the more stringent evidentiary approach to class actions as endorsed in the US Supreme Court in *Wal-Mart v Dukes*[15] has little application to Canadian class actions.[16]

Importantly, the Supreme Court of Canada outlined the three important advantages class proceedings have over a multiplicity of individual suits:[17] First, by aggregating similar individual actions, class actions serve judicial economy by avoiding unnecessary duplication in fact-finding and legal analysis. Second, by distributing fixed litigation costs amongst a large number of class members, class actions improve access to justice by making economical the prosecution of claims that any one class member would find too costly to prosecute on his or her own. Third, class actions serve efficiency and justice by ensuring that actual and potential 'wrongdoers' modify their behaviour to take full account of the harm they are causing, or might cause, to the public.[18]

In Canada, in order to commence such an action, the person who seeks to represent the class and institute the class action must present a demand for an order authorizing the action as a class action and recognizing them as the representative of the class, according to a list of criteria by which a judge is to assess whether the class should be certified or authorized.[19] The judgment

---

[15] 131 S Ct 2541 (2011).

[16] *Infineon Technologies AG v Option consommateurs* [2013] SCC 59; *Sun-Rype Products Ltd v Archer Daniels Midland Company* [2013] SCC 58; *Pro-Sys Consultants Ltd. v Microsoft Corporation* [2013] SCC 57.

[17] *Dutton* (n 14) [27] – [9].

[18] *Dutton* (n 14); also see *Fehr v Sun Life Assurance Company of Canada* [2012] ONSC 2715 (CanLII) [40]. Most Canadian provinces have enacted legislation enabling class actions. In provinces that do not have class action legislation, the Supreme Court of Canada has extended the right to bring class actions notwithstanding the absence of legislation, effectively creating a 'common law' class action.

[19] As per Quebec's art 575 CPC, the court authorizes the class action and appoints the class member it designates as representative plaintiff if it is of the opinion that (1) the claims of the members of the class raise identical, similar or related issues of law or fact; (2) the facts alleged appear to justify the conclusions sought; (3) the composition of the class makes it difficult or impracticable to apply the rules for mandates to sue on behalf of others or for consolidation of proceedings; and (4) the class member appointed as representative plaintiff is in a position to properly represent the class members. See recent Supreme Court of Canada case of *L'Oratoire Saint-Joseph du Mont-Royal v JJ* [2019] SCC 35 (*L'Oratoire Saint-Joseph*). S 5 Ont CPA was recently amended as per Bill 161, Smarter and Stronger Justice Act, 2020. The Smarter and Stronger Justice Act introduced a more demanding approach to certification by requiring that the class proceeding be the superior procedural means of 'determining the entitlement of the class members to relief or addressing the impugned conduct of the defendant' and by requiring that questions of fact or law common to the class members predominate over questions affecting only individual class members. Although the effects this newly adopted requirement will have on class actions practice in Ontario remain indeterminate, the

authorizing a class action describes the class whose members will be bound by the class action judgment, appoints the representative plaintiff and identifies the main issues to be dealt with collectively and the conclusions sought in relation to those issues. It also describes any subclasses that have been created and determines the district in which the class action is to be instituted, orders the publication of a notice to class members, and determines the opt-out period.[20] No multi-jurisdiction, Multi-District Litigation (hereafter 'MDL') or other co-ordinating procedure currently exists in Canada for class actions brought in multiple jurisdictions, although the judiciary is prepared informally to co-ordinate to achieve judicial economy.[21]

14.2.2 Economic Enablers,[22] Risk Assumptions and the Actual State of Class Action Financing

The context of class litigation is complex: the cost of litigation is prohibitive, the delays too long, and the system not only unequal and asymmetric, but inefficient as a whole. Significant economic barriers confront a group that has allegedly been harmed by a wrongdoer and seeks relief. There is, of course, the high cost of obtaining legal services to litigate the claim – collectively or individually. Part of this cost is the adverse costs award payable to the defendant, thereby constituting a significant cost exposure to the representative plaintiff

'preferability' criteria is inspired by US Rule 23 and thus will be interpreted in light of this. Despite this change, the framework developed by the Supreme Court of Canada in *AIC Limited v Fischer* [2013] SCC 69, for determining if class proceedings were preferable will likely continue to be relevant.

[20] Art 576 CCP.

[21] There are nonetheless three Canadian protocols that address multi-jurisdictional class proceedings in Canada: the Canadian Judicial Protocol for the Management of Multi-Jurisdictional Class Actions https://www.cba.org/getattachment/Our-Work/Resolutions/Resolutions/2011/Canadian-Judicial-Protocol-for-the-Management-of-M/11-03-A-Annex01.pdf accessed 5 July 2021; the Notice Protocol: Coordinating Notice(s) to the Class(es) in Multi-jurisdictional Class Proceedings https://www.cba.org/getattachment/Our-Work/Resolutions/Resolutions/2011/Notice-Protocol-Coordinating-Notice(s)-to-the-Clas/11-03-A-Annex03.pdf accessed 5 July 2021; and the Protocol on Court-to-Court Communications in Canada – US Cross-Border Class Actions https://www.cba.org/getattachment/Our-Work/Resolutions/Resolutions/2011/Protocole-de-communication-entre-les-tribunaux-dan/11-03-A-Annex02.pdf accessed 5 July 2021. These protocols do not have the scope or latitude of the US MDL.

[22] See Camille Cameron, Alon Klement and Jasminka Kalajdzic, 'Economic Enablers', in Deborah Hensler, Christopher Hodges and Ianika Tzankova (eds), *Class Actions in Context: How Economics, Politics and Culture Shape Collective Litigation* (Edward Elgar 2015); also see e.g., Michael J. Trebilcock and Elizabeth Kagedan, 'Economic Assessment of Third-Party Ontario Class Actions' (2014) 55:1 *Canadian Business Law Journal* 54.

and a barrier to access to justice. Representative plaintiffs are responsible for costs in Quebec and Ontario,[23] if the class action is unsuccessful, but class members are not.[24] While this exposure may be significant in Ontario, costs payable in Quebec remain more moderate – even nominal,[25] as certification costs awards are capped in Quebec. As the Ontario Superior Court of Justice has rightly stated, '[a]ccess to justice, even in the very area that was specifically designed to achieve this goal, is becoming too expensive'.[26]

The only three possible responses to this economic barrier to initiating class proceedings are (i) third-party private funding initiatives, (ii) public fund assistance, and (iii) indemnification of the representative for his or her 'services'.[27] In order to avoid any conflicts of interest, indemnification of the representative for his or her services is not permitted in Quebec,[28] subject to the courts discretion to grant the representative an award under section 593 CCP for their disbursements and to cover legal costs and the lawyer's professional fee. As a result, third-party funding initiatives as well as public funding assistance remain the most popular alternatives for financing class actions. We will address these two economic responses to the growing need for financial assistance within the class actions ecosystem below.

---

23 S 31 Ont CPA.

24 Art 579 (1) (6) CCP provides that the notice published or notified to class members should state 'that no class members other than the representative plaintiff or an intervenor may be required to pay legal costs arising from the class action'; see also *Desgagné v Quebec* [2010] QCCS 4838 [567].

25 See e.g., *Buonamici v Blockbuster Canada Co* [2007] QCCA 468 [25]–[29]; *APA v Canadian Honda Motors Ltd* [1980] RP 331, EYB 1980 137554 (Protonotary Mercier), confirmed by JE 81-1019 (CS), EYB 1981-138919 (Justice Phelan) (where the court limited the amount of costs payable to $253 instead of $650–675 stating that the estimated value of the litigation is undeterminable pursuant to the costs tariff regulation).

26 *Rosen v BMO Nesbitt Burns Inc* [2013] ONSC 6356 (Ont SCJ) [1]. Also see *Crisante v DePuy Orthopaedics* [2013] ONSC 6351 (Ont SCJ); *Dugal v Manulife Financial* [2013] ONSC 6354 (Ont SCJ); *Brown v Canada (Attorney General)* [2013] ONSC 6887 (Ont SCJ); *Sankar v Bell Mobility Inc* [2013] ONSC 6886 (Ont SCJ). In these decisions, Belobaba recommended changes to the prevailing approach to cost awards on certification motions in Ontario. If adopted, these changes will turn Ontario into a 'no-costs regime'. Another justice, Justice Perell, has added to the discussion in a later case, stating that 'The assessment of costs (and of lawyer's fees) must adapt to a changing and evolving class action regime and every case requires individual treatment.' See *The Trustees of the Drywall Acoustic Lathing v SNC Group Inc* [2013] ONSC 7122 [18].

27 *Fehr v Sun Life Assurance Co of Canada* [2012] OJ No 2029 (Ont SCJ) (*Fehr*) [53].

28 *Attar c Fonds d'aide aux actions collectives* [2020] QCCA 1121.

14.3 PRIVATE FUNDING OF CLASS ACTIONS IN CANADA

14.3.1 Rationale and Context for Private Funding

Around the world, there has been a palpable increase in private third-party litigation funding (hereafter 'TPLF'), also defined as the practice of providing money to a party to fund the pursuit of a potential or pending lawsuit in exchange for a portion of the proceeds.[29] Lord Jackson outlined the advantages of TPLF in his *Review of Civil Litigation Costs – Final Report – 2010*,[30] a report commissioned by the UK Parliament. The access to justice component was highlighted, as well as the advantage of reducing the pressure of litigation and of assuring a certain degree of litigation expertise by sophisticated investor companies.[31]

In Canada, TPLF has garnered collective acceptance by both the courts and legislators as a means of promoting access to justice.[32] This recent development comes despite the legal communities' initial concerns over the legitimacy and acceptability of such funding.[33] Despite the apparent conflicts of interest surrounding private litigation funding agreements and their potential to create agency problems, courts have overwhelmingly come to view TPLF as a mechanism to fund class actions which otherwise would not have seen the light of day, thereby promoting the objectives underlying class actions legislation.[34] With the ever-growing costs of litigations and oftentimes unpredictable adverse costs and disbursements in class actions, the need and pertinence of TPLF in this type of litigation has become evident.

---

[29] See e.g., Peter Cashman and Amelia Simpson, 'Research Paper 5 – The Costs and Funding Commissions of Class Actions' [2020] University of New South Wales Law Research Series 87; Rachel Howie and Geoff Moysa, 'Financing Disputes: Third-Party Funding in Litigation and Arbitration' (2019) 57:2 *Alta L Rev* 465.

[30] Rupert Jackson, *Review of Civil Litigation Costs: Final Report* (2010) 117–125, 464.

[31] Ibid.

[32] *9354-9186 Québec Inc v Callidus Capital Corp* [2020] SCC 10 (CanLII) [95]; *Bayens v Kinross Gold Corp* [2013] ONSC 4974 (CanLII) [34].

[33] The initial worries surrounding third-party private litigation funding are further explored in Piché (n 1).

[34] *Drynan v Bausch Health Companies Inc* [2020] ONSC 4379 [19]; *Bayens v Kinross Gold Corp* [2013] ONSC 4974 (CanLII) [34].

14.3.2 Private Funding Approval Mechanisms

Part of the favourable reception to TPLF in Canada stems from the thorough judicial scrutiny which originally governed the enforceability of such agreements and thereby ensured their legitimacy. Acting to ensure the best interests of class members, courts have embraced the role of class guardians, protecting absent class members against potentially egregious or unfair agreements. Originally, these protections were in large part developed by the courts 'relying on common sense, knowledge of the problems of access to justice and of the administration of justice, and academic commentary'.[35]

A particularly important precedent in the field was established by the Ontario Superior Court of Justice in *Bayens v Kinross*[36] where the court laid out a series of general principles governing third-party litigation agreements in the context of class actions.[37] Courts across the country implemented within their jurisdiction the *Bayens v Kinross* model-criteria for enforcing TPLF in class actions.[38] Most recently the Ontario Superior Court of Justice examined the leading principles regarding this type of funding in *Houle v St Jude Medical Inc.*[39] After an extensive review of the case law surrounding such agreements in Ontario, the court explained that agreements must be approved judicially following their prompt disclosure, and summarized the law governing third-party agreements as follows:

> [63] … to approve a third-party funding agreement, the court must be satisfied that: (a) the agreement must be necessary in order to provide access to justice; (b) the access to justice facilitated by the third-party funding agreement must be substantively meaningful; (c) the agreement must be a fair and reasonable agreement that facilitates access to justice while protecting the interests of the defendants; and (d) the third-party funder must not be overcompensated for assuming the risks of an adverse costs award because this would make the agreement unfair, overreaching, and champertous …
>
> [64] … Further, … the third-party funding agreement must not interfere with: the lawyer-client relationship; the lawyer's duties of loyalty and confidentiality; or the lawyer's professional judgment and carriage of the litigation on behalf of the representative plaintiff or class members … The representative plaintiff must retain the right to instruct and control the litigation and the representative plaintiff must

---

35 *Bayens v Kinross Gold Corp*, ibid., [33].

36 Ibid.

37 Ibid., [41].

38 In New Brunswick: *Hayes v the City of Saint John et al* [2016] NBQB 125 [4]; In British Columbia: *Stanway v Wyeth Canada Inc* [2014] BCSC 931 [15]; In Saskatchewan: *Schneider v Royal Crown Gold Reserve Inc* [2016] SKQB 278 [8].

39 *Houle v St Jude Medical Inc* [2017] ONSC 5129 (CanLII) (*Houle*) [63].

> not become indifferent in giving instructions to class counsel in the best interests of the class members …[40]

Importantly, the court affirmed that the defendant should be given notice of the motion for court approval of the third-party funding agreement and should be provided with an opportunity to make submissions.[41] In addition, it held that the representative should be provided independent legal advice about (a) the law firm's contingency fee agreement, (b) the third-party financing agreement and (c) the inter-relationship between the third-party funding agreement and the contingency fee agreement.[42] Subsequent cases have since applied these same principles.[43]

Most recently, private funding in the context of class actions was embraced by the Ontario legislator. Pursuant to the proposed reforms advanced by the Ontario Law Commission,[44] the Ont CPA was amended to include a section on TPLF agreements. Thus, section 33.1 (1) Ont CPA governs the enforceability and validity of third-party litigation funding agreements. The scope of a 'third-party funding agreement' is thereby defined, and agreements are made contingent on court approval to be enforceable, codifying long-established caselaw requiring transparency in this context.[45] Section 33.1 (4) of the Act further requires that the defendant be notified of such funding agreements. Any and all 'information that may reasonably be considered to confer a tactical advantage on the defendant' must be redacted.[46]

Ultimately, S 33.1 (9) provides factors governing the court's approval. To approve a funding agreement, the court must be satisfied that:

---

[40] Ibid., [63]–[64].

[41] Ibid., [69].

[42] Ibid., [70].

[43] *JB & M Walker Ltd / 1523428 Ontario Inc v TDL Group* [2019] ONSC 999 (CanLII) [6]; *Drynan v Bausch Health Companies Inc* [2020] ONSC 4379 [17]; *Flying E Ranche Ltd v Canada (Attorney General)* [2020] ONSC 8076 (CanLII) [28]; *9354-9186 Québec inc v Callidus Capital Corp* [2020] SCC 10 (CanLII) [94].

[44] Law Commission of Ontario, *Class Actions: Objectives, Experiences and Reforms: Final Report* (Toronto, July 2019) https://www.lco-cdo.org/wp-content/uploads/2019/07/LCO-Class-Actions-Report-FINAL-July-17-2019.pdf accessed 5 July 2021. Understandably, the Class Proceedings Fund is exempt from these rules, see s 33.1(16) Ont CPA.

[45] *Fehr v Sun Life Assurance Company of Canada* [2012] ONSC 2715 (CanLII) [89] ('Third party funding of a class proceeding must be transparent and it must be reviewed in order to ensure that there are no abuses or interference with the administration of justice.')

[46] S 33.1(5) Ont CPA However, an unredacted copy is still provided to the judge, who may require disclosure of certain information: see Ont CPA, s 33.1(6) (7).

(i) the agreement, including indemnity for costs and amounts payable to the funder under the agreement, is fair and reasonable,
(ii) the agreement will not diminish the rights of the representative plaintiff to instruct the solicitor or control the litigation or otherwise impair the solicitor-client relationship,
(iii) the funder is financially able to satisfy an adverse costs award in the proceeding, to the extent of the indemnity provided under the agreement, and
(iv) any prescribed requirements and other relevant requirements are met ...[47]

Further, section 33.1 (9)(b) requires funders to consensually agree to abide by confidentiality requirements and the deemed undertakings rule. Importantly, courts must consider whether the representative received independent legal advice about the agreement, as per section 33.1(10) Ont CPA.

In many ways the new legislative scheme for approving third-party litigation agreements largely resembles the pre-existing common law requirements developed by the courts to scrutinize such financings. Judges will continue to play an important role as 'guardians'[48] of the class, ensuring most importantly that the agreements are 'fair and reasonable'.[49] Overall, greater certainty and stability to the emerging private funding litigation industry is provided with this new Ontario development. Of course, lenders in Ontario will still need to be careful in how they draft their agreements if they hope to avoid the old torts of 'champerty & maintenance', still in force under An Act Respecting Champerty.[50]

Prior to the enactment of section 33.1 Ont CPA, funders of class actions needed to show the 'necessity' of the funding agreement in order to determine

---

47 S 33.1 (9)(a) Ont CPA.

48 Law Commission of Ontario, *Class Actions: Objectives, Experiences and Reforms: Final Report* (Toronto, July 2019) 86.

49 S 33.1 (9) Ont CPA.

50 An Act Respecting Champerty RSO 1897, c 327; In *Houle v St Jude Medical Inc* [2017] ONSC 5129 [50], the Ontario Superior Court of Justice described the Champerty Act's original intent as follows:

> The public policies supporting the torts of champerty and maintenance are the goals of discouraging unnecessary litigation prompted by a non-party stirring up strife in order to profit from it and of preventing a non-party from meddling and perhaps controlling somebody else's litigation.

that their support to the litigation did not constitute champerty and maintenance. As Perell J explains in *Houle v St Jude Medical Inc:*[51]

> The rationales for allowing what otherwise would be champerty and maintenance, which is to say the officious intermeddling of a non-litigant in another's litigation are that: (a) but for the third-party's financial assistance, the litigant would have no access to justice; and, or (b) but for the third-party's financial assistance, society would be bereft of a means to modify the behaviour of wrongdoers who have harmed a group. One or the other of the rationales for a litigation funding agreement; *i.e.*: (a) enabling access to justice; or (b) discouraging or deterring wrongdoing, must be present or the agreement should not be approved.[52]

Although the newly adopted legislation makes no mention of the 'necessity principle', we believe that this criterion has been implicitly incorporated in the 'fair and reasonable' test set out at section 33. 1(9)a) i) Ont CPA. Prudent funders should therefore ensure that the funding provided in the litigation will promote the objectives of class actions and contribute to access to justice.

In the province of Quebec, by comparison, various forms of class litigation financing exist. Financing can be provided by class representatives or by class members, especially in instances where the class is smaller and cohesive, and class members may be easily identified.[53] Although no specific legislation in Quebec regulates TPLF agreements, courts in Quebec have approved such agreements.[54]

In parallel to recent judicial and legislative developments regulating TPLF agreements, litigation funding code of conducts have been adopted in many jurisdictions around the world.[55] Although no such code of conduct currently exists in Canada, such a development may help further legitimize the role of third-party litigation funders in the context of class actions.

Despite the emergence of private funding assistance, public assistance remains a favourable initiative in terms of access to justice both in Quebec and in Ontario, and as such, Quebec is a pioneer in establishing a public assistance fund for this very purpose. As we discuss below, public financiers such

---

51 *Houle v St Jude Medical Inc* [2017] ONSC 5129.

52 Ibid., [75].

53 See, e.g., *Nantais v Telectronics Proprietary (Canada) Ltd* [1996] OJ No 5386 (Ont Gen Div) (QL), where the representative loaned money to the class counsel on a contingency basis.

54 Marcotte c Banque de Montréal (CS, 2015-05-05), 2015 QCCS 1915.

55 As an example, see *Bayens v Kinross Gold Corp* [2013] ONSC 4974 [6]. In this case, the court notes that the third-party funder is a member of the Litigation Funding Association and thereby abides by the Code of Conduct for litigation funders in England and Wales. Similar observations were made most recently in *Flying E Ranche Ltd v Canada (Attorney General)* [2020] ONSC 8076 [20].

as the *Fonds* cannot be accused of providing champertous assistance when they assist with a proper motive, in exchange for a very reasonable 'compensation' – that is not a compensation *per se* as it is a means of subrogation. This 'compensation' does not serve to compensate; rather, it serves only to self-finance the entity, as opposed to making profit, with minimal intervention and intermeddling. Our view is that the *Fonds* has a socially-focused access to justice objective and a mandate that gives it a proper motive to assist litigants, and that it is fully justified by its public status as a Government-funded entity to provide the assistance required.

14.4 PUBLIC FUNDING OF CLASS ACTIONS IN CANADA

14.4.1 Funding Half of Quebec Class Actions: The *Fonds d'aide aux Actions Collectives*

Cognizant of the important financial hurdles intrinsic in advancing class action litigation, the Quebec legislator demonstrated exceptional foresight when it introduced the *Fonds d'aide aux recours collectifs* (now called *Fonds d'aide aux actions collectives* – hereafter the '*Fonds*') as a financial intermediary designed to promote access to justice.[56] Since its establishment in 1979, the *Fonds* has constituted an integral part of the legislative scheme governing class actions in Quebec and has profoundly impacted the funding landscape for advancing such cases.[57] As such, it has conclusively played a leading role in promoting access to justice within the province. To this day, despite the emergence and growth of TPLF, the *Fonds* continues to play an important role in financing and advancing class actions litigation in Quebec. As recent statistics of the *Fonds'* activities reveal, the growth in popularity of TPLF in Quebec has decreased neither the demand, nor the issuance of public funds in class actions in the province.

A creature of statute, the *Fonds* falls under the Quebec Ministry of Justice and is composed of three administrators named by the government.[58] The object and mandate of the *Fonds* is to ensure the financing of class actions in first instance or on appeal and to disseminate information respecting the

---

56 See Journal des débats, 16 May 1978, vol 20, no 34, 1475; Frikia Belogbi, 'Le fonds d'aide aux actions collectives' in Barreau du Québec, Service de la formation continue, *Colloque national sur l'action collective - Développements récents au Québec, au Canada et aux États-Unis (2017)*, vol 428 (Éditions Yvon Blais 2017) online, 29–30.

57 Belogbi (n 56) 29–30.

58 Act Respecting the Fonds d'aide aux Actions Collectives, ch F-3.2.0.1.1, art 8.

exercise of such actions.[59] Pursuant to section 20 of the Act Respecting the Fonds d'aide aux Actions Collectives,[60] every representative and every person intending to be ascribed such status may apply in writing for assistance from the *Fonds*, outlining the basis of the claim and the essential facts determining its exercise, and describing the group on behalf of which they intend to bring or are bringing the action.[61] Prospective applicants must also state their financial condition, and that of the putative class members, as well as indicate the purposes for which the assistance is intended to be used, the amount required, and what other revenue or service is available.[62]

Importantly, the criteria the *Fonds* will consider in its decision to assist or not is whether the class action may be brought or continued without such assistance, and the probable existence of the right intended to be asserted and the probability that the class action will be brought.[63] Ultimately, the *Fonds* may defer the study of a part of the application, refuse assistance or grant it, in whole or in part, and in all cases, it shall render its decision within one month following receipt of the application.[64] In any event, reasons for a decision to refuse or defer assistance must be provided,[65] as well as the conditions for assistance.[66] A negative decision may be contested by the applicant in front of the Administrative Tribunal of Quebec.[67]

When a favourable decision is rendered, and assistance is granted, the recipient is entitled to payment by the *Fonds* of the expenses expedient for the preparation or bringing of the class action, including attorney and expert fees of the recipient, the recipient's costs and other court expenditures including costs of notification, and any other expenses related therein.[68] Most importantly, the *Fonds* does not charge any interest fees. Furthermore, an agreement may be made to indemnify representative plaintiffs for adverse costs awards.[69] Importantly, the recipient or his attorney shall reimburse the *Fonds* the

---

59 Ibid., art 7.
60 Ibid.
61 Ibid., art 21.
62 Ibid.
63 Ibid., art 23 (2).
64 Ibid., art 23 (4).
65 Ibid., art 24.
66 Ibid., art 25.
67 Ibid., arts 35, 37.
68 Ibid., arts 27, 29.
69 Ibid., art 29.

amounts paid by it up to the amounts received from a third party as fees, costs or expenses.[70]

As of 2020, the *Fonds* has granted funding to 45 per cent of all active class actions in Quebec.[71] According to the *Fonds*' Annual Report, it had provided financing to 242 active class actions throughout the province out of a total of 541 active cases.[72] The annual report further revealed that between 1 April 2019 and 31 March 2020 alone, the *Fonds* had provided over 3.6 million dollars towards financing class actions litigation.[73]

A significant portion of the *Fonds* success in financing class litigation stems from how well capitalized it is. In fact, since its creation, the *Fonds* has been almost entirely self-sustainable. Although the *Fonds* was initially supported with capital injections provided by government subsidies, it has since emerged as a self-financed entity, allowing it to maintain its annual contributions without requiring further governmental financial assistance. Currently, its three annual sources of revenue are: subrogation revenues; a percentage of recoveries pursuant to the Regulation respecting applications for assistance for a class action; and interests on investments. Naturally, the *Fonds* withholds the power to be subrogated in the rights of the recipient or his attorney up to the amounts paid to them.[74] The recipient is obligated to reimburse to the *Fonds* the amounts paid by it, up to the amounts it receives from a third party as fees, costs or expenses.[75] This reimbursement only occurs when the action is successful; otherwise, the financing is not reimbursed, and the financing risk is assumed entirely by the *Fonds*.

The second source of financing for the *Fonds,* and the most substantial, is the percentage of all class action recoveries made pursuant to article 42 of the Act Respecting the Fonds d'aide aux Actions Collectives and the Regulation

---

70 Ibid., art 30. In addition, art 31 provides that:

> In the cases where the representative was granted assistance, if the defendant in whose favour the final judgment has been rendered shows to the satisfaction of the *Fonds* that it is impossible for him to obtain the full payment of the judicial costs on the property of the representative, the *Fonds*, after examining the financial condition of the defendant, may pay these judicial costs in the name of the representative. The *Fonds* then becomes subrogated in the rights of the defendant up to the amount paid to him.

71 See *Fonds*' Annual Report, *Fonds d'Aide aux Actions Collectives Rapport Annuel* (2019–2020) http://www.faac.justice.gouv.qc.ca/doc/RapportAnnuel2019-2020.pdf accessed 5 July 2021, 22.

72 Ibid.

73 Ibid., 21.

74 Act Respecting the Fonds d'aide aux Actions Collectives, ch F-3.2.0.1.1, arts 25 and 30.

75 Ibid., art 30.

respecting applications for assistance for a class action.[76] By this mechanism, the *Fonds* may seek and obtain a percentage of the balance from collective recovery or of individual recoveries.[77] Essentially, the *Fonds'* right to compensation applies to all class actions in Quebec, regardless of whether it had provided financing to advance the action. Given this feature, every class action case initiated in the province – whether it is funded or not – helps finance the next one.

As a result of the unique structure of the Quebec funding system, plaintiffs are strongly incentivized to apply for financing. Unlike other funding systems around the globe, which seek a percentage of any successful recovery as a condition for funding, the *Fonds* does not claim rights in the form of a special levy for successful cases which its funds. Further, unlike traditional third-party private financiers, the *Fonds*' mission and incentive in providing assistance is not to make money, but rather, to promote recovery and provide access to justice. These dynamics present applicants with a unique funding opportunity, where the interests of all parties align in order to advance litigation and promote access to justice. Accordingly, applicants have fully embraced the Quebec public financing system with nearly half of all active class actions in the province currently financed publicly. Encouraged by this positive experience, countries around the world, such as France and Belgium, have undertaken reforms of their own class actions systems in order to provide self-sustaining public financing for class actions, similar to the model established in Quebec.[78]

14.4.2 The Ontario Class Proceedings Fund

By way of comparison, the Ontario government established a *Class Proceedings Fund* (hereafter the '*Fund*') right after its class proceedings legislation came into effect in 1992 and contributed the sum of $500,000 to establish it.[79] Pursuant to section 59. 1(2) LSA, the *Funds'* mandate is to provide 'financial

---

[76] Regulation respecting applications for assistance for a class action, c R-2.1, r.1. art 42 of the Act Respecting the Fonds d'aide aux Actions Collectives provides that:

> In the case of a collective recovery of the claims, the Fonds shall withhold a percentage fixed by regulation of the Government on the balance established under articles 596 and 597 of the Code of Civil Procedure (chapter C-25.01); in other cases, the Fonds shall withhold a percentage fixed by regulation of the Government on every liquidated claim.

[77] According to art 38a) of the Act Respecting the Fonds d'aide aux Actions Collectives, the Government may, by regulation, 'fix, for the application of art 42, the percentage withheld by the Fonds from the balance or from a liquidated claim'.

[78] Belogbi (n 56) 42.

[79] Law Society Act, RSO 1990, c L8, § 59.1(1) (hereafter 'LSA').

support for plaintiffs to class proceedings …' as well as provide 'payments to defendants in respect of costs awards made in their favour …'. Discussing the *Funds'* purpose, courts in Ontario have long recognized the need for such a funding entity, particularly to protect against large adverse costs awards and as a means of encouraging the advancement of meritorious litigation.[80]

While counsel fees are not recoverable, Ontario funding covers approved disbursements and adverse cost awards,[81] and is provided based upon several factors including the strength of the claim and the public interest involved. It should be noted that in the jurisdiction of Ontario, adverse costs awarded against unsuccessful litigants in the context of class actions follow the English rule and therefore can amount to substantial sums.[82] When the *Fund* finances the action and it is unsuccessful, the defendant is entitled to apply to the *Fund* for recovery of the defendant's costs.[83] Alternatively, if the action is successful, the plaintiff will have to repay the contribution to the plaintiff's costs made by the *Fund*. In addition, the *Fund* will be entitled to receive 10 per cent of the judgment awarded in favour of the class.[84]

Pursuant to section 59.3 (4), in deciding whether to grant financial support to the plaintiff, the Committee may consider:

(a) the merits of the plaintiff's case;
(b) whether the plaintiff has made reasonable efforts to raise funds from other sources;
(c) whether the plaintiff has a clear and reasonable proposal for the use of any funds awarded;
(d) whether the plaintiff has appropriate financial controls to ensure that any funds awarded are spent for the purposes of the award; and
(e) any other matter that the Committee considers relevant.

---

80 In *Bayens v Kinross Gold Corp* [2013] ONSC 4974, the court recognizes that '[instead] of employing a no-costs regime, the Ontario Legislature responded to the problem of the economic barrier of an adverse costs award by introducing funding from the Class Proceedings Fund of the Law Foundation of Ontario.'

81 LSA, RSO 1990, c L8, § 59.3 and 59.4.

82 Discussing costs awards, the court in *Houle v S. Jude Medical Inc* [2017] ONSC 5129 (CanLII) [43], notes that 'Ontario's class actions regime, unlike other Canadian jurisdictions (such as British Columbia), follows the "ordinary costs" or "loser pays" rule, which provides that the losing party can expect to pay costs to the successful party at any stage of the proceeding.'; However, c 31 (1) CPA, 1992, SO 1992, c 6, allows the court to consider in awarding fees whether the action was a 'test case, raised a novel point of law or involved a matter of public interest'.

83 LSA, RSO 1990, c L8, § 59.4(1).

84 LSA, RSO 1990, c L8, § 59. 5g) and § 8 of the Ontario Reg 771/92.

Importantly, cases supported by the Ontario *Fund* must seek to advance the *Class Proceedings Act* and jurisprudential objectives. As such, these funded cases seek to enhance access to justice and judicial efficiency, to advance the public interest, to achieve behaviour modification and to further the establishment of new legal principles.[85] Ontario courts have recognized certain inherent limitations involved in the public financing of class actions, notably that the *Fund* possesses a finite amount of resources and that it cannot fund every single application it receives. As a result, courts have firmly held that the decision not to fund any given case cannot be taken as a signal as to the merits of the case.[86]

Although the annual sums of funding awarded have continuously improved, the Ontario *Fund* remains to date, vastly underused having funded approximately only 10 per cent of all cases advanced since 1993.[87] For example, in 2019, only eight new applications for funding were approved.[88] Some authors have suggested that the elevated *public interest* criteria may explain in part why a smaller percentage of active class actions in the province of Ontario are funded by the Fund in comparison to the situation in Quebec.[89] Similarly, the inflexible and weighty 10 per cent levy applicable to funded cases may also be a deterrent to potential applicants, particularly since certain third-party lenders have previously provided funding at lower rates.[90] Finally, the notable difference in adverse cost awards normally granted in class actions between Quebec and Ontario may also explain the more cautious approach to funding undertaken by the Ontario *Fund* in comparison to the Quebec *Fonds*. For instance, in 2019 alone, the *Fund* was liable to pay $7M in adverse costs, whereas it collected only $4M in levies.[91] Although it has since solidified its

---

85 § 5 of the Ontario Regulation; also see Class Proceedings Fund, Class Proceedings Fund 20 Years in Review (2013) http://www.lawfoundation.on.ca/wp-content/uploads/CPF-Brochure-2013.pdf accessed 6 July 2021.

86 *Bayens v Kinross Gold Corporation* [2013] ONSC 4974 (CanLII) [28]–[29].

87 Law Commission of Ontario, *Class Actions: Objectives, Experiences and Reforms: Final Report* (Toronto: July 2019) 84.

88 See The Law Foundation of Ontario, 'Bringing legal help to people across Ontario' (2019 Annual Report) https://lawfoundation.on.ca/download/2019-annual-report/ accessed 6 July 2021, 31.

89 André Durocher, 'Une grosse carotte, un gros bâton: l'accès à la justice et les aspects financiers de la pratique en matière de recours collectifs' in Barreau du Québec, Service de la formation continue, Colloque national sur les recours collectifs: développements récents au Québec, au Canada et aux États-Unis (2013), vol 362 (Éditions Yvon Blais 2013) online, 349.

90 See *Marriott v General Motors of Canada Co* [2018] ONSC 2535 (CanLII) [6]–[9]. In this case an interest rate of 7 per cent was charged, which is less than the Fonds' 10 per cent levy.

91 The Law Foundation of Ontario (n 88) 29.

financial position, maintaining a balance of nearly 13 million dollars on its balance sheet as of 31 December 2019,[92] the risk of a 'black swan' [93] adverse costs award persists.

After extensive review of the question of costs in the context of class actions, the Law Commission of Ontario recently proposed amending the CPA to introduce a modified no-costs regime for certification and ancillary motions.[94] Although such amendments were not included in the Smarter and Stronger Justice Act[95] and recent amendments to the Ont CPA, the issue of rising costs is irrefutably an important barrier to justice. As a result, courts in Ontario and throughout Canada have recognized the relevance of TPLF when appropriate to help advance litigation. Most recently, in *JB & M Walker Ltd / 1523428 Ontario Inc v TDL Group*,[96] the courts considered the *Fund*'s incapability to provide financing for class counsel fees as a factor in determining whether third-party litigation was necessary given the circumstances, in order to advance access to justice and promote the objectives of class actions legislation.[97]

14.5 FINAL WORDS – TOWARDS ENHANCED TRANSPARENCY IN CLASS ACTION FUNDING MECHANISMS

Pursuant to the newly amended legislation, the Ont CPA bestows upon courts the role of 'guardians' of TPLF agreements. The prevailing argument in favour of private funding in class actions is that courts can ensure that fundamental fairness principles of law are followed and that class members are protected precisely because of their ability to screen and subsequently approve such agreements. Given the rise in popularity of TPLF in class actions, the issue becomes whether the court-created mechanisms, which have now been codified in Ontario, are sufficient in order to protect class members, promote access to justice, and advance the objectives of class proceedings.

Parallel to private funders, public financing entities such as the Quebec *Fonds* act as powerful gatekeepers of class action systems by screening for cases which are potentially worthwhile to advance. Unlike third-party litigation funders, public funding entities are socially focused and seek to promote

---

[92] Ibid., 31.

[93] Law Commission of Ontario, *Class Actions: Objectives, Experiences and Reforms: Final Report* (Toronto, July 2019) 84.

[94] Ibid., 9, 85-86, 88.

[95] Bill 161, Smarter and Stronger Justice Act (2020).

[96] *JB & M Walker Ltd / 1523428 Ontario Inc v TDL Group* [2019] ONSC 999.

[97] Ibid., [11]–[12].

recovery and access to justice over and above any material objectives. By way of comparison, funders finance litigation and primarily seek to raise capital. It would therefore seem that state funders are inherently better positioned to further the public policy objectives underlying class actions, while mitigating the ethical risks.

Nonetheless, we conclude that the criteria developed by the courts regarding third-party funding in class actions and reaffirmed by the Ontario legislator are appropriate and contribute to enhancing access to justice. The reality is that only TPLF can help fund the prohibitive cost of experts and hundreds of hours of work necessary to bring a case to authorization. Public funding remains, to this date, insufficient, even in Quebec. However, we maintain a previously evoked position that the mandate of class action public financing entities should be redefined to include a specific oversight mechanism of class action litigation.[98] Overall, by expanding the oversight mechanism functions of state funding entities, the class action system as a whole would become more transparent, to the benefit of all litigants – actual and future.

Transparency can properly be characterized as a fundamental issue in the Quebec and Canadian justice system.[99] Increased oversight, accountability, and transparency will lead to an improved class action system and is a welcomed development for both state funding entities as well as for the third-party litigation funding industry. Courts have repeatedly held that in order to be enforceable third-party funding agreements must be transparent.[100]

As herein discussed, following the recent amendments to the Ont CPA only court-approved funding agreements are enforceable.[101] Importantly, pursuant to section 33.1(9) Ont CPA, courts must determine whether agreements are 'fair and reasonable' in light of the particular circumstances of the case, and advancement of the goals of class actions legislation. The statute further requires courts to find that the agreement will not impair the solicitor-client relationship. By limiting the ability for third parties to control or interfere with

---

98 See Piché (n 1).

99 Canadian Bar Association, National Task Force on Systems of Civil Justice, *Report of the Task Force on Systems of Civil Justice* (August 1996):

> accountability of the system to the public it is intended to serve cannot be accomplished unless the functioning and operations of the system are understandable to the public. Further, and significantly, a genuinely accessible system cannot be achieved unless additional ways are found to make the system comprehensible and transparent to potential users.

100 In *Fehr v Sun Life Assurance Co of Canada* [2012] ONSC 2715 (CanLII) [89], the court held that: 'Third party funding of a class proceeding must be transparent, and it must be reviewed in order to ensure that there are no abuses or interference with the administration of justice.'

101 S 33.1 (2) and 33.1(3) Ont CPA.

the litigation, courts can ensure that agreements are not *champertous,* thereby protecting the interests of class members.

When examined through the lens of access to justice, TPLF agreements permit otherwise meritorious litigation to be pursued notwithstanding any seeming insurmountable financial hurdles to advancing the litigation.[102] Due to their structure, TPLF entities are incentivized to advance class litigation which has a high probability of success. Eager to generate returns, and owing a fiduciary obligation to preserve capital, funders are motivated to minimize risk by funding cases which have a strong likelihood of success. Further, reputational considerations strongly incentivize funders to avoid funding frivolous or otherwise abusive lawsuits. Private funders are asked to play an important role where other sources of funding such as state or counsel funding would not otherwise be available, thereby promoting the prime policy objectives of class actions legislation. Private funding therefore meets an untapped need in the litigation market and is most likely to arise where other sources of financing, such as public financing are unavailable or inadequate.

In instances where public financing is available, applicants have strong reasons to pursue it. This is particularly true in Quebec, given that the *Fonds* does not claim rights in the form of a special levy for successful cases which its funds. Rather, because the *Fonds'* right to compensation applies to all class actions in Quebec, every class action case initiated in the province – whether it is funded or not – helps finance the next one. In terms of incentives, the *Fonds* is – even if only implicitly –motivated to finance cases that have a greater chance to succeed, especially since the loan provided to the class action initiator is reimbursed only in the event of success in litigation. The *Fonds'* decisions are kept confidential, but once an announcement is made that a case has been funded, a strong indication is sent to the legal community and to the parties that the case is well worth litigating.[103]

Beyond their functions as capital providers, we propose that the mission of state funding entities should be expanded to include an oversight function of class action activities. This development would allow for a more data driven

---

[102] *Dugal v Manulife Financial Corp* [2011] ONSC 1785 (CanLII) [32]:

> If class counsel is not prepared to accept the risk of an adverse costs award, then the plaintiff's only option is to either abandon the claim or apply to the Fund. The fund may or may not accept the application. If it accepts the application, its fee is an inflexible 10 per cent of the recovery. Law Commission of Ontario, *Class Actions: Objectives, Experiences and Reforms: Final Report* (Toronto, July 2019) 86.

[103] *Québec (Commission de la santé et de la sécurité du travail) v Pillin*, EYB 1983-142308 (Que CA). In that case, the Court of appeal remarks how the *Fonds'* written decision appears as a decision of the merits of the case.

approach to class actions, which at a minimum would serve an informative function to the public, while also allowing for better decision making on behalf of all the stakeholders in the class actions system. Data is critically important to researchers of course, but also to the legislator, to the courts and to the public in general. Increased supervision and oversight would not only make the class action litigation process less obscure, but it would also shed light on key measurements such as claim rates and settlements. Only then would the overall success of the class action in relation to the three class action objectives be empirically assessed.

The *Fonds* can contribute by acting as an official overseer of class actions in Quebec and by requesting clearer and more definite data from the parties and lawyers. And in fact, should it not be that government or semi-governmental entities like the *Fonds* have an utmost obligation to be so transparent in their legal activities and reporting? With greater information could come greater access to justice, another public policy objective of the class action, as more citizens would understand and trust the procedure, and more cases would be initiated in the courts. As for the rights of absent class members more specifically, an enhanced presence by the *Fonds* would lead to a greater protection; with greater information would come increased participation in the class action litigation. The involvement, eventually, of the *Fonds* in class settlements would, furthermore, make proceedings beneficially more adversarial.[104]

Overall, state funded entities are in an advantaged position to help advance access to justice because of their ability to finance worthwhile cases, all the while creating a more transparent and therefore more efficient, class actions system. Even so, the enforcement of 'fair and reasonable' funding agreements is a welcomed development in the Canadian class action ecosystem, which has the potential to act as a legitimate tool for funding collective litigation.

---

[104] See generally Catherine Piché, 'Fairness in Class Action Settlements' (Carswell 2012) (doctoral thesis), for a discussion on the Canadian class actions settlement law.

Index